JAMAICA Fi Real!

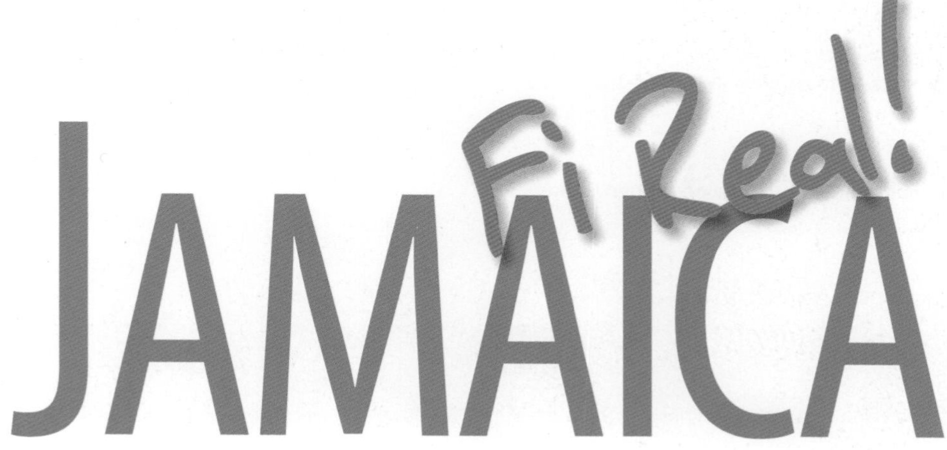

BEAUTY, VIBES AND CULTURE

Kevin O'Brien Chang

IAN RANDLE PUBLISHERS
Kingston • Miami

Published in Jamaica, 2010 by
Ian Randle Publishers
11 Cunningham Avenue
P.O. Box 686
Kingston 6
www.ianrandlepublishers.com

National Library of Jamaica Cataloguing in Publication Data

Chang, Kevin O'Brien
Jamaica fi real : beauty, vibes and culture / Kevin O'Brien Chang

p. : ill., maps; cm.

Bibliography : p.

ISBN 978-976-637-397-9 (pbk)

1. Jamaica - Description and travel - Guide books 2. Jamaica - Guide books

I. Title

917.292 - dc 22

Front cover images courtesy of Maria LaYacona, Getty Images and Charlene Collins

Back cover images courtesy of Vaughan Turland, Berette Macaulay, Carlington Wilmot and the Gleaner Company Ltd.

Cover and book design by Heather Kong
Printed in Malaysia

Contents

SALT RIVER

SPORTS

RELIGION

ARTS+LITERATURE

ECONOMY

FOOD

SCENERY

THE EXPERTS SPEAK

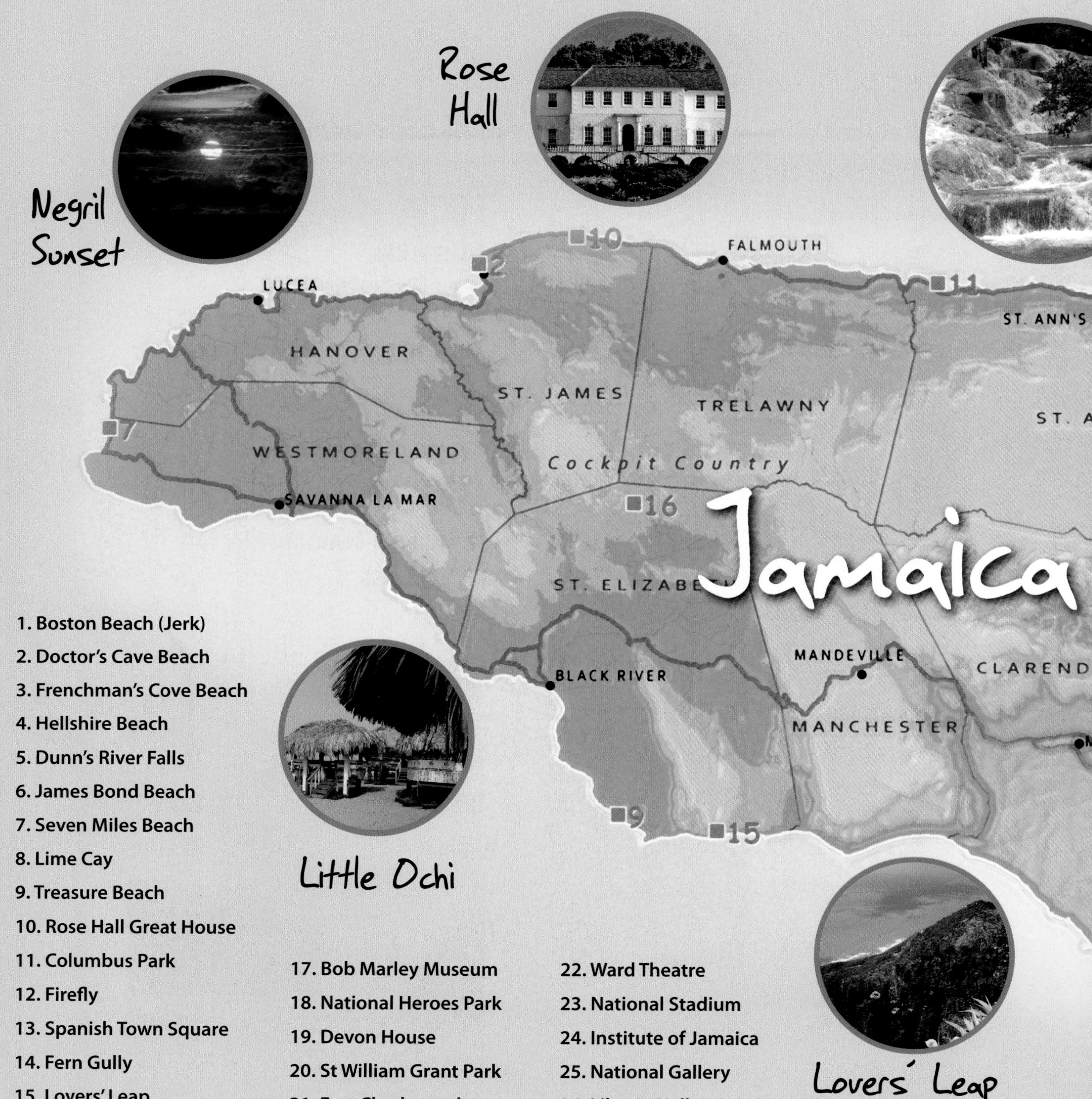
Negril Sunset
Rose Hall
LUCEA
FALMOUTH
HANOVER
ST. JAMES
TRELAWNY
ST. ANN'S B
ST. AN
WESTMORELAND
Cockpit Country
SAVANNA LA MAR
Jamaica
ST. ELIZABE
MANDEVILLE
BLACK RIVER
CLARENDO
MANCHESTER
10
2
11
7
16
9
15
Little Ochi
Lovers' Leap
1. Boston Beach (Jerk)
2. Doctor's Cave Beach
3. Frenchman's Cove Beach
4. Hellshire Beach
5. Dunn's River Falls
6. James Bond Beach
7. Seven Miles Beach
8. Lime Cay
9. Treasure Beach
10. Rose Hall Great House
11. Columbus Park
12. Firefly
13. Spanish Town Square
14. Fern Gully
15. Lovers' Leap
16. Cockpit (Accompong)
17. Bob Marley Museum
18. National Heroes Park
19. Devon House
20. St William Grant Park
21. Fort Charles and the Giddy House
22. Ward Theatre
23. National Stadium
24. Institute of Jamaica
25. National Gallery
26. Liberty Hall

MAP COURTESY OF MONA GEOINFOMATICS INSTITUTE

© S. Hodges

THE TITCHFIELD PENINSULA, PORTLAND

Foreword

TONY REBEL

Help me big up Jamaica
The land of wood and water
The systems might noh proper
But we love the vibes, the
food and the culture

Woi, can't you see
The beauty of this country
Me never know a serious thing
Until me reach a foreign.

Say what a nice place fi live
Sweet Jamdown

As an entertainer I have circled the globe, and it is easier to tell of the places that I have not been rather than those I have seen. With all the persuasive invitations and broad opportunities offered, I still make Jamaica my home. Why? Because there is nowhere more beautiful, no people more friendly, no culture more vibrant. Yes, there is crime and poverty and not enough social justice, which we cannot stop fighting for. Yet the attractive qualities of this country far surpass the negative elements.

The systems might no proper
But we love the vibes, the food and the culture

Jamaican artistes have showcased our music in almost every country on the planet, demonstrating our culture, which has elements of our Africanness but is very unique to us. There is hardly any place where Rastafari is not established regardless of the language, colour, culture or creed, thanks to Bob Marley and Burning Spear and others who have educated and entertained the world.

Everything Jamaican is embraced wherever we go. Everyone loves Jamaican food and music, and even wants to speak Jamaican. We can safely say that we are the most imitated persons of the twenty-first century. Nobody can say exactly why this is so. Is it the food, the drink, the herb, the geographical location?

Jamaicans are so openly proud of who we are, that others embrace in us what they wish they had. Maybe this pride is embedded in our DNA and the constant sunshine and surrounding carry-us-beyond sea magnifies everything larger than life.

Marcus Garvey's voyage from St Ann to the wider world became an inspiration to many, including Earl Little, the father of Malcolm X, Malcolm X himself and Martin Luther King, Jr just to name a few. Fortunately for us we have seen the first black president of the United States, Barack Obama, who was inspired by Martin Luther King. Do you see the Jamaican connection?

If half the story of Jamaica's history is recorded and preserved in a safe archive, the future generations of the world will have a field day reading and learning about us.

My good brethren Kevin O'Brien Chang has made a great start in this direction. He has clearly observed life in Jamaica in great detail, and what he has not personally seen or experienced, he has consulted and discussed with those of us who have.

Jamaica Fi Real is a consummate description of Jamaica and its people: analysing the past and predicting the future, Kevin navigates us through the hills and gullies of our culture. He evokes emotions, asks questions, and tries to provide answers. It is the reality of this country, the good, the bad, the ugly and the pretty. You will be reminded where the greatest creators of ambiguous terminologies come from.

So prepare yourself for an edutaining experience. If you hate facts, dislike laughs, and don't want to learn about Jamaica – don't read this book!

Tony Rebel

JAMAICA

Preface

I have been trying to understand and explain Jamaica for over ten years in my columns for the *Gleaner* and *Observer*, but I keep finding more questions than answers. What do Jamaicans want? Well yes, like all people they wish for a higher per capita GDP and less crime and more education. Yet apparently they also desire what cannot be quantified, namely the maximum enjoyment of life.

Whatever else they might be, the people of this endlessly contradictory island are not and never will be purely rational economic animals. No matter how hard things get, the sense of gladness is never far away. For if there's no fun in life, then what's the point? Sure Usain Bolt might have run faster in the 2008 Bejing Olympics 100 metres had he not been so caught up in enjoying the moment; but records come and go (as Bolt has since shown), while the sensation of pure delight is priceless. Not everything can be measured by a clock, and certain things money just can't buy. That perhaps is Jamaica's message to the world.

This book tries to explain today's Jamaica from a Jamaican point of view, while highlighting its distinctive features. It also ponders present realities in the context of the past – history without the boring parts, or at least that was the goal. Strong threads of continuity run through the entire Jamaican experience; we did not jump from the 1865 Morant Bay Rebellion to the 1938 demonstrations, as Alexander Bustamante built on the work of Marcus Garvey, who was indebted to Robert Love. Mento and pocomania helped create ska and rocksteady, which gave birth to reggae and dancehall. Slim and Sam celebrated folk culture before Louise Bennett, without whom there could have been no Bob Marley. Arthur Wint begat Don Quarrie, who paved the way for Usain Bolt. Rastafarianism has elements of kumina, and links with Bedwardism. If you don't know where you're coming from, you can't know where you're going.

I wish to thank all those who have helped me with this book, especially Nicole Watson for her constant encouragement, Kiana Adams for her excellent editing, Heather Kong for her lovely design, Christine and Ian Randle for their patience and advice, Ann Marie Bailey, Camille Chin, Stephanie Chen See, Tony Rebel, Yasus Afari, Ian Boyne, Cliff Hughes, Oliver Clarke, Lloyd Lovindeer, Marion Hall, Diana McIntyre-Pike, Ray Chen, Viv Morris-Brown, David Buckley, Trevor Munroe, Omar Davies, Mel Cooke, Ity and Fancy Cat, Tony Becca, Simon Crosskill, Geoffrey Maxwell, Paul Auden, Tommy Cowan and Carlene Davis, David Boxer, Hazel Ramsey-McClune, Wayne Chen, Carolyn Cooper, Grace Cameron, Thelma McCarthy, Robert Lalah, Jill Byles, Garfield Davidson, Leonie Harvey, Fay Plunkett, Ruthlyn Sherwood, Caulene Forbes, Ivy Palmer, Victor Wilson, Carl Chang, Norman Peart, Paul Francis, Michael Beaumont, Davia Davidson, Vaughan Turland, Debbie Kalczynski, Roberta Tilp, Suzanne Jordan, Catherine Chang, Stephanie Lockwood, Ann Chang, Ray Therrien and of course my father and mother, Bobby and Angela Chang.

Above all, thanks and praise to the most high for giving me the health, strength and wherewithal to complete this labour of love. Eternal Father, bless our land.

HORSEBACK RIDING AT HELLSHIRE BEACH

Introduction

Twenty-First Century Jamaica: The World's Most Fascinating Island?

'The fairest isle that eyes have ever beheld'.

This supposedly is how Christopher Columbus described Jamaica to Queen Isabella. Another story says he depicted its verdant hills with a crumpled piece of green velvet.

Well, considering nobody is even sure if Columbus was buried in the Dominican Republic or in Spain, who knows what he really said 500 years ago? Yet as we say in these parts, 'if it no go so, it near go so.' Whether factual or not, these tales express an inherent truth.

Beauty is in the eye of the beholder, and gorgeous scenery comes in many forms – snowcapped mountains, gleaming lakes, immaculate gardens. To most people, however, paradise is a tropic isle, and there is none lovelier than Jamaica. From the powder white beaches and sky blue seas of Negril, to the rolling green hills of Manchester, to the luxuriant forests of Portland, it would be difficult to imagine a greater variety of tropical scenery in an area of similar size.

Or one with a more perfect climate – nearly always sunny, just enough rain to keep the land constantly green and temperatures rarely below 70°F or above 90°F (20°C to 30°C). Yet nature's bounty is never unadulterated. The price of all-year-shirtsleeve weather is the annual threat of hurricanes which keeps Jamaicans wary of late summer weather bulletins. The old mariner's poem goes:

June, too soon; July, stand by; August, look out you
must; September, remember; October, all over.

However, despite regular brushes, this lucky island (knock wood!) tends to escape the worst. In the last half century, only 'Hurricane Gilbert' in 1988 has hit directly. In a perverse way, this sense of 'possible but not likely disaster', adds to the island's addictive 'living pon di edge' ambience.

Jamaicans who know no other country take its splendour for granted. However, Jamdowners abroad realise what they are missing, and can never be wholly satisfied by foreign surroundings. They yearn unceasingly for the sensual lushness and intoxicating beauty that made the poet M.G. Smith exult – 'I saw my land in the morning, and O but she was fair!' Every country has attractive areas, but Jamaica's loveliness is never ending (except perhaps, say out-of-towners, for Kingston!).

In my younger days I visited the Greek islands. The guidebooks said Samos was the prettiest; and it was pretty, but nothing like Jamaica. The scenery was nice, but of a kind. There were no wonderfully varying vistas with each bend in the road, no endless variety of trees, no infinite shades of green. This was it? Apparently yes. Yet it couldn't begin to compare to what I was used to and took for granted.

CATHEDRAL ST JAGO DE LA VEGA,
SPANISH TOWN

Then it dawned on me that if this was the most scenic of the famed 'isles of Greece' which poets have rhapsodised over for centuries, my homeland must be special indeed. The more I read and travelled, the more obvious it became that, at least scenically, 'When me check it out lawd, nowhere no better than yard.'

A Beautiful Contradiction

To the world at large Jamaica means sunny beaches, reggae and rum. Yet beneath the music and beauty lies a passionate ambivalence. This may be an island of only 2.5 million people, but pound for pound, as they say in boxing, it's possibly the most contradictory country on the planet. Jamaica combines a Third World standard of living with an almost First World life expectancy. It is one of earth's most stable democracies, yet has one of its higher homicide rates. It is reputed to have both more churches per square mile, and a higher out-of-wedlock birth rate, than any other place on the globe. It is a largely black country, whose most famous sons Marcus Garvey and Bob Marley are international symbols of racial pride, yet which has more than once elected a light-skinned prime minister.

Jamaica is blessed with a strongly embedded liberal democratic tradition, with freedom of speech and choice being assumed as birthrights. The result is a very open society, where worldwide currents of change are usually felt sooner rather than later. Also, because of its small size, such changes begin to take effect rather quickly. So Jamaica's 4,411 square miles often seem a stage on which many of the great problems confronting the modern world are being worked out in advance. Is there such a thing as too much democracy too early? Will female educational dominance change the rules of mating? How do societies function when the nuclear family is the exception and not the norm? Can indigenous cultures resist the forces of globalisation? Is 'McDonaldisation' (or in Jamaica's case 'KFCisation') a good or bad thing? Can full racial tolerance among differing ethnic groups be achieved? How important is religion to a nation's well being? These may be theoretical academic issues in most countries, but they are questions the Jamaican nation is in the process of actively answering.

One intriguing aspect of living here is that the 'invisible hand' of change can almost be glimpsed in action. For though not small enough for any one person or group to dictate events, the island is not so large that individual actions become lost among irresistible social forces. Those trying to effect change can often feel themselves being changed, becoming at once both cause and effect.

Adding to the fascination is the engagingly open and emotionally expansive Jamaican character. You don't have to dig deep here to gauge the general mood. Self-consciousness is almost unknown, and people speak their minds exceedingly freely. To get a feel for the national psyche, you only have to turn on the radio talk shows.

Yet the customary top-of-the-voice assertiveness can't hide the fact that most folks aren't sure what direction they wish the country to take. Yes, everyone desires a modern, technologically advanced First World Jamaica; but they also want to preserve the unhurried natural rhythms of life, and the distinctive national identity. Not that these are mutually exclusive goals over the long haul, but you can't suck and blow at the same time. Countries that are hesitant to put economic priorities above all else won't get rich, or at least not as quickly as those that are single-minded in the pursuit of wealth. The Jamaican temperament also contains more than a hint of 'For what shall it profit a man, if he shall gain the whole world, and lose his own soul?' doubt. If this island is ever going to become the world-class success story everyone says it has the potential to be, its people will first have to make up their minds about what they want. Until then, daily life here will remain a riveting conflict between the dictates of reason and the desires of instinct. For good or bad, Jamaica is human nature in the raw.

To the world at large Jamaica means sunny beaches, reggae and rum. Yet beneath the music and beauty lies a passionate ambivalence.

A DONKEY RACE IN TOP HILL, ST CATHERINE

People

OUT OF MANY, ONE OF A KIND

Exuberant; talkative; aggressive; humorous; passionate; resourceful; unpredictable – there are many adjectives which the word 'Jamaican' brings to mind, but 'boring' is not one of them. Whatever their faults, Jamaicans have an inimitable style that fascinates people everywhere.

And everywhere means just that. Despite the small population, Jamaicans are remarkably well-travelled, and there is scarcely a place on earth where a 'yardie' cannot be found. So no matter what the country, if you encounter a group of people talking excitedly at the top of their voices, gesticulating animatedly, and every once in a while bursting into full-blooded belly laughter, chances are you have come across a bunch of Jamaicans.

Or maybe a group of Italians or Nigerians, for Jamaicans are hardly the world's only outgoing people. Indeed some find the people here 'boasty', and even 'boasty' about being 'boasty'. It could be a matter of taste. When Usain Bolt won world record 100 metres gold in Bejing 2008, was he spontaneously enjoying the moment or arrogantly showboating, when he spread out his arms and slapped his chest before the finish, and then danced with joy?

A few observers, though none of his opponents, deemed Bolt unsportsmanlike. Yet most foreign reporters hailed him and his compatriots as a breath of fresh air in a marvelously organised but often soulless spectacle. As Michael Rosenberg in the *Detroit Free Press* put it:

> Nobody jams like the Jamaicans. This is true in the sprints, after the sprints and as far as I can tell, in life. I've heard a lot of athletes say they are 'just happy to be here.' I've never seen anybody show it like Usain Bolt and [women's 100 metres winner] Shelly-Ann Fraser.

One local scribe, possibly drunk on Olympic gold but perhaps not totally off the mark, babbled thus.

> Watching the unbridled victory celebrations of Usain Bolt and Shelly-Ann Fraser, the thought occurred yet again that Jamaicans

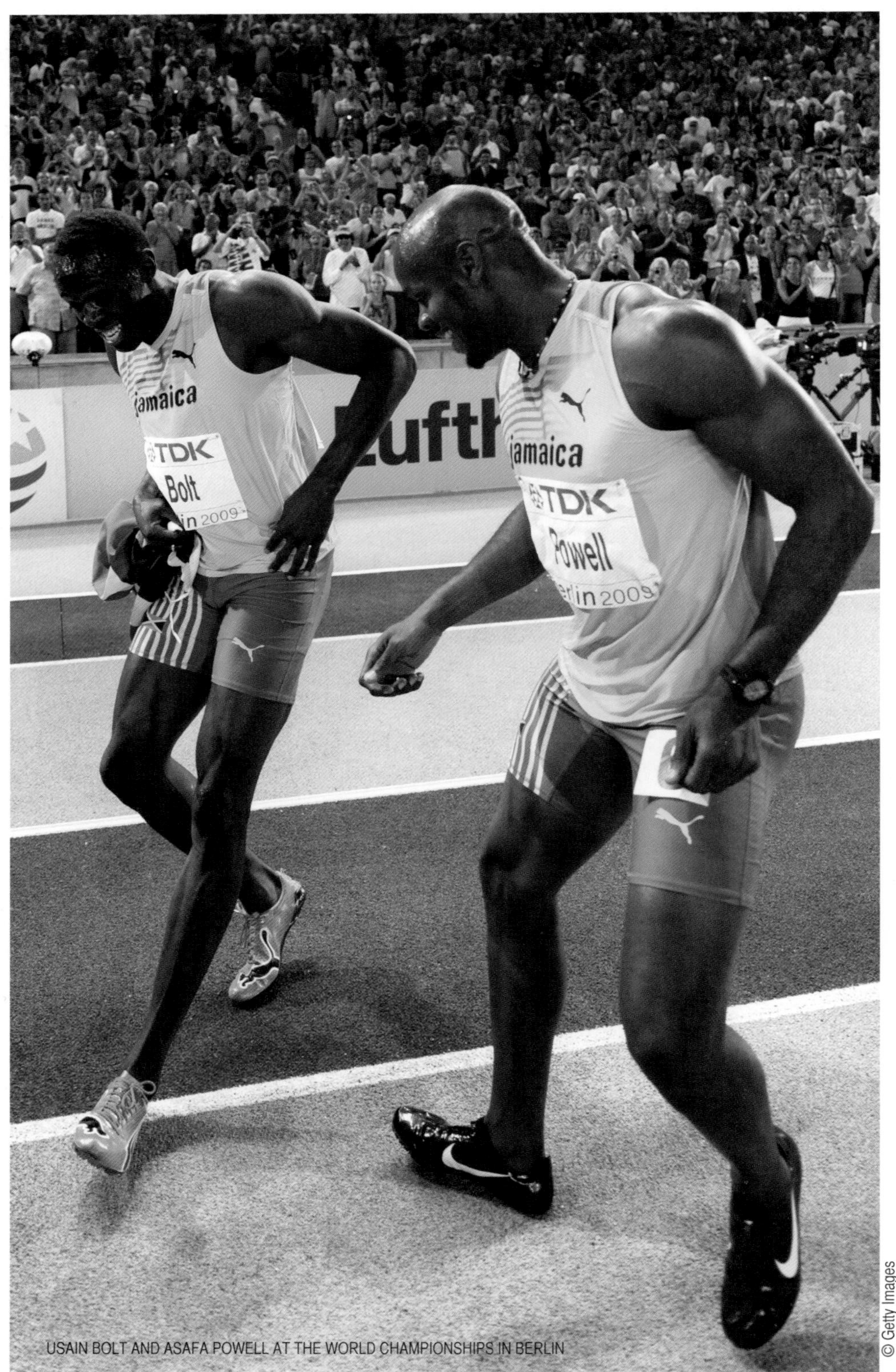

USAIN BOLT AND ASAFA POWELL AT THE WORLD CHAMPIONSHIPS IN BERLIN

ITY AND FANCY CAT

were put on earth to show the rest of the world how to enjoy themselves. As Ity and Fancy Cat say, 'Me wouldn't want to born in no other country!'

Yet even the most jingoistic yardies rubbed their eyes in disbelief as Bolt dancehalled around the track draped in black, green and gold while reggae thundered through the Bird's Nest. Earth's biggest stage was transformed into Jamaica before the eyes of billions. Once again this 'likkle but tallawah' island had captured the planet's imagination, and made itself the envy of countries a hundred times richer and bigger.

What makes this place so larger than life? After all, world–influencing nations are usually ancient, populous, or wealthy. Independent for less than 50 years, with not even one-twentieth of one per cent of the global population or GDP, Jamaica should be an obscure dot on the map. Why does it resonate so forcefully around the earth?

Dub poet Yasus Afari has contemplated this outsized prominence firsthand in many countries.

Me wouldn't want to born in no other country

He attributes it to Jamaica's role as a conduit of 'Africanness' to the West, and increasingly the East. Since all humans outside the mother continent descend from a small band that left Africa perhaps 120,000 years ago, he may be on to something. Is the attraction of other lands to things Jamaican perhaps the unconscious recognition of a primal commonality?

In the poet Yasus's words, 'Jamaica is the cultural cornerstone that the builders refused. Shipped in captivity to distant lands, we have become catalysts to unlocking the genetic memory codes of Africa. We are the leaven that leavens the whole'.

World-travelled singjay Tony Rebel agrees, and says the national personality magnifies this impact. 'Everyone admires our strong sense of self-identity. Maybe it's inborn character. Or maybe it's middle passage survivor resilience. Yet Jamaicans are so openly proud of who we are, that others embrace in us what they wish they had.'

Professor Barry Chevannes also makes the crucial point that 'Rastafarianism has been the chief repository of African consciousness in modern Jamaica'.

The larger Afro-dominant populations of the US and Brazil have also spanned the globe culturally. Yet they are surrounded by a chiefly European ethos, while Jamaica's 'Africanness' is unconstrained. This small island is also the world's most populous, mainly non-white, solely English-speaking country. So Jamaica expresses humanity's oldest culture in the lingua franca of our age. Many feel this accessible profundity is what makes 'brand Jamaica' so universally potent.

Its epitome of course is the standard English phrased, world beat tinged reggae of half-black, half-white Bob Marley. Music producer Tommy Cowan says Marley was definitely conscious of making his music more accessible to non-Jamaicans:

> Once I went to visit Bob and he was playing a Bee Gees album. I asked him why he was listening to stuff like that. He answered 'Look. These guys sold ten million records last year. They must be doing something right and I'm trying to figure out what it is.'

Now Jamaicans not only share the general monoglot arrogance of English-speaking nations, it strongly influences their mental world map. They pay close attention to events in the US, Britain, Canada, and the other ex-British West Indian territories. Yet except for events like the Olympics and the football World Cup, or disasters and wars, usually the rest of the earth might as well be on another planet. Cuba, Haiti and the Dominican Republic are next-door neighbours, but most Jamaicans generally don't pay much attention to them. Yet unusual events in Trinidad and Barbados, which are thousands of miles away, make front-page headlines. Furthermore, while Jamaicans may be largely of African descent, most would feel more at home in London or New York, than in Lagos or Johannesburg. This island is living proof that language, even more than geography, religion or race, is destiny.

Like most places Jamaica has developed its own dialect or patois – referred to here as 'patwa'. English is the language of business, academic and other formal discourse, patois the everyday social and emotional tongue. However, there is a serious linguistic cleavage, one many consider more divisive than either race or class as all Jamaicans talk patois, but not all can speak English – or code switch in academic jargon –

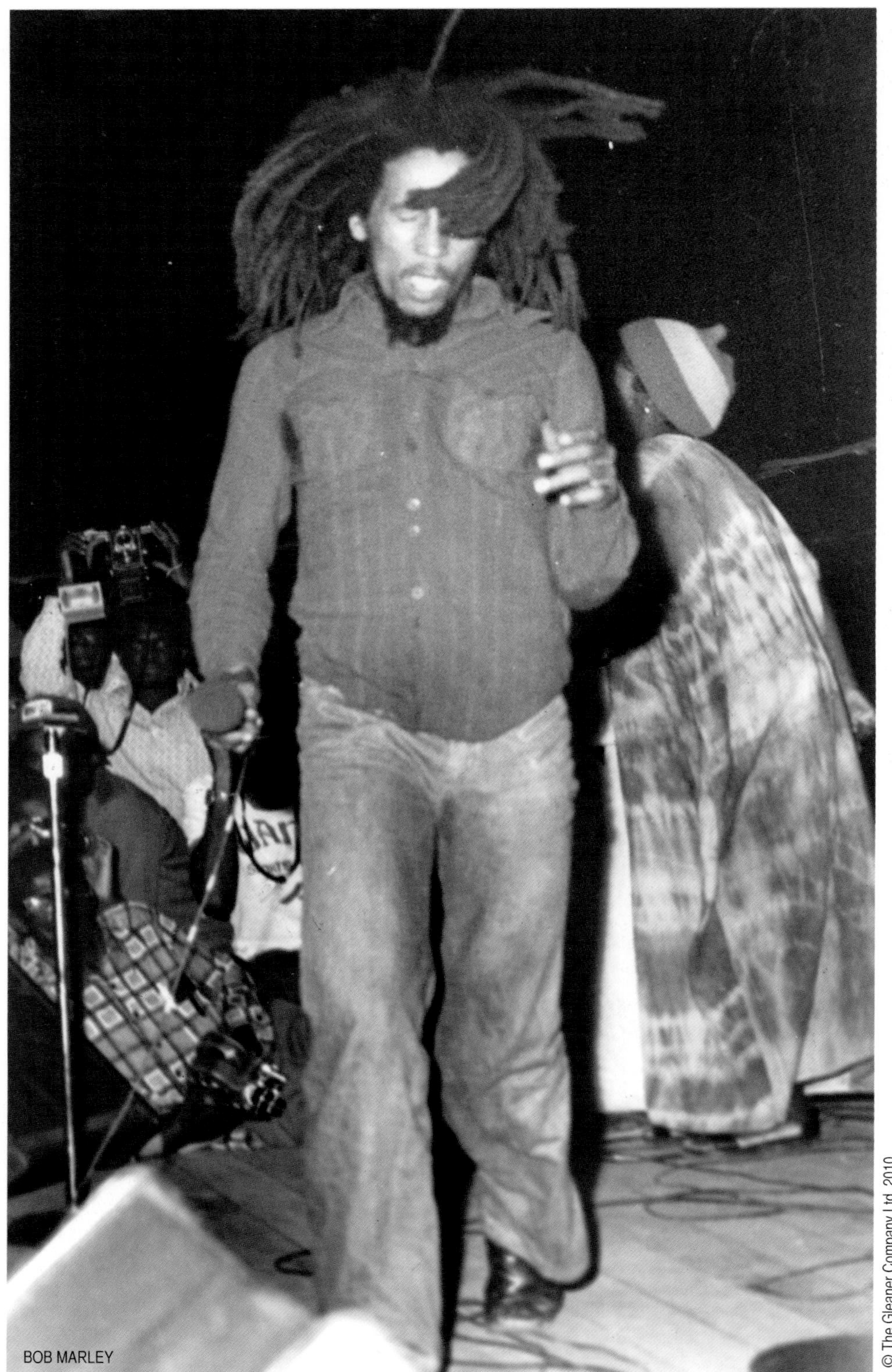

BOB MARLEY

when it is necessary.

The condescending manner in which many 'proper' speakers address their verbal inferiors can be extremely annoying. Even more irritating is the often cringing subservience of those who cannot express themselves clearly in English towards those who can. You hear a lot of talk here, especially among the intelligentsia, about 'mental slavery', but this will never be a fully free nation until all Jamaicans are able to converse on equal terms.

Linguists say patois's vocabulary, grammatical structure and intonation can be partly traced to West African languages. As to what some regard as its 'Irish lilt', well, the English speakers who had most direct contact with slaves were plantation bookkeepers and overseers, a significant proportion of whom were Irish.

Yet while the Irish accent is often described as 'gentle', that certainly can't be said about the forceful staccato in which Jamaicans converse with each other. They delight in aggressive verbal duels and believe any opinion worth holding is worth holding at the top of one's voice. Maximum volume arguments are without doubt the country's favourite pastime.

This is a famously unpunctual nation – some say 'soon come' is the unofficial national motto. Usually when people are late, it's because they got caught up in some engrossing conversation, and lost track of time. No wonder, that despite ranking in the bottom half of the world per capita GNP list, Jamaica is in the world top 20 cellular phone usage per person and that cellphone billboards dominate roadside advertising. One downside of this constant chatting is generally lousy customer service, with store clerks often showing barely concealed resentment at having their gossip fests interrupted.

The national penchant for being direct comes through in the language, for patwa is, in a sense, English with the non-essentials pared away. Jamaicans don't believe in beating around the bush, or indulging in niceties, but they are fond of injecting humour into the proceedings, and love to make fun of themselves and others. You rarely hear Jamaicans talking for long without an eruption of laughter. People who can't see the funny side of things are never going to like this country, nor will the thin-skinned. Those who can't give as good as they get are apt to be dismissed as meek or even worse 'soft' (or 'saaf'), a term of great disrespect to Jamaican men, especially when tauntingly uttered by a woman.

Respect is a big thing here. Jamaicans insist that their innate worth as human beings be properly acknowledged at all times. Perceived or actual 'disrespect', such as talking down to or rudely ignoring someone, is a frequent source of heated verbal quarrels and even violent confrontations – 'You must learn how to talk to people!' The contradictory flipside is that polite tones of entreaty sometimes don't elicit much response. It often takes aggressive loudness to

Respect is a big thing here. Jamaicans insist that their innate worth as human beings be properly acknowledged at all times.

get people's attention, or in local lingo, 'You haffi get ignorant before them notice you!'

Conversations are often salted with terse, word picture proverbs. *Stone a river bottom never feel sun hot* (Those who have not undergone an experience cannot understand how it feels). *Don't put butter in puss mouth* (Don't place temptations before those who may not be able to resist). *Cockroach no business inna fowl fight* (Don't get involved in what is not your concern). Many have made their way into famous reggae

PARTY ADVERTISEMENT ON THE BACK OF A CAR

Cockroach no business inna fowl fight (Don't get involved in what is not your concern)

songs. *Chicken merry, hawk de near* (Danger lurks even in the midst of happiness). *Wha sweet nanny goat, a go run him belly* (What tastes good to a goat now may soon upset his stomach – What you enjoy today you may regret tomorrow). *Sorry fi mawga dog, mawga dog turn round bite you* ([mawga = meager] – Those we help are often ungrateful).

Complicated situations are summed up in pungent concrete terms. Many are sexually related, for instance *bun* = cheat on partner; *jacket* = a woman making a man think he is her baby's father when he is not; *raffle* = a woman persuading the most financially well off of her sexual partners that he is the actual father of her child; *joe grind* = a sexually expert man with whom a woman is cheating on her partner.

A man might warn his friend 'If you bet everything on that racehorse and lose, *dog nyam yuh supper* (you will suffer like a hungry man whose supper a dog has eaten).' A woman might advise another 'You and your date might quarrel, so carry your *get vex money* (that is, enough money to take a cab home if he leaves you stranded)'. A man who makes a fool of himself over women is a *gal clown* and anything extremely enjoyable or extremely popular *sell off!* While '*What don't kill fatten, what don't fatten soon forgotten*' captures the stoic optimistic Jamaican philosophy of life.

DO YOU HAVE A PROBLEM? IS S
WRITE TO: TELL ME PAST
PO BOX 188, KING STREET, KING
EMAIL: PASTOR@J

Tell Me Pastor

He is a deceiver

Dear Pastor,

I am living in Canada and I'm in a relationship with a married man. I previously had a child with him knowing that he was married, however, I was unaware of his marriage prior to meeting him.

His wife found out about our child and it seems as if he does not want to spend time with us anymore. He takes care of the baby financially, but I need more than that for my son. This is my only child and I just need to know what to do to make this man be a part of our lives.

Please tell me what to do.

M.C.

Dear M.C.,

This man has been supporting his child, but you want him to do more. And, by that, you mean you want him to leave his wife and come to you totally. Evidently, he is not prepared to do so. Frankly, he is a deceiver. He lied to you and caused you to believe that he was a single man when you met. He even went further by getting you pregnant. That is why I called him a deceiver.

But, now my dear, his wife has found out about you and the baby and so he has decided to stay with her but support his child. His wife has more claim over him than you because they are legally married. He was just doing a 'thing' with you and he got caught.

He played with your emotions and it is tough on you. But keep courage, my dear. Pray and ask God to help you to cope without this man. Carve out your future without him. Don't do anything to encourage him to stay with you because he would use you, again and again and again. He should be allowed to play only one role and that is father to his son.

The love you have for him will not suddenly die but you can learn to put the past behind you and move forward.

Pastor

More than just money, house, land

Dear Pastor,

I believe that both male and female should be credited individually for his/her own success, instead one crediting the other for his/her success. I will say though that a man of strong principle and influence in life should demonstrate to a woman the importance of success.

S., New York, United States

Dear S.,

I understand you to mean that no one has a right to take credit for the success of another, who might be his/her spouse. What I think we need to understand is that if there is anybody in this world who needs to be given credit for the success of anyone is our teachers. Nobody would have become anything that is good in life without being taught by men and women who have dedicated themselves to teach.

Of course, I realise that is not what you are saying. I made that point because you raised the matter of one's success. I want to say that if two people love each other, they share everything that they have together, which may mean their time, knowledge and resources. They can say to each other, I have done my part in allowing you to become successful and I am proud of it. No one does it alone. Only fools brag that they have done it alone.

Sometimes, credit must be given to grandma, who was not literate but who saw the value of education and encouraged their grandson or granddaughter to pursue a good education or a career. It might be a dad who was rough on his daughter while she was growing up but who deserves credit for going without certain necessities of life to see that his daughter went through college without getting pregnant.

But, it could also be a young man who got a girl pregnant and she was thrown out of her parents' house. And the young man made great sacrifices to help her become a teacher, a nurse, a lawyer, etc. He deserves credit for what he has done for her. And what about that young woman who took her younger siblings under her arms, so to speak, and gave them shelter and sent them to school. She deserves credit for being a tremendous role model.

That is how it goes, my friend, we need each other, no one can do it alone.

Pastor

The in of s

Dear Pastor,

It is so nice to listen to
any marriage. Boredom
focusing on the relations
wealth, the bills, school
family life but some pe
dead to the touch and fe
Sometimes, it seem
material aspect of life a
other material things th
we are through. That is
to pray and then year
wrong places.

C.R.

Dear C.R.,
A good relationsh
cation, etc. It is an
who are in love an
biological needs.
I agree with yo
things that a relati
things are not for
other for greener
On the other ha
if there is no love
Because the truth
uine love. That is
same time genu
lose sight of eac
other.
Pastor

The

Dear Pastc
I am a 21-
believes tha
ones who
women thr
They motiv
women. O
young mer
What they
selves and
satisfied.
I am no
a man wh
than I am
what I sa
from exp
himself.

Foreigners often laughingly remark on the Jamaican habit of carrying on conversations with oneself. It's not uncommon to hear persons muttering to themselves and 'kissing-teeth' in indignation, usually at some remembered folly of their own, such as – *'Man I forget to mail the blasted letter. Stewps. Me head a get tough to rahtid'.*

Stewps, or kiss-(you)-teeth, means sharply sucking in wind against the teeth or back of the tongue to show vexation, contempt, or amused disbelief. The greater the emotional arousal, the louder and longer the sound. It is a sign of extreme disrespect when made towards parents or elders. This everyday oral gesture is common across the English-speaking Caribbean, and is probably of West African origin.

Jamaican drivers even like to communicate with their car horns, 'hailing up' any friend they see with a 'toot', and getting a 'toot toot' in return. Also when there is a long line of traffic, and a car is trying to get out from a side street, someone in line will often 'toot', as if to say 'go on through'. The driver let through will then give a 'toot toot' thank you in gratitude.

Outsiders can find this disconcerting. 'This constant blowing drives me crazy!' an American once complained to me. 'In the US we only blare our horns when there's an emergency or we get angry. All this honking keeps me wondering what I'm doing wrong!'

Even car lights are a mode of communication, as when oncoming drivers flash you to 'beware of a police speed trap ahead'. A recent new dimension to this 'chatting by car' is the printed sign advertising of upcoming parties on car rear windows.

Given that life in Jamaica is essentially one continuous conversation, with occasional interruptions to deal with life's logistics, it is no accident that deejay chanting – which is essentially talking in the natural rhythms of everyday speech over a beat – was invented in Jamaica. Or that it was a Jamaican who introduced the concept to America, where it was transformed into rap, and then spread across the world.

When you love something as much as Jamaicans love expressing themselves in their own language, and spend so much time doing it, well wasn't the next logical step to try and get paid for doing it? Which other people could ever have thought of such a concept and then actually have carried it off successfully?

What is whispered elsewhere, dancehall music chants here rhythmically at full volume. Sex, violence, love, laughter and spirituality – it's all there unadorned.

A Heartical Nation

Ten years or so ago, 'heartical' (also spelled hortical or artical') – roughly meaning a real man – was one of the biggest compliments in Jamaican dancehall lingo. Of course street slang constantly changes, and the term is now slightly dated, but it neatly sums up the unfailing Jamaican preference for heart over head. Few places give the emotions freer reign, and logic that disagrees with instinctive desires is always an unwelcome intruder.

Relationships here are especially rich sources of hilarity. The daily newspapers brim with melodramatic stories of love gone wrong, especially in the working class favourite the *Star*. Its 'Dear Pastor' agony column is filled with mostly females seeking advice about often unbelievably complicated situations, as for instance

> My husband has gotten my 15 year old sister pregnant, and my mother wants him arrested for carnal abuse [Sex with even willing under 16 females is illegal]. But I know she seduced him, and as a man he couldn't help himself, and I still love him. What should I do?

One unfortunate side-effect of all this free floating emotion is frequent crimes of passion. Lovers' quarrels end in death lamentably often.

All this is vividly reflected in song. What is whispered elsewhere, dancehall music chants here rhythmically at full volume. Sex, violence, love, laughter and spirituality – it's all there unadorned. Since political upheaval often stems from a society's inability to express its frustrations peacefully, many see music as a major component of Jamaica's democratic stability. Dancehall lays bare the dreams and realities of its people with perhaps unparalleled forthrightness. Nothing is suppressed.

THE GHETTO REALITY OF SLACKNESS

Deejay Lloyd Lovindeer is famous for his humorous social commentary in topical tunes like 'Wild Gilbert' and 'Find Your Way Back Home'. Perhaps the closest thing the country has to an oral historian, he is also Jamaica's most accomplished exponent of suggestive songs. So here is his expert's take on the ghetto reality of 'slackness' – a Jamaican expression for 'out of order' behaviour, but meaning in musical terms 'explicit song lyrics'.

'When we talk about slackness…there's a time and place for everything, and the only thing wrong with slackness in some of these songs nowadays is that it is exposed to children, and those who don't want to hear them. But in the confines of the dancehall, where anything goes, and for the people who want to hear this kind of thing, there's nothing wrong with it. The slacker the lyrics you can come up with, the more gun salute and pram-pram you get. The people in the dancehall, they enjoy it. And as they say, what consenting adults do behind closed doors is OK.

…the same lyrics you hear those DJs using, cursing women and all that, that's the same kind o' lyrics those women use to curse other women. Because that's where the DJs get their lyrics from….Most of these DJs they do this thing strictly for the money, the straight economics of it. A guy has to survive. And remember DJ language is the language of the street so the lyrics they use are the lyrics that they are exposed to in their everyday life. Sex sells, as they say, and in Jamaica sex sells even better with a dancehall 'riddim.' There was a time when only the male dancehall DJs performed explicit sex lyrics. Then Lady Saw came on the scene. She was a well-rounded performer who could both sing and DJ. Her style was considered to be raunchy because she would DJ the same kind of lyrics as her male counterparts but from the female point of view. She became the voice of all the women who were not afraid to talk openly about sex and their own sexuality. As a lyricist and a performer she could stand shoulder to shoulder, toe to toe with any male DJ. But she didn't do slackness for the sake of being slack. Her lyrics were honest, real, thought provoking and humorous. When she did 'If Him Lef' she was merely boasting about a woman's sexual prowess in the same way that the male DJs boast about theirs in a very explicit way.

It is ghetto talk, ghetto language, ghetto experience. Not that the ghetto experience is any different from the uptown experience. It's just that the uptown experience usually happens behind closed doors and you don't really see how it goes. But living in a tenement yard, you find you're exposed to more of this kind of thing. And children are more exposed to this kind o' living when they live in the ghetto, because you can't lock yourself up in the bedroom and discuss certain things while the child is in the living room watching TV, because there's just one room. So these children are exposed to all kinds o' lyrics in dem head, and dem no see nothing wrong with it. So whereas we might cringe when we hear certain lyrics, it is second nature to them. And in the dancehall, sorry to say, but anything goes, and the more a DJ can come up with those kinds of lyrics, the more he'll get across….

So it's a totally different culture from what we are exposed to uptown and even slightly midtown. Totally different. You have to really go back to school when you goin' to these places.'

It is ghetto talk, ghetto language, ghetto experience...

LLOYD LOVINDEER

© The Gleaner Company Ltd, 2010

Dancehall also mirrors Jamaica's intense homophobia. Male homosexuality is almost universally regarded with extreme distaste, though lesbianism doesn't attract the same opprobrium. It's perhaps not so much homosexuality that upsets Jamaicans, but rather its open display. Quite a few discreet public figures are suspected of being gay, yet are still treated with great respect. This is not the place to discuss the rights or wrongs of a highly controversial topic; though no one knows exactly why, Jamaicans remain overwhelmingly opposed to the legalisation of homosexuality. Whatever the personal opinions of politicians, any government crossing the public on this issue would be swept from office.

Jamaica often seems to be a place without social norms, a land where the 'anything goes for grown-ups' cliché holds true more often than not. Context is crucial of course – you don't smoke ganja at Sunday church. Yet with flaunted homosexuality being about the only unacceptable lifestyle for consenting adults, it's often up to individuals to set their own boundaries. Transgressions from the accepted norm which might make people elsewhere gasp in astonishment – such as a late former prime minister 'stealing' and marrying his ex-best friend's wife – usually elicit laughing comments like 'But dem no easy!'

In fact, Jamaicans appear to almost celebrate the absurdity of life, as if the more ridiculous you behave, the more human you seem. What is in most places the province of novels and movies, is on this island the common stuff of daily existence. Living here can cause one to lose the taste for fiction. Who needs made up stories when everyday life is so full of passion and drama?

Not that unrestrained emotion is unique to Jamaica. There's plenty for instance in Verdi's operas and Dostoevsky's novels. Indeed, one commentator summed up Dostoevsky thus:

> Humanity in a state of tranquility appears to have held no interest whatever for [him]. He could only tolerate existence provided that no element of serenity was permitted to invade his personal life....[He] was a seeker of strong mental sensations or, to put it differently, he usually preferred to be violently unhappy rather than mildly happy.

This is a pretty good snapshot of the Jamaican soul.

Neither does this island dwell much on times gone by. There are few physical markers of what has been, only occasional plantation ruins that bring to mind Carl Sandburg's poem – 'I am the grass; I cover all'. Too little history may be as bad as too much, but one great benefit of indifference to the past is a lack of 'in the bones' hatred. There is little generalised ethnic or religious animosity here. The last racial disturbance, the 1965 Chinese riots, took place 40 plus years ago and shed little blood.

A striking example of the inclusive national personality is Jamaican popular music's welcoming attitude to foreigners. Every once in a while a German or Japanese or Israeli or whatever performer appears on a local stage show, mostly to initially warm applause. However, if they're not up to scratch, the no-nonsense Jamaican audience will 'boo' off foreigners as quickly as they would unsatisfactory 'born and bred yah' artistes. As the fans would say, 'we no partial'.

In 2002 a Japanese girl actually won the national dancehall queen contest – where contestants parade the latest dance styles and moves, and are judged by audience applause. Far from arousing resentment, the victorious Junko became a local celebrity, getting 'big ups' all around.

HALF WAY TREE COMES ALIVE AS JAMAICANS CELEBRATE OUR ATHLETES SUCCESS AT THE WORLD CHAMPIONSHIP GAMES

HELD IN BERLIN

Happy Go Lucky?

Are Jamaicans a happy people? Well it's hard to say; while few people go hungry, there are pockets of real poverty, and a fair amount of physical discomfort. Polls say about half of Jamaicans would emigrate to the US if they could, and a high crime rate is not usually the sign of a contented populace. Then there is the constant complaining, for people here are world-class grumblers. Yet Jamaicans interact with such vitality and humour, that it's hard to conceive of them as being fundamentally miserable and disgruntled. There can't be many places where people laugh as easily or as often, and no matter how bad things get, folk here always find reasons for outbursts of merriment.

The national suicide rate is among the world's lowest, and polls consistently show a strong majority of Jamaicans claiming to be happy. In fact, the country ranked third out of 143 countries on the 2009 Happy Planet Index. I asked newspaper columnist Mark Wignall – whose work and lifestyle makes him familiar with inner city realities – if this included the ghettos. 'I hate to admit it, but I have to say yes.' he responded, and related this story:

> I remember talking to one of these unemployed and uneducated youths you see so many of. To me his future seemed pretty dim. But the man was so cheerful and content, that one day I exclaimed to him that 'You have no right to be so happy!' He just laughed at me. He had a girlfriend he said, and he could juggle a little money, and he loved his music, and there was a dance every weekend. Why shouldn't he be happy?

We are all one big family of Jamaicans!

Most visitors and resident expatriates express a genuine affection for Jamaica. Yes they complain about the bad roads, power cuts and water lock-offs. On the whole, however, they seem to really like the people and country. What many find most attractive is the lack of pretence. This is not a land of 'happy smiling natives'. When people here are feeling angry or miserable, you see it on their faces and hear it in their voices. Yet when feeling good about life, which is most of the time, they laugh and joke constantly. Whatever they are, Jamaicans are not plastic people. What you see is what you get.

This is strongly evident at entertainment events, where local crowds are notoriously tough to please. The late reggae legend Alton Ellis, who performed all over the world, once remarked that his greatest satisfaction as a singer was getting cheers from a Jamaican crowd. He said audiences abroad were usually gracious, and even if you really didn't do a good show, they clapped politely. On the other hand, if a Jamaican audience isn't pleased, they're not going to clap, and might even 'boo' you off the stage, or worse. Yet if they like what you are doing, they let you know it in no uncertain terms. When he got applause here, he knew he had earned it.

Many feel it's this emotional authenticity that makes music from this tiny island resonate so strongly around the globe. Foreign audiences may not always be able to understand the lyrics, but they feel the genuine passion. Here is Toots Hibbert, the man who named the musical genre:

> Reggae is real music that come from the heart. Everything I write about happen to me, or to somebody I know. It's not no make up or pretend something.

This 'heart on a sleeve' attitude makes everyday life here, depending on the circumstances and one's outlook, either infuriatingly frustrating or engagingly unpredictable. For this island is a strange mix of political stability, social disorder, and religious conviction. It's almost as if the Jamaican populace has subconsciously calculated that cleaving to the certainties of Westminster and the Bible will allow it to indulge every emotional whim, and yet still have a functioning society. Theirs is a truly 'carpe diem' culture.

There certainly are downsides to this outlook, but Jamaicans show absolutely no indication of wishing to change their way of

SPECTATORS CELEBRATE AT A MANNING CUP FOOTBALL MATCH

THE AUDIENCE SHOWS THEIR APPRECIATION FOR A PERFORMANCE

life. They seem to have collectively decided that the benefits of virtually complete emotional freedom outweigh the negative consequences. Perhaps this partially explains why despite the low per capita GDP, the country scores relatively well on the healthy life expectancy scale.

The people and the nation both have an unmatched penchant for embracing chaos, while somehow avoiding true disaster. The girl who gets pregnant for an 'old dawg' that doesn't even acknowledge the baby, always finds someone to help her raise the child. Localised roadblock demonstrations may be common, yet post-independence Jamaica has never experienced a serious insurrection.

Jamaicans seem to have perfected the art of worrying just enough about the future, and doing just as much as is necessary to prevent catastrophe. 'Adrenaline addiction' is how some describe this national partiality for living 'pon di edge'. Maybe this is why so many emigrant Jamaicans who have attained economic success abroad still pine for their native land. After the passionate intensity of this isle, other places can seem a trifle boring.

A distinguishing feature of Jamaicans living elsewhere is the strong attachment to their land of birth. They tend to visit often and hold on tenaciously to their cultural identity. A high per cent return home to live when financially able. The worldwide popularity of the country's music is partly due to Jamaicans taking it everywhere with them. Jamaicans are adaptable, and tend to get on well with others anyplace they go, but whatever their abode, they are always first and foremost Jamaicans.

Mixed with their apparent penchant for the unpredictable, is a fondness for tradition. Jamaicans don't believe in fixing what 'aint broke', and what they like, they like for a long time, no matter how styles and fashions may change elsewhere. 'Oldies' music for instance is very popular even among the young, who frequent weekly retro sessions, and sing along happily to the decades old ballads by the likes of Sam Cooke and The Drifters that dominate Sunday radio.

One centuries old custom that still thrives is an informal cooperative savings system called 'partner'. This usually takes the form of weekly contributions from each member called a 'hand'. The total weekly contribution of all members, called a draw, is paid to each member in rotation, minus a small fee for the 'banker'.

The practice is common across the Caribbean under different names, including 'susu', derived from 'esusu', the name for a similar system among the Yoruba people of Nigeria. 'Susu' is recognised by law in Trinidad. The system is called a 'Meeting' in Barbados, 'Box' in Guyana, 'Sam' in the Dutch islands, and 'Syndicate' in Belize. Caribbean immigrants have taken the system to North America under the name 'Susu'.

Though no interest is paid and despite modern advances such as cell phone banking, most Jamaicans refuse to give up their 'partner'. Apparently group pressure makes participants feel obliged to put away what they might otherwise squander, and this sense of compulsion is deemed to be more than worth the bank interest foregone. It's also another indication of how interconnected people are, with 'no man is an island, entire of itself' being an unconsciously accepted fact of life. Hard as things might get, loneliness is not a major worry here.

A woman we name so we born lucky...

– Lady Saw

A WOMAN WE NAME

PORTIA SIMPSON MILLER

A century ago universities were nearly all male. In the West today female undergraduates outnumber and outperform males. Few nations are experiencing greater female academic domination than Jamaica, where the literacy rate is significantly higher among women than men, 86 per cent versus 74 per cent according to UNESCO. Only Lesotho has a greater reverse gender gap. Girls here outclass boys academically at every level and an alarming 80 per cent of university graduates are female.

Jamaican women are as liberated and uninhibited as any on earth. This is also fast becoming the first country in history where women are not only more emotionally aware than men, as females everywhere tend to be, but more intellectually developed as well. The national suicide rate is quite low and although men the world over commit suicide more often than women, Jamaica's almost 10:1 sexual dispariy is virtualy unprecedented. Proof perhaps of novelist Anthony Winkler's assertion that 'Jamaican culture produces a female personality that is stronger, hardier, and more adaptable than its male equivalent'.

Portia Simpson Miller was hailed as a pioneering glass-ceiling breaker when she became the nation's first female prime minister in 2006. Current education trends suggest she is unlikely to be the last, although curiously only 8 of 60 Parliamentarians are women. Business people already consider female employees more honest, hard-working, disciplined, and productive than their male counterparts. There is a growing and unhealthy tendency to see the majority of men as good for only manual labour. 'If women could lift cement bags, I wouldn't have a man in the place' half-jokes a business acquaintance.

No one knows for sure what long-term effects female educational superiority will have on Jamaican society. What will happen to personal relationships? Most women seek mates of an equal or superior educational level. A female friend says women find it easy to manipulate men emotionally and sexually, so a man who can also be dominated intellectually seems inferior and not good enough.

GRADUATES OF UNIVERSITY OF THE WEST INDIES, MONA

However, if only 20 per cent of main university graduates are men, how can all of the 80 per cent who are women find a comparably educated partner? What about the uneducated men deprived of potential mates? Will they become frustrated and violently bitter towards females? For it's a sad fact that when women are better educated, males often validate themselves in the only way left, physically.

Jamaica's mating patterns are already unusual by global standards. It has the world's highest median marriage age – 35 for men and 33 for women, versus a worldwide 27 and 23 average. In addition 85 per cent of children are born out of wedlock, and over 50 per cent have no registered father.

BOYS' DAY AT A LOCAL PRIMARY SCHOOL

In the island's three main universities...an alarming 80 per cent of graduates are female.

A male teacher told me this thought-provoking story. One of his 13-year-old students confided that

> …he hated women because his home was controlled by women. Like most Jamaican children he had an absentee father and lived with his mother and his school was controlled by women [the teaching profession in Jamaica is over 90 per cent female].

In short, the authority figures in his life were all women, and he associated the female sex with being ordered around.

To compound the problem, the girls in his class were generally much brighter than the boys and treated them with barely disguised disdain. Indeed gender disparity is now so great that many schools now have 'Boys' Days', when girls stay home, and successful men are brought in to give 'I did it lads, and you can too' motivational speeches.

Perhaps as Jamaican women come to dominate the private and public sectors, they will restructure society. Maybe there will be a fundamental transformation of gender roles, although it is difficult to imagine four million years of genetic hard wiring changing in a few generations. Revamped educational and legal systems could over time conceivably modify male behavioural patterns. More educated women might choose mates who get actively involved in their offspring's lives and provide positive role models. All Jamaica can do – and soon perhaps the world – is wait and see.

White, Brown and Black

It is often said that almost everything found in Jamaica came from somewhere else. This is an open island, constantly exposed to outside influences, and quick to adopt whatever it finds useful or attractive, no matter the origin. Yet we're not a copying country. Anything that comes here seems to undergo some kind of transformation that makes it uniquely ours. Rhythm and Blues may have originated in New Orleans, and Kumina in the Congo, but we combined them into Jamaican ska and reggae.

The distinctive flavour of Jamaican music, food and Jamaican talk has made them popular and copied worldwide. Many developing countries worry about western cultural imperialism obliterating native traditions, but Jamaica is probably the world's smallest net cultural exporter. In a world of increasingly globalised and often soulless conformity, this country and its people are definitely one of a kind.

This is not surprising, as our national identity was built from scratch. Most New World countries are, in varying degrees, cultural hybrids of European invaders and indigenous inhabitants. The originally sparsely populated US and Canada were more or less remade in Britain's image. The Spanish imposed their language on most of South and Central America, but surviving Amerindian natives stamped their traditions on the nations that emerged.

In Jamaica however, the original Taino inhabitants died out in a generation after the Spanish arrived. The governing white slave masters were largely British in thought and deed. However, while they dominated socially, economically and politically, their small numbers meant they could never fully impose their mores on the entire population.

The African descended slave majority brought with them only jumbled memories of their various homelands – though some argue that being largely West African, their differences were only regional variations of a common culture. With no common tribal identity, they did not even have a shared tongue, and could only communicate with each other in English. Yet their Africanness was self-evident, and one had only to look around to realise that, whatever language it spoke, this predominantly black country was not a little new Britain.

Jamaica was, from the beginning, then, neither fish nor fowl, neither mostly European, nor mostly African. Even today 'motherland' can mean, depending on context, either Africa – the land to which most Jamaicans trace their ancestry, or England – birthplace of the language all Jamaicans speak. In a sense this tension has defined the island's history since 1838.

The first to grapple with this reality were the mixed race 'mulatto' offspring of white overlords and slave women. These 'coloureds' were slaves by law, but white fathers who could afford to, and many could not, usually purchased the freedom of their accidental progeny. Coloured children often grew up in the paternal home, absorbing the speech patterns and deportment of their white relatives. Frequently they learned to read at a time when few slaves were literate.

Coloureds were the largest freeborn class, and the most Jamaican of Jamaicans, exhibiting the strongest attachment to their island. Whites might dream of going back to Britain, and blacks to Africa, but browns knew they would be unwelcome in both. Here was all they would ever have.

Local whites refused to recognise mixed bloods as full equals, even after legal discrimination was abolished, while coloureds in turn looked down at blacks. This middle class insecurity made coloureds accentuate the European part of their social heritage, and minimise the African aspect. It also produced a compensatory exaggerated loyalty to Britain.

The bitter old proverb, put to song by Peter Tosh, still often rings true – 'white alright, brown stick round, black get back'.

1979: PETER TOSH

Still, the whites' miniscule numbers made them welcome coloureds as fellow defenders of European heritage against the black hordes, while for coloureds, any association with whites made for greater social respectability. This situation in time applied to immigrants who were neither white nor black. The Jews, Chinese, and Lebanese, who came to Jamaica in regular streams during the late nineteenth and early twentieth centuries, at first kept to their own kind, and focused on making money. However, as they became assimilated, they mirrored the attitudes of coloureds, as did upper class, business-oriented East Indians.

At the same time, the East Indians who came as indentured labourers in the mid-1850s, integrated extensively with the black working class. They brought with them two future Jamaican staples, curry goat and ganja. Another Indian import was the plaid cotton material (with principal colours of red, yellow and white) formerly much favoured by market higglers, and now incorporated into Jamaica's national costume. It is popularly called Madras plaid or bandana – which derives from the Sanskrit 'bandhna' for 'tying'.

REVELLERS AT CARNIVAL

The US is often said to have a 'one drop' rule, where even a trace of black blood makes a person black. The situation in Jamaica became almost the reverse, with any non-black blood aiding social mobility. Whatever highlighted blackness was frowned on, while European features such as straight or 'pretty' hair were prized.

Social station tended to be fixed according to skin colour, plus an endless variety of subtle differentiations, such as hair 'quality'. The social ladder grew progressively darker with each descending rung and at the base stood the blacks, the vast majority of the population, characterised as much by homogeneity of colour, as by poverty and ignorance.

There has been considerable progress over the years, but to some this pernicious situation continues today. A glance though the business press suggests that the economic heights are commanded mostly by whites, light browns, Indians and Chinese. The make-up of groups like the Private Sector Organisation of Jamaica (PSOJ) and the Jamaica Chamber of Commerce confirms this.

There are many gatherings of the good and great, and not a few gated communities, where practically the only black faces to be seen are waiters, maids and gardeners. By contrast light complexions are virtually unknown in the ghettos and prisons. The bitter old proverb, put to song by Peter Tosh, still often rings true – 'white alright, brown stick round, black get back'.

Given this history, it is amazing that post-1865 Jamaica has never had a serious racial disturbance, and indeed is often considered an exemplar of racial tolerance. What accounts for this? Some praise the patient wisdom of the Jamaican masses, who instinctively realised that centuries of injustice could not be remedied overnight, and that trying to do so usually ends in disaster. Others condemn the mental slavery of the black majority who, even after the advent of universal adult suffrage, still deferred to whites and browns, and acquiesced to the notion that blacks were not fit to lead themselves.

Maybe it's just demographic chance, with

black weight of numbers counterbalancing light-skinned economic and educational dominance. Jamaican whites have always been too few to set up the kind of self-sufficient society that created official apartheid in South Africa, or the unofficial kind some still perceive in places like Barbados. In addition, the Jamaican common man has always been essentially conservative, distrusting sudden change, and preferring evolution to revolution.

For all its faults, colonialist Britain did bequeath independent Jamaica a reasonably well functioning country. Perhaps the poor illiterate black masses intuitively calculated that they did not yet possess enough education or management skills, and that the economy could not function without the productive capital and financial know-how of the whites and browns. So, unlike many newly independent African countries, Jamaica never fell into the 'Africa for Africans only' mindset that pushed improperly trained persons into positions because of their colour, and which often led to a crippling brain drain of qualified non-blacks.

It is almost as if an unwritten bargain prevailed. Though their numbers might have allowed them to do so if they wished, it was not in the black populace's self-interest to physically drive out the ruling lighter minority. Conversely, being vastly outnumbered made whites and browns careful not to exploit blacks to the point where they would rise up and exterminate their oppressors as in Haiti. Thus was 'Out of Many One People' born.

The masses had little voice before universal adult suffrage in 1944. However the ruling classes relentlessly promoted the idea of Jamaica as a virtually equal mixture of all races living in blissful accord, although this was clearly at odds with the 85 per cent black reality. Prior to 1962 the black majority had limited access to the island's better quality schools – as reflected by pre-independence yearbook photos of places like Jamaica College and Decarteret College. Furthermore most of the whites and the more prominent browns lived in the politically and economically dominant Kingston, and the tourism capital Montego Bay. This meant the well educated and well connected were far more varied in skin tone than the general population.

Since visiting journalists mostly interacted with this racially disparate upper echelon, the foreign press also bought into and helped spread the 'out of many' legend. An old advertising axiom says people will believe anything if it is repeated often enough. So it proved with 'out of many', as the idea of a land where the races lived in perfect harmony became part of the national consciousness. In his 1961 address to the US National Press Club, then Premier Norman Manley extolled Jamaica as a 'non-racialist' haven and a living model for the modern world. The entire country applauded with pride, even

Martin Luther King Jr after a 1965 visit…said he had never felt more at home anywhere else in the world, and that 'in Jamaica I feel like a human being.'

© The Gleaner Company Ltd, 2010

MARTIN LUTHER KING, JR ADDRESSING A CROWD AT THE NATIONAL STADIUM IN KINGSTON

if at that time non-white bank tellers were still a rarity, and blacks were not welcome in swankier hotel swimming pools.

Yet imperfect as they were, race relations here were still better than in most other places. At least this was the view of Martin Luther King Jr after a 1965 visit. He said he had never felt more at home anywhere else in the world, and that 'In Jamaica I feel like a human being.' He later added:

> The other day Mrs King and I spent about ten days down in Jamaica…I always love to go that great island which I consider the most beautiful island in all the world…we traveled all over Jamaica. And over and over again I was impressed by one thing. Here you have people from many national backgrounds: Chinese, Indians, so-called Negroes, and you can just go down the line, Europeans, European and people from many, many nations. Do you know they all live there and they have a motto in Jamaica, 'Out of many people, one people.' And they say, 'Here in Jamaica we are not Chinese, [Make it plain] we are not Japanese, we are not Indians, we are not Negroes, we are not Englishmen, we are not Canadians. But we are all one big family of Jamaicans.' One day, here in America, I hope that we will see this and we will become one big family of Americans.

The attitude of Jamaican leaders to the colour issue has been critical. All have made conscious efforts to resist any attempts at polarisation. The Bustamante-led 1938 mass demonstrations essentially transferred political power from the light-skinned merchant/planter minority to the black majority. Yet he never allowed his 'mental revolution' to take on any racial or ideological tones, and his example has been more or less continued by all regimes.

For instance Hugh Shearer – the first 'visibly black' head of government – instituted a deliberate policy of gradual 'Jamaicanisation'. This meant the white English expatriates, who held most senior civil services positions at independence, were slowly replaced by locals. Shearer had previously urged then Prime Minister Bustamante to appoint the black former schoolteacher Clifford Campbell as the first Jamaican Governor General, when others had been recommending someone from the light-skinned elite. Yet Shearer's government dealt quite strictly with 'black power' activists like Stokely Carmichael and Walter Rodney.

At the same time Jamaica has always been at the international forefront of the fight for racial justice. Even though Jamaica was not yet technically an independent country, in 1959 Premier Norman Manley banned trade with apartheid South Africa, setting an example many others would follow. In 1966 Acting Prime Minister Donald Sangster brokered a Commonwealth declaration calling for UN sanctions against minority ruled Rhodesia.

THE RODNEY RIOTS AND BLACK POWER

In October 1968 the black power activist Walter Rodney was a lecturer in History at the University of the West Indies' Mona Campus. He attended a black writers' conference in Montreal, but on his return was refused re-admittance to Jamaica, for 'carrying on activities which constituted a danger to the security of the nation.' This sparked a demonstration by University students, which degenerated into riots in which three died.

A Parliamentary motion upholding the government's decision to ban Rodney was passed without dissent. Then Opposition Leader Norman Manley said:

> It is good for Jamaica to know that the reason why Dr Rodney was expelled from this country was because he was engaged in organising activities which advocated violence and the overthrow of those things which are highly treasured in this country – our progress toward a multi-racial society in which a man is not as good as his skin but as good as his merit. And anything that tends to undermine our motto – in spite of our hardship, in spite of our suffering, in spite of our troubles…is bad for Jamaica.

Years after, Shearer reflected on the action he had taken:

> I thought, based on all the security reports presented to me, that it was in the interest of the nation to do as I did. I knew that it would be unpopular among those who embraced the Black Power Movement without analysing what Rodney professed to be. But I remained true to an assurance I gave this country when I became prime minister, that I would never seek to 'butter' nor to please any clique or section of this country to the detriment of the nation.

WALTER RODNEY

That is why I subsequently described Black Power as black ambition, black equality of opportunity, black dignity, economic strength and self-respect. That's Black Power! When Sir Alexander Bustamante made Isaac Barrant a Minister, a man who started his working life as a sideman on a truck, and the middle class opposed the appointment, that was Black Power in operation!

CLIFFORD CAMPBELL

When Edwin Allen, Minister of Education, prescribed that 70 per cent of the places in Secondary Schools should be reserved for Primary School children who passed the Common Entrance Examination, and 30 per cent for Preparatory School children, that was Black Power!

When Sir Clifford Campbell was appointed Governor General, that was a move in furtherance of Black Power! Don't forget, too, the strong and vulgar criticism about the appointment of this black man to the highest post in the land.

When we decided to send for the body of Marcus Garvey to give him eminence in his own country, that was Black Power! Yet there were some people who went to the ceremony to disrupt it, almost causing a riot. That was not Black Power! Definitely not!

Furthermore, as I said before, and I repeat now, the people who shout Black Power loudest are hypocrites masquerading in black skins by day and sleeping with white skins by night!

...as I said before, and I repeat now, the people who shout Black Power loudest are hypocrites masquerading in black skins by day and sleeping with white skins by night!

UNIVERSITY STUDENTS FLEEING THE POLICE DURING THE RIOTS

A SHOP IN THE COUNTRY

UPTOWN VS DOWNTOWN: COUNTRY VS TOWN

Jamaicans separate the island mentally in two: 'town' refers to Kingston and St Andrew, while everywhere else is considered 'country'. Of late, the population growth in Portmore and Spanish Town has created a third 'neither nor' category: often thought of as part of 'country' by Kingstonians, and part of 'town' by 'country people'.

Out-of-towners are apt to disparage the capital as hot, hectic and crime-ridden, though they cannot deny Kingston's economic, political and cultural pre-eminence. Kingstonians on the other hand love to sneer at the naivety of 'country' folk, but cannot hide their envy of a generally more polite and grounded rural lifestyle.

'Town' itself is divided into 'uptown' where the well-off live, and 'downtown' where the poor dwell. Implicit in this division is a 'midtown' of working class Jamaicans who are neither 'upper class' nor 'ghetto.' Physically, 'uptown' is above Half Way Tree, and 'downtown' is below Torrington Bridge. The area in between, encompassing Half Way Tree and Cross Roads, is a sort of 'midtown' melting pot.

This is only a rough simplification, with the 'up' and 'down' partition being more mental than geographic, for there are 'ghetto' areas scattered

TORRINGTON BRIDGE

DANCEHALL ARTISTES VYBZ KARTEL (LEFT) AND MAVADO

all about. These include the 'Gullyside' of Cassava Piece in Constant Spring, and 'Gaza' of Waterford in Portmore, now rivals in song via the lyrics of deejays Mavado and Vybz Kartel.

Uptown is quite racially mixed and generally colour unself-conscious, but downtown reflects the reality that Jamaica has few poor non-blacks. Kingston's geographic divide has become a metaphorical one across the country. Former prime minister, and trained anthropologist, Edward Seaga has even described the dynamism of Jamaican culture as 'a unique mix of the largely Eurocentric lifestyle of "uptown", with the African retention traditions of "downtown"'.

Yet even the old 'Torrington Bridge' division may be crumbling. Once there was a widespread implicit assumption that the only genuine Jamaicans were working class black 'sufferers', everyone else being dismissed as 'stoosh' (pretentious) uptowners. It was as difficult to imagine a middle class dancehall deejay as say a suburban delta blues singer.

Music has helped to break down some of these class barriers. Producer Mikey Bennett says dancehall has allowed downtown-spawned deejays and producers to move into uptown neighbourhoods, and pulled uptown patrons down into Kingston's inner city streets. Well-to-do youths no longer have to pretend to understand the state of affairs in Kingston's ghettos. As such, they do not have to bypass the gatekeepers of authenticity, the audience. 'They don't have to pretend that they know,' he says, 'because they do know. Every kid uptown has a good friend who lives in the inner city. Though they may not have first-hand experience, they still have knowledge from their second-hand experience.'

To quote Tanya Batson-Savage and Mel Cooke of the *Gleaner*, 'So, while dancehall has long been synonymous with downtown, with the ghetto, more and more those from uptown are staking their claim in what is a Jamaican identity, no longer just that of a segment of society'.

Sean Henriques had Portuguese and African grandfathers, Jewish and Chinese grandmothers, and went to the 'stooshest' high school in the Kingston. Yet no one now sees international superstar deejay Sean Paul as anything but 100 per cent Jamaican.

Jamaican race relations continue to be considerably influenced by class. Many state categorically that Jamaica does not have a race but a class problem. With blacks becoming more educated and moving into positions of prestige, over the years colour has become less of a factor in the make-up of upper and upper middle class Jamaica. Even then, 'colour' sometimes has as much to do with attitude as skin shade.

A friend recalls a 1970s university debate where then Prime Minister Michael Manley was insistently labelled black, and his predecessor Hugh Shearer condescendingly branded white. In reality Manley was a fair-complexioned son of privilege, while Shearer was a dark-skinned man of the working class. To the speakers, however, Manley's talk of socialist empowerment for the masses made him black, while Shearer's rejection of the black power movement as 'shallow and hypocritical' made him white.

Which is not to say this schoolboy rebel view of Shearer as a 'roast breadfruit' – black on the outside and white on the inside – was correct. As a union leader he worked tirelessly to win better conditions and wages for poor black workers. He was also Jamaica's most effective prime minister in terms of increasing measurable welfare, though some charged him with not giving his full attention to politics, and losing touch with the masses.

HUGH SHEARER

1970s: MICHAEL MANLEY HUGS HIS WIFE, BEVERLEY, WHILE ADDRESSING A CROWD OF SUPPORTERS

Manley's ex-wife Beverley – he was 48 when they wed – had these insights:

> [Michael] used to say that if there was anything he could do to become black, like the majority of Jamaicans, he would. I would reply that the masses of people saw him as black and referred to him as black. But this never sufficed – he wanted to be a black man more than anything in this world.... Michael was very class conscious, and although his life's work was for the masses, he knew little or nothing about them at an individual level and was uncomfortable around them.... Michael taught me how the other half of Jamaica lived and I did the same for him.... I introduced him to Jamaican music, such as the works of Bob Marley, Peter Tosh and Ken Boothe, and to Jamaican foods like stew peas and cooked down chicken.

His daughter Rachel concurred.

> For all our dedication to the oppressed and the working classes, our family was quaintly British middle class in our habits, even in our choice of food.... My father had spent his adult life representing a world with which he shared very little social intimacy. He never went into a rum bar or cruised the constituency the way Douglas did. He would go to a little rural home on the campaign trail, where someone had painted the house for his visit, and when offered a drink he'd ask politely for a glass of white wine, or his tonic water, and then try to hide the annoyance when the perplexed host would present him with some Wincarnis, a local 'tonic wine'. But this made no difference to most Jamaicans. This was who he was, and that was the way they loved him. They knew he could represent their case anywhere in the world. This was their bond.

In the final reckoning, whenever Jamaicans are asked to pick their favourite prime minister, Michael Manley always tops the polls.

Gleaner proprietor Oliver Clarke concurs that race in Jamaica often has as much to do with behaviour as appearance. In his experience, those seen as actively contributing to the national welfare are considered true Jamaicans, in other words, black, while those who are not are considered interlopers or non-black. Some might dismiss this as a comforting self-justifying myth of a minority aristocrat, but the lack of racial animosity here suggests he may be on to something fundamental. Indeed a number of key fighters for workers' rights have been light-skinned figures – for example William Knibb, Alexander Bustamante, Edward Seaga and Michael Manley – who were at times mistrusted by their own upper classes, but beloved by the poor black masses.

The mostly relaxed Jamaican attitude to race is heard in the blunt and stereotypical ethnic references of everyday discourse. Any East Indian is a 'Coolie'. An Oriental-looking person is a 'Chiney'. Someone from the Middle East is a 'Syrian'. Those of lighter complexion are often simply 'brown man' or 'white man', but no malice is intended, and no offence is taken. It's simply a spade being called a spade.

At the same time there are class niceties. Frank racial language is generally used by the black working class majority in reference to minorities perceived as wealthier, and it doesn't work the same way in the other direction. So while a taxi driver may say to a prospective oriental passenger 'Need a ride chiney man?', a reply of 'No, black man' would not be deemed appropriate. Between acquaintances of equal status, teasing – or 'mouthing' – about racial matters is commonplace.

The fairly strong charitable tradition, started by persons like William Knibb, has also helped to dampen class and colour resentment. Rita Marley once alluded to this in an interview:

> The prejudice didn't make me bitter, because I didn't understand what this was about until I started to read about Marcus Garvey and Selassie, and met Bob. They started to show me that black is good, and you should be proud to be black, and hold your head up for you are a queen. Before this we were conditioned to feel inferior. I would never get out of this situation. I was always going to be black and poor. But it didn't make me angry, because you didn't have anybody to be angry with. Cause when you saw a brown person or somebody of a different calibre, they always came to help. I used to go to the Catholic Church for milk powder and rice and things every Friday. And I would get old clothes and high heel shoes – ol brukers we called it! – and dress up and feel good about myself. So you didn't have time to fight against. Because it was the only aid you had.
>
> The anger against prejudice is much stronger now that black consciousness has grown, but mostly Jamaica has learned to live with it. Because we are forced to work together. And you find the intermingling, with the uptown people coming downtown, and the uptown kid now smoking spliff and doing what the locals do. We have definitely overcome a lot of things that used to happen when I was growing up, where black people couldn't go there and work, and black stay back. Hey that's wiped out! They can't bring that anymore.

The anger against prejudice is much stronger now that black consciousness has grown, but mostly Jamaica has learned to live with it.

RITA MARLEY

The colour question continues to shift. When P.J. Patterson became prime minister in 1993, some upper St Andrew verandahs whispered that Jamaicans would never vote for a black prime minister. All previously elected leaders – Bustamante, Norman Manley, Sangster, Michael Manley, Seaga – had been brown or white. Black Hugh Shearer, who was appointed prime minister after Sangster died, had been trounced at the polls by three quarters white Michael Manley. However Mr Patterson led his party to three straight general election victories, so no one talks anymore about Jamaicans being unwilling to elect a black leader. In fact some began wondering if they would vote for a visibly non-black one.

The election of Bruce Golding answered that question. Though light brown-skinned himself, his father was visibly black, as are his wife and children. Golding considers the colour question irrelevant, once dismissing a critic who raised the question with a sharp 'Who are you to question my blackness?'

In the business sector too, there has been slow but discernable progress towards balanced racial representation. A 1970s academic paper purported to show that nearly all directorates of the nation's major companies were in the interlocking hands of 21 all-white families. Whatever the truth then, the situation has changed significantly. For one, most banking sector senior managers are now black, and the current 'rich list' is far from lily white. In addition most major companies are now publicly listed, and so 'owned' by tens of thousands of mostly black shareholders. There may be a ways to go, but the money train is gradually moving in the right direction.

The same is true culturally, though thorny problems still exist. While the young nowadays mostly view their African heritage with pride, some psychological effects of slavery and colonialism remain. Four hundred years of mental oppression do not vanish overnight and media globalisation has given the question of race and identity a new dimension.

Courtesy of the Jamaica Tourist Board

Take the annual beauty contests, Jamaica may be 85 per cent black, but historically few 'Miss Jamaicas' have been of the same complexion as the majority. The sardonic once jested that the lightest-skinned contestant was always the safest bet.

As far back as 1931, a blonde blue-eyed Miss Jamaica prompted the pioneer writer and broadcaster Una Marson to wryly comment that perhaps

> Some amount of expense and disappointment could be saved by numbers of dusky ladies, who year after year enter the Beauty competition, if the

1955: A SPECTRUM OF JAMAICAN BEAUTY

> promoters of the contest could announce in the daily press that very dark or black 'beauties' would not be considered.... There is a growing feeling that 'Miss J' should be a type of girl who is more truly representative of the majority of Jamaicans.

Yet the modern day mostly black promoters and judges strenuously deny any preconceived bias, and they are probably being honest. The forces at work in beauty contests are not individual but societal ones, for the judges' verdicts usually agree with the crowd's. The preponderance of Caucasian-featured, light-skinned Miss Jamaicas in a mostly black country was likely not the result of prejudiced adjudicators, but history and globalisation. The phenomenon has diminished noticeably over the past few years. Miss Jamaica Universe 2007 Zahra Redwood was not only dark-skinned, but a dreadlocked Rastafarian to boot (incidentally, three Miss Jamaica winners have become Miss World – Carole Joan Crawford in 1963, Cindy Breakespeare in 1976 and Lisa Hanna in 1993).

Yet the 'white is beautiful, black is ugly' mentality, so drummed into Jamaicans through plantation slavery and British colonialism, still persists in many quarters. Sadly, people still openly refer to straight hair as 'good' and light skin as 'quality', while 'bleaching', or lightening your complexion with chemicals, is alarmingly common among teenage girls, and even boys.

The video screen also greatly influences attitudes towards physical appearance. As elsewhere, most Jamaicans now spend the majority of their leisure time watching television, and to many, what they see on screen is as valid as everyday reality. Hollywood may be more multi-hued than it once was, but the overwhelming majority of faces on cable TV and DVDs are still white, thus reinforcing the Caucasian concept of beauty.

Not that this phenomenon is new; over 70 years ago, Una Marson's poem 'Cinema Eyes' spoke of a mother who 'grew up with a cinema mind', and thus when young 'saw no beauty in black', and adored 'beautiful white faces'. So she wants to shield her daughter from the same conditioning:

> Come, I will let you go [to the cinema]
> When black beauties
> Are chosen for the screen;
> That you may know
> Your own sweet beauty
> And not the white loveliness
> Of others for envy.

Still, Jamaica is only one tiny country and television and movies are themselves only a part of larger social influences. Globalisation and the internet are creating a 'one big world' mentality of similar tastes, habits and thinking. The logical end would be an integration of all aspects of human existence, including physical appearance.

Who knows, it may be humanity's destiny to interbreed completely and create a uniformly mixed race. It's notable that Miss World and Miss Universe are no longer predominantly Nordic type blondes. Recent winners have been Indian, Jewish, African, Trinidadian, Turkish, South American and Chinese. This may portend a future where the average person reflects the planet's racial make-up, and is about half Mongoloid, one third Caucasian, one sixth Negroid with traces of aborigine and pygmy (though some say these terms are outdated, now we know all our genomes are 99.99 per cent the same).

In global metropolises like New York and Toronto, something of the sort is already happening. In London, perhaps the world capital of miscegenation, the great majority of young black males reportedly have non-black partners. A totally mixed world might be a very good thing. If we all had roughly the same colour and features, racial prejudice would be non-existent. It would also be an ironic return of sorts to humanity's original state. Are we not all descended from the same African Eve?

1963: CAROLE JOAN CRAWFORD

1976: CINDY BREAKSPEARE

1993: LISA HANNA

2007: ZAHRA REDWOOD

Democratic Triumph, Economic Disappointment

'History is nothing but a record of the crimes and misfortunes of man' wrote Voltaire. A famous Chinese proverb agrees – 'Fortunate countries have no history'. Compared to the often chilling chronicles of its nearest neighbours – Cuba, Haiti and the Dominican Republic – Jamaica's past makes pretty tame reading. It has no 'Remember the Maine' invasions, Citadelle Lafferriere horrors, or Trujillo massacres to contemplate with fascinated dismay.

Jamaica's historical highlights – the 1655 Battle of the Rio Nuevo, the 1831 Sam Sharpe slave uprising, the 1865 Morant Bay Rebellion, the 1938 Frome riots – would scarcely rate footnotes in these countries a mere 100 miles away. Jamaica did have to endure the unspeakable brutalities of slavery. This was an almost universal New World experience. Even then, slaves in the British Caribbean were freed by decree a generation before anywhere else, and experienced no brutal liberation wars as in Haiti.

Granted a bloodless independence and untouched by war, modern Jamaica has also been exceptionally fortunate in escaping violent upheaval. If history was strictly Darwinian, this peaceful past should have created a quiet and docile people. Yet rarely a week goes by without a demonstration protesting bad roads, poor water supplies, or police brutality with the common refrain 'We want justice!' Excitable and aggressive in defending whatever they view as their rights, Jamaicans have a reputation for belligerence even among other Caribbean nations.

This makes Jamaica's political history all the more striking. Since becoming independent in 1962, the country has remained uprising free, suffered no major political assassination, adhered to the rule of law, maintained a free press, and held regular multi-party elections in which incumbent leaders are often voted out. This might seem a rather commonplace achievement, but over the past 48 years, very few countries of over a million people can make the same collective claim. Indeed you can count them on fingers and toes: Britain, Canada, Australia, New Zealand, Ireland, Germany, France, Austria, Belgium, Denmark, Holland, Finland, Norway, Japan, Switzerland, Costa Rica.

It is remarkable how many places fail such basic criteria. The US saw the 1963 assassination of John Kennedy and the 1981 attempt on Ronald Reagan. Trinidad suffered a 1990 coup attempt, where Prime Minister A.N.R. Robinson was shot and wounded. Italian Prime Minister Aldo Moro was kidnapped and found dead in 1978. Swedish Premier Olaf Palme was murdered in 1986, as was Israeli Prime Minister Yitzhak Rabin in 1995. India suffered the 1984 and 1989 assassinations of Indira and Rajiv Ghandi.

As for the rest of the world, the Far East has experienced political freedom only intermittently – its oldest democracy Singapore is still in essence a press and opposition stifling one-party state. Uninterrupted democracy of substantial length is unknown in the Arabian Middle East. The same is true of Africa, except in Senegal, which suffered a coup attempt in 1962, and Botswana, which has yet to change its ruling party. In Latin America only Costa Rica has known unbroken democracy, while free elections are a

Since becoming independent in 1962, the country has remained uprising free, suffered no major political assassination, adhered to the rule of law, maintained a free press, and held regular multi-party elections in which incumbent leaders are often voted out. This might seem a rather commonplace achievement, but over the past 48 years, very few countries of over a million people can make the same collective claim.

POLITICAL PARTY SUPPORTERS

> Granted a bloodless independence and untouched by war, modern Jamaica has also been exceptionally fortunate in escaping violent upheaval.

fairly recent novelty in Eastern Europe

None of this argues that Jamaica is a more successful society than Sweden, the US or even Trinidad. It shows rather that freely ordered societies are rare, and that peaceful change is the exception, not the rule. Jamaica is no Jeffersonian utopia, but power here has never come through the barrel of a gun. Drug 'don' controlled garrisons still haunt the Jamaican body politic, but they have never prevented the will of the people from ultimately prevailing. Every leader of this country has been constitutionally chosen, and all losing candidates have accepted the ballot count.

Karl Popper once defined democracy as 'the type of government which can be removed without violence'. From this perspective, independent Jamaica is unquestionably a great democratic success. What accounts for this? Three obvious factors come to mind: responsible leadership, especially from founding fathers Alexander Bustamante and Norman Manley; the common sense of the Jamaican masses; and historical fortune. For almost none of the dynamics that caused so many newly emerged democracies to fail were present here. Jamaica has been untouched by war, has no tradition of a politically active military, and has no significant ethnic, linguistic or religious divisions. In short, there was nothing to distract its people from devoting all their energies to governing themselves.

Whatever else their sins might have been, British colonial masters left Jamaica with as clean a democratic slate as any new country ever had, even giving guided lessons in choosing leaders from 1944 to 1962. Their record is not flawless, as places like Nigeria and Iraq show, but the British do democracy better than anyone else. Except for Switzerland and Sweden, the only countries to enjoy uninterrupted democratic rule between 1914 and 1945 were Great Britain, the United States, Canada, Australia and New Zealand.

Being a British colony then, was a bit like old age – not so bad, considering the alternative. The century of British rule between emancipation in 1838 and the first stirrings of nationalism in 1938, clearly impressed enough Westminster into the Jamaican soul to make any other political system unthinkable. These democratic traditions were severely tested in the violent run-up to the1980 elections, when a parliamentary candidate was killed, and the possibility of bullets and not ballots determining political power became a frightening reality. However, in the end, British instilled tradition prevailed again – people voted, ballots were counted, and all sides accepted the results.

Outsiders have often jokingly called Jamaicans and other West Indians 'Afro-Saxons', but politically we have had the last laugh. Only in 1983 Grenada has a West Indian government ever changed hands violently, a one-off never repeated. Outside Western Europe and North America, the English-speaking Caribbean is the most continuously democratic region – if a region can be defined by language – on earth.

Now Britain is the world's oldest democracy, America the richest, India the largest, and Jamaica is a strong contender for the most exuberant. Party conferences and meetings here are electrifying spectacles of almost palpable excitement. The tens of thousands strong JLP or PNP mass rallies at Half Way Tree are strikingly natural cultural exhibitions. Candidates' speeches are highlighted with pounding reggae music, and the roars of the crowd are punctuated with firecrackers in a ganja smoke-filled atmosphere. They resemble nothing so much as gigantic dancehall stage shows. Few, if any other, nations celebrate democracy with such unbridled passion.

At the same time however, the Jamaican economy has languished. In 1962 Singapore, South Korea and Jamaica were in the same underdeveloped bracket, but these Asian tigers now have a much higher per capita GDP than the Caribbean tortoise. Even West Indian cousins like Barbados and Trinidad and Tobago have far outperformed us economically. There is not much obvious physical suffering here, and life expectancy is relatively high, meaning official figures may not reflect black market realities. Yet by any reckoning Jamaica remains a poor nation.

So here is the Jamaican paradox: this country of highly volatile people with a demonstrated propensity for violence, has nevertheless proven itself one of the world's most stable democracies. At the same time despite a free press, multi-party democracy, and an independent judiciary, it nevertheless remains mired in poverty. In short, almost alone among the roughly 200 countries on the planet, independent Jamaica has managed to be both a political success and a relative economic failure.

No other country with such a low per capita GDP has witnessed comparable political stability. However, if no unbroken democracy has ever lasted so long on so little, then none has lasted so long and produced so little. Should we marvel at the heroic preservation of liberal democracy in the face of sometimes crippling financial pressures? Or lament the gross economic mismanagement that has produced minimal real official growth since 1962, despite the absence of any serious social disruption?

Whatever the verdict, this country still enjoys free speech, fair elections and due process. It's not oppressed by memories of devastating invasions, despoiling revolutions, divisive civil wars, kleptocratic dictatorships or shattering natural disasters. In the context of its size and location, Jamaica since independence has more or less decided its own destiny. For good or bad, its fate will continue to lie 'not in our stars but in ourselves'.

Now Britain is the world's oldest democracy, America the richest, India the largest, and Jamaica is a strong contender for the most exuberant.

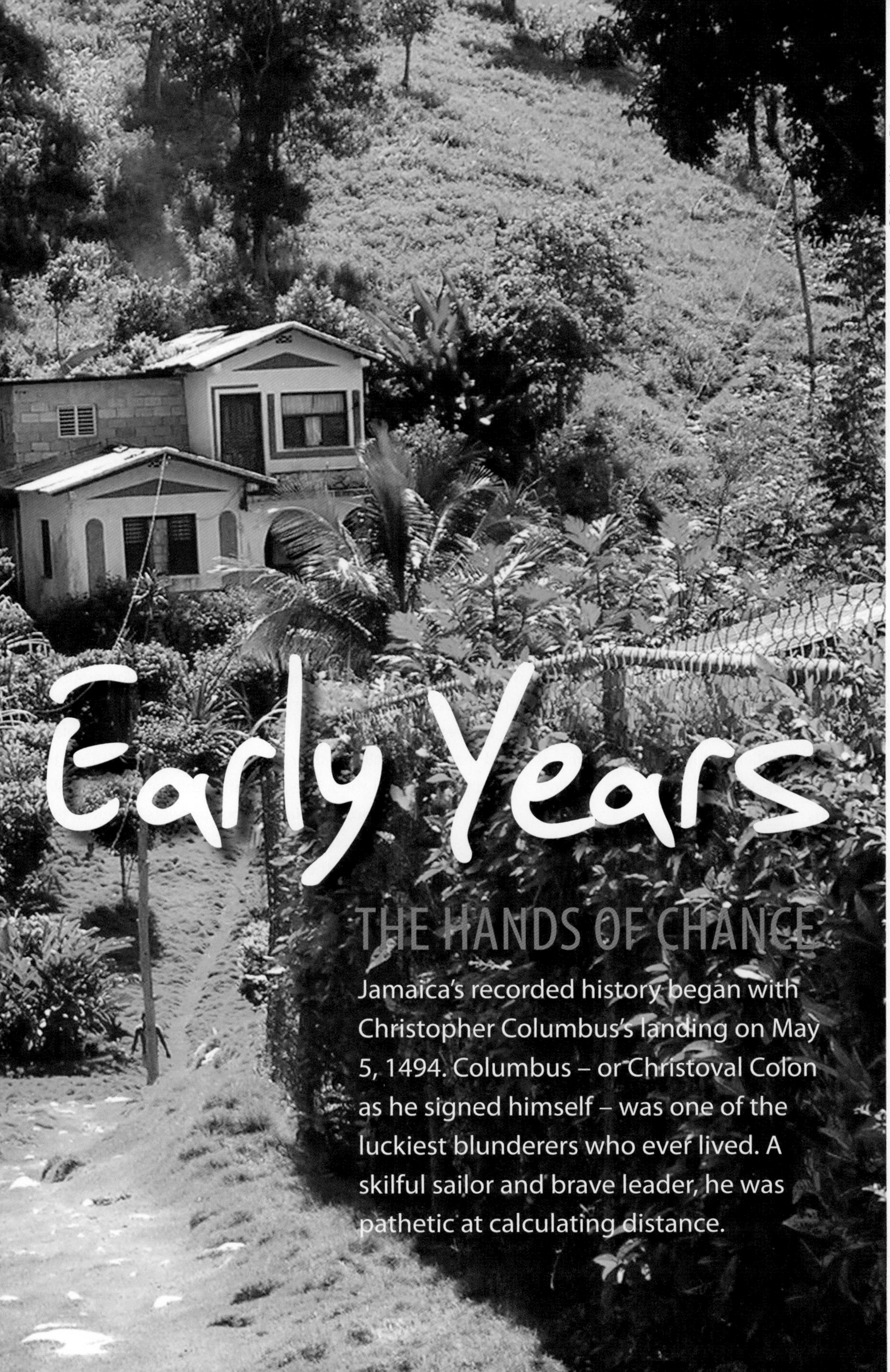

Early Years

THE HANDS OF CHANCE

Jamaica's recorded history began with Christopher Columbus's landing on May 5, 1494. Columbus – or Christoval Colon as he signed himself – was one of the luckiest blunderers who ever lived. A skilful sailor and brave leader, he was pathetic at calculating distance.

Columbus was certainly not the only man of his time to believe the world was round. All geographers since the ancient Greeks acknowledged that the earth was a sphere, but Columbus disagreed with accepted opinion about the distance between Europe and Asia. He reckoned roughly 2,000 miles (3,218 kilometres), while almost everyone else said over 10,000 miles (16,093 kilometres) – which it actually is.

Had they not stumbled upon the Americas, whose existence no one even hypothesised at the time, Columbus and his crew would likely have died of disease or starvation long before reaching land. Indeed Columbus never set foot on the North or South American mainland, and maintained until his dying day that the lands he encountered were part of Asia – hence the absurdly named 'West Indies'.

When Columbus landed, Jamaica was populated by the Tainos, who had probably displaced the previous inhabitants, the Ciboneys, in about 1,000 AD. The Stone Age Tainos had no writing, and

Courtesy of The National Library of Jamaica

THE JAMAICAN COAT OF ARMS

their only surviving archeological artifacts are wood and stone carvings, and rude graffiti on natural rock faces. Their name for the island was *Xamayca* – the land of wood and water – later corrupted to Jamaica. The Tainos were an Amerindian Arawak-speaking tribe, and ethnologists formerly labelled them Arawaks, which is what most Jamaicans still call them.

Around the time of Columbus's arrival the Tainos were being pushed out of the eastern Caribbean by the warlike Caribs of South America. The Caribs, from whose name comes the word cannibal – though it's uncertain whether they were truly maneaters – sacrificed Taino men to their gods, and abducted the women. The Caribs might well have exterminated or displaced the Tainos in the region, had the Spanish not interrupted proceedings. As it was, Jamaica's Tainos were nearly all dead in a generation, though some of the woman likely interbred with Spanish conquistadors. Perhaps too-scattered bands fled to the mountains, and contributed to the island's Maroon element. Estimates of their 1494 population vary. However, nearly all Taino settlements were within six miles of the sea, and given the normal density of the time and region, it was probably under 10,000.

In his 'Brief Relation of the Destruction of the Indies' Bartolome de las Casas gave a horrifying account of the atrocities perpetrated on the natives of Hispaniola. The Spanish in Jamaica were likely no less cruel, but were present in far fewer numbers. The estimated population of Jamaica in 1611 was a mere 1,510, only 523 of whom were adult Spaniards, so it was probably the Tainos' lack of immunity to European diseases that led to their demise. Today they linger in the Jamaican memory mainly through the imagined portrayal of an 'Arawak' couple in the national coat of arms.

Other than the Tainos' wholesale extinction, not much happened to Jamaica in the next 150 years or so after Columbus landed. The island was a backwater, overshadowed first by the much larger islands of Hispaniola and Cuba, and even more so later by the discovery of South and North America. While these other places became administrative centres with large cities and universities, Jamaica remained a sleepy settlement, whose inhabitants survived mainly by keeping cattle and trading with passing ships.

In 1655 Oliver Cromwell launched his 'western design', intended to gain British control of the West Indies seaways. In April, Admiral Robert Venables and General William Penn led an attack on Santo Domingo in Hispaniola. This was a disaster, with a third of the English army being left behind as dead or missing. In an attempt to retrieve the expedition from total disgrace, they turned on the sparsely populated and well-situated Jamaica. The less than 200 able-bodied Spanish defenders were quickly overwhelmed by the 7,000 strong English force. Penn and Venables then returned home to face Cromwell's wrath and imprisonment.

The last Spanish Governor, Don Cristobal Ysasi, made a bid to recapture Jamaica in 1658 and was defeated by Colonel Edward D'Oyley at Rio Nuevo. This was the most important battle ever fought in the island, for though only about 300 died, it made Jamaica a permanently English-speaking land. Ysasi fought on for a few years, but left for Cuba in 1660 when all hope of recapturing the island vanished.

Apart from a few place names like Ocho Rios, Savanna la Mar and Rio Cobre, the most lasting legacy of Spanish rule was the Africans who had accompanied them. On account of the sparse population in Jamaica, racial barriers weakened, and the Africans fought with the Spanish as equals against pirates. Indeed a priest from Angola had acted as a peace envoy between the English and Spanish, before being hung by militant Spaniards opposed to peace.

The British offered the Africans their liberty, but since they were already free in practice, they ignored the notice. They fought on as if the country belonged to them, and a large number collected in the Clarendon mountains under Juan Lubolo, later known as Juan de Bolas. Realising their importance the British tried to win them over, and after the Battle of the Rio Nuevo, de Bolas and his followers accepted the British offer of land and full citizenship.

The other Africans, whose foremost leader was Juan de Serras, refused to give up their independence, and fought on. About three years later, having failed to break their resolve, the exasperated British sent de Bolas to destroy them. However, his ambushed forces were cut to pieces, and he was slain. A reward was offered to anyone who killed Juan de Serras, but it was never collected. His bands formed communities in the hills, which the British first referred to as 'Rebellious Blacks' and then later as Maroons.

Whereas the island was relatively unimportant to the Spanish, Jamaica became Britain's main base in the Caribbean. However, it was a rough beginning. With food and medicine scarce, soldiers died like flies from tropical diseases and hunger, with an estimated 5,000 perishing in the first ten months. In early 1664 the Second Dutch War broke out, and the British Admiralty could not spare a fleet for the West Indies. So Sir Thomas Modyford, Jamaica's non-military Governor, based the island's defense on the buccaneers. He actively encouraged them to use Port Royal as a base, since the presence of heavily armed ships would discourage potential invaders. As he also explained to his superiors in England, granting buccaneers 'letters of marque' – which authorised them to act against hostile nations – was the only way to prevent them becoming enemies of Jamaica.

The plundered Spanish treasure they brought in, of which the crown claimed ten per cent, made Port Royal the 'richest and wickedest city in the world'. These technically legal pirates were known as privateers, but they remained a disordered rabble until Modyford allied himself with Henry Morgan. Ruthless and unscrupulous, Morgan was also a resourceful and skilful commander. He moulded the indisciplined buccaneers into a fighting force capable of attacking Spanish strongholds, thus keeping Jamaica free from invasion. The historian Long later wrote that 'It is to the Bucaniers that we owe the possession of Jamaica at this hour'.

The 1670 Treaty of Madrid officially acknowledged the British presence in the Caribbean. Morgan was knighted and appointed Lieutenant-governor of Jamaica, dying in 1688. In 1692 an earthquake destroyed Port Royal, leaving much of the city's defenses shattered or under water, thus making the island vulnerable. Two years later the buccaneer Governor of French Hispaniola Jeane Du Casse attacked with a 3,000 man strong French fleet. His forces ravaged the eastern coast, burning plantations, kidnapping slaves and killing white colonists. They were turned back at Carlisle Bay in Clarendon by Jamaica militiamen. This was the only time after 1655 that Jamaica was actually invaded.

Encouraged by British reverses in the American War of Independence, France, Spain and the Netherlands all declared war on Britain, with the West Indies the main theatre of operations. A powerful French fleet threatened Jamaica in 1779, and among those manning the defenses against the invasion that never came, was the then 20-year-old Horatio Nelson, future hero of the Battle of Trafalgar. Nelson commanded the batteries of Fort Charles in Port Royal, and a marble tablet at the old fort now reads:

IN THIS PLACE DWELT HORATIO NELSON
You who tread his footprints
Remember his glory

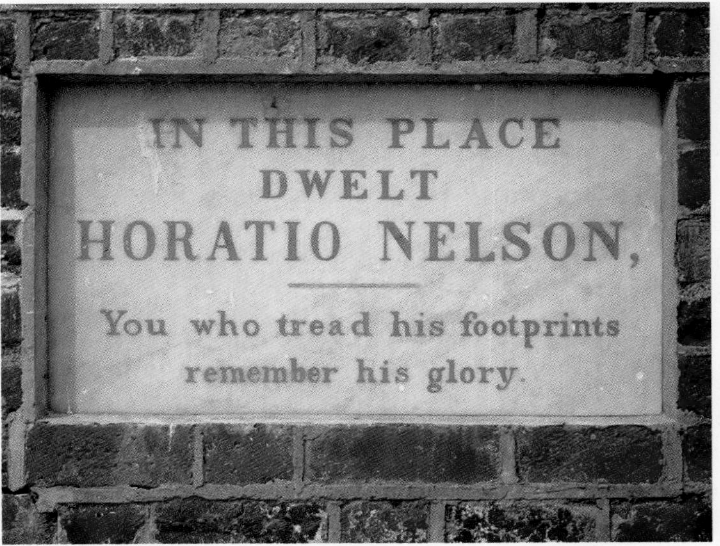

© Ian Randle Publishers

By 1782 Britain had lost the American War of Independence, and was in grave danger of losing its remaining Caribbean territories. French Admiral de Grasse joined with the Spanish to launch an invasion of Jamaica which was widely expected to succeed. The Franco-Spanish fleet was intercepted by British Admiral George Rodney off the island of Dominica, and defeated in the Battle of the Saints. British prestige was restored, and Jamaica remained an English-speaking country.

The American Revolution cut off important supplies like corn, flour and salt fish, causing severe privations in which many slaves reportedly starved to death. So new food crops were introduced from abroad, such as ackee and mango, and in 1787 an expedition was mounted to obtain the 'South Sea plant that produced bread'. Captain William Bligh sailed the HMS Bounty to Tahiti, collected breadfruit suckers, and headed for Jamaica. A month out of Tahiti, the crew under first mate Fletcher Christian mutinied, set Bligh and a few crew members adrift in an open boat, and piloted the Bounty to uninhabited Pitcairn Island. Numerous novels, plays and films have since celebrated 'The Mutiny on the Bounty'.

Bligh navigated the boat back to land safely, and in 1793 successfully brought breadfruit to Jamaica, plus other crops like otaheite apples and jackfruit. During his stopover in Jamaica, Bligh collected over 800 tropical plants for Kew Gardens in England. One was the then unclassified ackee, which was subsequently given the botanical name *blighia sapida*.

By now however, Jamaica had become what it remained until 1838, a vast slave sugar plantation.

Photos © Ian Randle Publishers

FORT CHARLES IN PORT ROYAL

BUCCANEER MYTH AND REALITY

Buccaneers were pirates who operated in the Caribbean and around the South American coast during the seventeenth and early eighteenth centuries. The term loosely describes both lawless adventurers who preyed on any ships they encountered, as well as men like Henry Morgan who made war on Spain with commissions from the English Governor of Jamaica.

JAMAICA NATIONAL TRUST COMMISSION
HISTORIC MARKER
WELCOME TO
PORT ROYAL
Once called "the richest and wickedest city in the world." Port Royal was also the virtual capital of Jamaica. To it came men of all races, treasures of silks, doubloons and gold from Spanish ships, looted on the high seas by the notorious "Brethren of the Coast" as the pirates were called. From here sailed the fleets of Henry Morgan, later lieutenant-governor of Jamaica, for the sacking of Camaguey, Maracaibo, and Panama - and died here, despite the ministrations of his Jamaican folk-doctor. Admirals Lord Nelson and Benbow, the chilling Edward "Blackbeard" Teach, were among its inhabitants. The town flourished for 32 years until at 20 minutes to noon, June 7, 1692, it was partially buried in the sea by an earthquake.
Jamaica National Heritage Trust

The original buccaneers were French hunters from Hispaniola who cooked meat on wood frames – *boucaner* (adapted from a Carib term) is French for smoke dry. Driven out of the interior by Spanish soldiers, they were joined on the north coast by deserters and escaped criminals. In the 1620s the offshore island of Tortuga became their base for attacks on passing merchant ships and Spanish treasure

galleons. At first there was little organisation, but they soon developed a loose confederation known as the Brethren of the Coast.

A pirate ship captain was elected by his crew, and could be so deposed. At the start of each voyage, written articles were drawn up which every member signed. These varied, but all regulated the distribution of plunder, compensation for injuries, and punishments for rule breakers. It's often argued that pirates' democratic customs made them welcome blacks as equal partners, and that runaway slaves found freedom on buccaneer ships. Yet like other whites of the time, pirates regarded black slaves as commodities to be bought and sold, and used them for heavy labour. Henry Morgan's death estate included 109 negro slaves.

The most vivid contemporary written account of buccaneer life was the 1678 *The Buccaneers of America* by Alexander Exquemelin, who lived among buccaneers for 12 years as a surgeon. An instant best-seller packed with details about buccaneer life and bloodthirsty stories of pillage, it remains the standard work on the subject. Nearly half of the book was devoted to Henry Morgan's legendary exploits on the Spanish Main, including the 1671 sacking of Panama, the last major buccaneer action. The pirates who followed in Morgan's wake were freelance raiders, who attacked ships of all nationalities, and rarely carried commissions.

'Calico Jack' Rackham for instance, commanded a modest sloop that attacked small fishing boats and local trading ships. British authorities captured his ship in 1720, and tried the crew in Jamaica. Two crew members turned out to be female: Ann Bonny and Mary Read.

Ann Bonny was Rackham's 'baby mother'. One story, worthy of Shakespeare or *Playboy*, relates that when Mary Read joined the crew dressed as a man, Ann Bonny found herself strongly attracted to 'him/her'. Ann privately revealed herself as a woman to the handsome new recruit.

Mary, 'knowing what she would be at, and being sensible of her own capacity in that way, was forced to come to a right understanding with her, and so to the great disappointment of Ann Bonny, she let her know that she was a woman also'. To avoid further misunderstandings, Calico Jack was let into the secret.

All Rackham's crew were found guilty, and the males hung. Calico Jack's body was put in an iron cage and hung from a gibbet on Deadman's Cay, a small island off Port Royal now called Rackham's Cay. However Mary Read and Ann Bonny revealed themselves pregnant, and were thus reprieved. Read contracted fever and died in prison. The fate of Bonny and her child remains unknown.

The public learned of Calico Jack and his women pirates from the 1724 *A General History of the Robberies and Murders of the Most Notorious Pirates* by Captain Charles Johnson. This remains the prime source of the so-called golden age of piracy that the Royal Navy effectively stamped out in the 1720s. It gave almost mythical status to villains like Edward 'Blackbeard' Teach and Captain Kidd, who were subsequently celebrated in ballads, plays and novels. Works like *Treasure Island* and *Peter Pan*, and movie stars like Errol Flynn and Johnny Depp, continued to paint buccaneers as romantic outlaws.

Yet piracy was, and is, simply armed robbery at sea. Real life pirate captains were often vicious and sadistic villains whose careers rarely lasted more than three years. They were far more likely to drown in a storm or suffer death by hanging than to retire in luxury with their plunder. Most pirates were casually brutal young men who routinely tortured or murdered victims who did not co-operate, and those attacked by pirates found it a terrifying ordeal. Modern day machine gun toting, speed boat pirates who shoot to kill, differ from so-called 'golden age buccaneers' only in their tools of trade.

THE REALITY OF SLAVERY

Every continent has known slavery. Indeed the word slave derives from *Slav*, the name given to the Eastern Europeans enslaved in great numbers during the early middle ages. Slavery was common in all ancient civilisations including Egypt, Babylon, China, India, Greece and Rome. The Caribbean knew its misery even before the middle passage, as the original Taino inhabitants were often captured and put into bondage by the warlike Caribs from South America.

In Africa too, slavery had existed since time immemorial. Edward Reynolds in his book *Stand the Storm* writes:

> The common denominator in all definitions of a slave is that such a person is the property of another politically, is socially at a lower level than the rest of society, and performs compulsory labour… slavery in Africa was unlike that of the Western plantations, where it was an exploitative economic as well as social institution. However the fact that African slavery had different origins should not lead us to deny what it was – the exploitation and subjugation of human beings.

Moslem merchants traded slaves in Africa long before Europeans discovered the Western Hemisphere. More slaves were sent from Africa to Arab countries than were shipped across the Atlantic – 14 million as compared to 11 million, though over a much longer period. The death toll among slaves imported by Islamic countries, who often had to walk across the burning Sahara desert, was twice as high as in the infamous middle passage.

The first African slaves to arrive in Jamaica were Iberian blacks brought here by the Portuguese, the earliest Europeans to engage in the African slave trade.

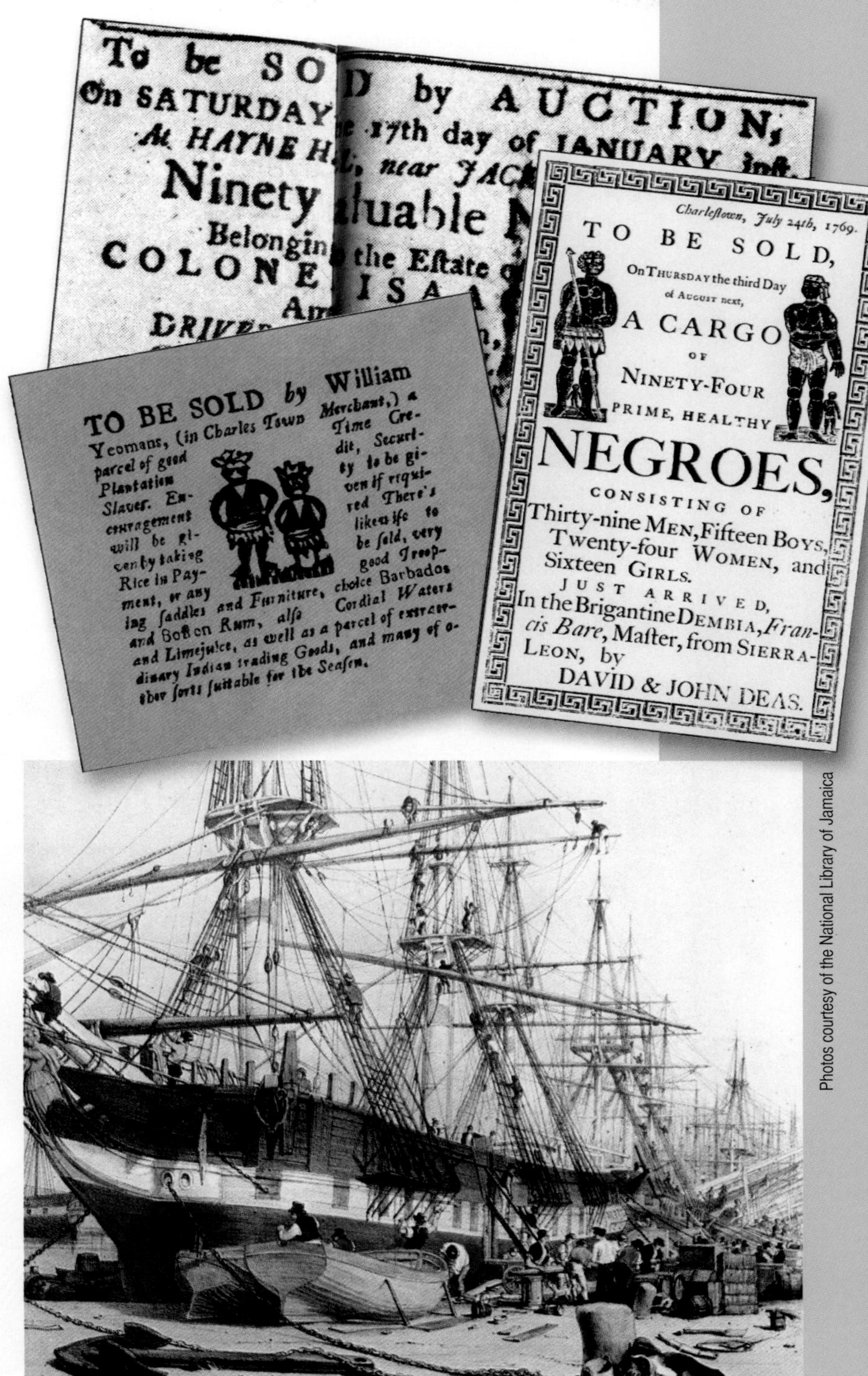

Photos courtesy of the National Library of Jamaica

The Dutch and then the English followed as major traders. What made the Atlantic slave trade uniquely horrible was its sheer scale, and the consequent reduction of human beings into chattel or merchandise. This dreadful and complex institution would not have been possible without co-operation between black African chiefs, who caught and supplied the future slaves, and white merchants who bought and shipped them. The majority of slaves sent across the Atlantic were purchased rather than captured by Europeans.

In the beginning most slaves were prisoners of war, and many traffickers asserted that selling prisoners was better than killing them. However, as demand increased, raiding parties went into the African interior specifically to capture slaves for the Atlantic trade. African societies rarely sold their own people or those who were culturally close to them, but rather they sold foreigners obtained through trading networks and markets.

Just as Europeans argued that the slaving would only have been immoral if the Africans were human beings with souls like themselves, so too did Africans rationalise the trading of 'foreigners' and 'troublemakers'.

The Triangular Trade

The usual voyage of a European slaver was three-sided. It left Europe with trade goods to barter in Africa for slaves, who were sold in the West Indies for sugar and rum, which was brought back to Europe. The 'middle passage' leg from Africa to the West Indies, lasting from six to twelve weeks, was perhaps the most dreadful experience new world slaves had to endure. Traders crammed as many slaves aboard their ships as possible. Shelves about one metre apart were attached to the sides, and slaves were stacked side by side, chained to each other, without sufficient space in which to sit upright. Only greed tempered the horrific circumstances, for pragmatic standards of hygiene

and nourishment resulted in more slaves being delivered alive, and hence greater profits.

The slaves who survived this journey called each other shipbrothers and shipsisters. Their deep and lasting relationships, as strong as family bonds, could endure across generations. They treated each other's children as their own, and these often called their parents' shipmates 'Aunt' and 'Uncle'.

Between 1660 and 1808, 3,429 slaving voyages were made to Jamaica, with a total of 915,015 enslaved Africans embarking. In all, perhaps 15 to 20 million Africans were forcibly transported to the Americas, with an estimated ten per cent dying in transit. The gender structure was heavily skewed, as over 80 per cent of those shipped were men and children.

Brazil received 36 per cent of the total, Spanish America 22 per cent, the British West Indies 18 per cent, the French Caribbean 14 per cent, the United States and the Dutch West Indies five per cent, and the Danish and Swedish Caribbean under one per cent. This geographic distribution has little correlation with the subsequent distribution of black populations, as the key factor in the treatment of slaves was not nationality, but a society's ability to replenish its supply from Africa.

The United States was the farthest from Africa and Brazil the closest. With distance and mercy being inversely related, the US had a much lower slave death rate and consequently a larger resident population, even though Brazil imported over six times as many slaves. Places like Haiti, Cuba and Jamaica fell between both extremes.

Sugar estates also had higher slave mortality levels than coffee, tobacco or cotton plantations. Cane harvesting season demanded up to 20 hours of continuous labour, and many sugar slaves survived only eight to ten years.

In 1802, Denmark became the first European nation to abolish the slave trade, banning it in tiny St Thomas, St Croix, and St John. However the first blow had been struck by the 1791 St Domingue Revolution, which led to Haitian emancipation and then independence in 1804. The 1805 Haitian constitution declared that any enslaved person who arrived in Haiti would become a citizen. Runaway slaves from across the Americas fled in boats to Haiti seeking freedom. Haiti became the Atlantic symbol of black redemption and liberation.

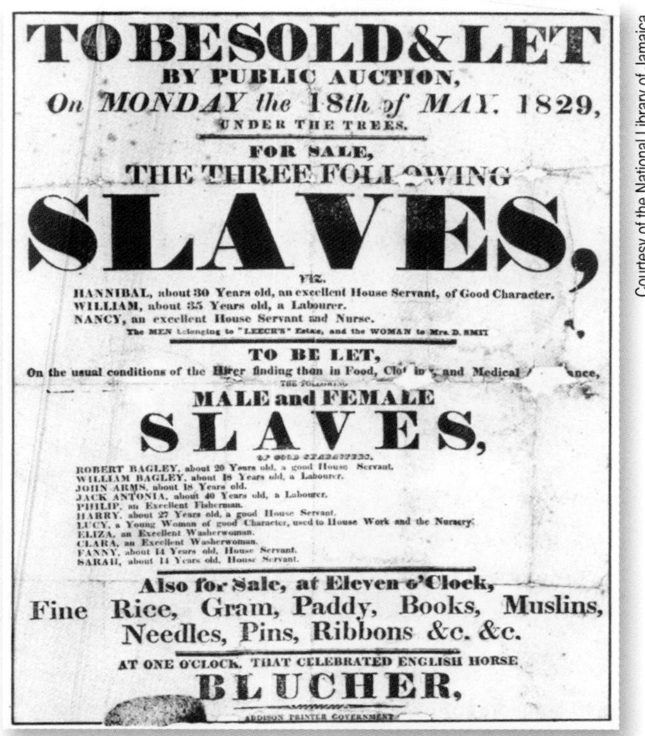
TO BE SOLD & LET
BY PUBLIC AUCTION,
On MONDAY the 18th of MAY, 1829,
UNDER THE TREES.
FOR SALE,
THE THREE FOLLOWING
SLAVES,
VIZ.
HANNIBAL, about 30 Years old, an excellent House Servant, of Good Character.
WILLIAM, about 35 Years old, a Labourer.
NANCY, an excellent House Servant and Nurse.
The MEN belonging to "LEECH'S" Estate, and the WOMAN to Mrs. D. SMIT
TO BE LET,
On the usual conditions of the Hirer finding than in Food, Clot[illegible] and Medical [illegible]ance,
THE FOLLOWING
MALE and FEMALE
SLAVES,
OF GOOD CHARACTERS.
ROBERT BAGLEY, about 20 Years old, a good House Servant.
WILLIAM BAGLEY, about 18 Years old, a Labourer.
JOHN ARMS, about 18 Years old.
JACK ANTONIA, about 40 Years old, a Labourer.
PHILIP, an Excellent Fisherman.
HARRY, about 27 Years old, a good House Servant.
LUCY, a Young Woman of good Character, used to House Work and the Nursery.
ELIZA, an Excellent Washerwoman.
CLARA, an Excellent Washerwoman.
FANNY, about 14 Years old, House Servant.
SARAH, about 14 Years old, House Servant.
Also for Sale, at Eleven o'Clock,
Fine Rice, Gram, Paddy, Books, Muslins,
Needles, Pins, Ribbons &c. &c.
AT ONE O'CLOCK, THAT CELEBRATED ENGLISH HORSE
BLUCHER,
ADDISON PRINTER GOVERNMENT

Courtesy of the National Library of Jamaica

In 1807 Britain became the first major power to abolish the slave trade. Eric Williams and others argue that slaving was abolished primarily because it was no longer contributing positively to Britain's economy. Yet British West Indian imports and exports were greater during the period of abolition than 50 years earlier. West Indian planters valued their plantations at 85–100 million pounds in 1807, as against 50–60 million in 1775. Indeed the major attack on the British slave trade came during its most profitable period.

Still, economic changes made the abolition of the slave trade possible. Even in 1776 Adam Smith had argued that slavery was uneconomic. The industrial revolution, which started in Britain, shifted resources from agriculture to industry. Except for a few places like Cuba and Brazil, where plantations were still growing, demand for slaves levelled off as slave populations began reproducing themselves.

West Indian planters lost the sympathy of the British people on moral and economic grounds. They repeatedly rebuffed urgings to improve the conditions of slaves, including the

Photos courtesy of the National Library of Jamaica

SLAVES BEING SOLD AT A MARKET

1830 amelioration directives. These recommended, among other things, that Sunday markets should be stopped and slaves given an extra free day to sell their produce, that whipping in the field and flogging of women should be forbidden, and that slaves should be allowed religious instruction. The Jamaica House of Assembly refused to revise its slave laws, and some members even threatened to transfer allegiance to the United States.

Most West Indian planters were absentee proprietors living in Britain off their profits leaving management of their plantations to attorneys and overseers, who squeezed what they could out of the system by cutting corners on reinvestment and overworking slaves. Many plantations slid towards bankruptcy. Nearly all the six million pounds Jamaican slave owners received as compensation when their slaves were freed, went to English creditors.

This economic mismanagement led to higher production costs than European beet sugar and cane sugar rivals like Mauritius, Brazil and Cuba. To protect her colonies, Britain placed a heavy duty on sugar from other sources, and prices rose so high in 1829 that many found it unaffordable. To the British public, the only possible justification of slave plantations was cheap sugar. If slavery could not produce this, it was a clearly unnecessary evil that might as well be abolished.

Yet none of the other major slaving nations Spain, the US, Portugal, France or the Ottoman Empire – took the same steps as Britain, which almost single-handedly and at considerable expense, carried out a crusade to eliminate the slave trade throughout the world. The compensation to slave owners in the Empire alone totaled the then huge sum of 20 million pounds. Emancipation freed 800,000 in the British Caribbean, which at the time was only one seventh of the New World's slaves, and fewer than three per cent of all coerced labour in the world.

Britain maintained an anti-slavery naval patrol for generations, and often unilaterally imposed anti-slavery edicts on other sovereign nations. The battle was not fully won until well into the twentieth century. For instance slavery in Arab-dominated Zanzibar was only stamped out in 1922 when the British were in firm control.

Sources: *History of Jamaica*, Clinton Black. *History of Slavery*, Susanne Everett. *Africa*, John Reader. *Conquests and Cultures*, Thomas Sowell. *Stand The Storm*, Edward Reynolds. *The Story of the Jamaican People*, Philip Sherlock and Hazel Bennett. *The Slave Trade*, Hugh Thomas

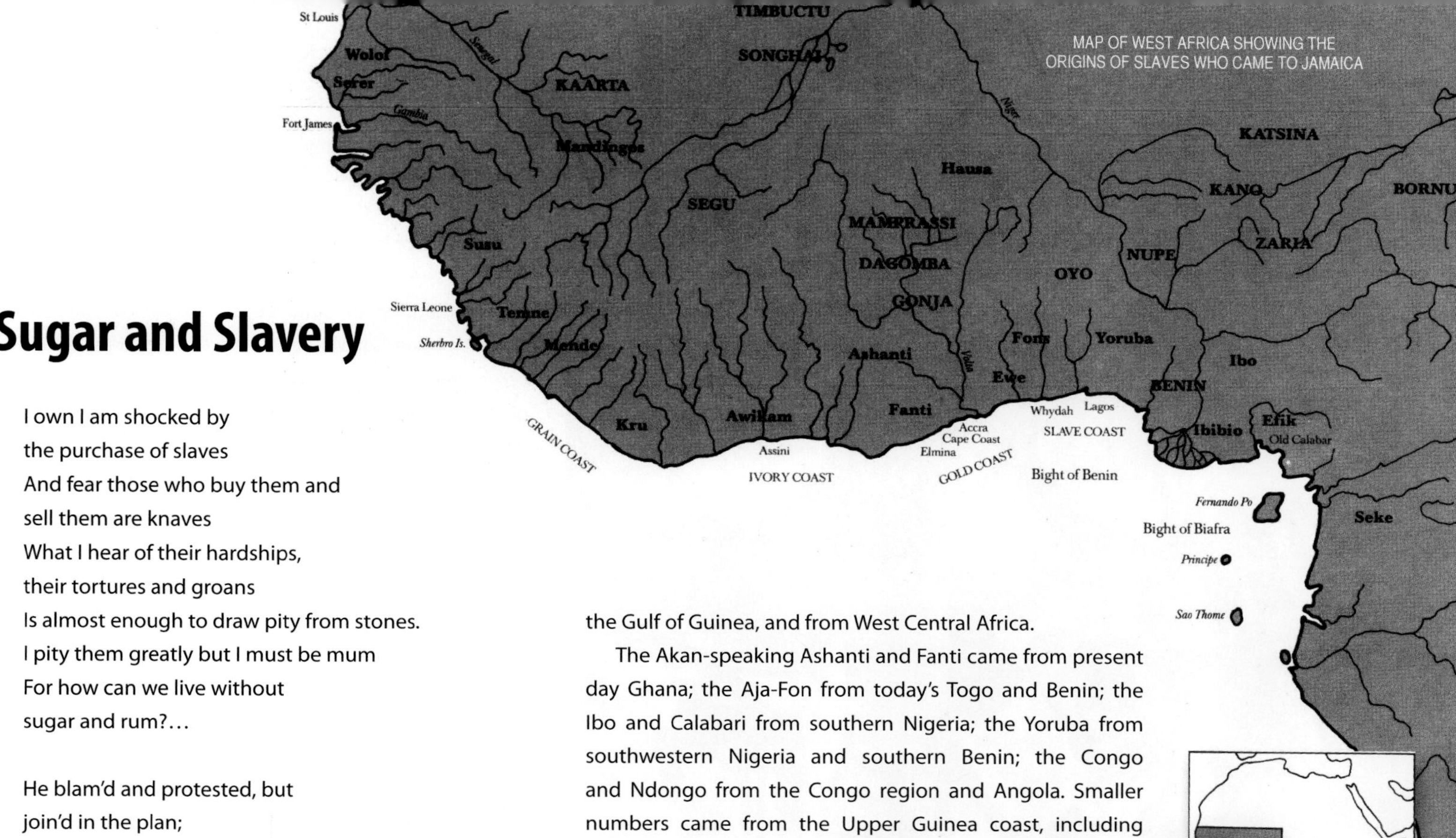

MAP OF WEST AFRICA SHOWING THE ORIGINS OF SLAVES WHO CAME TO JAMAICA

Sugar and Slavery

I own I am shocked by
the purchase of slaves
And fear those who buy them and
sell them are knaves
What I hear of their hardships,
their tortures and groans
Is almost enough to draw pity from stones.
I pity them greatly but I must be mum
For how can we live without
sugar and rum?...

He blam'd and protested, but
join'd in the plan;
He shar'd in the plunder, but pitied the man.

'Pity for Poor Africans', William Cowper (1788)

Sugar first appeared in the Caribbean in 1637, when Dutch merchants from Brazil brought the sugar cane plant to Barbados. Growing demand in Europe made it an extremely profitable crop. However, successful sugar production then required huge amounts of cheap labour, which was only available through slavery. The Spanish began importing black slaves from Africa as early as 1517, when the numbers of Amerindian natives began to dwindle. However, it was not until the plantation system became widespread in the mid-seventeenth century, that the huge population shift known as the Atlantic slave trade began in earnest.

The Africans who came to the Americas were thrust into a society whose existence depended on their degradation. Jamaica itself was a trans-shipment port – perhaps 5,000 of the large number of slaves that landed each year remained on the island, the others being re-exported to other parts of the Caribbean. Most of the Africans who came to Jamaica were from the Gold Coast eastward to the Niger Delta on the Gulf of Guinea, and from West Central Africa.

The Akan-speaking Ashanti and Fanti came from present day Ghana; the Aja-Fon from today's Togo and Benin; the Ibo and Calabari from southern Nigeria; the Yoruba from southwestern Nigeria and southern Benin; the Congo and Ndongo from the Congo region and Angola. Smaller numbers came from the Upper Guinea coast, including the Temne, Limba, and Mandingo – some of whom were Moslem. Most later indentured Africans were Congo, Ibo and Yoruba. However many so-called tribal names are imprecise and often refer only to slave shipping ports.

The tribes were said to differ greatly in character. The Ibos for instance had long been enslaved in Africa by stronger tribes, and so were docile and rather sad by nature, with the women in particular making good field labourers. The Coromantees on the other hand were considered strong, proud and fierce. They tended to keep to themselves, were generally disliked by other tribes, and were not easily broken to gang labour.

The term Coromantee was first used to describe all slaves shipped from the slave fort of Koromantine, the present day Kromantse, but it later came to describe a cultural group with distinctive characteristics, consisting mainly of warlike Akan speakers, especially Ashanti and Fanti. Thomas Thistlewood, a slave owner wrote in his diaries:

> ... firmness both of body and mind; a ferociousness of disposition; but withal activity, courage, and a stubbornness, or what an ancient Roman would have deemed an elevation of soul, which prompts them to

enterprises of difficulty and danger; and enables them to meet death, in its most horrible shape, with fortitude or indifference.

Coromantees led almost every slave revolt, and made up the majority of Maroons, who still perform 'Kromanti' ceremonies. Some colonies refused to have them because of their rebellious nature. Yet despite their warrior disposition, their hardiness and courage made them a favourite with Jamaican planters. They made up perhaps a quarter of the slaves imported to the island from 1655 to 1807.

The Dutch established the first Caribbean plantations, followed by the French and British. Until the nineteenth century, the Spanish focused on shipping home gold and silver from Mexico and Peru. This largely accounts for the difference in racial mixture between say Jamaica and Cuba, or the Dominican Republic and Haiti.

Most plantation slaves were field workers, with a minority doing domestic duties in the great house and overseer's residence as cooks, maids, butler, grooms and the like. As this was much easier than field labour, domestic slaves dreaded being transferred to the fields. Rebellions were often betrayed by 'loyal' house slaves.

In Jamaica, slaves were given provision grounds on which to grow their own yams, potatoes, plantains and other foodstuffs. These were worked in the few free hours allowed, mainly on Saturday afternoons and Sundays (out of crop time). They produced almost all the food needed, with only salt fish needed from outside sources. Surplus produce was sold at Sunday markets, and in this way a very few slaves earned enough in time to buy their freedom.

There were a few opportunities for recreation, such as Christmas and New Year holidays. Lady Nugent wrote of Boxing Day 1801:

> Nothing but bonjoes, drums and tom toms going all night and dancing and singing, and madness all the morning.

Colourful Jonkannu (Jon Canoe) bands, possibly

JONKANNU

According to Jackie Ranston in her book *Bellisario: Sketches of a Character*, Jonkannu is not a play on the French word 'gens inconnu.' Rather, as first posited by the historian Long and supported by others, it is a corruption of the name Jon Konny, a Ghanian chief who waged a successful war against the Dutch for almost two decades in his hometown called Prince's Town. Around 1720, Jon Konny was eventually captured by the Dutch and sent as a slave to Jamaica. There he became a folk legend, and the subject of slave performances that bear striking resemblance to rituals practised in Prince Town even today. Ranston's hypothesis is partly based on the oral tradition passed on to her by the present-day chief of Prince Town, His Majesty, Nana Ndama Kundmuah IV, a direct descendant of Jon Konny. Subsequent DNA tests have uncovered a match for the chief's DNA samples in a businessman from Virginia, US. Similar tests will soon be conducted in Jamaica, which might reveal others in the lineage of the chief and Jon Konny.

based on the real life Ghanian chief John Konny, roamed the street, and teams of pretty Set Girls dressed up in their mistresses' rich clothes and jewellery competed with one another in the lavishness of their costumes. On the other hand, many plantation owners and overseers routinely forced sex upon female slaves. Planter Thomas Thistlewood chronicled some 4,000 sex acts with 138 women during his 35 years on the island.

As the planter-historian Bryan Edward stated: 'In counties where slavery is established, the leading principle on which government is supported is fear: or a sense of the absolute coercive necessity which…supersedes all questions of right'. Subjection was enforced by savage penalties, including dismemberment, mutilation and torture. 'Drivers' kept field slaves hard at work with lashes from cowhide whips, especially in crop time when mills rolled day and night – there was no such thing as being tired or sick.

John Newton, the one time slaveship captain who later penned 'Amazing Grace', was assured by planters that it was cheaper to work slaves out and replace them, and that slaves rarely lived more than nine years after importation. Conditions gradually improved, though only in the waning years of slavery did the Jamaican slave population approach reproduction levels.

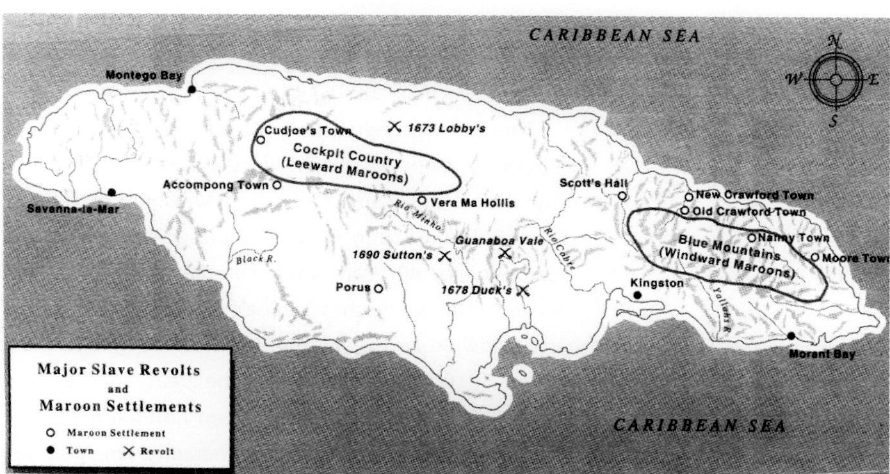

Major slave revolts and Maroon settlements

Unrelenting brutality then, was the lot of the vast majority of Jamaicans before slavery was abolished. The only noteworthy 'political developments' before 1838 were those that moved the black majority closer to freedom. There were many of these: nine uprisings and two Maroon wars took place between 1673 and 1798.

THOMAS THISTLEWOOD'S REMARKABLE DIARIES

We don't know what he looked like, but the overseer and small landowner Thomas Thistlewood (1720–86) kept remarkably frank and thorough diaries. Their 10,000 pages detailed his life in Jamaica from arrival in 1750 until his death. They give a unique 'warts and all' portrait of the brutal contradictions of eighteenth-century British colonial slave plantation life.

While distinguished by an unusual love of books, Thistlewood was very normal in his sexual, social, and physical relationships with slaves, and never questioned the morality of slavery. He regularly subjected his slaves to horrific punishments, including savage whippings and sadistic tortures. His descriptions often seem one of a society at war, and he relates the fear that gripped white plantation society during Tacky's Rebellion.

He had sex with defenseless runaway slaves, and paid others for their favours. Yet the slave Phibbah became his common law wife and they had a son. Through her association with Thistlewood and selling her crops, Phibbah came to possess pigs, poultry, and horses and even owned another slave whom she sometimes hired out for wages, and she regularly lent large sums of money to Thistlewood. They both had frequent affairs with others, and he chronicles their mutual jealousy. In his will he left her two slaves, and provided money for her to purchase her freedom and a house and land.

Source: In Miserable Slavery: Thomas Thistlewood in Jamaica 1750-86, Douglas Hall, (Kingston: University of the West Indies Press, 1999).

The Maroons

The Maroons were not only Jamaica's first freedom fighters but one of the first in the New World. Before Toussaint L'Ouverture of Haiti or Washington of the US or Bolivar of Latin America, there was Cudjoe of the Maroons. For 49 years his forces defied the might of Britain, until fearing that Cudjoe's warriors would inspire an islandwide slave revolt, the British felt obliged to make peace. This fight for freedom was the great Jamaican epic that still sends a thrill through even non-Maroons, and strongly influenced the national character. For Jamaica's self-image is in large part a reflection in a Maroon mirror – an indomitable country of resourceful fighters who never give up regardless of the odds.

CUDJOE SIGNS A PEACE TREATY WITH THE BRITISH

Courtesy of the National Library of Jamaica

Due to their experience in Africa, black slaves were often employed by the Spanish to chase and herd cattle running free in the bush. These were called 'cimarrons', Spanish for wild or untamed. In time the herders themselves came to be referred to as 'Maroons'. Many of these escaped to the mountains, with scattered bands in time becoming sizeable communities. First used in Jamaica, the term 'Maroon' was later applied to runaway slave settlements across the Americas.

Jamaican Maroon oral history numbers 'Arawaks' (Arawak-speaking Tainos) among their ancestors, and Taino artefacts have been found in archeological excavations of the eighteenth-century Maroon settlement of Nanny Town. After the fall of Nanny Town, the eastern or Windward Maroons settled on the northern slopes of the Blue Mountains in Old Crawford Town. After the signing of the 1739 treaty, they moved to New Crawford Town, then split up into what are now called Charles Town and Moore Town in Portland, and Scott's Hall in St Mary. The western or Leeward Maroons concentrated in the former Trelawny Town in St James, and present day Accompong in St Elizabeth near the trackless Cockpit Country.

In 1663 Maroons ignored an offer of land and full freedom to everyone who surrendered. In 1690 the Cudjoe-led Clarendon slaves rebelled and escaped to the Cockpit Country, where they were joined by other rebel groups. Cudjoe's fame spread, and aided by his brothers Accompong and Johnny, he became leader of the Leeward Maroon community.

This episode is often said to mark the start of the First Maroon War. Yet there had been continuous fighting between the British and the Windward Maroons since 1655. What Cudjoe did was to open up a second front in an ongoing war, and increase the number of Maroon combatants. A 1731 census estimated 2,000 'rebellious negroes', as against 7,648 whites and 74,525 black slaves.

Skilled in guerilla warfare, the Maroons avoided open combat and relied on ambush, taking a heavy toll on British troops. They communicated with the abeng, a cow horn with a hole at the tip and a blow hole at one side. Its sound carried many miles, enabling isolated bands to send coded signals to each other. With the help of portable canons, the British successfully stormed the

© Werner Zips

A MODERN DAY MAROON BLOWING AN ABENG

Windward Maroon stronghold of Nanny Town, high in the Blue Mountain wilderness in the 1730s. However, a stalemate developed, and after the 1739 Battle of the Spanish River in Portland, the British signed treaties with Cudjoe on March 1, 1739, and with Quao on Nanny's behalf on June 23, 1739. Cudjoe was still known to be alive in 1764, then well over 80.

In return for ceasing hostilities the Maroons were guaranteed full freedom, allowed to keep their lands, and permitted virtually full internal self-government, except for cases involving the death penalty. The Maroons also agreed to recapture runaway slaves for the British, and to assist the government in suppressing local uprisings or foreign invasions.

The Maroons occupy a somewhat ambivalent place in Jamaican history. They are much admired for their intrepid spirit and martial prowess. On the other hand, they became in effect a black auxiliary arm of the British government. Perhaps in the circumstances they had no choice but to play both sides. Maroons were said to accept bribes to allow runaways to escape, and to return only a comparative few to their masters. However, in the 1790s the Governor accused some of the leading planters of paying 'protection money' to the Maroons, in order to safeguard their properties. Maroons consorted freely with slave women on estates they visited, a practice condoned by planters who felt Maroon-fathered offspring would be stronger and hence more valuable.

Maroons also played a major role in suppressing almost every slave revolt, including the largest in the island's history, Tacky's Rebellion in 1760–61.

Skilled in guerilla warfare, the Maroons avoided open combat and relied on ambush, taking a heavy toll on British troops. They communicated with the abeng.

Tacky's Rebellion

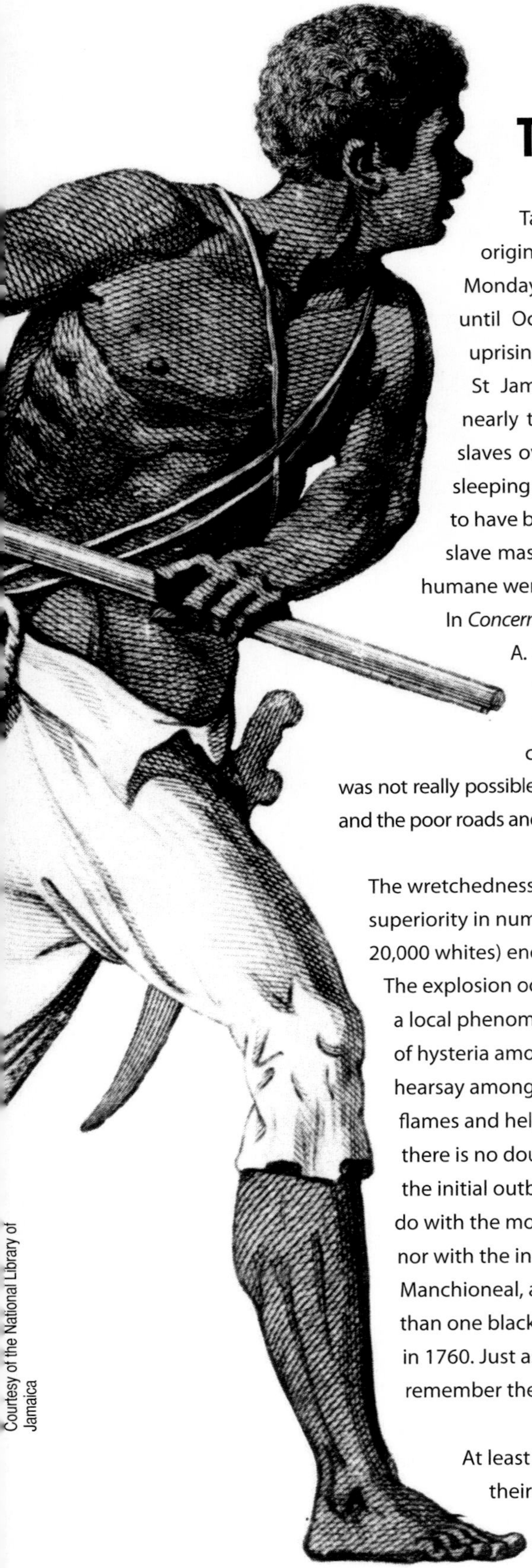

Tacky's Rebellion, named after its original ring leader, began on Easter Monday 1760 and was not finally suppressed until October 21, 1761. Though the major uprisings were in St Mary, Westmoreland and St James, there were disturbances across nearly the entire country, with hundreds of slaves overrunning estates inland and killing sleeping white masters. Maltreatment seems to have been a factor in the uprising, as several slave masters who were reputed to have been humane were allowed to go unharmed.

In *Concerning Jamaica's 1760 Slave Rebellions*, Carl A. Lane argues that the 'single conspiracy view of the 1760 rebellions flies in the face of common sense'. To him, a slave conspiracy embracing the entire island was not really possible given the restrictive plantation system and the poor roads and limited communications of the time.

The wretchedness of their condition as well as their superiority in numbers (roughly 150,000 blacks to 20,000 whites) encouraged Jamaica's slaves to rebel. The explosion occurred in 1760. Each uprising was a local phenomenon, although an atmosphere of hysteria among the whites and rumour and hearsay among the blacks may have fanned the flames and helped the rebellions to spread. While there is no doubt that Tacky was responsible for the initial outburst in St Mary, he had nothing to do with the more serious revolt in Westmoreland, nor with the insurrections at Tryall, Windsor, Manchioneal, and Kingston. In other words, more than one black hero and leader fought and died in 1760. Just as history remembers Tacky, let it remember the others too.

At least 50 whites and perhaps 500 slaves lost their lives either in battle, or in the grisly retributions that occurred after Tacky was shot dead and the rebels defeated by English and Maroon regiments. In terms of its shock to the imperial system, only the American Revolution surpassed Tacky's Rebellion in the eighteenth century. If the Maroons had thrown in their lot with the rebels, the outcome might have been very different, and the course of Jamaican history drastically altered.

The Second Maroon War supposedly started because two Trelawny Town Maroons were caught stealing pigs, then sentenced and flogged by runaway slaves, whom Maroons had recaptured. This act of perceived disrespect added to simmering tensions, such as a need for more arable land, and the replacement of the popular British Maroon Superintendent by a less respected man. Matters boiled over in August 1795. The Trelawny Maroons burned Trelawny Town – then the largest Maroon settlement in the island – and went into battle. As there was an ongoing feud, they received no help from their fellow Leeward Maroons in Accompong.

With the authorities fearing a repeat of the still ongoing Haitian Revolution, these troubles were magnified as war and dealt with as such. Almost the entire island was disrupted, one writer commenting that Jamaica seemed 'more like a garrison…than a country of commerce and agriculture'.

With the aid of bloodhounds, the British put the Maroons on the defensive, but won no real victories. Worried that the Windward Maroons intended to join the fray, the authorities offered the Trelawnys a peace treaty, which was ratified in February 1796. A crucial clause stated that they would not be banished from Jamaica. However, against the wishes of the field officers who signed the treaty with them, the Trelawny Maroons were betrayed by the Governor and Assembly, and banished to Nova Scotia in Canada. They were later sent to Sierra Leone, the first New World Africans repatriated to Africa.

The Maroon communities of Charles Town, Moore Town, Scott's Hall and Accompong still retain a semi-independent status. Even as late as 1865, the Maroons helped the authorities suppress the Morant Bay Rebellion.

Courtesy of the National Library of Jamaica

THREE FINGER JACK

Sometimes slave revolt was individual, as with the famous bandit 'Three Finger' Jack Mansong. Accounts of his life vary – the name Mansong did not even appear in print until 19 years after his death. Yet one consistent story is that Jack fled the slave plantation and holed up at the head of the Cane River, where he could swoop down on travellers. He moved to higher ground and settled in a Blue Mountain cave. From there he robbed passers-by, raided nearby plantations and launched his own private guerilla war against the authorities of the time.

Jack is said to have been over two metres tall and amazingly strong, with a long face and fierce black eyes. In addition to a sword and musket, he always carried a small 'Obeah bag' which supposedly made him invulnerable. He got his 'Three Finger' nickname after losing two fingers in trying to ambush a maroon called Quashie, who was also badly injured in the skirmish.

The area between Bull Bay and Grant's Pen, St Thomas, where a monument in his memory stands today, became Jack's main hunting ground from where he reputedly carried out many daring robberies and kidnappings. In popular legend he was a classic folk hero-villain, who allegedly targeted government officials and slave owners, did not harm women or children, and freed a number of slaves.

The February 1780 razing of the Crawford Town district in West Portland has been widely attributed to 'Three Finger' Jack, who recruited disgruntled slaves as his deputies. The Maroons were hired to quell the disturbance, and dispersed Jack's gang of rebels. A free pardon was offered to the rebellious slaves and all accepted, except Jack, who fought on alone.

JACK MANSONG
OR
THREE FINGER JACK
North of this road, in the hills and valleys behind
this Marker, was the territory of the famous Jack
Mansong or Three Finger Jack. It is not certain
whether he was born in Jamaica or came from
Africa, but it is known that in the years 1780-81,
he fought, often singlehandedly, a war of terror
against the English soldiers and planters who held
the slave colony. Strong, brave, skilled w h machete
and musket, his bold exploits were equalled only
by his chivalry. He loved his country and his people.
He was said to have never harmed a woman or child.
His life became a legend. Books and plays about
him were written and performed in London theatres.
He was ambushed and killed near here in 1781.

© Ian Randle Publishers

A December 12, 1780 government proclamation described him as a 'daring rebel' who 'had eluded every attempt to capture him'. Officials offered a £300 reward and full freedom to any slave who could bring the feared rebel to justice, dead or alive. On January 27, 1781 he was surprised near the entrance of his cave by Quashie, now a Christian convert named John Reeder, a small slave boy called 'A Good Shot', and Sam Davy.

Jack only had time to grab his cutlass, but was shot three times, and threw himself down a 40-foot precipice in an effort to escape. Reeder followed him down the slope, and the two engaged in a deadly fight, with both being badly injured. Jack was eventually overpowered and slain after Sam Davy bashed in his head with a rock. As proof for the £300 reward, his head and three-fingered hand were put in a bucket of rum and taken to Spanish Town, where it was preserved for 20 years.

He passed into folklore, being celebrated in literature, drama, art and music. Almost 20 biographies were written about him – more than about any West Indian other than maybe Bob Marley – all in Britain by anonymous authors. They variously describe him as the 'Terror of Jamaica', a 'famous negro robber', a bold and daring defender of the rights of man', a 'gallant hero'. Several were written by evangelical missionary advocates of human dignity for West Indian and African blacks. The pantomime musical 'Obi – or Three Finger Jack' was a sensation in England and ran for nine years. Jack's hideout was prominently displayed on nineteenth-century Jamaican maps, including the first detailed survey of the island in 1802.

An old song, somewhat at odds with his 'Robin Hood' reputation and possibly written for a play, describes the general relief at his death:

Beat big drum – wave fine flag
Bring good news to Kingston Town, O!
No fear Jack's Obeah-bag –
Quashie knock him down, O!

GRANDY NANNY OF THE MAROONS

The only female National Hero of Jamaica, Nanny was a spiritual leader of legendary prowess. A 1741 patent granting land to 'Nanny and the people residing with her' still survives. Though her name is mentioned only four times in official documents, 'Grandy Nanny' has been a powerful living presence for Windward Maroons for more than two centuries. She is in a way reminiscent of the founding mothers of matrilineal Akan-speaking societies of West Africa, being regarded not only as the 'queen' but as the 'mother' of the clan-like Windward Maroon 'family'. Its members refer to themselves as Grandy Nanny's 'yoyo', a Maroon word denoting children, progeny or generation.

Consciousness of the Maroon past is intimately bound up with this notion of descent from Nanny. Tradition relates that during the early days of war with the British, she was from a young age groomed for her role as queen by the male Maroon leaders, who then submitted to her authority. While the exploits of other legendary Maroons are also commemorated in oral history, she receives the most attention.

The ceremony known as Kromanti Play nurtures much of what remains distinctly Maroon in world view, language and music. Only the 'yoyo' descendants and spiritual heirs of Grandy Nanny can practice the true Kromanti rites, from which outsiders are excluded. The majority of Maroons no longer participate, but ritual specialists, known as 'fete-man' or 'fete-woman', summon the powers of Nanny and other ancestors in times of need.

MONUMENT TO
THE RIGHT EXCELLENT NANNY OF THE MAROONS
Nanny was leader of the Maroons at the beginning of the 18th Century. She was an outstanding military leader, skilled in guerrilla warfare practised by the Eastern Maroons to confuse the British. Said to have had supernatural powers, Nanny was an important figure in the fierce fight with the British during the First Maroon War 1720 - 1739. She led with courage and inspired her warriors to maintain that special spirit of freedom and independence.
This monument designed by Compass Workshop Ltd. was dedicated on October 14, 1999. The abeng, the sound of which was critical to Maroon tactics, forms an integral part of the monument. The vertical structures symbolize Nanny surrounded by her guerrilla Warriors.
Nanny was declared National Hero in 1975.

MONUMENT AT THE NATIONAL HEROES PARK

'Grandy Nanny' has been a powerful living presence for Windward Maroons for more than two centuries.

THE SAM SHARPE REBELLION

Perhaps the most significant Jamaican slave uprising was the Sam Sharpe rebellion of Christmas week in 1831.

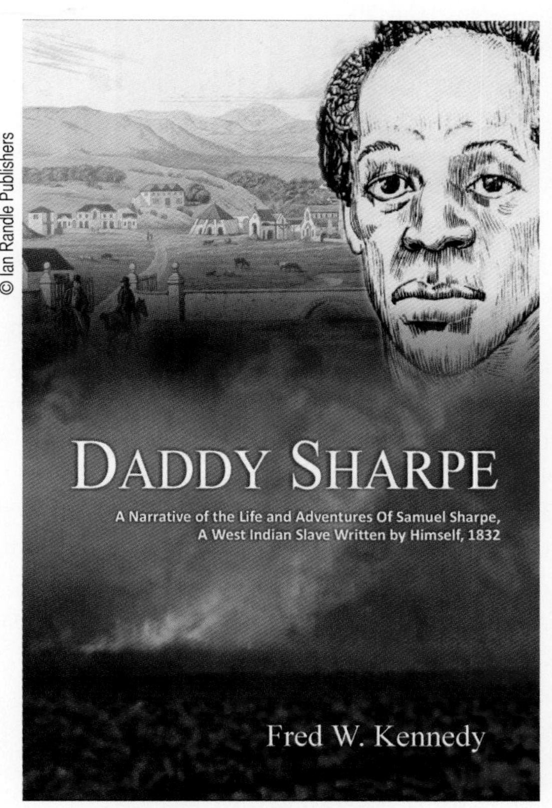

DADDY SHARPE
A Narrative of the Life and Adventures Of Samuel Sharpe,
A West Indian Slave Written by Himself, 1832
Fred W. Kennedy

© Ian Randle Publishers

COVER OF THE BOOK DADDY SHARPE

Although an ostensible failure, this revolt was the final hammer blow on the door to freedom. If moral arguments were not sufficient, the threat of more such rebellions made slavery obviously untenable. On August 29, 1833, four weeks after Wilberforce's death, the Bill to free all slaves was passed in the House of Commons. It specified that all slaves in the British Empire were to be freed on August 1, 1834, but that a period of apprenticeship should be served. Full freedom came on August 1, 1838 amidst devout prayer and joyful thanksgiving.

The outstanding leader of the 1831 Christmas week slave revolt, often referred to as the 'Baptist War' because of the denomination of most participants, was Deacon Samuel 'Daddy' Sharpe. Wesleyan missionary Henry Bleby described him as the most remarkable and intelligent slave he had ever met. Sharpe argued that the Bible proclaimed the natural equality of men, and denied the right of whites to hold blacks in bondage. He persistently quoted the text 'No man can serve two masters', which became a slogan among slaves. Sharpe also read the newspapers of the day, and came to believe that Britain had freed the slaves, or planned to do so. His sense of urgency was also fuelled by the violent anti-abolitionist planters, who openly talked of joining the United States as a slave state, thus postponing emancipation indefinitely. Rumours even spread among slaves that whites planned to kill all black men and keep the women and children in bondage.

What Sharpe had envisaged, a century before Mahatma Gandhi and Martin Luther King, was a movement of passive resistance, a sit down strike of all the slaves in the western parishes. He hoped

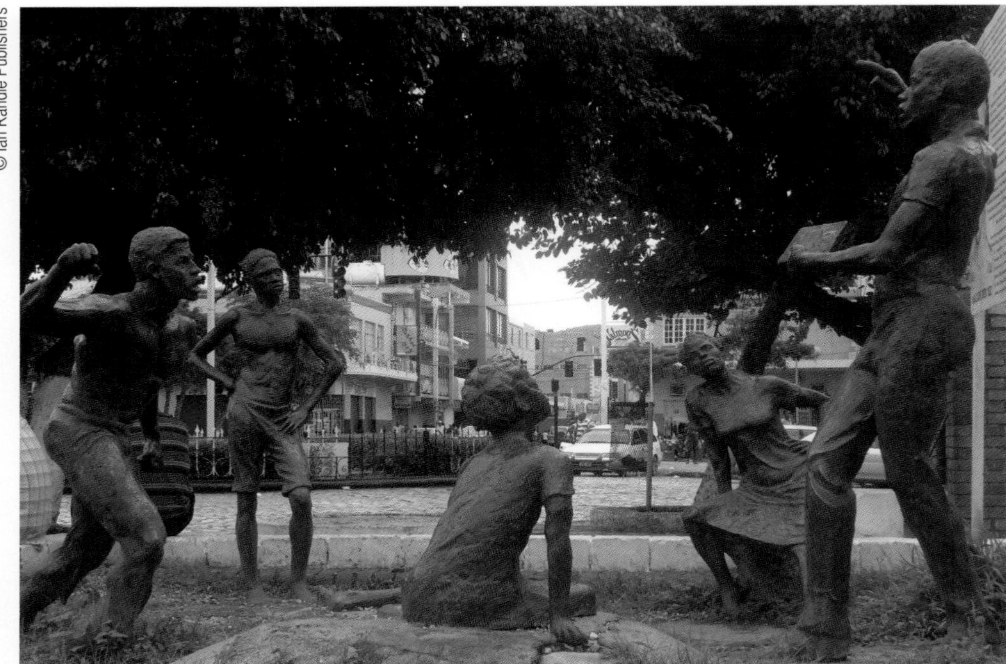

MONUMENT TO SAM SHARPE IN MONTEGO BAY

to force the plantation owners to pay them for their work, and thus affirm their freedom. Drivers on each estate were delegated to tell overseers returning from the three-day Christmas holidays that slaves would work no more without wages. However if an attempt was made to force them back to the fields as slaves, they would fight for their freedom. To this end a black regiment about a 150 strong was formed, with 50 guns among them, led by Thomas Dove and Robert Gardiner. It was believed that royal troops would not fight the slaves whom the King had freed, so only the planter militia might challenge them in the field. No one was to be killed, except in self-defense. Word was spread in nightly prayer meetings, and Sharpe swore conspirators to secrecy by asking them to 'kiss the book'.

However rumours reached the planters. Troops were sent into St James in case of trouble, and warships were anchored in the harbour. On the last night of the holidays December 27, the occupants of Kensington Great House fled to Montego Bay, and the St James militia marched on the estate to ensure slaves returned to work. The slaves reacted to the militia's presence by setting fire to Kensington estate, which was located on the highest hill in St James. By midnight, 16 other western estates were burning, and a rebellion was on the way, led by some of Sharpe's most trusted lieutenants.

The rebels routed the first militia that confronted them and roamed over the countryside, destroying plantations. Terrified planters and their families fled, leaving 50,000 slaves suddenly freed and uncertain what to do. Sharpe moved among the estates, counselling and praying, but matters were now beyond his control. Martial law was declared, and the untrained and uncoordinated rebel forces were soon overwhelmed by superior military force. Armed resistance was virtually at an end by the first week of January.

Though property destruction was widespread, loss of life was very low, and even armed rebels fought only against whites who attacked them. Those offering no opposition met with no harm, and there were only two acts of violence against whites throughout. This restraint was noted by a Presbyterian missionary:

> Had the masters when they got the upper hand been as forbearing, as tender of their slaves' lives as their slaves had been of theirs, it would have been to their lasting honour, and to the permanent advantage of the colony.

The civil authorities retaliated brutally. While less than 20 whites were killed in the revolt, nearly 600 slaves were executed in its aftermath. Perhaps influenced by the jailing of white missionaries like William Knibb and Thomas Burchell, Sam Sharpe gave himself up to the authorities. He admitted responsibility, cleared the missionaries of any blame and said destruction of life and property was not part of his plan. Even in jail he never lost his composure, praying and preaching to his fellow prisoners. On May 23, 1832 he was hanged, having told Bleby 'I would rather die upon yonder gallows than live in slavery'. His body is said to have been removed from its original burial place to a grave beneath the pulpit of the Montego Bay Baptist church. The location of his gallows is now the Sam Sharpe Square in Montego Bay.

'I would rather die upon yonder gallows than live in slavery'
- Sam Sharpe

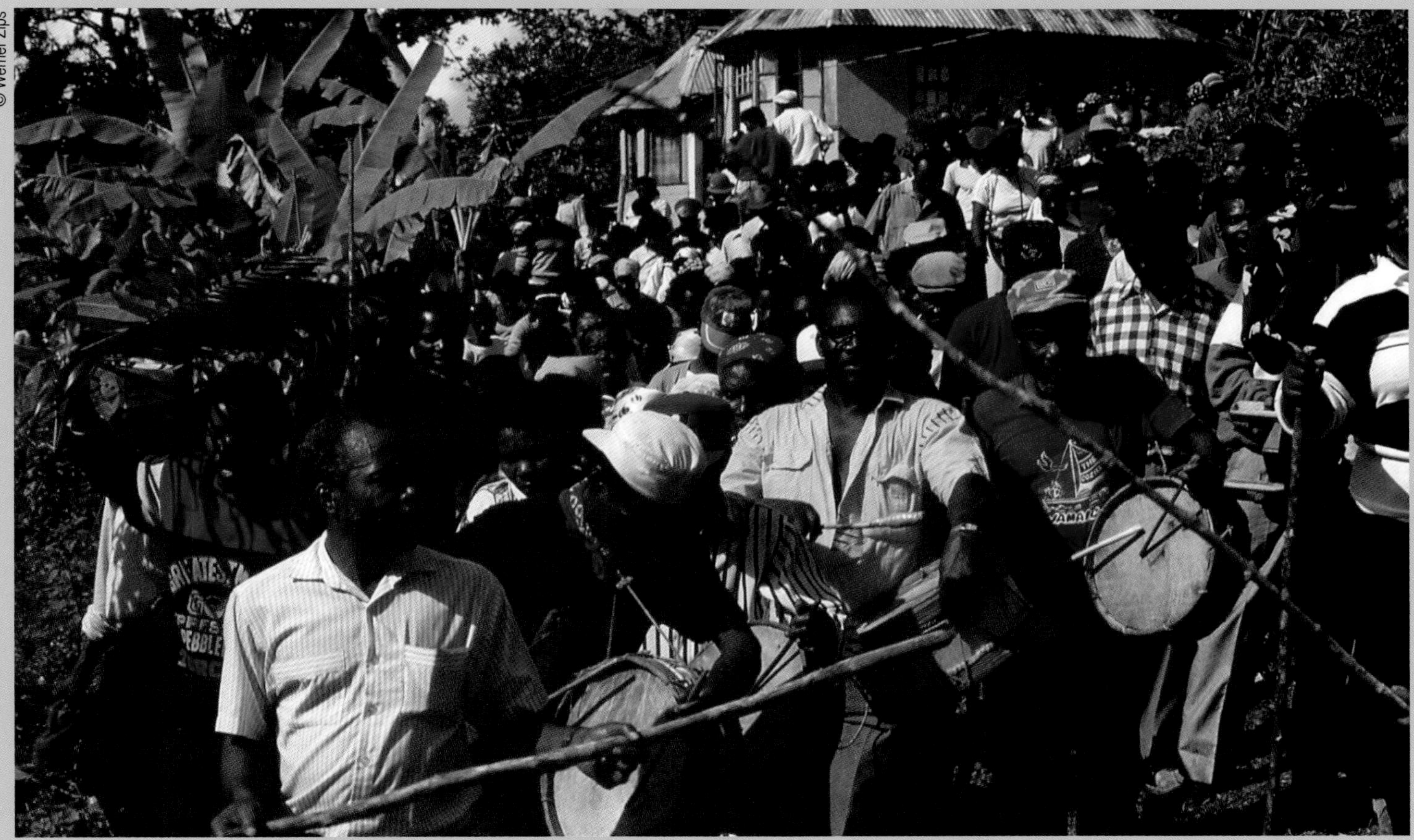
PROCESSION AT A MAROON CELEBRATION

INTERVIEW WITH A MODERN-DAY MAROON

Colonel Frank Lumsden has been the Moore Town Colonel – 'Colonel' being the title of the elected leader in each Maroon community – for the past five years. He was born in Charles Town, but his grandaunt Tun Tun was before him Colonel of Moore Town:

> There are four main Maroon communities today. The Leeward Maroon town of Accompong has a population of about 3,000. In the Windwards, Moore Town has about 2,800 people, Charles about 1,500 and Scott's Hall about 950. Accompong is the most well known, partly because it is more accessible and has the January 6 celebrations open to tourists. But the Maroon culture is strongest in the Windward communities. This is mostly because of language.
>
> In the Leewards Cudjoe had banned the speaking of any language except English to facilitate better communication among the various African tribes that made up his forces. But in the older Windwards we have preserved the Twi language and still use it widely on an everyday basis. The drumming and kromanti play used in the spiritual communication is also found only in the East.
>
> We have recently adopted a new mindset of preserving and strengthening the culture, and using it to develop industries such as agro-tourism. For instance we want to set up a museum of Maroon culture where we can sell Maroon produce like cassava and bammies and jerk pork done the original authentic way. After all it is only here that these things are done using original methods that are hundreds of year old.
>
> Maroons today are very conscious of their heritage, and perhaps there is a sense of superiority in some. I wouldn't say there is anything that distinguishes us physically. But we can tell immediately who is a Maroon and who is not by talking to them. You know Maroons didn't use to call themselves Maroons. They originally called themselves the yongugu family. And to be honest there are certain things we still do not share with outsiders.

MARY SEACOLE: BLACK WOMAN PIONEER

Courtesy of the Mary Seacole Hall, University of the West Indies, Mona

Nightingale and her nurses were based in a hospital several miles from the front. Yet Seacole treated wounded soldiers from both sides on the battlefield, often under fire.

Mary Jane Grant was born in Kingston in 1805 to a Scottish army officer and a free creole woman. Her mother ran the Kingston hotel Blundell Hall at 7 East Street, and was also a 'doctress' versed in the use of African herbal remedies, a knowledge she passed on to her daughter. Many of her guests and patients were British soldiers, often suffering from tropical diseases.

In 1836 Mary married Edwin Horatio Hamilton Seacole, rumoured to be Horatio Nelson's godson, who died in 1844. She was an inveterate traveller, and before marrying visited the Bahamas, Haiti, Cuba, Central America and England, where she complemented her knowledge of traditional healing with European medical ideas. Yet, the medical profession of the time was riddled with ignorance and quackery. For instance a study of inquests in 1838 showed that 28 out of 100 neonatal infants died because of the opium used to 'quiet them'. Mary on the other hand was said to have once boasted that she had never lost a mother or child. She inherited Blundell Hall from her mother, and when it burnt down in 1843, rebuilt and expanded it. It is now the site of the National Library of Jamaica.

In 1851 she visited her half-brother in Panama. Shortly after her arrival, cholera struck, and she pitched in with her expertise. The rich paid, but she treated the poor for free. On returning home to Jamaica in 1853, she was asked by the Jamaican medical authorities to minister to victims of a severe outbreak of yellow fever. She organised a nursing service at Up Park Camp, composed of fellow Afro-Jamaican doctresses.

She returned to Panama in 1854 and, succumbing to the gold fever in the air, invested in a mine. She read about the cholera-riddled British Army in the Crimean War, and 'The inclination to join my old friends of the 97th... and other regiments...took such exclusive possession of my mind that I threw over gold speculation altogether'. She travelled to London to put her extensive knowledge at the army's disposal. At the time, disease was a far greater threat to soldiers than the enemy. Over 21,000 British soldiers died in the Crimean War, but only about 5,000 perished from battle injuries.

Yet despite her expertise in treating cholera, she was turned down by the War Office, the Quartermaster-General's Department, the Crimean Fund, and Florence Nightingale's organisation. The undaunted Mary travelled to the Crimea at her own expense. She visited Nightingale, who had little practical experience of cholera, but her offer of help was refused. So Mary opened the British Hotel, fondly known as Mother Seacole's Hut, a few miles from the battlefront. Here she sold food and drink to soldiers, using the earnings to finance the medical treatment she gave. Nightingale and her nurses were based in a hospital several miles from the front. Yet Seacole treated wounded soldiers from both sides on the battlefield, often under fire.

Photos © Ian Randle Publishers

THE INSTITUTE OF JAMAICA

She was mentioned with affectionate admiration in many first-hand accounts of the war, tending the sick and wounded with warmth and good humour, and becoming famous for her fine meals. In fact the most famous French chef of the mid-nineteenth century, Alexis Soyer, considered her an equal. Florence Nightingale mistrusted her, mainly because she served alcohol at her hotel and prescribed it to her patients. Nightingale aimed to change the system. Seacole simply wanted to make her 'sons' feel better.

The sudden signing of a peace treaty left Mary with a large stock of unsalable provisions and unpaid debts. It was the only failure of her business career. She returned to England destitute and ill. The press highlighted her plight, and a benefit for her in July 1857 attracted thousands of people. She then published *The Wonderful Adventures of Mrs Seacole in Many Lands*, the first autobiography written by a black woman in Britain. She re-established herself in Jamaica in the 1860s, but then returned to England.

Queen Victoria's nephew Prince Victor, who as a young Lieutenant had been one of her customers in Crimea, carved a marble bust of her in 1871. She also became personal physiotherapist to Alexandra, Princess of Wales, later the queen of Edward VII. On her death in 1881 she left an estate valued at the then significant sum of over £2,500. In 1991 Mary Seacole was posthumously awarded the Jamaican Order of Merit, and in 2004 was voted the greatest black Briton ever.

Emancipation

On the eve of emancipation Jamaica was divided into three main groups. The first was a small number of whites: officials, plantation owners, merchants, professional men, attorneys, overseers, bookkeepers, master craftsmen. They controlled the country's economic and political life, and were practically self-governing in local affairs.

The second group consisted primarily of free people of colour, or mulattoes, who were largely the offspring of white planters and slave women. Their situations varied; some masters developed caring, de facto marriages with slave mistresses, and left their children money and property, other masters were serial rapists, or kept slave women harems, and were indifferent to their offspring.

While mixed-blood children were by law slaves, white fathers with the means usually secured their freedom. However, lower class whites like overseers and bookkeepers often could not afford to buy their mulatto offspring's liberty. So at emancipation there were probably as many coloured slaves as free coloureds.

By the 1820s free coloureds far outnumbered whites, and made up a high proportion of the militia, which the island largely depended on for defence. Still their rights as citizens were limited. They owned property, and could carry arms and give evidence in court. Free blacks had a similar 'in between' status – free blacks separated themselves socially from slaves, and some even owned slaves. Indeed, by 1838 coloured and black freedmen owned some 70,000 slaves, nearly one quarter of the total slave population. Visitors to the island during the last decade of slavery consistently commented on the abuse meted out to black slaves by coloured slave masters. A common Jamaican saying of the time went 'If me fe have massa or misses, give me Buckra one – no give me mulatto – dem no use neega well'. So class and colour attitudes have never been straight forward matters in Jamaica.

EDWARD JORDON

ROBERT OSBORNE

Photos courtesy of the National Library of Jamaica.

The freedmen newspaper, the Watchman, launched by the coloured Edward Jordon and Robert Osborne in 1829 and the first newspaper to engage in revolutionary journalism.

Free coloureds and blacks had both unsuccessfully petitioned the Assembly in the past to be allowed to vote. However by 1830 Jamaican planters felt so threatened by the powerful anti-slavery lobby in Britain that they offered full civil rights to coloured and black freedmen in return for their support in resisting emancipation. Once granted full rights, the freedmen tended to side with the Crown against planters, whom they felt had little interest in the island or its people. Freedmen were born and would die in Jamaica, and so were committed to its future. To white planters the island was merely a temporary stopover, to be quickly abandoned once their fortunes were made.

In 1831 planters refused to act on slave amelioration legislation passed in Britain, and threatened to secede and join the United States as a slave state. The freedmen newspaper the *Watchman*, launched by the coloured Edward Jordon and Robert Osborne in 1829 and the first newspaper to engage in revolutionary journalism, warned that any attempts by whites to transfer allegiance would be met by the combined force of free coloureds and blacks and slaves supporting the Crown's amelioration policy. In 1832 Jordon wrote an article calling upon 'the friends of humanity to give a long pull, and a strong pull, and a pull altogether,

EMANCIPATION SQUARE, SPANISH TOWN

until we bring the system [of slavery] down'. He was unsuccessfully charged with sedition and treason, punishable by death, but later convicted for libel, and jailed for six months before being freed on appeal.

The third and by far the largest component of Jamaican society were the mostly illiterate black slaves, who had no direct part in the island's political life. Some carried out domestic duties while others were the technicians of the plantations, the carpenters, masons, boiler-men and such but the overwhelming majority – about three quarters were field workers. The slaves had rights by custom as well as by law. They were entitled to allowances of food and clothing, had the use of land on which to grow food and were usually allowed to keep small stock. They also had every Sunday and every other Saturday for their own work.

Emancipation made the newly freed blacks equal to other British subjects before the law, but only on paper as the basic structure of slavery society remained virtually intact. The governmental system remained oligarchic, the masses were excluded from politics, and skin colour determined status and social mobility. There was no common base of ideas, no shared values, no unifying national sentiment.

Jamaica's history since 1838 has thus been a variation on two themes. One was the forging of a truly Jamaican identity, reflecting both a British-based language and political tradition, and the African derived sensibilities of its people. The other was the transfer of political, economic and social power from a light-skinned minority to the black majority. The white planter class and its mulatto allies only grudgingly ceded any of their advantages, often using income, property and even education eligibility measures to deny most of the black populace voting rights. However, change did come, in a lengthy, generally peaceful, but still unfinished process.

The freed slaves received no compensation, no guidance and no training to enable them to rearrange their lives independent of the plantation system. Prior to emancipation, slaves lived on their owners' estates in plantation

After emancipation, exorbitant rents and harsh trespass laws forced many newly freed blacks from their former estate homes.

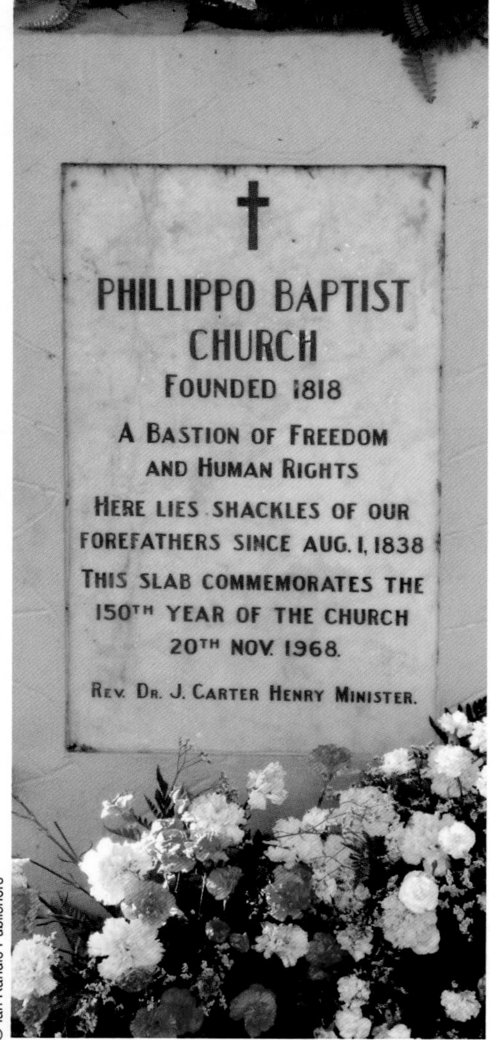
PHILLIPPO BAPTIST
CHURCH
FOUNDED 1818
A BASTION OF FREEDOM
AND HUMAN RIGHTS
HERE LIES SHACKLES OF OUR
FOREFATHERS SINCE AUG. 1, 1838
THIS SLAB COMMEMORATES THE
150TH YEAR OF THE CHURCH
20TH NOV. 1968.
REV. DR. J. CARTER HENRY MINISTER.

villages or 'slave yards'. No matter how terrible the conditions, the slaves were attached to these homes, which had often been occupied by the same families for generations. In addition to the provision grounds on the backlands of the estates, they were allowed to cultivate land around their huts and also buried their dead nearby.

After emancipation, exorbitant rents and harsh trespass laws forced many newly freed blacks from their former estate homes. The planters reasoned that with nowhere else to live, the ex-slaves – now a landless proletariat – would remain a cheap, captive workforce. Yet the emancipated slaves sought their own land to cultivate in any way they could. They squatted on mountainous Crown lands or abandoned estates, rented or leased marginal lands from cash-strapped owners, and in some instances managed to purchase small plots. Only the most destitute without any option became tenants of the estates.

Organised assistance came from Baptist missionaries such as James Phillippo and William Knibb, who used loans obtained from English connections to buy up old estates. They subdivided these into lots for their church congregations, and dubbed them 'free villages'. In fact Phillippo had foreseen the upcoming problem as early as 1834, and secured an estate above Spanish Town, which later became Sligoville. Free villages were a study in co-operative effort, with villagers helping each other to clear the land, prepare fields and construct houses. The first buildings were often a church and a school.

Only six years after emancipation, over 19,000 freed slaves had been settled in free villages. Governor Sir Charles Metcalfe, who arrived in 1839, had this to say in his first dispatch to London: 'The character… acquired by the people in their transition from slavery to freedom, seems to be more that of independence than of submission to the will of others. They are…as little subservient, as any labouring population in the world'.

In response to the labour shortage on plantations, the authorities began importing workers from abroad. Some Germans, Scots and Irish came, but they too soon turned their backs on plantation work. Then indentured Indian and Chinese labourers were brought in, with some limited success. Even large scale migration from Africa was tried, with some 7,500 coming between 1840 and 1865. These latter were mainly Africans from the interior rescued by the Royal Navy from slaving ships. They were originally taken to Sierra Leone and St Helena, but when these settlements proved overcrowded, both liberated slaves and Britain found the West Indies a suitable alternative.

The 1846 Sugar Equalisation act meant that Jamaica's sugar, rum, coffee and other exports soon had no protection against cheaper products from slave-owning countries like Cuba, Brazil and the US. Coupled with a commercial crisis with Britain, this all but ruined the planter class. Many plantations were abandoned, with especially painful consequences for the recently emancipated ex-slaves.

Asiatic cholera swept across the globe in the late 1840s, reaching Jamaica in 1850. Over the next five years some 32,000 died here, about eight per cent of the population. One of those who helped alleviate the situation was Mary Seacole.

Courtesy of the National Library of Jamaica

Prelude to a Rebellion

Elected politics in Jamaica was an all white affair up to 1830, when coloured and black freedmen were granted the vote. The coloured Assemblymen Edward Jordon and Robert Osborne used the *Watchman* newspaper to encourage people of colour into political activism, and by 1837, there were over ten coloureds in the Assembly.

William Knibb was the first to see the electoral possibilities of grassroot organisation, encouraging Baptist church members to endorse pro-slave candidates in the pre-abolition 1830s. The broadened franchise of 1840 opened the way for Knibb to organise the black and coloured electorate to challenge the Anglican church establishment, and attack the tax increase on land and animals. Governor Elgin however called early elections in which newly registered Baptists could not vote, so their actual successes were few. Knibb's death in 1845 deprived the movement of a leader whose energy and vision were never replaced, but he had created a new awareness among blacks of their rights and latent electoral power.

In 1847 the small landowner Edward Vickers became the first black man to win a seat in the Assembly. In office he argued for agricultural diversification, increased educational grants and penal reform. He was the first – and for a long time only – Jamaican politician to call for universal male suffrage. Another black man to win a seat was Charles Price, who often voted with the white establishment. In the 1865 Morant Bay Rebellion, Price was killed by a member of Bogle's army, who described him as 'a black man with a white heart'.

By 1852 blacks and browns made up 36 per cent of the Assembly. This prompted the imposition of a 'hereditaments' tax which sharply reduced the electorate. Ironically the motion was introduced by the brown Edward Jordon, who had once sided with Sam Sharpe and agitated for abolition, but who had grown increasingly conservative.

In 1863 the population consisted of 13,816 whites, 81,065 coloureds, and 346,374 blacks, for a total of 441,255. However only 1,543, or less than one half of one per cent, could vote, and the great education and capital gap meant the lighter-skinned minority still dominated economically and socially. The English Baptist missionary Edward Underhill estimated that nearly 70 per cent of voters in the 1860s voted on the basis of paying taxes or receiving salaries. He concluded that small occupiers of land were not represented in the House, and that planters, attorneys, agents, clerks and shopkeepers controlled the vote.

Between 1849 and 1854, 17 coloureds and three blacks sat in the Assembly. None won a seat in 1863, and the all-white Assembly used its power to keep increasing taxes on the poor – between 1840 and 1865 the tax on salt fish went up by 366 per cent, mackerel 433 per cent, donkeys and horses 1,580 per cent. The black masses already resented their lack of land and the exorbitant rents charged to small farmers. A particular grievance was the corrupt judicial structure, where court costs were prohibitive, and employees had little hope for redress against employers.

The subsequent 1865 Rebellion then, was very much the consequence of a dysfunctional electoral system that gave the masses no say in how they were governed.

PAUL BOGLE AND HISTORICAL MEMORY

In a young country like Jamaica it's almost possible to see historical memory being shaped in real time. Take the famous Edna Manley statue of 'Paul Bogle' erected in front of the Morant Bay courthouse in 1965, and which was taken up for restoration in 2009. When remounting plans were announced a year later, town residents demanded that the statue, supposedly based on a grandson of Bogle, be replaced by his 'true image'.

According to Dorette Abrahams, president of the African Heritage Development Association,

> Paul Bogle was described by newspapers as a tall man with a dominant personality and the imperious character of an African chief. He was born in slavery times, but came to own 500 acres, and out of a total island population of 440,000 in 1864, was one of only 1,903 who could vote. So he was a man of means. Give us the real Paul Bogle possibly mounted on the white horse that he rode and dressed in his waistcoat, so that when parents or teachers take their black children to look at this black man, they look at his true likeness and feel the energy emanating from him and the children can be inspired to believe that by dint of hard work and natural ability, they too can achieve great things in their lives and in this country.

What most Jamaicans think of as a 'true to life' depiction of Bogle is the widely disseminated photograph that was put first on a $2 note and then on the 10 cent coin. However,

STATUE OF PAUL BOGLE AT THE MORANT BAY COURTHOUSE

David Boxer's monograph on Edna Manley says she rejected this increasingly controversial photo that portrays a smooth faced man aged about 25 to 30. Bogle was 45 at the time of the Morant Bay Rebellion, and the October 18, 1865 *Colonial Standard* which carried a reward of 2,000 pounds for his capture gave this description:

> …a very black man, with shining skin, bearing heavy marks of smallpox on his face, and more especially on his nose; teeth good, large mouth with red thick lips; about five feet eight inches in height, broad across the shoulders, carries himself indolently, and has no whiskers.

Can it really matter how a man who died nearly 150 years ago is depicted today? Well before Bogle was made a National Hero, some St Thomas residents blamed him for the repression by the militia that put down the rebellion, and even for the resulting under-development of the parish. His descendants suffered a good deal of persecution, and many were forced to flee the parish or change their names years after the 1865 rebellion. Zedekiah Inglington remembered that

> As a child growing up, the Bogle name was a disgrace because people use to claim that them kill white people and so nuff people never want to say dem is a Bogle.

After the granting of National Hero status, however, the Bogle name became a badge of pride and an association with greatness – vivid proof that official historical narratives can have real effects even centuries after actual events.

Sources: *Jamaica Observer* March 21, 2010 'Bogle Statue Model was Hero's Grandson', 'Bogle Name was Mud after Morant Bay Rebellion', 'Statue Should Reflect Real Bogle', 'Bogle Statue Debate Taking Unfortunate Turn'. *Gleaner* March 25, 2010 'That Unacceptable Statue of Paul Bogle, Devon Dick.

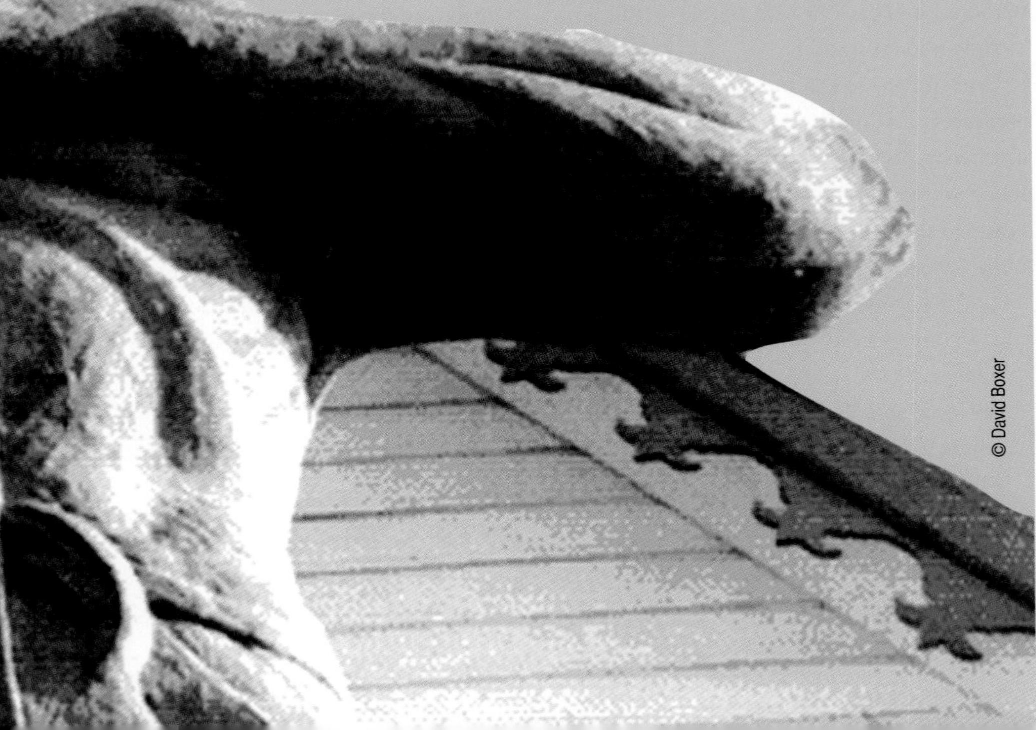

© David Boxer

Courtesy of the National Library of Jamaica

GEORGE WILLIAM GORDON

The Morant Bay Rebellion

By 1865 the American civil war and a severe drought had dramatically increased food costs, while collapsing sugar prices had cut estate wages and made work scarce. In January, Edward Underhill wrote a letter describing 'the extreme poverty of the people' who had to 'steal or starve'. He criticised the Jamaican Legislature for high tax levels and denying blacks political rights.

'Underhill' meetings of persons wishing to change the system sprang up across the island. The people of St Ann even addressed a petition to Queen Victoria, complaining of hardships and asking to be rented Crown land at low rates. Governor John Eyre (previously a famed explorer of Australia

all I ever did was to recommend the people who complained to seek redress in a legitimate way...it is the will of my Heavenly Father that I should thus suffer in obeying his command to relieve the poor and needy...I thank him that I suffer in such a case.

– George William Gordon

and still considered a hero there) forwarded the document but he blamed the people's problems on 'their natural disposition to indolence.'

The Colonial Office responded with 'The Queen's Advice' telling labourers that 'it is from their own industry…that they must look for an improvement in their condition.' Many missionaries refused to circulate it, maintaining that the Queen would not have replied so unsympathetically. The emancipated blacks viewed the British Crown as a guarantor of freedom because white planters had talked openly of Jamaica reimposing slavery by joining the US as a slave state.

Matters came to a head in the parish of St Thomas, which significantly had received some 8,000 indentured labourers from the Congo region of Africa between 1841 and 1865. Having never known slavery, these recent immigrants were perhaps more prone to rebel against perceived injustice than their Jamaican-born counterparts.

In August 1865 the brown St Thomas vestry (assembly) member George William Gordon attacked Eyre for sanctioning 'everything done by the higher class to the oppression of the negroes' and reportedly raised the spectre of Haiti. One area of Gordon's electoral strength was Stony Gut, where the Native Baptist preacher Paul Bogle was his political agent. At an open air meeting in the St Thomas capital of Morant Bay Bogle was appointed to lead a delegation to march 80 kilometres to Spanish Town, and lay the complaints of the people before the Governor but they were refused a hearing.

Bogle began to hold secret meetings and drill his men. He visited the Hayfield Maroons to enlist their support, as the Maroons were greatly feared for their violence in quelling unrest. They later claimed to have offered him no encouragement, but Bogle said they had agreed to help him in a quarrel he expected to have with the bukra. 'The Maroons is our back' he said. Gordon at this time had fallen seriously ill.

On October 7, Bogle and a group of men were involved in a skirmish with police at court, and arrest warrants were issued. However, when the police went to apprehend Bogle, about 300 men disarmed them. Bogle complained in a petition to the Governor that:

> …an outrageous assault was committed upon us by the policemen….We therefore call upon your Excellency for protection, seeing we are Her Majesty's loyal subjects, which protection if refused we will be compelled to put our shoulders to the wheel, as we have been imposed for a period of 27 years with due obeisance to the laws of our Queen and country, and we can no longer endure the same.

Here was the essence of the revolt:

On October 11, 1865 several hundred black persons led by Paul Bogle marched into Morant Bay. They confronted the white and brown militia protecting the St Thomas vestry, and fighting erupted. By nightfall the crowd had killed 18 people and wounded 31 others, while seven members of the crowd died. Disturbances spread across the parish and martial law was declared. By the time it ended a month later, 29 whites and browns had been killed, and nearly 500 mostly black persons executed in retaliation.

Bogle insisted he was not rebelling against the Queen but whites saw the St Thomas outbreak as a massive conspiracy of blacks intent on taking over the island, and the government ruthlessly put it down. The Maroons played a key role in suppressing the rebellion, and committed many of the worst atrocities.

Eyre identified Gordon with the rebellion and had him arrested. He denied involvement, and indeed was in bed at the time. However, he was convicted and hung on October 23. In his final letter to his wife Gordon wrote:

> …all I ever did was to recommend the people who complained to seek redress in a legitimate way…it is the will of my Heavenly Father that I should thus suffer in obeying his command to relieve the poor and needy… I thank him that I suffer in such a case.

Also on October 23 the Maroons captured Paul Bogle. He was hung the next day, going calmly to his death.

The harshness of the suppression led to

MONUMENT TO
THE RIGHT EXCELLENT GEORGE WILLIAM GORDON
December, 1815 - October 23, 1865
AND THE RIGHT EXCELLENT PAUL BOGLE
Died October 24, 1865
George William Gordon and Paul Bogle emerged as defenders of the rights of the underprivileged during the 1865 period. Gordon, the son of a slave mother and Scottish planter, was a champion of the poor and oppressed. Despite earning the wrath of the political directorate, as a member of the local assembly, he staunchly defended the rights of the underprivileged and urged them to resist strongly the oppression and unjust conditions of the time. He was also deeply religious and started an independent Baptist organisation, opening chapels in the countryside and ordaining deacons.
Among the deacons Gordon ordained was Paul Bogle of Stony Gut. Like Gordon, Bogle saw the social and economic hardships that prevailed and led a series of protests against them. Seeking some redress for the injustices being meted out, Bogle and his supporters walked 45 miles from Stony Gut to Spanish Town to petition the Governor. He refused to see them so they returned dejected.
On October 11, 1865, Bogle led another protest march to the Morant Bay Courthouse where a violent confrontation with official forces took place. Nearly five hundred (500) people were killed in the uprising and many were flogged and punished before order was restored. Both George William Gordon and Paul Bogle were executed for their role in the protests.
The 1865 protests paved the way for change in the official attitude, which made possible a move to improve the social and economic conditions of the people as well as the change to Crown Colony Government.
In this Monument designed by H. T. Repole, sets of five concrete arches curve towards a centrepiece of "unformed" marble that contains the busts of Gordon and Bogle. The arches are symbolic of the ten fingers on a pair of hands, rough-ened to symbolize hands that once toiled during slavery and show the lines and bruises of bondage. The centrepiece of "unformed" marble is a freedom symbol. The eyes of both heroes are fixed on the freedom symbol, indicative of their mission to liberate all who were oppressed.
In recognition of their contribution to the political, social and economic development of the country, Gordon and Bogle were conferred the status of National Heroes in 1969.

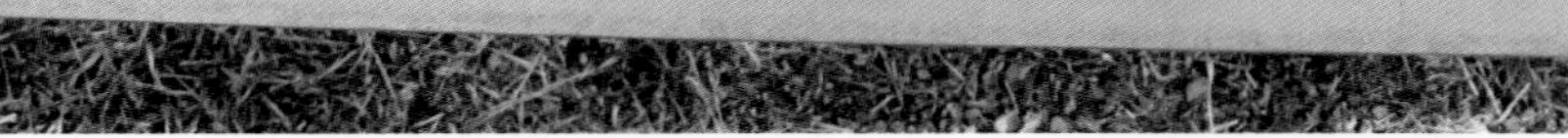

MONUMENT AT NATIONAL HEROES PARK

the Jamaica Royal Commission inquiry in England. This praised Eyre for acting, promptly, concluding there was no general conspiracy, but that given the 'general excitement and discontent' the rebellion might have spread to other parishes if not quickly suppressed. It condemned him for prolonging the period of martial law, for the injustice of Gordon's trial, and for the barbarous retributions. It attributed the uprising to demand for land, and a breakdown in the justice system. Yet many of the Jamaican upper classes regarded Eyre as a saviour who had prevented a general massacre, and he had never been so popular as after the rebellion.

While the rebellion failed, planter class rule remained under threat, and the prospect of a non-white majority in the Assembly still loomed. At the first Assembly meeting after the rebellion's suppression, Eyre offered planters the only available alternative to the rule of an emerging black majority – the dissolution of the Assembly by a vote in favour of Crown Colony government. The vote was passed and for the next 18 years there was no voting, as Jamaica was ruled by a Governor-appointed legislative council.

DEVON HOUSE, KINGSTON

Modern Times

CHARTING A NATIONAL DESTINY

Modern Jamaica may be said to date from 1866, when the new Governor Sir John Peter Grant began restructuring the administrative apparatus. New courts were established, a new police force was created, and the Church of England was disestablished in Jamaica. Road and irrigation systems were improved, more money was spent on health and education, and in 1872 the capital was moved from Spanish Town to Kingston. The new system of governance was also free of nepotism and local favouritism, which made civil servants harder to bribe. So in the end Gordon and Bogle did get a good measure of what they bravely fought and died for: fair and competent government.

Another important development was the start of banana exports in 1866, when Yankee skipper George Busch took a boatload of bunches back to Boston. However, it was Captain Lorenzo Dow Baker who started shipping in large quantities. By 1890 bananas had outstripped sugar as Jamaica's major export, and from 1876 until 1929 when it was overtaken by Honduras, Jamaica was the world's largest banana producer. To help defray passage costs, later banana traders promoted the island's scenic virtues to would-be travellers, thus creating the local tourism industry.

Many Jamaicans had emigrated to Panama between 1850 and 1855 to help build the railway there. Even more went from 1880 to 1889 when the French began cutting the Isthmus canal, and there was another upsurge during the 1904–14 US completion phase. Back and forth travel between the two countries became the norm. Perhaps 174,000 Jamaicans emigrated to Panama between 1850–1915, and maybe 63,000 failed to return – significant numbers in a then current population of about 500,000.

Jamaica at the time offered few economic opportunities or social outlets for the working class, and ambitious young people literally fought to get on departing ships. The strong urge to leave left many parts of the island depopulated, while the Panama port city of Colon became half-Jamaican. Most emigrants were young men and the birth rate fell significantly during construction periods. It's an era still remembered in the folk song 'Colon Man'. Today there are an estimated 60,000 persons of West Indian descent living in the Canal zone, chiefly in Colon and Cristobal.

Jamaicans continued to seek better fortunes in foreign lands. During the decade 1911–21 for instance, the total net movement was about 146,000. Some 46,000 went to the US, 45,000 to Panama, 20,000 to Cuba and 43,000 to other places such as Costa Rica, Colombia, Nicaragua and Honduras. This migration served, then and later, as a safety valve in relieving economic and social tensions. The willingness of Jamaicans to go abroad in search of opportunity has continued throughout its history.

Though precise figures are not available, it's estimated that the number of second and third generation Jamaicans abroad – mostly in the US, Britain and Canada – may equal the number of people living on the island. Those who travelled abroad, and returned with the first-hand knowledge that things did not have to be as they were in Jamaica, often became catalysts for social change.

Among those seeking their fortune was George Stiebel, who left Jamaica a poor carpenter, found his fortune in South American gold, returned to Jamaica the country's first millionaire of African descent, and became custos of St Andrew. In 1881 he built a massive home that is today one of the country's most famous buildings, Devon House.

Courtesy of the National Library of Jamaica

CONSTANT SPRING HOTEL

The 1891 Great Exhibition that showcased the island's products was Jamaica's earliest attempt to sell itself to the world, and is often seen as the beginning of the formal tourist industry. It was also perhaps the first time Jamaicans asked themselves how they were viewed by outsiders, and what they had to offer economically or culturally. Though it was well supported by locals, not many foreign visitors showed up, and the Exhibition lost money. Most of the hotels built for the occasion went bankrupt, including the former Constant Spring Hotel that now houses the Immaculate Conception High School, while the Moorish style buildings where the Great Exhibition was held is now occupied by Wolmer's High School.

Towards Electoral Empowerment

Although it undoubtedly brought administrative improvements, Crown Colony rule hindered local political development. No black man, for instance, had been nominated to the Legislative Council or any official position in the administration – though brown politicians such as Edward Jordon attained senior appointments.

In the face of local and international pressure, the Colonial Office reintroduced limited elected representation in September 1884. Tax and income qualification meant that there were out of a population of over 580,000, only 7,443 could vote – 3,766 blacks, 98 East Indians, 2,578 coloureds, 1,001 whites. Those who qualified under this financially restrictive franchise did not necessarily share the interests of the majority.

Non-white politicians who attempted to mobilise the masses or raise the colour question were accused of fomenting violence as seen in the case of Morant Bay or Haiti. Take for instance the coloured businessman Charles Campbell, who in 1874 had founded the newspaper the *Budget* to campaign for the restoration of representative government. In 1884 he campaigned openly on the basis that 'he alone, of all the candidates in the election, truly represented the coloured and black sections of the population, and on this ground must be elected to the Legislative Council to advance the interest of this class'.

He immediately came under attack from the

MARCUS GARVEY PRESIDING AT 1922 CONVENTION, LIBERTY HALL

Photos courtesy of the National Library of Jamaica

white planter/merchant class in the columns of the *Daily Gleaner*. His detractors found a black shoemaker to denigrate Campbell on the platform, and inadequate facilities prevented many of his supporters from voting, ensuring his defeat. Similar tactics were used when Campbell ran for the Municipal Board, with the same shoemaker being put up as his opponent. A white Jewish politician later called Campbell 'Perhaps…the first black man who had come forward…as distinctively a representative of his class, and a worthy representative'.

In 1885 the basic requirement was lowered to a payment of ten shillings in direct taxes annually, approximately the tax on a donkey and one acre of land. There was active mobilisation among the black petty bourgeoisie – successful smallholders, teachers, parsons, low level civil

ROBERT LOVE

servants and clerks. So by 1889 black voters far outnumbered whites and coloured voters. In response the authorities introduced a literacy clause preventing those unable to read and write from voting. This produced the desired all white Legislative Council.

Robert Love, a Bahamian born black physician who settled in Jamaica after living in the US and Haiti, set out to change this. He called for more black Justices of the Peace, more black members of boards and commissions, and greater black representation in government. Perhaps the largest grouping that supported Love's philosophy were the 1,700 teachers who constituted the island's single largest block of qualified professionals. They formed the Jamaica Union of Teachers in 1894 and with membership spread across the island, provided a decentralised body of potential leaders, who became central to the Jamaican political process.

Love was perhaps the first leader to publicly challenge the assumption of black inferiority.

Courtesy of the National Library of Jamaica

J.A.G. SMITH

An anti-colonialist, he believed that the primary goal of any black country should be self-rule. However his experiences in Haiti and the US inclined him to the view that possibly:

> …the best hope for black people lay within the British legal and political system….In spite of some faults which we see and feel, there is much that is good and sound in the great heart of England, and we have confidence in Her good intentions.

When the *Daily Gleaner* refused to publish his letters, Love started his own weekly *Jamaica Advocate* in 1894. In order to erase the belief that blacks were not interested in politics or would make unsuitable candidates, Love publicised lists of persons with suitable educational and financial qualifications. Accused of preaching race hatred, Love replied: 'Loveism' chooses a white man, as its exponent, when he is a good man; a black man when he is worthy; and any other kind of man if the right principles are found in him.'

Love also highlighted women's rights:

> …the conditions in which the black people of the British West Indies are found today is due to the fact that no effort has been made to lift the black women up and to put her on the plane that women ought to occupy in society.

It was not until 1919 however that Jamaican women won the vote.

In 1893 only four coloured men presented themselves as candidates and only one gained a seat. Still the number of black and coloured representatives grew, with Love himself being elected in 1906. By 1935 they formed the majority in the legislature. The most prominent and popular was the black barrister J.A.G. 'the giant killer' Smith – so nicknamed for his scathing criticisms of colonial officialdom. Norman Manley called him 'the most outstanding, incorruptible politician this country has ever seen'. He was also chief draftsman of the 1944 Universal Adult Suffrage Constitution.

Smith apart, the Legislative Council was not highly regarded by the public. It was no longer a matter of colour alone, for its members were now predominantly negro and 'The traditional type of candidate would now rarely consent even to run, fearing that he would be defeated on account of his white skin'. Whether black, white or brown, the 'ten shilling' voters, tended to side with the merchant plantocracy against workers.

In 1896 the *Advocate* suggested a public memorial for George William Gordon. It encouraged blacks to assert their equality, express their political views, educate themselves, and develop pride in their African heritage. Among those influenced was Marcus Garvey, to whom Love gave elocution lessons. Garvey declared in 1920 that 'Much of my early education in race consciousness came from Dr Love…if Dr Love was alive and in good health, you would not be attacking me, you would be attacking him'. Garvey would develop the political strategy initiated by Love, and take the message of race consciousness worldwide.

No other Jamaican has had such a profound international impact as Marcus Garvey. In an era that treated the idea of black inferiority almost as a given fact, Garvey shouted 'No!' in a voice heard across the planet. As Martin Luther King later said, Garvey was 'the first man, on a mass scale, to give millions of Negroes a sense of dignity and destiny....He gave us a sense of personhood, a sense of manhood, a sense of somebodiness'.

Garvey saw the key to racial harmony in the open acceptance of racial differences, and respect for them. He advocated race consciousness as critical to self-worth, and a crucial element in national development. Yet he was no racist, as he pointed out in the 1929 Jamaican context:

> My opponents say I am against white and fair-skinned people. This is not so. I am against the class system here, which keeps the poor man down, and the poor are mostly black people. It is only natural, therefore, that their interest should be nearest and dearest to my heart….Let us all work together as fellow Jamaicans, and ring in the changes for a new Jamaica.

Born in 1887, Garvey had a life changing experience at 14:

> …the place where I lived…was adjoining that of a white man. He had three girls and a boy. All of us were playmates….The little white girl whom I liked most knew

Courtesy of the National Library of Jamaica

HARBOUR STREET IN DOWNTOWN KINGSTON AFTER THE 1907 EARTHQUAKE

> no better than I did myself. We were two innocent fools who never dreamed of a race feeling and problem.... At fourteen my little white playmate and I parted. Her parents thought the time had come to separate us and draw the colour line. They sent her...to Scotland, and told her that she was never to write or get in touch with me, for I was a 'nigger'. It was then I found for the first time that...there were different races, each having its own separate... social life.

Garvey was a foreman at the city's largest printery when a great earthquake killed over 600 people and devastated Kingston on January 14, 1907. The resulting financial hardships badly squeezed the working class. The printers' union – Jamaica's first – asked for better wages and working conditions. When turned down, they struck. Garvey was offered a pay increase in the hope that he would keep the plant operating. He refused and walked out with his men, who chose him to organise the strike.

The strike was eventually broken and, blacklisted by private printers, Garvey took a government job. The strike experience strengthened his desire for an organised effort to improve black working class conditions. He founded a periodical called *Garvey's Watchman*. It did not do well, and in 1910 Garvey broadened his horizons by travelling to Central and South America, England and Europe. He was struck by the inferior social and economic status of blacks everywhere. In England he worked for the world's leading Pan African journal, the *Africa Times* and *Orient Review*. Though he did not visit Africa, this job kept him abreast of African history and current affairs and brought him into contact with influential Africans.

There he conceived the idea of one great international organisation of proud, educated and financially independent black people, who would take their place as equals on the world stage. He returned to Jamaica in 1914, and on Emancipation Day, August 1, launched the Universal Negro Improvement Association. The UNIA was dedicated to improving the conditions of black people the world over, encompassing America, the Caribbean, and Africa. Its famous motto was 'One God! One Aim! One Destiny!' However the UNIA found it difficult to make headway in Jamaica, where Garvey found no clear race consciousness. He felt Black America would answer his call and moved there in 1916.

He later described the difference between the American and Jamaican slave experience to UNIA member Amy Bailey:

> Marcus used to say to me that in Jamaica we thought we had suffered. But it was not a total suffering, our souls had not gone through the mill. For blacks in America the iron went into their souls through their slavery, but in Jamaica it did not go so far. The American Negro would therefore cry out in his spirituals to be able to walk around God's heaven. In Jamaica we have no spirituals, we have folk-songs where we laugh at each other. The white man stripped the black man in America of his inner dignity. The English were born colonisers. They knew it was a mistake to strip the person of the 'I am' within you. He wouldn't say to you, you can't have this job because you are a nigger. He would say I'm sorry but that vacancy is filled. That bitterness never entered the soul of Jamaican slaves.

SHOP
CAN ALIENS FIGHT
ENGLAND WOULD DO WELL TO LET GHANDI GO
The UNIA spread to almost everyplace in the world with a significant number of African descended people....Malcom X was a son of a UNIA organiser and attended meetings as a child.

Photos courtesy of the National Library of Jamaica

UNIA MARCHERS 1924

THE UNIVERSAL NEGRO IMPROVEMENT ASSOCIATION

The UNIA was headquartered in New York City, which contained a polyglot African community, about 20 per cent of whom were West Indian. In addition there was a sprinkling of persons from Africa itself and the larger African Diaspora, who passed on news of the movement to their home territories. Garvey's earlier contacts in his travels also helped spread word of the fledgling organisation.

The UNIA colours were red, black and green, signifying the blood of the Negro race nobly shed, the colour of the skin, and a promise of a better life in Africa. The newspaper *Negro World* played a key role in the internationalisation of the Garvey Movement. Started in 1918, it was by the early 1920s the most widely circulated African newspaper in the world. Sections were printed in Spanish and French as well as English, and it carried news of UNIA branches and race matters of interest to people everywhere. The UNIA also disseminated its ideas through political and practical instruction, providing its membership with opportunities for literary and artistic expression.

The UNIA spread to almost every place in the world with a significant number of African descended people. At its height it had an estimated four million members with over 1,000 branches in over 20 countries, including the US, Britain, Australia, Canada, Cuba, Haiti, Brazil, Mexico, Panama, Costa Rica, Ecuador, Venezuela, South Africa, Liberia, and the colonial territories encompassing future countries such as Nigeria, Ghana, the Democratic Republic of Congo (Zaire), Sierra Leone and Senegal. It had over 800 branches in the US, and is generally considered the largest mass movement in Afro-American history. The New York local alone had over 40,000 members.

Many major African political figures were directly or indirectly influenced by Garvey. Kwame Nkrumah, independent Ghana's first leader, attended UNIA meetings in New York as a young man and testified in his autobiography to the overwhelming impact of Garvey's 'Philosophy and Opinions' on his political development. Jomo Kenyatta of Kenya considered himself a Garveyite as early as the 1920s, and later lived in a house in London rented by Garvey for African students. Nnamdi Azikiwe, first Governor General of independent Nigeria, recalled in his autobiography his first copy of the *Negro World*. In 1920s South Africa, much of the top leadership of the African National Congress belonged to the UNIA. In Afro-America, Elijah Muhammad patterned his Nation of Islam (the so-called Black Muslims) to a large extent after the UNIA, of which he was a member. Malcom X was a son of a UNIA organiser and attended meetings as a child. Vietnamese leader Ho Chi Min attended UNIA meetings in Harlem and gave financial contributions.

LET'S PUT IT OVER

The Indispensable Weekly
The Voice of the Awakened Negro

Reaching the Mass of Negroes
The Best Advertising Medium

A Newspaper Devoted Solely to the Interests of the Negro Race

VOL. XIX. No. 8 — NEW YORK, SATURDAY, OCTOBER 3, 1925 — PRICE: FIVE CENTS IN GREATER NEW YORK. SEVEN CENTS ELSEWHERE IN THE U. S. A. TEN CENTS IN FOREIGN COUNTRIES

IN BUILDING EMPIRE NEGROES ARE DOING WHAT IS FEASIBLE AND POSSIBLE; RACE WILL BENEFIT FROM MISTAKES OF OTHERS

ABSENCE OF SYMPATHY AND HUMAN LOVE CAUSE OF DOWNFALL OF EARLIER EMPIRES

Striking Example Seen in British Empire, Which Is Now Tottering to Its Fall

IF KRIM CAN HOLD OFF GREATEST MILITARY POWER, WHAT IS IMPOSSIBLE FOR 400,000,000 ORGANIZED NEGROES?

Fellow-Men of the Negro Race, Greeting:

I desire to say a few words this week on "Empires and Their Fall." Empires have risen; empires have fallen, and empires in the future will fall because of the misconduct of those who rule. We have come a long way in the history of governments; we have come a long way in the history of empires. We had Assyria, Babylon, Rome, Greece. We had the German Empire, and we are still living in the age of empires—empires that will fall.

From my observation I have come to the conclusion that empires have fallen because of those who rule—their failure to consider the feelings, the sufferings, the afflictions of those whom they rule or those whom they govern. The fall of nations and empires has always been caused by the disorganized spirit, the disorganized sentiment of those who make up the nation or empire; the one class opposing the other, fighting against the other class; the other class seeking to deprive them of the essentials of life that are necessary for the good and well-being of those who make up the nation or the empire. Hence you have had social revolutions, you have had civil strife which ultimately resulted in the downfall of the nation or the empire. History teaches us that and we are seeing it today.

Benefit From the Past

It is because we have studied history that we of the Universal Negro Improvement Association have started toward empire. In traveling toward the destiny of empire we must see to it that we do not make the mistakes others have made in the past; otherwise we shall fall even as they fell.

Some people say that Garvey and those who lead and make up the Universal Negro Improvement Association are endeavoring to do the impossible, because Africa is controlled by great forces; that Negroes will never be able to compete with the British Empire and other great European nations that have dominion over a large part of Africa.

Those who make such a statement do not take into consideration the history of the rise and fall of empires. What has happened in the past will happen again. The handwriting is now on the wall. Peoples, whether Turk, Indian, Egyptian, or Arab; Chinese, Syrian, or Bantu, are today rising in their might, the scales at last removed from their eyes, and asserting their right to live their own lives in their own land; to wipe out the plague of oppression visited upon them for centuries. And "with what measure ye mete, it shall be measured unto you again."

I am not attempting to prophesy the destruction of any of the existing empires or nations, but am merely stating the overt fact that unless there comes a striking change in the mentality and attitude of the strong and powerful on the earth today—and that speedily—destruction and ruin will inevitably ensue.

When the Few Err

We have industrial monopoly; we have commercial monopoly; we have economic monopoly that places power in the hands of a select few, and on account of the selfishness of the administration by this conceited, self-centered few, the masses barely exist. It is but natural, then, that dissatisfaction follows. And from this springs a desire to correct evil, with the resultant dethronement of the oppressor, and the destruction of empire.

Empires have fallen in the past and they will fall again; the handwriting is on the wall; and we of the Universal Negro Improvement Association are organizing for the rearing of a greater African Empire of tomorrow.

But, as I have said before, in traveling toward the destiny of empire, let us not make the mistakes others have made in the past and others are making now. If we fail to give consideration and to extend fellowship to all who make up the African Empire, the Empire will fall. And who can tell that we are not the people to teach the world the qualities of mercy and justice, of human freedom and democracy? Who can tell but that out of the wreck of empires the Negroes of the world will build up a model empire that will teach man how to rule and govern?

The Case of the British Empire

If, for example, those who laid the foundation of British imperialism had laid it on righteousness and treated all men as they would like to be treated themselves, there would be no discord; there would be no dissatisfaction within the empire. All would work for the continuity of empire. But because of the oppression, high-handed dealing, and inhumanity that was practised, the exploited and robbed and oppressed, as we see today, are turning upon the empire to rend it. The empire's statesmen failed to consider the higher development of the people and to legislate to meet that higher development. The methods you adopt toward savages or pagans cannot be adopted toward civilized and Christian men. Continue those tactics, and they will rebel. Continue to refuse to interpret the spirit of the people in the age in which they live, and you are headed toward destruction.

We are not going to start any fight. We are just going to walk into the "New Jerusalem"—I mean the New Africa. Take Spain and France and little Morocco. Those Moors, just a handful of them, have given the Spaniards a thrashing, and are now successfully opposing the combined efforts of the two to rob them of their independence. If Abd-el-Krim and his handful of valiant tribesmen can make the Spaniards a laughing-stock, can engage, on apparently equal terms, the might of the greatest military power in the world, how long will it take the combined forces of 400,000,000 trained in military tactics to rid their soil of the invader?

Let me say to you, men and women, freedom, complete freedom for Africa is not impossible. The freedom of Africa may come at any minute. It is for us to become race conscious, to learn to co-operate, to pool our resources, to strike out, and all else will come. Pick out the best in every government, whether that government be monarchical, democratic, or soviet, and model our government in such a way that all the citizens of that government will be satisfied and in sympathy with each other. The thing you call sympathy, the thing you call human love, is the thing that binds humanity. Much of the rest is dross. When you show love and tolerance and sympathy toward your brother, he in turn loves and respects you, and will die, if need be, hand in hand with you.

The world is suffering from a lack of sympathy and human love. Embrace these attributes, Negroes, and redeem humanity.

I have the honor to be,

Your obedient servant,

MARCUS GARVEY,

Founder and President-General, Universal Negro Improvement Association.

LIBERTY HALL

All UNIA divisions were required to have 'Liberty Hall' community headquarters for social, cultural, intellectual, and economic activities. Liberty Hall was so named because of Garvey's admiration for the Irish independence movement and the Irish Transport and General Workers Union, whose headquarters in Dublin was named Liberty Hall in 1912. Around 1924, Liberty Halls and other UNIA properties in the US were valued at more than half a million dollars.

Liberty Hall, Kingston was established in July 1923 at 76 King Street. It was the first meeting hall in Jamaica fully owned and operated by blacks, and provided the working class with their own social club and intellectual centre, things they were largely denied by the era's racially constraining colonial environment. The two-storey building housed administrative offices, a laundromat, a canteen, a job placement service and co-operative bank. It also served as headquarters for various UNIA units such as the Black Cross Nurses, the Juveniles and the African Legion.

In addition it hosted lectures, debates, training courses and cultural programmes. Many Jamaicans benefited from the educational activities afforded, including the well-known educator Sir Phillip Sherlock, Excelsior founder Wesley Powell, the noted teacher Dalton James, women's rights advocate Amy Bailey, and Father Gladstone Wilson – the first Negro tutor at the Urban College in Rome.

LIBERTY HALL

...a place where 'people could relax and refresh themselves after the heat and burden of the day'.

Seeing the need for a larger venue, Garvey transformed Edelweiss Park, an old home at 67 Slipe Pen Road, into a place where 'people could relax and refresh themselves after the heat and burden of the day'. Before this, the arts in Jamaica were dominated by local and touring expatriate drama groups, and a black face on stage was a rarity. So Liberty Hall and Edelweiss Park had a transformative effect, attracting huge crowds to concerts, dance troupes and plays. Many Jamaican entertainers got their start at these venues, including the famous comedian Ranny 'Mas Ran' Williams.

Garvey left Jamaica in 1935, but Liberty Hall remained operational as an entertainment centre for decades, providing an outlet for budding musicians. It was also a popular sporting arena particularly for boxing. However, over time the building fell into disrepair. In 1987, the centenary of Garvey's birth, it was purchased by the Government of Jamaica. The Jamaica National Heritage Trust declared it a national monument in 1992. Now restored and open to the public, it houses the Garvey Museum, the Garvey Research Library and the Garvey Multimedia Centre. The second floor Garvey Great Hall hosts symposiums, lectures and cultural events.

Garvey's message of African nationalism, anti-imperialism and black upliftment through education, resonated strongly with African people in the US and elsewhere. By 1922 it was the largest black association yet known.

Garvey's 'Back to Africa Movement', which imagined Liberia as a base for black self-determination, has often been dismissed as mass repatriation utopianism. However, as Garvey explained:

> It does not mean that all Negroes must leave America and the West Indies and go to Africa to build up a government. It did not take all the white people of Europe to come over to America to lay the foundation of the great republic.

In Rupert Lewis's words

> The Liberian project foundered on two rocks. First, the Liberian government was pressured by US, French and British interests hostile to Garveyite nationalism. Secondly, the Americo-Liberian ruling elite itself wanted Afro-American capital, but without Garveyite anti-colonial nationalism.

Like many visionaries, Garvey was not the most practical of businessmen. His Black Star Line Steamship Corporation, conceptualised to transport blacks back to Africa, proved a financial disaster. It also gave the American authorities, who saw Garvey as a threat to the Jim Crow status quo, the opportunity to neutralise him. He was charged for fraud, sentenced to five years in prison and eventually deported back to Jamaica in 1927.

Thousands hailed Garvey's return. The *Daily Gleaner* reported that '...no denser crowd has ever been witnessed in Kingston....Deafening cheers were raised and remarks heard on all sides in the huge crowd showed the high esteem in which he is held by the ordinary people of this country'.

MARCUS GARVEY

Courtesy of the National Library of Jamaica

Among Garvey's staunchest supporters were ex-servicemen who had fought for Britain in the First World War and been part of the 1918 revolt of the British West India Regiment in Taranto Italy.

Though the black working classes made up the majority of the Jamaican populace, restrictive franchise requirements made them passive observers rather than active participants in the political process. Garvey's UNIA gave them a taste of organised political and social life, and a forum for talking about their problems and aspirations.

In 1929, Garvey entered local politics, forming the People's Political Party. He lashed the plantocracy, that less than one per cent of the populace who owned nearly all the land, yet kept it idle,while the poorer 95 per cent had no place to build on and no farm to work. He was sharply critical of the banana multinational United Fruit Company and other foreign companies, who repatriated all their profits, arguing for reinvestment in Jamaica. However the practical minded Garvey was a staunch anti-communist.

The PPP's manifesto was Jamaica's first practical and realistic anti-imperialist programme, summing up the economic, political, legal and educational aspirations of the working people. Among other things it called for Jamaican representation in the British Parliament, a Jamaican university, a free government high school and public library in each parish capital, promotion of native industries, public housing, land reform and minimum wage and eight hour day legislation.

This manifesto was a first in the island's electoral history. In pre-Garvey Jamaica individual merchants and planters were returned to the legislature not because of a programme, but on the basis of their class and ability to dispense patronage. 'Influential persons' often retained seats uncontested.

The tenth plank of the PPP platform proposed that there should be a law to impeach judges who, in defiance of British justice, entered into underhand agreements with lawyers to deprive ordinary individuals of their judicial rights. When Garvey elaborated on this clause at a public meeting, he was charged with contempt of court, and sentenced to three months in jail. Popular legend has it that the prosecuting lawyer was Norman Manley but the case Manley won against Garvey was a suit defending a woman against libel in the UNIA *Blackman* magazine. While in prison Garvey won election to the Kingston and St Andrew Corporation. He was released only a month before the national election, thus putting his new party at a severe disadvantage.

Not surprisingly, Garvey was seen by the planter and merchant elite as a threat to their privileged status quo, and they hounded him mercilessly. The *Gleaner* editor H.G. de Lisser – of *The White Witch of Rose Hall* fame – was especially vitriolic. One attack went:

> It is with profound regret that we view the arrival of Marcus Garvey in Jamaica. And it is with more profound regret that we picture any leader of thought and culture in this island associating himself with a welcome given to him. But…a new spirit has passed over the lower classes which has nothing to commend it except its ignorance.

This vilification campaign was sadly so successful that many still believe Garvey never had a large following in his native land.

While the PPP drew massive crowds, none of its three candidates was elected to the Legislative Council. The bitter fact was that most of Garvey's supporters could not meet the stringent electoral property requirements, which meant less than eight per cent of the populace were registered voters. The majority of these voters were black, but Garvey was not popular with the civil servants and small proprietors who dominated the electoral list. He was also attacked by conservative elements of the black clergy and teaching profession, the most influential leaders of thought, and criticised them in turn. The PPP defeat was perhaps more a question of class than colour.

Yet as Garvey said afterwards 'The thousands who attended and cheered at the Party's meetings indicate that if you, the poor people had a vote, our Party would have been sent to the Legislature'. In the *Blackman* of August 23, 1930 he advocated full adult suffrage. When his call was finally answered in 1944, the party of the masses (Jamaica Labour Party) won decisively.

The colonial administration added to the pressure on Garvey by enforcing a $30,000 judgment handed down against the old UNIA in New York. Such adversities, made worse by the great depression, broke him financially in Jamaica. In 1935 Garvey emigrated to England, where he died five years later. Before he left, Garvey lamented to Alexander Bustamante, who was to become Jamaica's first prime minister:

> …if one wants to know what sorrow is, try and do good for the masses of the country and 'big brains' will plot, conspire, and do everything to destroy you and your name…until your spirit is broken….

However, as Bustamante proclaimed in 1944:

> …thousands today still stick to the memory of that good man [Garvey]. They have not forgotten his good deeds. They still remember that he suffered for them, that he went to prison for them…. [A]lthough he is gone, perhaps his spirit still hovers around us, and his work is being carried on....

In 1964 he was declared Jamaica's first National Hero. His remains were exhumed, taken to Jamaica, and reinterred at a shrine in National Heroes Park.

Towards Universal Suffrage

Garvey had warned that if conditions were not improved, the oppressed would rise up. His prediction came true in 1938, as demonstrations swept the island and erupted into violence on the Westmoreland sugar plantations. As in the case of the 1865 Morant Bay Rebellion, these disturbances were partly due to outside circumstances. The worldwide Great Depression had made the normally hard life of the Jamaican peasant often intolerable.

One of Garvey's most prominent followers was St William Grant, whose main stomping ground was the park in the centre of Kingston which now bears his name. Dressed in military-style uniform and bearing the Garvey flag, Grant drew large crowds to his Back-to-Africa speeches. However, the hard times turned his attention to more urgent issues of wages, working conditions and unemployment. Alexander Bustamante made his first public address at one of these UNIA meetings.

This future leader of the 1938 protests was christened Alexander Clarke. He left Jamaica when about 20 in 1904, and travelled widely in the Americas and perhaps Spain and Morocco – only he knew for sure and his accounts varied. Somewhere along the line he adopted the name Bustamante. Very tall and thin with a striking face and a great shock of hair, Bustamante was dramatic in speech and appearance. When he returned to Jamaica in 1934 from the US, he was greatly disturbed by the poverty in Kingston, the ineffectiveness of the Legislative Council and the lack of concern among employers.

In April 1935, Bustamante sent a letter to the *Gleaner* criticising its opposition to a planned demonstration. He argued that 'Hungry men… have a right to call attention to their condition and to ask of people fulfillment of promises made to them, so long as they do so without using violence.' Over the next 18 months he wrote maybe 100 more letters on strikingly varied topics, which gained him a national reputation as a defender of the poor. His language was forthright and rich in biblical imagery, and he displayed an impressive range of knowledge, an ordered mind, a lively wit, and a courtly regard for adversaries. He proved the most effective letter writer in the country's history.

Courtesy of the National Library of Jamaica

YOUNG BUSTAMANTE

© The Gleaner Company Ltd, 2010

ST WILLIAM GRANT

He began travelling 'from Port Morant to Negril Point investigating the conditions of the land'. In early 1938 he wrote to British Parliamentarians and British newspapers, calling for a Royal Commission of Enquiry into the dreadful condition of the Jamaican masses. Sympathy for the poor and unemployed, criticisms for the rich and uncaring, no hesitation in attacking the colonial administration, a strong attachment to economic liberalism, with a corresponding marked antipathy for monopolies – these were the positions that emerged clearly in Bustamante's letters, and which he adhered to throughout his political life.

Though of mixed blood, with a 'whiteish' father and 'dark-skinned' mother, considerations of race and colour placed the young Bustamante as a member of European Jamaica, as opposed to African Jamaica. Yet his 'poor white' rural

TOUGH LIKE BUSTA BACKBONE

Preparing dock workers for the fray in a fiery speech on the morning of May 23, Bustamante prophetically observed: 'This is not a military revolution – it is merely a mental revolution'. When a police baton charge scattered the crowd, Bustamante and St William Grant led a march to Parade, where Bustamante climbed up on Queen Victoria's statue and addressed the huge throng. Lady Bustamante, then Gladys Longbridge, relates what happened next:

> As he descended from the statue, a squad of policemen…marched on the crowd…Inspector Orrett pulled his revolver and gave the command… 'Click your heels and aim!' Then he ordered the people to disperse. Baring his chest Bustamante confronted Orrett and declared, 'If you are going to shoot, shoot me, but leave these defenceless, hungry people alone'.
>
> The Inspector was speechless. The policemen lowered their arms and I stood there almost frozen to the spot, wondering if the end had come….I wanted to move away but the crowd stood firm with the discipline Bustamante had so often preached. Before Orrett could say another word, Busta called upon the people to sing the British National Anthem and as God Save the King rang out from the mass of discordant voices, the police were forced to stand at attention and could advance no further. Bustamante then moved away with the large crowd following him.
>
> At that moment I realised that something new was happening in Jamaica; that the poor had passed the stage

STATUE OF ALEXANDER BUSTAMANTE ERECTED IN ST WILLIAM GRANT PARK

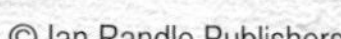

where they could be bullied and pressed into submission by guns and bayonets.... Years later, the *Daily Gleaner*, in reviewing the events of 1938, commented that Bustamante had inflamed the crowds with violent speeches. But it was not violence that Bustamante was preaching. Rather it was the replacement of disorganised resentment with organised resistance.

The incident is commemorated by Bustamante's statue in St William Grant Park, a replacement for the one of Queen Victoria on which he had climbed. His courage is still celebrated in folk memory by the hard coconut sweet named after him, because 'it tough like Busta backbone'.

Recipe for Busta Backbone

Ingredients:

1 cup grated coconut (drained)
1 tablespoon finely grated fresh ginger
1/4 cup water
2 cups very dark brown sugar
1 tablespoon lime juice or cream of tartar powder

Method:

Mix the sugar and water. Add the ginger and lime juice. Boil until when dropped in water it forms a ball (about 1/2 hour add the coconut and stir well. Pour onto a buttered cookie sheet. Slice with a knife when cooled a little, or with a pair of scissors.

upbringing meant he understood and identified emotionally with the peasant working class. As a light-skinned budding capitalist, he could have joined the privileged ranks, but chose to align himself with the have-nots.

Years later in an interview at the National Press Club in Washington when asked about his racial mixture, he responded 'I am one third Irish, one third Negro, one third Arawak, and one third white'. A reporter replied 'But that makes you 120 per cent sir?' Bustamante flashed a smile and said: 'That is why I am better than other leaders.'

Some members of the crowd actually objected to his colour when St William Grant first invited Bustamante to speak on a UNIA platform. No Jamaican of his complexion had ever been seen at a street meeting making common cause with the poor. However, once he showed himself willing to openly criticise the colonial authorities and even risk physical harm for the rights of the oppressed, an unbreakable bond was established between Bustamante and the workers.

With his sincerity proven, the mentality of the times paradoxically made Bustamante's colour an advantage. When he and St William Grant were arrested in 1938, the police brutally beat the black Grant, but they instinctively obeyed the 'one of their own' Bustamante's order of 'Don't dare touch me with your batons!'

Several pioneers of the Jamaica labour movement were either Garveyites or had been connected with the UNIA, including Bustamante's one time mentor and later rival A.G.S. 'Father' Coombs. When disturbances rocked the island in 1938, Bustamante himself swiftly developed into Garvey's successor as champion of the Jamaican masses.

The situation first came to a head in May of that year on Frome sugar estate, where police opened fire on a crowd and killed four demonstrators, including a pregnant woman. The unrest spread to the capital, culminating on May 23 in a revolt of the Kingston working classes that gave Jamaica a new sense of direction and national purpose. By day's end marauding workers had brought all services and business activities to a standstill. Kingston lay in the hands, and at the mercy, of the discontented and disenfranchised.

The next day Bustamante and Grant were arrested, and thus immobilised. Urged by his wife Edna, Norman Manley – Jamaica's leading lawyer and Bustamante's distant cousin – offered to represent striking workers. The offer was eagerly accepted by Governor Sir Edward Denham and headlined in the press. While Gladys Longbridge sought legal help for Bustamante and Grant, Edna Manley helped organise relief meals for the striking workers.

Manley later wrote 'The shippers had agreed to all my demands on the part of the workers. They were certain that this eliminated the demand for Bustamante's release and that once they got what they wanted, loyalty would seem less important....' Yet after the meeting with Manley, truckloads of workers drove through the city shouting to cheering onlookers, 'No work! No work! We don't want shilling an hour. We want Bustamante!'

Unrest spread and eventually Bustamante's lawyer J.A.G. Smith persuaded Denham that the longer Bustamante was held, the more explosive the situation would become. Denham agreed to release Bustamante, providing his good behaviour was guaranteed by affidavits, including Manley's. On May 28 Bustamante and Grant were freed.

By refusing to work unless their chosen leader was released, the workers of Jamaica had imposed their will upon the colonial administration. As Bustamante had predicted, a mental revolution had taken place. That night a vast throng of 15,000 workers greeted

Bustamante and his colleagues with delirious cheers. When he left the waterfront, the crowd followed singing 'We will follow Bustamante till we die'. 'Busta' had become the most popular figure in Jamaican history.

The country really now had two leaders. In the following weeks, the increasingly familiar duo of Bustamante and Manley toured the island to calm the aroused workers. They would dominate Jamaican politics for the next 40 years. Bustamante was worshipped by the labouring masses, Manley by the intelligentsia, middle class and commercial elements.

Manley was by common consent the best lawyer in Jamaica and the West Indies. He was habitually retained by large firms to handle their affairs on a permanent basis, meaning he often fought cases on the employer's behalf. This frequently made it appear to some as if he was against the workers' interests and did not help his reputation as a supporter of the people.

In 1937 Manley founded Jamaica Welfare, the first large scale social welfare organisation in the island. It originated from suggestions he made to United Fruit Company president Samuel Zemurray, while acting as lawyer for the Jamaica Banana Producers' Association. Zemurray offered one cent per stem of United Fruit's Jamaican banana exports, 'to form a fund to be administered by an organisation to be created…for the good and welfare of the people of Jamaica, with emphasis on the rural people'. With the banana export trade at its height, the initial amount was over US$250,000.

Jamaica Welfare's programme consisted largely of practical adult education, co-operative training, cottage industries, and group activity in agriculture and manufacturing. After the 1938 disturbances, the British government adopted it as the model for improving the people's welfare throughout the troubled West Indies.

ALEXANDER BUSTAMANTE

Though they had a common grandmother, Alexander Bustamante and Norman Manley were very different. Bustamante was a rough and ready man of the people with little formal education, and made no major mark on the world until he had passed 50. For Manley, achievement of excellence was the norm. He was an outstanding high school athlete, Rhodes scholar, decorated First World War military hero, prize man of Gray's Inn, acknowledged as the Caribbean's finest legal mind and the first Jamaican to appear before the Judicial Committee of the Privy Council.

The two also had very different personalities. Bustamante was a charming and affable extrovert. The *London Times* had this to say in the 1950s:

> Mr Bustamante is as remarkable as the circumstances in which he came to prominence. Uneducated in the strict scholastic sense of the word, he makes up for this deficiency with an apparently limitless store of common sense, shrewd intelligence, and an uncanny way of making friends and influencing people.... He has a sharp wit, an amazing memory, a daring imagination and tremendous physical capacity.

To the last British Governor General Sir Kenneth Blackburne, he was 'the most generous and honest of men'.

One observer reported 'Alexander Bustamante had what could be described as an obsessive loyalty to his relatives, particularly to his cousin, Norman Manley, for whom he had a special "soft spot" and for whom he repeatedly expressed love and admiration.' On one occasion he declared 'I love my cousin. Norman is weak as shredded oats; he may even be a sneak – willing to wound but afraid to strike. But he is so innocent, he could be a saint and if he were to die now he would go straight to heaven'. Bustamante was also fond of Michael Manley, reportedly comparing Michael to himself and Michael's brother Douglas to Norman. 'Michael takes after me....Douglas is like Norman.'

The Gleaner Company Limited, 2010

NORMAN MANLEY

Manley tended to be reserved and formal, and did not suffer fools gladly. Theodore Sealy described him as 'Gamin and genius, shy yet arrogant, coldly analytical yet given to much emotion'. In his own self-analysis

> I suffered from a quick flaring temper which it took me half a lifetime to control. Indeed, I doubt if I ever learnt. Constant, inhibiting violent efforts at control gradually wore it down till it seemed to disappear, with its place being taken by a sort of arrogant indifference which was eventually mistaken for the real me.

He was born to a black father and white mother, and his early years were filled with 'stress and gore'.

> I grew up as a bushman. I earned my pocket money cleaning pastures and chipping logwood. I would go out in the morning...and get home late at night after 12 to 14 hours on the constant move. The result was that I was tough as hell and developed a stamina I have never seen surpassed...till I was 70 I did not regard a 15 hour day of concentrated work as excessive.

He lost his father when very young, his mother in high school, and his brother in the trenches of the First World War, where he himself won a Military Medal for bravery. Some claim the colour prejudice Manley encountered in the army made him anti-British, but his unfinished autobiography contradicts this.

EDNA MANLEY

GLADYS LONGBRIDGE BUSTAMANTE

He was incomparably the greatest lawyer in Jamaican history. A visiting colonial authority concluded 'Whenever a man in this country gets into trouble, he first flies to Mr Manley, and if Mr Manley is already retained, he next flies to Cuba'. Hotheads often threatened 'I will kill you and get Missah Manley to get me off!' A great lover of the classics, he was for a time the *Gleaner's* music critic.

On his death Theodore Sealy wrote:

> Norman Manley…had the mind and measure of the truly great anywhere… his faults lay mainly in his virtues – his righteous sense of consistency; an almost fanatical loyalty to those who marched the rugged course of life beside him; a commitment to principle even when in political terms the practical course was sharply different on the nation's compass.

Busta and Norman both drove recklessly fast. In his wife's words, Bustamante 'drove like a madman.' Few of Manley's friends would willingly travel with him at the wheel, for he held nearly all the rumoured 'point to point' records over the early rugged marl roads. He seemed to revel in the narrowness of the margin by which he avoided the other vehicle. He nearly paid for his daring with his life in 1946 when his car catapulted into the valley on the Gordon Town Road.

Both also married remarkable women. Manley and his wife Edna were first cousins, their mothers being sisters. Both were also second cousins with Bustamante. Edna was the country's most important sculptor, and a pioneering leader of Jamaica's indigenous artistic movement. The Manley home Drumblair was the hub of the nascent nation's cultural activities, and a gathering point for its leading intellectuals.

Gladys Longbridge was 28 years younger than Bustamante, but she was his confidante, right hand and memory bank. They only married in 1962, because the Catholic Bustamante could not remarry until his previous wife died. He talked over all important matters with her, and readily took on board her advice. In discussions he would turn to her incessantly about particulars, and such was her memory that she would recall instantly what had taken place three or four years previously. She was also from its inception the treasurer and principal day-to-day caretaker of the Bustamante Industrial Trade Union, then by far the largest single organisation in Jamaica. As she put it:

> We women were the mainstay of the Union's organisation, though we could hardly have functioned without the brave men who toiled day and night…. Bustamante was the busiest of us all….I was by his side, taking note of important details, seeing to his personal welfare and offering advice based upon my own experience, close contact with the people, and, of course, a woman's intuition.

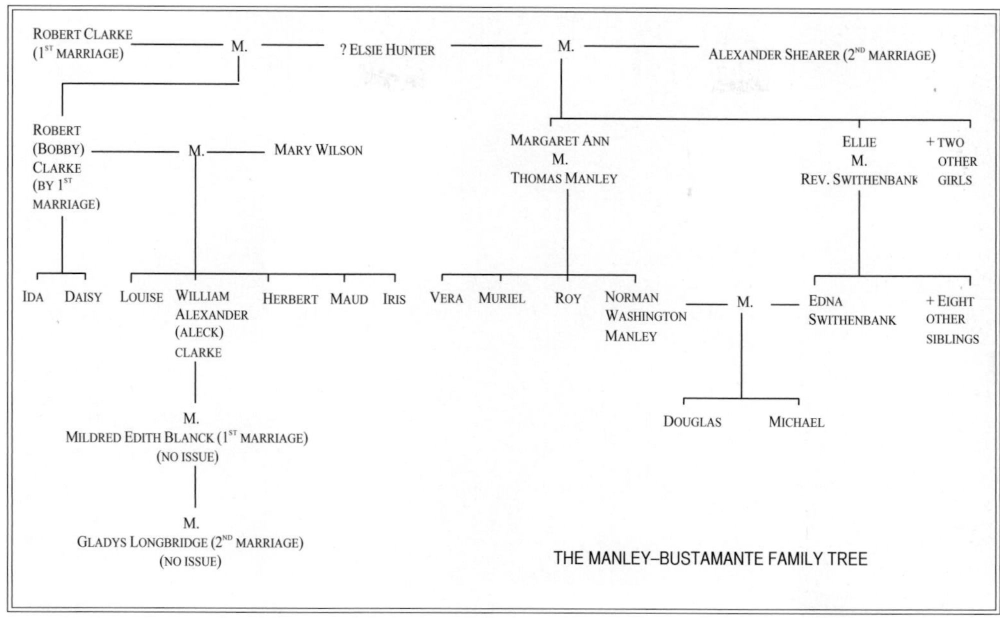

THE MANLEY–BUSTAMANTE FAMILY TREE

One might have expected the 'establishment' Manley to be politically conservative, and the 'outsider' Bustamante to possess revolutionary tendencies and yet Bustamante had quite conventional economic and political views. A moneylender by trade before entering politics, he was unabashedly pro-free enterprise, declaring that 'We can only attract investors if we ensure them a fair profit'. Despite his antipathy to the colonial government, he shared the strong attachment of the Jamaican working class to the British monarchy, which was seen as a bulwark of the people's rights against the plantocracy and its middle class allies.

Bustamante's experience of revolution-prone Latin American republics had also deepened his respect for British political institutions. In 1938 he proclaimed, 'I am very glad we are a colony of Great Britain'. The *Jamaica Standard* of the day opined 'In no other place than the British Empire could Bustamante find his place and survive. In other countries not a thousand miles from Jamaica, he would either have become a dictator following revolution or else a victim of early assassination.'

Manley from the beginning professed himself a staunch socialist. At the 1940 PNP conference he declared 'Socialism is not a matter of higher wages, of better living conditions for workers… it involves the concept that all the means of production should in one form or another come to be publicly owned and publicly controlled'. He was also an early champion of self-government, while Bustamante was adamant that 'We have to walk before we can jump'.

After the 1938 uprising Bustamante concentrated on creating a structured union, which was named the Bustamante Industrial Trade Union, with Bustamante president for life. These moves disturbed many, including then Governor Sir Arthur Richards, who tried without success to have both altered. Lady Bustamante defended the name and lifelong presidency as group executive decisions that workers fully endorsed – they ensured the union was clearly distinguishable from others, prevented jockeying for the leadership position, and reassured workers that their fates remained in their beloved Busta's hands. However, Bustamante would be criticised for having dictatorial tendencies throughout his political career.

In September 1938 Manley was invited to head the country's first major political organisation, the People's National Party, by party architect O.T. Fairclough. Bustamante was originally a member of the PNP, but soon broke with it. While he disagreed with the PNP's socialist agenda, the rift was likely an inevitable outcome of the naturally adversarial nature of democracy.

In September 1940 Bustamante again found himself behind bars, this time on account of remarks he reportedly made to restive waterfront workers. 'I have stood for peace from the first day I have been in public life, but my patience is exhausted. This time if need be there will be blood from the rampage to the grave.' Governor Sir Arthur Richards deemed this dangerous to public peace in wartime conditions, and Bustamante was detained for 17 months. Thus he suffered the martyrdom of imprisonment which was almost de rigeur for British colonial independence leaders. Norman Manley again came to his cousin's aide, offering to oversee the BITU during Bustamante's incarceration.

Bustamante was released in February 1942 and shortly after, he and Manley parted political company for good. Bustamante charged that certain PNP members, though not Manley, had tried to assume control of the BITU during his absence. In July 1943 he launched the Jamaica Labour Party.

In November 1944 a new constitution was proclaimed. Thirty-two House of Representatives members were to be elected by universal adult suffrage, meaning every Jamaican over 21 could now vote. Previously, voters had to pay taxes of not less than ten shillings per year, and earn more than £50 a year.

NORMAN MANLEY AND ALEXANDER BUSTAMANTE AT A CONFERENCE IN LONDON

Males had to be over 21 and females over 25, and there was a literacy test. These restrictions meant less than one tenth of the population were on the electorate list in the 1933 general elections. A 1943 census showed over 700,000 were now eligible to cast ballots, as against fewer than 20,000 under the old system.

The newspapers billed the election as a straight contest between the socialist PNP and the businessman's Jamaica Democratic Party. According to Theodore Sealy, Norman Manley had by now 'changed his image as the national mediator and become brash and almost reckless in his support of the more rabid left wing elements of the party.' On the day the constitution was first proclaimed with a great parade in Kingston's main square, he was seen waving a clenched fist from high on top of a bell tower. The thought that Norman Manley was now a rabid political personality created shock waves throughout the upper and middle classes.

Bustamante denounced the PNP's socialism as atheistic and expropriatory, asserting that independence would mean 'brown man government', and a political return to slavery. This mirrored the views of the black masses, especially the land conscious, small plot owning peasants, who profoundly distrusted the condescending brown middle classes. Coupled with Bustamante's overwhelming popularity, this swept the JLP to victory. It received 41 per cent of the vote, independents 30 per cent, the PNP 23 per cent and the JDP four per cent. The seat count was 23 JLP, five independent, four PNP, with Manley failing to win his constituency. The winning JLP candidates included six trade unionists, six businessmen, four school masters, two farmers, two lawyers, two religious ministers, and one electro-dermatologist. Bustamante's boast, that he would put the common man in the seats of government, had largely come true.

Bustamante now wielded more power than any local leader before or since, and likely could have taken the country in any direction he chose. He had already demonstrated the powerlessness of the colonial powers in the face of mass worker mobilisation. As *Gleaner* columnist Morris Cargill later put it:

> He might have been a communist agitator, concerned not with Jamaica, but with Russian imperialism. He might have been a Marxist bent upon the destruction of the only economic system…appropriate to our continued development. He might have been a Latin American type of Fascist, bent upon setting up a personally profitable dictatorship. That he was none of these, and that he brought, or helped to bring, self-government and a new life to this country without at the same time disturbing unduly our historical or economic continuity is something that should stand to the lasting credit of Sir Alexander and to the good sense of our people.

The Road to Independence

Jamaica's march to independence was a model of gradualism. Under the 1944 constitution, official, nominated and elected members took joint responsibility for policy creation and execution. In 1953, elected members were given a majority in the Executive Council, and a Chief Minister appointed. In 1957, Cabinet Government with mostly elected members was instituted, and virtual internal self-rule was granted. Only bills relating to defense and international relations were reserved for the special assent of the Queen, meaning the Governor was becoming a figurehead.

Both main parties moved toward the centre. Assiduous work by its left-leaning trade union arm increased the PNP's support among workers, with union leaders gaining strength within the party and growing increasingly Marxist. In 1952 matters came to a head when in order to preserve party integrity and his leadership position, Manley oversaw the expulsion for 'communistic' activities of the notorious four Hs – Richard Hart, Ken Hill, Frank Hill and Arthur Henry. To many, this left wing purge vindicated the charge Bustamante made from as early as 1938, that the PNP contained communist elements who aimed at political dictatorship.

BUSTAMANTEADDRESSING PARLIAMENT

At the same time the JLP tried to make its policies and attitudes more attractive to the middle and upper classes. So the ideological differences between the parties gradually shrunk from capitalist workers against socialist intelligentsia, to centre right versus centre left.

A major economic development was the first shipment of bauxite, the ore from which aluminum is produced, in 1952. Bauxite was first discovered here in 1942 when local planter Sir Alfred D'Costa became frustrated with poor yields on his St Ann property. He had the soil analysed, and it was found to be almost pure bauxite. The government declared all bauxite the property of the Crown under wartime regulations, but the war delayed commercial exploitation, and it took a decade for real mining to begin. Jamaica soon became one of the world's largest bauxite exporters.

The British Caribbean Federation Plan, which included most of the English-speaking West Indian islands, was drawn up in 1953, and elections were held in 1958. Still there were always doubts about how economically viable a body consisting of widely scattered small islands could be. In a 1961 referendum, Jamaicans voted to withdraw from the West Indies Federation, though the idea lives on in the West Indies cricket team and the University of the West Indies. In 1962 Jamaica became a fully independent country.

Manley led the discussions in London and justified the non-radical form of the Constitution by saying:

> We had a system which we understood; we had been operating it for many years with sense. It is a system that has endured in other countries for generations successfully. It is a system that is consistent with the sort of ideals we have in this country, and it was not difficult to decide that we should follow the familiar system with those modifications which we thought the circumstances of independence deserved.

One constant through all these developments was the presence of 'BustaManley'. As the undisputed leaders of the two main parties, they traded the roles of elected government leader and opposition leader – Bustamante winning in 1944 and 1949 and 1962, Manley in 1955 and 1959. Few countries have been blessed with such contrasting yet complementary founding fathers. Though cousins – in itself a blessing, as their disagreements seldom rose above the level of a good-natured family squabble – they were polar opposites in nature and outlook. Both rigidly adhered to British parliamentary tradition, but diverged on almost everything else. Busta was a capitalist businessman, Norman a socialist lawyer. Manley wanted immediate independence, Bustamante was a one-step-at-a-time man. Norman was a great believer in plans, Busta saw overly detailed plans as distractions from pressing concerns.

Thanks to this governmental 'yin and yang', Jamaica achieved political maturity in a remarkably short time, and in an astonishingly incident-free manner. Rigged elections, civil wars, revolutions, coups, assassinations and guerilla uprisings have been distressingly common throughout the Third World. Yet not a single major political disturbance occurred in Jamaica between the 1938 riots and independence in 1962, or even to the present day.

For the outstanding aspect of Jamaican political history since 1944 is that no elected government has tried to entrench itself, nor had its legitimacy challenged, which in the end are the true tests of democracy. Every ruling regime has allowed mostly free and fair elections, all defeated parties have unhesitatingly accepted the will of the people, and peacefully awaited the next electoral contest. That above all is the magnificent legacy of Alexander Bustamante and Norman Manley.

Independence

Independent Jamaica began 'punching above its weight' on the world scene almost immediately. In the nation's first United Nations address, future Prime Minister Hugh Shearer called for an International Year of Human Rights, and received a standing ovation from the General Assembly. A year later the UN designated 1968 the International Year of Human Rights. Also in 1963, Jamaican Carole Joan Crawford was crowned Miss World.

While the aging Bustamante remained nominal Prime Minister, it was deputy Prime Minister Donald Sangster who really held the reins of government. A former lawyer, the meticulous Sangster was also finance minister, and ran a tight fiscal ship under which the economy prospered. A great supporter of the Commonwealth, he used Jamaica's betwixt and between standing to smooth over many disagreements between Britain and its former

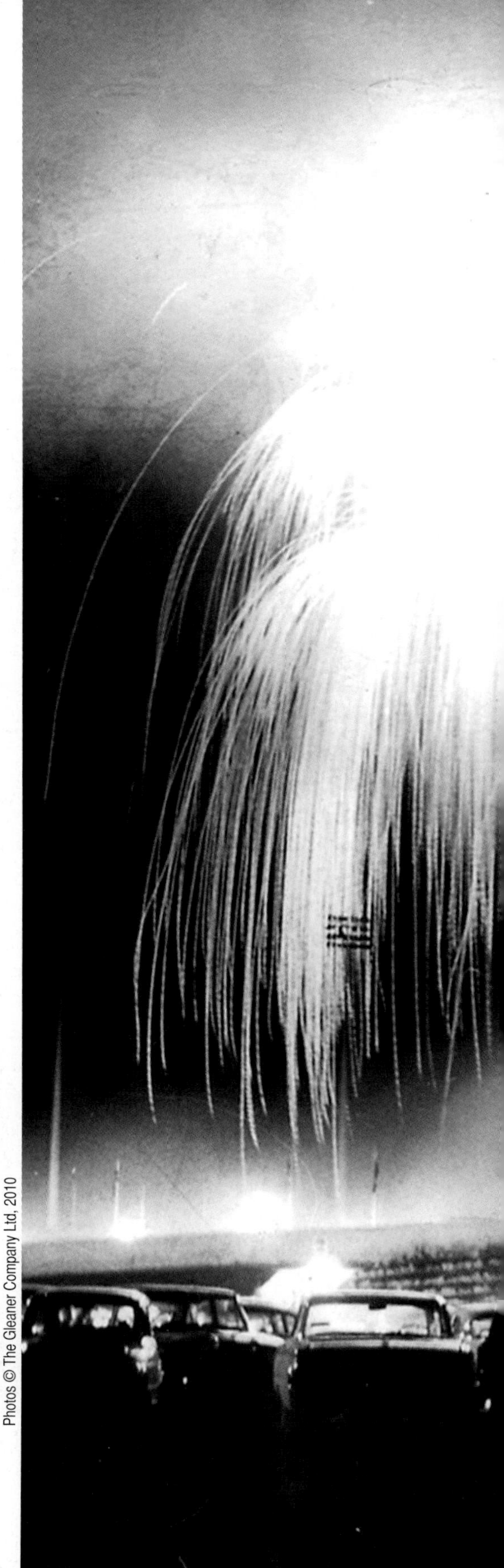

FLOAT PARADES AND FIREWORKS WERE PART OF THE INDEPENDENCE CELEBRATIONS IN 1962

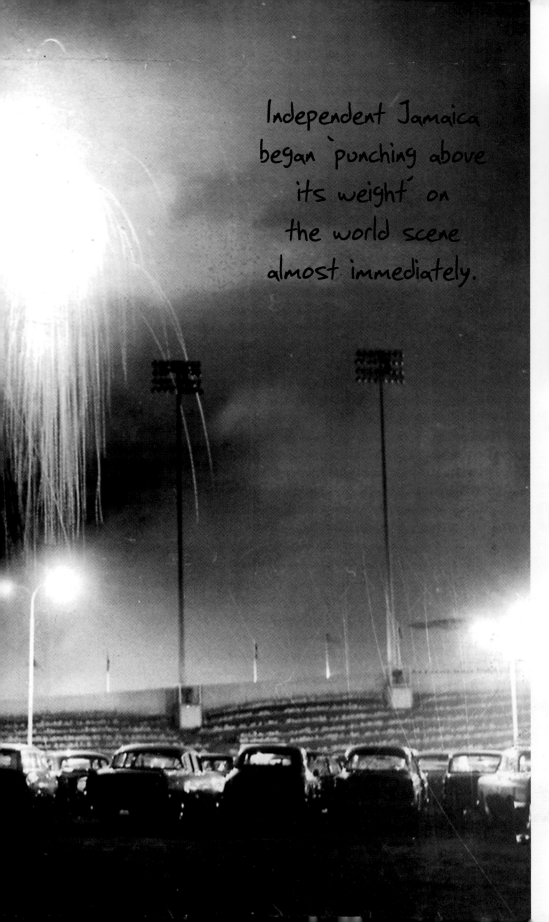

Independent Jamaica began 'punching above its weight' on the world scene almost immediately.

HUGH SHEARER

African colonies, particularly with regard to minority ruled South Africa and Rhodesia.

In 1967 Jamaica held its first general elections as an independent nation, and the JLP was narrowly re-elected. A few weeks after being officially sworn in as Prime Minister, Sangster suffered a cerebral seizure from which he died soon after. On the first ballot to choose his successor Clem Tavares received 12 votes, Hugh Shearer ten and Robert Lightbourne eight, with Shearer reportedly spoiling his ballot. On the second count Shearer gained 16 votes to Tavares's 15. Thus is history made.

Shearer was a lifelong trade unionist, who won many improvements in wages and living conditions for workers. However, as shown by his hesitation to vote for himself, he was a reluctant politician. He may also have been distantly related to Bustamante, and Norman Manley's mother was a Shearer. Interestingly, Sangster's mother was the sister of Bustamante's first wife. Bustamante was of course a cousin of Norman Manley, Michael's father, making Jamaica's first five heads of government kin of sorts. Manley junior obviously benefited from instant name recognition, but the other family relationships had no political consequences, and are just historical curiosities.

Shearer continued Sangster's gradualist policy. One significant symbolic move was the establishment of Jamaican National Honours and Awards to replace British ones. Under Sangster and Shearer, Jamaica had one of the world's highest economic growth rates, but in spite of this paper boom, serious social tensions became apparent. In 1966 clashes between PNP and JLP supporters led to a state of emergency declaration, and in 1968, a student march over the deportation of black power activist Walter Rodney turned into a riot that claimed three lives and caused over one million pounds of property damage.

The murder rate also surged alarmingly. Up to independence, Jamaica's murder rate was a little higher than Britain's, and a little lower than that of the US. However, in 1969 it began to outstrip the US rate and the sinister syndrome of 'garrison' politics – whereby constituencies were transformed into one-party enclaves through cash handouts, housing grants and sheer brute force – reared its ugly head.

In 1972 the governing JLP was crushed at the polls, proving that the official economic boom had not trickled down to the masses. The new prime minister was the former trade union leader Michael Manley, son of Norman. He combined Bustamante's charisma with his father's urbane eloquence, and an ecstatic populace acclaimed him a new Joshua leading his people into the promised land. Manley had skilfully used local music stars on his 'Better Must Come' campaign 'bandwagon', and a popular victory anthem 'hailed the man' and 'the coming of a brand new day'.

Manley saw his massive triumph as a mandate to implement the socialist doctrines his father had espoused. However as with every socialist experiment on record, the economic results were disastrous. Between 1972 and 1980 per capita GDP plunged by 30 per cent, and the murder rate soared by over 500 per cent. For the first time Jamaica became the scene of ideological battles between armed gangs. 'Garrisons' so multiplied that in perhaps 20 per cent of constituencies, the result was known before a ballot was cast.

Manley implemented many needed social reforms, and broke down many class and colour barriers, but he proved a better orator than administrator, and sometimes got carried away by his own rhetoric. He waxed ecstatically about 'walking to the mountain top' with Cuban dictator Fidel Castro, causing many to wonder in alarm if his 'democratic socialism' was but a prelude to communism.

Manley also told those who disagreed with his policies, that there were 'five flights a day to Miami'. Scared businessmen shipped money abroad, and the resulting government crackdown on capital outflows started a vicious downward spiral of investment. The 1973 oil crisis that quadrupled fuel prices only exacerbated matters.

In the meantime former finance minister Edward Seaga had become JLP leader, and the relationship between Manley and himself grew increasingly hostile. In 1976 a state of emergency was declared, purportedly to curb growing political violence. Three JLP candidates

The Sunday Gleaner

KINGSTON, JAMAICA, SUNDAY, JUNE 20, 1976 — PRICE: 25 CENTS — SECTION A — TWENTY-EIGHT PAGES

Governor-General on advice of Cabinet declares...

STATE OF PUBLIC EMERGENCY

Security forces to detain persons likely to endanger public safety

DAY-TO-DAY ACTIVITIES, ELECTIONS NOT AFFECTED

GLEANER POLITICAL REPORTER

A STATE OF PUBLIC EMERGENCY in which the Security Forces has been given instructions by the Government to use their powers to "lock up and keep locked up all persons whose activities are likely to endanger the public safety, and in particular, the gunmen and terrorists", has been declared by the Governor-General, the Most Hon. Florizel Glasspole on the advice of the Cabinet.

The emergency, declared under Section 26 (5) (b) of the Constitution, became effective at noon yesterday.

In announcing the State of emergency Mr. Manley said that the violence in the country had increased to "a scale unique to our history". At the same time, there were indications that the stage "was to have been set" for even further escalation of the violence which had already caused innocent people to be murdered in the privacy of their homes, on the streets and in business places.

9 years, 9 months after last declaration

How the Emergency works

Rattray: law-abiding have nothing to fear

Senator the Hon. Carl Rattray, Minister of Justice and Attorney General in a radio interview yesterday evening said that the ordinary citizens should carry on their day-to-day activities in a normal way during the State of Emergency. They should continue helping the security forces in their fight against violent crimes in the country.

The citizen has nothing to fear he said. The only person who had anything to fear was the person involved in disrupting activity and who had so far got away with it.

On the question of detention he said a tribunal would be set up to review the case of persons detained to determine whether they would be freed or their detention should continue.

Could deprive Opposition of its rights — SEAGA

3 JLP, one PNP held

PRIME MINISTER MICHAEL MANLEY. ...violence on a scale unique to our history

World so small, foreign language a necessity — GG

Police find shotguns

Courtesy of the National Gallery of Jamaica/ Howard Moo Young

BOB MARLEY HELD HANDS HIGH WITH MICHAEL MANLEY (LEFT) AND EDWARD SEAGA AT THE ONE LOVE CONCERT IN 1978

were among the 593 persons detained for various lengths of time, with deputy leader Pearnel Charles being held for nine months. In elections held while the state of emergency was still in effect, the PNP won 47 of 60 seats. Yet the bloodshed continued, stoked by rumours – still unproven either way – of American CIA destabilisation plots, and Cuban 'brigadista' militia infiltration.

Even reggae superstar Bob Marley was shot and nearly killed in 1978. A bandaged Marley staged a 'One Love' concert to celebrate the twelfth anniversary of Haile Selassie's 1966 visit to Jamaica. In a famous scene, he held hands high with Manley and Seaga while 25,000 fans sang 'One love, one heart, let's get together and feel alright.' Yet the guns still barked.

Tensions kept rising, and in 1979, Manley led his cabinet and a large crowd in a demonstration against the *Gleaner's* perceived anti-Cuba stance, declaring in front of the paper's North Street offices 'Next time! Next time!'

In the 1980 election year, violence reached almost civil war proportions. Somehow British-instilled parliamentary tradition held. People voted, the ballots were counted, and when Manley realised he had lost, he gracefully handed over the reins of power to Seaga. Jamaican democracy had walked through the valley of death and survived.

From a cold bottom line perspective, the 1970s were a disaster, from which some say Jamaica has never recovered. Even today official

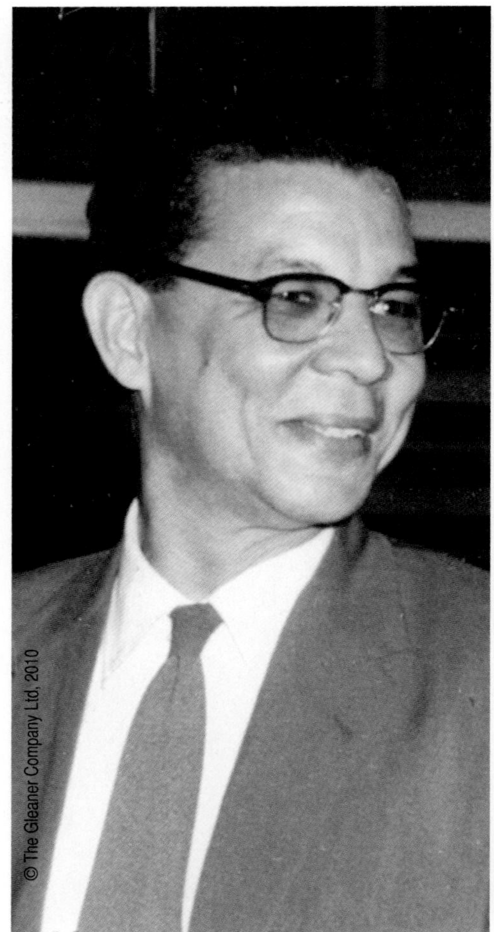

DONALD SANGSTER

MICHAEL MANLEY

EDWARD SEAGA

Whatever their faults, all Jamaica's leaders have been devoted to the welfare of the country, and firmly upheld the tenets of democracy.

per capita GDP is little higher than it was in 1972. Yet just as teenagers need to rebel against their parents to find themselves, so perhaps it is necessary for young countries to revolt against traditional mores to fully mature. The 'democratic socialism' experiment cured Jamaica forever of any ideological fervour, and rendered 'leftist' and 'rightist' political labels meaningless. Even Manley would later successfully reinvent himself as a market pragmatist.

The new Prime Minister Edward Seaga had first entered politics in 1959 when he became the youngest member of the Legislative Council, the pre-independence appointed upper house. In one of his first speeches, he warned of the dangers of being a country of 'Haves and Have-Nots', which led many to dub him a socialist. He was a man of startlingly varied interests: a pioneer in Jamaican anthropology; a driving force behind the local and international popularisation of ska and reggae; an originator of the annual cultural Festival; an award-winning poet; one of Jamaica's ablest finance ministers; the prime minister with the third longest term in office; the longest serving parliamentarian; and more recently a research fellow at the University of the West Indies. Perhaps no one has influenced independent Jamaica in so many

P.J. PATTERSON

PORTIA SIMPSON MILLER

BRUCE GOLDING

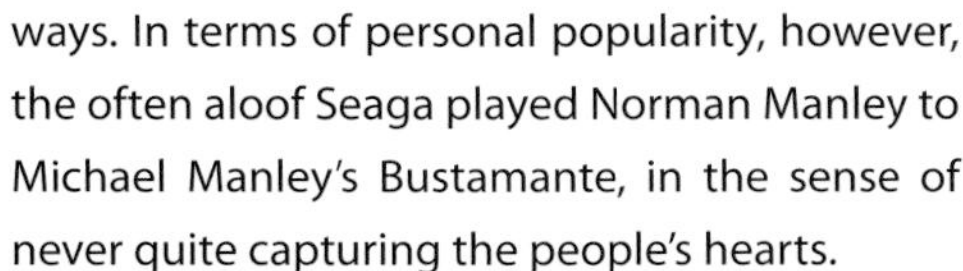

ways. In terms of personal popularity, however, the often aloof Seaga played Norman Manley to Michael Manley's Bustamante, in the sense of never quite capturing the people's hearts.

Prime Minister Seaga moved the country sharply to the right, cut ties with Cuba and made Jamaica sort of a poster child for Ronald Reagan's Caribbean Basin Initiative (CBI). A degree of economic normalcy returned, but a serious global recession drastically cut foreign earnings and there was no economic miracle as promised.

In 1982 a communist coup in the island of Grenada led to a US invasion, in which the Jamaica Defense Force played a significant role. Hoping to capitalise on the resulting popularity surge, Seaga called snap elections. Manley accused him of breaking a promise to reform the electoral system, and boycotted the elections. This meant that from 1983 to 1989, all 60 parliamentarians were JLP members. The spectre of one party rule arose, but British tradition was adhered to once more.

Crime declined in the 1980s and economic growth improved in the latter part of the decade. However Seaga's centralised statist approach seemed stifling to some, nor was his autocratic leadership style to everyone's taste. In 1989 the PNP swept back into power, with a 'new and improved' Michael Manley at the helm.

Though some outsiders looked askance at his return – 'Communists Return to Power in Jamaica' screamed one Canadian newspaper headline – Manley was as good as his word. The days of bushjacketed firebrand socialist rhetoric had truly given way to suit and tie globalisation. With the passion of a reformed addict, the PNP set about opening Jamaica to market forces and liberalising the economy.

In 1992, ill health forced Manley to retire, but his successor, the lawyer P.J. Patterson, continued where he left off. During his tenure Patterson also carried out in his typically unobtrusive manner perhaps the most fundamental electoral reform Jamaica has known since independence by creating and granting full powers to an independent electoral commission. This somewhat reduced, but did not eliminate, the 'Garrison' syndrome of all residents of an area being forced to vote for the designated party, whether they wanted to or not.

The great failing of his regime however was its inability to control crime, as between 1989 and 2005 the Jamaican murder rate more than tripled. Much of this surge was due to drug gang-related violence in the inner city and it has had surprisingly little effect on most Jamaicans' daily routine. Kingston's nightlife has never been more vibrant, and the rate of crimes against visitors remains low by world standards. This remains, however, the country's greatest challenge.

Many accused Patterson of entrenching patronage to an unprecedented degree. His defenders argued that he was merely empowering previously marginalised black entrepreneurs, and that his critics were sour grape defenders of the previous white and brown man neo-plantocracy. Perhaps there was some truth in both views.

Despite increasing violence, financial upheavals, and frequent scandals, the PNP's policies of openness to world markets and technological advances found great favour with the populace. Patterson won mandates in 1993, 1997 and 2003. Some say his best political asset was the refusal of the aging Edward Seaga to give up the JLP leadership.

In March 2006 Patterson demitted office, and party delegates voted Portia Simpson Miller his successor. The 60-year-old Simpson Miller, long the most popular politician in the country, entered office to almost unanimous acclaim. As someone of humble beginnings and the nation's first woman leader, 'Portia' was expected to have a special insight into the needs and wants of the people. The deep affection she inspired was reflected in her unprecedented 72 per cent positive rating.

However perceived indecision, allegations of corruption and a natural democratic impulse for change after 18 years of same party rule, gradually eroded both hers and the PNP's popularity. The JLP won the 2007 general election, albeit by only 0.4 per cent of the vote and 32 to 28 seats.

The new prime minister was Bruce Golding, former construction minister in the 1980s JLP regime, and once heir presumptive to Edward Seaga. Frustrated by Seaga's refusal to resign after two straight general election defeats in 1989 and 1993, he had left the JLP in 1995 to form the National Democratic Movement (NDM).

Launched on a platform of transparency and accountability, initial polls put the NDM even with the PNP and JLP. However its dry, political theory approach alienated the bread and butter oriented masses. The party won only five per cent of the vote and no seats in the 1997 elections. Golding resigned as NDM leader following a 2000 by-election loss, and began a brief stint as talk show host. The NDM was finished as a viable political entity, and so it seemed was his political career.

However in the run up to the October 2002 general election, a desperate JLP trailing badly in the polls persuaded Golding to rejoin the party. Though it lost for the fourth straight time, Labour made its best showing since 1980. Golding was once again the heir apparent, and took over when the 72-year-old Seaga resigned in 2005. Derided in many quarters for his 'slow and steady, substance not style' approach, Golding had the last laugh when he was elected Jamaica's eighth prime minister in 2007.

Once dismissed as a boring policy wonk, Mr Golding has shown himself a skilful communicator in office, even hosting a monthly 'speak to the PM live' talk show. If he can reduce crime, overhaul the public administrative structure, and make the political process more transparent and accountable, he might become an outstanding prime minister. If he fails to put in place what he has been preaching since 1995, he could be just another one-term leader.

Whatever their faults, all Jamaica's leaders have been devoted to the welfare of the country, and firmly upheld the tenets of democracy. For this they deserve their nation's gratitude.

MUTTY PERKINS & JOHN MAXWELL: A CONFLICT OF VISIONS

The best proof that all points of view are given free rein in Jamaica are the contrasting outlooks of the two doyens of local journalism, Wilmot 'Mutty' Perkins and John Maxwell. While Maxwell remains a more or less unreformed leftist, Perkins has become somewhat of a right wing anarchist. Ask the two former friends anything, and you are likely to get completely contradictory answers.

Perkins posits Singapore as the ideal for Jamaica to emulate, while Maxwell holds out Cuba as the model to be copied – strange positions indeed for men who bridle at any hint of government censorship. In the lands built by Lee Kwan Yew and Fidel Castro, where there is no such thing as a free press, both Perkins and Maxwell would be in jail for speaking out as they do here. Thankfully, in Jamaica these men of unquestioned courage and integrity are completely free to say it as they see it.

Their opinions of Jamaica's past leaders are particularly amusing. Maxwell dismisses Bustamante as 'an ignoramous and a gangster, the original two-fisted gunman', while Perkins found him 'very big hearted and generous and possessed of immense common sense'. To Perkins, Norman Manley was 'very arrogant and considered himself superior stuff to the common man, an aristocrat so to speak', but in Maxwell's eyes he was 'a brilliant man of the highest principles'.

Maxwell considered Michael Manley 'a very complex character and an excellent prime minister'. In Perkins' words:

> Michael Manley is reflective of the race and class prejudices of this country. As he was a handsome, high brown skin Adonis with what some called nice hair, and was named Manley and had a wonderful speaking voice and great powers of articulation – though he had no clear idea what to articulate – people thought he had to be a genius. But had he been black with what in Jamaica used to be called bad hair, and been named Jones, people would long have recognised him for what he was – a half-wit.

WILMOT 'MUTTY' PERKINS

JOHN MAXWELL

All this is as it should be. Perkins and Maxwell are excellent examples of the two competing political views described by Thomas Sowell in *A Conflict of Visions*. One is the 'constrained' vision, which sees human nature as unchanging and selfish. The other is the 'unconstrained' vision, in which human nature is malleable and perfectible.

As Sowell says, reality is too complex to be comprehended by any single mind or point of view. So a free press must not only accurately report what has happened, it should also present every plausible interpretation of the facts. One thing surely, on which John and Mutty can both agree!

A Free and Feisty Media

Were it left to me to decide whether we should have a government without newspapers or newspapers without government, I should not hesitate a moment to prefer the latter.

– Thomas Jefferson

The best reason to be optimistic about Jamaica's future is its media. Considering the country's size and relatively low journalistic pay, the press here is remarkably dedicated to the pursuit of truth. Though television and newspaper ownership is concentrated in only a few hands, proprietors tend to observe a long standing 'hands off' tradition. Jamaica ranked fourteenth out of 195 countries in the 2009 Freedom House Press 2009 Freedom global rankings.

There are three hard news oriented national newspapers – the *Gleaner*, the *Observer*, the *Herald*; three national television stations – TVJ, CVM, and Love, plus many cable channels; and about 20 radio stations. The *Gleaner* was formed in 1834, and is the oldest continuously published newspaper in the Western Hemisphere. An old saw says 'It's not news if it's not in the *Gleaner*'. It was often in the past a mouthpiece of the light-skinned elite, assailing any challenge to the status quo, with the harrying of Marcus Garvey a case in point. Nowadays it is more balanced, tending – as proprietor Oliver Clarke says – to be slightly against whichever government is in power. The *Gleaner* has seen off many competitors over the years, but the *Daily Observer* and the weekly *Sunday Herald* have for the past 15 years provided respected alternatives. The common man's paper is the *Star*, which focuses mainly on human interest stories, as do *X-News* and *Chat*.

The newspapers do a very good job of keeping the nation informed. Some find the print journalism level uneven and too often of first draft quality – though to be fair, the skimpy pay and undiscerning readership can make the effort of revision seem pointless. However this is a perhaps unavoidable problem with small media markets.

The television news shows also give excellent coverage of the goings-on in the country. Indeed the main goal of the frequent localised roadblocks against police brutality or water shortages or bad roads, seems to be to get their grievances aired on the national news, and so brought to the attention of the relevant authorities. TV correspondents go to great lengths to give the public the 'live and direct' story. During the near war zone conditions of the May 2010 'Tivoli Invasion' for instance, reporters bravely gave up to the minute coverage even while lying flat as bullets flew overhead. Not even the BBC could have done better.

Outside of prime time, local television often seems swamped by the scores of American cable stations available. Still, there are some fine news programmes such as long-running 'Profile', 'All Angles', 'Direct' and 'Impact'. An episode of 'Impact' – repackaged for FOX TV – won an American Television Emmy award for Cliff Hughes' interview with the mother of Jamaican born US mass killer Anthony Malvo.

The dominant medium for in-depth news coverage is radio, and 'behind the headlines' type shows on stations like RJR, HOT 102, Nationwide News, and Newstalk 93 are mostly high class. Interviewers are generally well informed and persistent, making it rather difficult for public figures to run and hide.

Then there are the talk shows that dominate daytime radio, on which callers vigorously debate every conceivable topic with popular hosts like Ronnie Thwaites, Kingsley 'Ragashanti' Stewart, Orville Taylor, Barbara Gloudon and Mutty Perkins. Even a brief listen makes it obvious that no country enjoys greater freedom of speech, or indulges in it with more gusto.

Ammar's DOWNTOWN 108 KING STREET UPTOWN THE VILLAGE / MALL

The Daily Gleaner

...is a girl's best friend!

LARGEST READERSHIP ESTABLISHED 1834 Price: THIRTY-FIVE CENTS

KINGSTON, JAMAICA, TUESDAY, SEPTEMBER 25, 1979

Vol. CXLV No. 215

Demonstrators clash over Cuba

JLP, PNP GROUPS MARCH IN CITY

POLICE IN KINGSTON USED TEAR-GAS YESTERDAY afternoon to break-up a stone-throwing clash between JLP supporters demonstrating against Cuban Ambassador Ulises Estrada and pro-Cuba demonstrators made up of PNP and Workers Party supporters.

The use of teargas by the police averted what could have been a more serious situation on Lady Musgrave Road, near to Hope Road, involving thousands of demonstrators.

There were also reports of gunshots being fired but there were no reports of any injuries.

The demonstrators regrouped with the JLP going to their Belmont Road headquarters and the PNP supporters going to Jamaica House gate where they were later addressed by Prime Minister Manley.

Later a crowd of PNP supporters, including several Ministers of Government staged an anti-*Gleaner*, pro Cuban demonstration in front of the Gleaner building, North Street.

'NO SPEECH

Prime Minister told the crowd "I have no speech to make. You have made the speech for me and you have made the speech for the progressive forces. But next time, next time, next time."

The demonstrations began before 11 o'clock yesterday morning with JLP supporters marching on the Cuban Embassy at 9 Trafalgar Road, bearing anti-Estrada placards and calling for his expulsion.

(On Tuesday Ambassador Estrada had called a press conference at his Embassy where he accused the JLP and the Gleaner of spreading lies against him. He threatened a Cuban reaction.)

The crowd, including Senator Pearnel Charles, General Secretary Bruce Golding and NPM chairman Michael Williams and Ed Bartlett of the Jamaica Freedom League, among other JLP officials distributed hundreds of pamphlets, and chanted: "Estrada must go."

Around 11.15 a.m. the crowd moved on to Knutsford Boulevard to the Ministry of Foreign Affairs, New Kingston. Along the busy street hundreds of people rushed to the windows of their high rise offices to watch the sea of people below.

Hundreds of pamphlets critical of Prime Minister Michael Manley were also distributed along the way. As quickly as some of the pamphlets were thrown on the street they were picked up, apparently by a van with PNP supporters. Some of the placards read: "Estrada DGI agent," "DGI help PNP to Kill," "Estrada DGI Spy," and "Manley sold Jamaica for less than 30 pieces of silver."

The crowd, was during this time escorted by the police who followed it along Oxford Road to the offices of the Jamaica Daily News and the Agency for Public Information. The demonstrators then went along the Half-Way Tree Road to the Jamaica Broadcasting Corporation on South Odeon Avenue. The group then moved on to Jamaica House where the Prime Minister has his

(Cont'd. on Page 13 Col. 1)

Householder burnt to death by robbers

In the early morning hours before daybreak on Sunday, intruders broke into a man's home in Trelawny, forcibly opened his mouth, threw gasolene in it, and set him afire.

Police reported that David Dixon, 49, of Bounty Hall, Trelawny, died from extensive burns that night, despite being transferred from the Falmouth hospital to the Kingston Public Hospital.

Dixon was at home about 3.00 a.m. on Sunday when two or three intruders reportedly crept up on him while he was asleep and set him afire.

They set his house ablaze and he managed to crawl out but despite all attempts to give him the best medical aid he died.

The Trelawny police are investigating a second case of suspected arson and murder involving Mr Herbert Jones, 65, who was found burnt to death in his house on Thursday.

ANTI-CUBA: J.L.P. demonstrators carrying placards reading "Manley is a traitor", "We Jamaicans don't love communists"; "DGI are killers" and other slogans at the corner of Hope Road and Lady Musgrave Road yesterday.

PRO-CUBA: Demonstration in support of Cuba against the 'Gleaner' in front of the Gleaner building at North Street, Kingston, yesterday afternoon, with Prime Minister, Michael Manley (centre, among placards).

MEDICAL ASSOCIATI[ON]

Drug short[age] may ha[ve] caused de[aths]

THE MEDICAL ASSOCIATION ... said yesterday that untimely deaths ... from the shortage of drugs affecting ...

Tourist cancellations
MORE SUPPORT FOR GLEANER REPORT

Gleaner Western Bureau

... speech would show up more among United States wholesale travel operators, rather ... all asked that their names be not published because of an attempt to block a possible showdown within the JHTA ... cancellations. Others reported that they were expecting cancellations which they hope would never materialise. Several hotel operators ... play politics with the industry.

Inside
- Aspirin again ......
- Strategic blunder
- Impertinence fr...
- of passage.........
- 4 MIGS shot dov...
- City punter wins

STEPHEN NEWLAND,
LEAD SINGER OF THE REGGAE BAND
ROOTZ UNDERGROUND

Music

HEARTBEAT OF A NATION

Jamaica is not for those who like peace and quiet. Music is everywhere, constantly blaring from cars and bars and streetside sound systems. Probably no country devotes a greater percentage of its income to music and Jamaica likely has the most recording studios per capita in the world, from which pour forth an estimated 500 releases a month.

Courtesy of Stone Love

SOUND SYSTEMS

Sound systems are a uniquely Jamaican phenomenon. Originally modest-sized outdoor playback systems, they have evolved into huge conglomerations of giant speakers and state-of-the-art musical equipment transported by lorry. Virtually every community or school function has a sound system blasting out wall-shaking music; even the smallest hamlets boast a 'champion sound' that plays at weekend dances.

At 'sound clashes', rival systems compete for the crowd's favour, with the applause level deciding the night's victor. Some systems like Stone Love have become internationally famous, playing all over the world. In fact sound systems have become a global phenomenon, proliferating across North America, Europe and Asia. 'World Champion' sound clashes held in Jamaica are often won by foreign systems like Japan's Mighty Crown.

The favoured sound system venues used to be 'lawns' – large open areas where volume could be cranked up to an ear-shattering maximum and dances could go on till dawn. However greater housing density means lawns far from residential areas have become scarce, and complaints by sleep-deprived residents angry about all night roof rafter-shaking parties, have spurred increased enforcement of night noise laws. So now promoters are supposed to obtain licenses before holding dances, and excessively noisy events are, in theory, ended at 2:00 a.m. However police enforcement of these laws is rather sporadic.

Some cultural extremists grumble about this 'Americanisation' of a 'fundamental aspect of Jamaican culture', claiming that moving dances to indoor clubs causes the 'genuine' tropical night ambience to be lost. Calmer heads in the music industry concede that everyone has a fundamental right to a quiet night's sleep, at least in theory. Police attempts to 'lock down' dances at the legislated time are not infrequently met with violent protests and roadblocks by patrons enraged at having their fun interrupted.

LOCKDOWN!

Residents protest as police enforce 'night noise' act in MoBay

BY ADRIAN FRATER
STAR Writer

WESTERN BUREAU

ANARCHY REIGNED IN downtown Montego Bay, St James, yesterday morning as patrons who attended the popular 'Japzy Thursday' party in the Barnett Lane community reacted angrily to the police's decision to lock-off the session at midnight.

Irate residents and patrons lit tyres and old household items along Barnett Street and at other strategic locations across the second city, causing traffic to back-up for several miles. Numerous persons on their way to work were forced to abandon their vehicles and walk long distances to their respective work places.

"Now we want to go to work and look what ugly cause," said an elderly woman, as the taxi in which she was travelling stopped along the Tucker Irwin main road. "This is madness, eno. Country can't run like this."

It took a large contingent of police and soldiers and the intervention of the promoter of the event, businessman Clive 'Japanese' Bowen, to restore order about 10:45 a.m. Units from the St James Fire Brigade put out the fires.

Police maintain a strong presence on Barnett Street in Montego Bay after protestors blocked the road.

PROMOTER DISAPPOINTED

While not condoning the violence, Bowen expressed disappointment with the actions of the police. He noted that in the four months since he started 'Japzy Thursday', it has been incident free in what is considered a volatile community.

"It is not really about me, it is about the people,' said Bowen. "This is a place where people feel safe and secure. If you lose your phone and you make an announcement, the person who find it just bring it back. It is just a good vibe thing for the people."

Deputy Superintendent of Police, Paul Stanton, who was among the security personnel seeking to restore order, said their action was a part of the drive to enforce the Noise Abatement Act.

"We had a press conference last week where we warned the various promoters about our new resolve to clamp down on night noise," said Deputy Superintendent Stanton.

At the press conference last week, Superintendent Steve McGregor and Area One divisional commander, Assistant Commissioner Clifford Blake, told some 30 sound system operators, promoters and owners of entertainment venues, that the flexibility they previously enjoyed would be curtailed.

The police say that no event will be allowed to progress beyond the cut-off times of midnight during the week and 2 a.m. on weekends.

Two die during shoot-out

KIMONI HARRIS
Staff Reporter

TWO OF FOUR gunmen who allegedly engaged ... was carried out in Riversdale. During the exercise four men armed with guns were seen in the community.

WHAT IS REGGAE?

Reggae is a generic name for all Jamaican popular music since 1960, but it also refers to the particular beat that was popular from about 1969 to 1983.

Jamaican music since 1960 can be roughly divided into four eras, which each had a distinctive beat – ska, rocksteady, reggae and dancehall. Ska dated from about 1960 to mid-1966. Rocksteady lasted from late 1966 to late 1968. The popular beat from 1969 to about 1983 was named reggae, and had two phases – 'early reggae', from about 1969 to 1974, and 'roots reggae', from about 1975 to 1983. From 1983 onwards the prevalent sound has been called dancehall.

Outside of Jamaica, dancehall is often called 'ragga' or 'dub'. However, in Jamaica 'dub' refers to instrumentals created by mixing out other instruments, and leaving the drum and bass only.

Reggae's global popularity is unique. No other indigenous music has attracted the same attention, or exerted similar influence. One extraordinary aspect of Jamaican music is its ability to continually reinvent itself. While many other indigenous musics have remained relatively unchanged over the years, reggae encompasses ska, rocksteady, deejay, roots, dub, lovers rock, dancehall and gospel. Joy, anger, love, sorrow, lust, laughter, contemplation, praise – there's a musical expression for every emotion. Also remarkably, almost every Jamaican sound has become hugely influential overseas.

Ska's popularity has made it an accepted music genre in itself, with North America and Europe boasting hundreds of ska bands. The drum and bass dub created by King Tubby and Lee Perry helped to transform club dance music everywhere. Bob Marley made roots reggae globally known. Deejay music gave birth to American hip hop, which indisputably began as an American version of Jamaican toasting. More recently dancehall has been 'Latin-Americanised' into Reggaeton. Rarely have so few influenced so many.

Music

Jamaicans have catholic musical tastes, listening to everything from rap to soul to country music to gospel. Yet not surprisingly in the land of its birth, the airwaves are dominated by reggae.

Reggae, says Orlando Patterson, illustrates the complexity of global cultural interaction perhaps more clearly than any other musical form. It is probably the only music of non-western origin heard in every country on earth, and is arguably the first modern example of a Third World country exporting its culture to such a diverse international audience. Indeed Jamaica is a music world power, probably surpassed in global influence only by the US and Britain. How did our rugged beat, 'sent forth from yard to conquer the earth', come to be?

Kumina, Quadrille and Mento

Jamaica, as Rex Nettleford famously put it, combines the melody of Europe with the rhythm of Africa. Not all African cultural retentions here are products of slavery. Between 1841 and 1865, over 8,000 Yoruba and Central African immigrants came to St Thomas parish as indentured labourers. Their most prominent cultural legacy is Kumina, an ancestor worship cult emphasising both singing and dancing. Kumina devotees considered themselves exiles and looked to the Congo-Angola and Guinea Coast regions of Africa as their ancestral homeland. Rastafarianism incorporated many Kumina customs; there is little difference for instance, between Rasta Nyabinghi and Kumina drumming.

Kumina fused with the great anglophone religious revival of the 1860s to produce Pocomania and today Kumina, Pocomania and Revivalism are often indistinguishable. However their influence on early ska and reggae are unmistakable and some emphatically define ska as a mixture of revival music and rhythm and blues.

Jamaica's first widespread native song form was dubbed quadrille, which is probably a country folk variation of nineteenth-century European dance music, such as the French quadrille. Quadrille song and dance groups still feature in heritage festivals.

MENTO BAND

The dominant music of Jamaica from its appearance in the late nineteenth century up to the 1930s was mento. It's most characteristic feature is the accent in or on the last beat of each bar. Olive Lewin links the accented fourth beat to gangs of men swinging pickaxes during field labour. In order to effect a strong downward movement on the first beat of each bar in songs used to accompany this common type of agricultural labour, there is an almost equally strong upward movement on the previous beat.

Trinidadian Calypso also impacted significantly on mento, as did Latin American music in general. The basic mento bass-drum rhythm is similar to that of Cuban rumba or son. Another influence was Jonkannu (or Jon Canoe), a once popular Christmas tradition dating to slavery days, in which bands of costumed dancers and musicians roamed the streets.

Mento closely follows local speech patterns, with bands using combinations of piccolo bamboo fife, guitar, rumba box, fiddle, banjo, shakers and scrapers. It demonstrates a Jamaican predisposition for bass, which predates the arrival of American records and electric instruments, and points to an aesthetic where rhythm takes priority over melody and harmony.

Mento's popularity diminished with growing urbanisation so that by the 1950s it became marginalised to rural festivities and tourist hotels. However, bona fide groups like the Blue Glades, St Christopher and Lititz Mento Bands still play regularly at funeral 'nine night setups' and festival celebrations, often accompanying quadrille dancers.

Paradoxically, mento became a national music just as it went into decline. Spurred by international interest in calypso, local entrepreneurs like Ken Khouri began recording mento. The first Jamaican commercial record was Lord Fly's tale of tribulation 'Whai! Ay!' Such records, and the arrival of radio, made performers previously known only to live local audiences famous islandwide.

Sound System Rhythm and Blues

Young migrants to Kingston, associated mento with rural deprivation. They preferred the black American rhythm and blues, which migrant sugar cane cutters brought back from the southern US in the late 1940s. Jamaican urban mass culture – as opposed to 'rural folk culture' – has probably been influenced by Afro-American music from the US since the late nineteenth century. For instance the 1930s street troubadors Slim Beckford and Sam Blackwood, the earliest popular singers to have their names recorded in print, often called their songs 'blues'. Yet Slim and Sam were purveyors of primarily Jamaican music, of whom Ranny Williams wrote (and exactly the same could be said of today's deejays) – 'The customs, whims, wiles and living conditions of the masses of the island are an open book in their hands'.

Courtesy of the National Library of Jamaica

SIR COXSONE DODD (LEFT) AND JOHNNY OSBORNE

North America probably influenced local music then as it would later – and as Europe did before – providing raw material to be reworked into distinctly Jamaican idioms.

Another strong inspiration was Gospel, as most Jamaican singers started in 'clap hand' churches. While the big bands, which were popular among the elite from the 1930s to 1950s, served as training grounds for the studio musicians who played on early Jamaican records.

Commercial radio broadcasting began in July 1950, but the middle class programming did not include the R&B popular with the masses. Some Jamaicans tried to fill this musical gap by tuning in to Miami and New Orleans R&B radio stations, but most turned to sound systems, which were essentially large mobile discotheques designed to fill the growing demand for R&B. Since most individual Jamaicans could not afford a playback system, these were in effect giant community record players. The first proper sound system was Tom Wong's 'Tom the Great Sebastien', which played at the corner of Luke Lane and Charles Street in downtown Kingston, creating perhaps Jamaica's first 'dancehall'. Other well-known early sounds were Clement Dodd's Sir Coxsone's Downbeat and Duke Reid's 'Trojan' located in the inner city.

In the late 1950s American R&B morphed into rock and roll, which Jamaican dance crowds didn't like. Business declined as the R&B supply dried up. So sound system operators tried recording their own songs.

Ska Ska Ska

Early record producers merely wanted to reproduce the American R&B sound their dance customers demanded, and made no conscious effort to create a definably Jamaican style. So how did these hesitant imitations develop into a new musical form? As one musicologist put it, 'Unless we hypothesise the existence of a vibrant – but almost completely undocumented – Afro-Jamaican folk music culture running parallel to the mainstream urban popular music, the rise of distinctive indigenous Jamaican forms in the 1960s remains inexplicable.'

The subtle differences from R&B became progressively more pronounced as the music evolved. The 1960 Prince Buster-produced 'Oh Carolina' may be the first recognisably modern Jamaican recording. With the Folkes Brothers on vocals, Rastafarian drummer Count Ossie providing African cross-rhythmic

> Ska – a mixture of rhythm and blues, mento, Revival and Rastafarian music – was born in poor west Kingston ghettos

accompaniment and background harmonies, Owen Gray playing contrasting American-styled piano, and guitarist Jah Jerry emphasising not the downbeat but the after beat, this song was unlike anything heard before.

The rastafarian element was significant. Rastafarians embraced Africa at a time when American black music was completely ignoring it, so that while part of the population was listening to Miami and New Orleans, rastas were urging Jamaicans to hold on to their cultural roots. Chris Blackwell says this has been a key dynamic in Jamaican music.

The attainment of independence in August

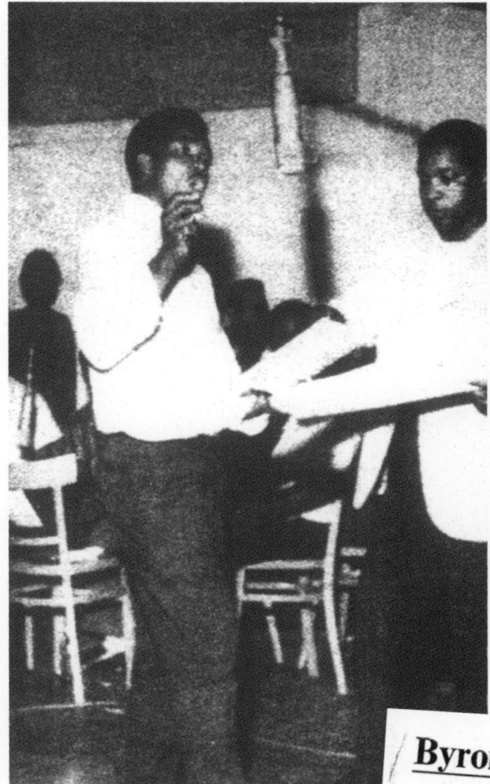

PRINCE BUSTER

Photos © The Gleaner Company Ltd, 2010

DON DRUMMOND

Courtesy of the National Library of Jamaica

COUNT OSSIE AND THE MYSTIC REVELATIONS OF RASTAFARI

Byron Lee Hits The North Coast!!
AGAIN WITH HIS GIGANTIC
"SKA SPECTACULAR"
BYRON LEE AND THE DRAGONAIRES
"THE BAND WITH SOUL"
★ ★ ★ ★ ★ ★
GUEST ARTISTS
THE FABULOUS
BLUES BUSTERS
- ON THE BANDSTAND OF -
CLUB MARACAS - Ocho Rios
THIS SATURDAY NIGHT - 20th MARCH '65 - From 9.00 p.m.
A Swinging Dance Date - Don't Miss It!
Cover ∴ 10/-
PRINTED BY: . ASSOCIATED PRINTERS LTD. 143 PRINCESS STREET, KINGSTON—'PHONE 24061

© Roy Sweetland/ Buzz Magazine

MARCIA GRIFFITHS

KEN BOOTHE

Photos © The Gleaner Company Ltd, 2010

DERRICK MORGAN

TOOTS HIBBERT

JIMMY CLIFF

...manipulations of reverbs and remixes gave birth to another entirely new branch of Jamaican music called dub

1962 spurred attempts to create a distinctive Jamaican sound. This was christened ska, a term of indeterminate origin. Ska – a mixture of rhythm and blues, mento, revival and rastafarian music – was born in poor west Kingston ghettos. However, it was introduced to the middle and upper classes, who could afford to buy records, by 'uptown' bands like Byron Lee and the Dragonaires, and Carlos Malcolm and the Afro-Jamaican Rhythms. Radio and live shows also helped to establish the local recording industry as more than just a fad. The first Jamaica Broadcasting Company (JBC) record chart in August 1959 had all foreign entries, and the first local chart record to enter the charts was Laurel Aitken's 'Boogie Rock' on October 9.

The era's top recording band was The Skatalites, which boasted most of the island's top instrumentalists, including the creative but eccentric trombonist Don Drummond. Among the early ska stars were Prince Buster, Derrick Morgan, Monty Morris, Jimmy Cliff, The Wailers, and The Maytals. The Maytals, whose songs were unmistakably rooted in rural folk and revival traditions, yet thoroughly modern in feeling, were especially influential in giving the new music a recognisably Jamaican sensibility.

An attempt by then Culture Minister Edward Seaga to market ska at the 1964 New York World Fair was hindered by uneven recording quality. Also in 1964 Millie Small's 'My Boy Lollipop', produced in Britain by Chris Blackwell, made the US and UK top ten, selling six million copies worldwide.

Get Ready for Rocksteady

In 1966 ska's profusion of percussive instruments, catchy guitar riff and abundance of horns, gave way to bold melodic bass lines in the background. Played in a laid-back style, this beat was said to 'rock steady'. A catchy and steady rhythm, or 'riddim', now became just as important as the vocals, and the bass began to assume a unique significance in Jamaican music. Songs also increasingly dealt with social realities; top acts included groups like Leroy Sibbles and the Heptones, BB Seaton and The Gaylads, Desmond Dekker and the Aces, John Holt and The Paragons, Slim Smith and the Techniques, and singers such as Alton Ellis, Bob Andy, Marcia Griffiths, Ken Boothe and Delroy Wilson.

The rocksteady era was perhaps Jamaican music's most melodically and rhythmically engrossing period. Yet it lasted less than three years, and in late 1968 The Maytals 'Do The Reggay' christened a new sound. As lead singer Toots Hibbert tells it:

> Raleigh and me and Jerry were talking some nonsense one day, and I just said 'Come on man, let's do the reggae'. Later we decide to make a song out of that. It was just a word you would hear on the streets. I don't remember why I apply it to music. At first reggae sort of mean untidy or scruffy. But then it start to mean like coming from the people. Everyday things. From the ghetto. From majority. Things people use everyday like food, we just put music to and make a dance out of it. Reggae mean regular people who are suffering, and don't have what they want.

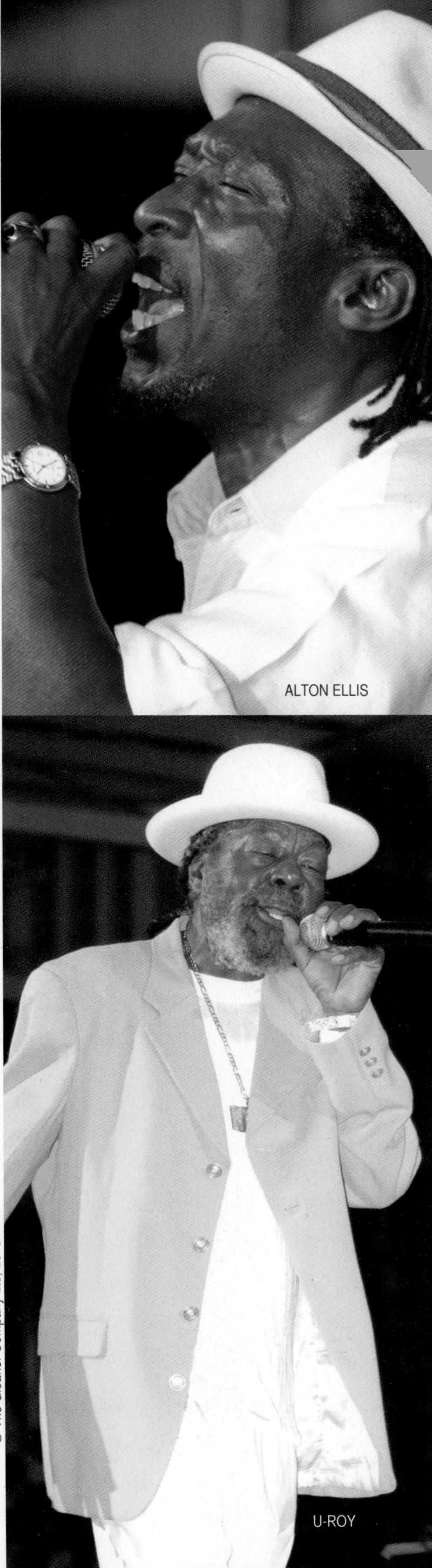

ALTON ELLIS

U-ROY

THE JAMAICAN ROOTS OF RAP

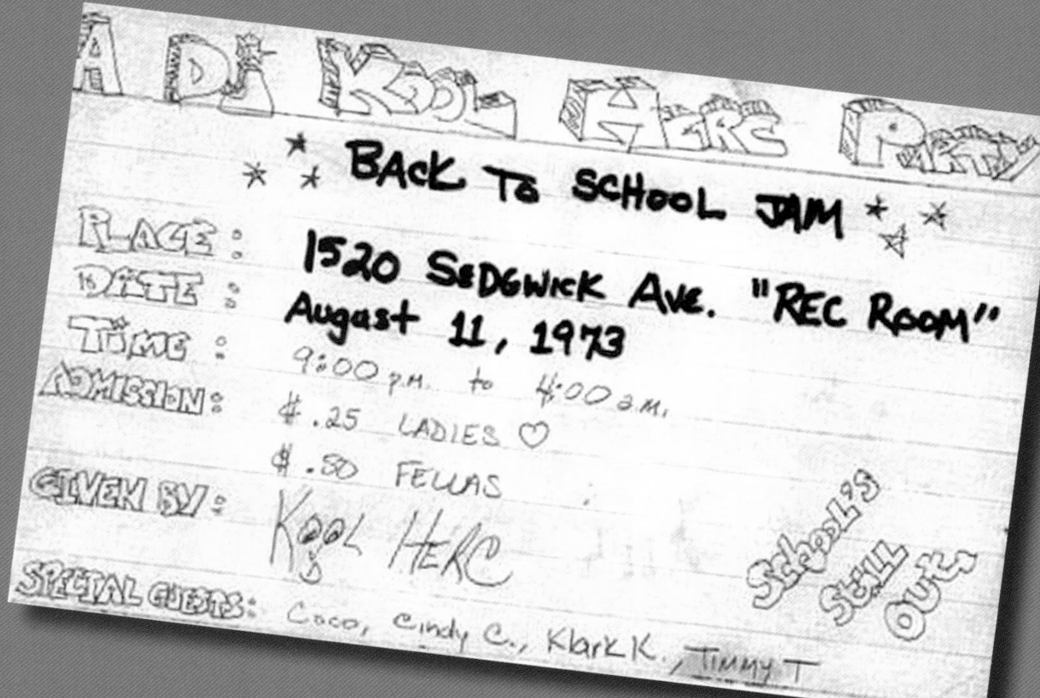
A DJ KOOL HERC PARTY

★ BACK TO SCHOOL JAM ★

PLACE: 1520 SEDGWICK AVE. "REC ROOM"

DATE: August 11, 1973

TIME: 9:00 p.m. to 4:00 a.m.

ADMISSION: $.25 LADIES ♡ $.50 FELLAS

GIVEN BY: KOOL HERC

SPECIAL GUESTS: Coco, Cindy C., Klark K., Timmy T

In 1967 at the age of 12, Clive Campbell moved with his family from Jamaica to the Bronx in New York. In 1973 he assembled a sound system like the kind he had grown up with in Kingston, and began throwing parties. The set was called Herculord and Campbell assumed the name Kool DJ Herc. Modelled after the huge sets necessary to compete in the heated sound system battles of Jamaica, Herculord was far more powerful than anything around and blew the competition away, establishing a ghetto-wide reputation. He murdered the competition with his 'clean' distortion free sounds, shattering frequency range, and massive volume (Above is an original hand-written flyer from August 11, 1973 promoting Clive and Cindy Campbell's first back-to-school jam).

The exact details of what came next are lost in the mists of time, because no one was really paying attention to what was only one of a million musical trends taking place. Still Herc probably sensed that while native American blacks didn't fully respond to the reggae rhythms he and his emcees toasted to, they liked the chanting. Even if they couldn't understand what the Jamaicans were saying and didn't talk like them, something in these verbal broadsides touched a chord. Chanting over funk and disco hits was the next natural step, and black American youngsters began adapting the form to their slang and rhythms of speech.

According to Afrika Bambaata

> [Herc] knew that a lot of American blacks were not getting into reggae. He took the same thing that the deejays was doing – toasting – and did it with American records, Latin records or records with a beat. Herc took phrases like what was happening in the streets, what was the new saying going round like 'rock on my mellow', 'to the beat y'all', 'you don't stop' and just elaborated on that...he would call out the names of people who were at the party, just like the microphone personalities who deejayed back in Jamaica.

One amusing aspect of rap's beginnings is how closely it paralleled the early days of Jamaican sound systems. Not only did they use toasters to give dances a live feel, but Kool Herc and his imitators like Afrika Bambaata and Grandmaster Flash would often have system battles, where rivals set up near each other and tried to blast away the opposition with superior wattage. Shades of Tom the Great, Trojan and Downbeat in the downtown Kingston 1950s!

The 1973 album *Hustlers Corner* by the Last Poets is often cited as rap's founding record. However, this was years after deejaying had been established as a legitimate musical form in Jamaica. 'Rapper's Delight', the first big commercial rap hit, didn't come out until 1979. Deejay music in Jamaica went through countless changes in style and form long before US rap music was recognised as anything more than a novelty.

The Jamaican link (and interestingly Grandmaster Flash, the earliest of rap stars, had Barbadian parents who collected both American swing and West Indian records), the similarity of musical methods, and deejaying's unquestioned chronological precedence, make it undeniably obvious that rap evolved from deejaying.

Some say Jamaican deejay music evolved from the southern black R&B radio disc jockeys, who in turn developed their style from jazz scat singers. Indeed both deejaying and rapping can be considered an extension of the West African oral tradition of the griot or storyteller, who recited the history of his tribal community, sometimes to the accompaniment of talking drums.

However, it was Jamaican deejays who first turned chanting/toasting/scatting into a commercial musical form that stood on its own and pushed all accompaniment into the background, and where people bought the records because of the rhythmic talking. So calling dancehall 'reggae rap' – as Americans sometimes do – is about as logical as referring to rhythm and blues as 'black rock and roll'.

Do the Reggae

To some, reggae combines all previous forms of Jamaican popular music – the ska riff on top of a slowed down rocksteady bass line, with a dash of mento. Like most of the world's popular music, reggae is in 4/4 time. However the strongly felt 'downbeats' are not beats 1 & 3, but 2 & 4. This is why non-Jamaicans who are used to the downbeat emphasis on beats 1 & 3, often find it difficult to dance to reggae.

Jamaican music was also expanding abroad. Performers like Max Romeo, Pat Kelly, Bob Andy, Marcia Griffiths and The Upsetters made the British charts. Desmond Dekker and The Aces' Leslie Kong produced 1969 'Poor Me Israelites' was a multi-million selling worldwide smash.

In 1970 U-Roy's 'Wear You to Ball' made deejay music widely accepted, thus becoming perhaps reggae's single most influential song. Strongly influenced by the dialect poetry of Louise 'Miss Lou' Bennett, deejaying was a unique music form where the vocalist chanted or 'toasted' in a kind of call and answer arrangement with the bass 'riddim'. The young Jamaican Clive Campbell, a.k.a. Kool DJ Herc, took this revolutionary mike chanting to America, and it gradually transformed into what was called rap.

About this time Oswald 'King' Tubby's studio manipulations of reverbs and remixes gave birth to another entirely new branch of Jamaican music called dub. This bass heavy instrumental music also had a worldwide impact as many international dance music trends like house, techno, industrial and jungle can be traced to the works of dub pioneers like King Tubby, Lee 'Scratch' Perry, and Augustus Pablo.

In 1972 *The Harder They Come*, the first Jamaican movie, hit the screens. Directed by Perry Henzell and starring Jimmy Cliff, this film became the single most powerful purveyor of

reggae internationally, and its sound track is still arguably the best Jamaican album ever.

In early 1973 The Wailers released *Catch a Fire*, their first album for Chris Blackwell's Island Records. It was perhaps the first reggae album conceived as a seamless unit and not just a collection of singles, and maybe the first instance of Jamaicans making music with a primarily foreign audience in mind. Bob Marley and The Wailers became reggae's biggest name and their subsequent studio albums – *Burnin* (1974), *Natty Dread* (1975), *Rastaman Vibration* (1976), *Exodus* (1977), *Kaya* (1978), *Survival* (1979), and *Uprising* (1980) – defined the decade.

European and North American audiences could identify with the charismatic, dreadlocked, half-white Marley, who was becoming a true international star when tragically cut down by

GREGORY ISAACS

...Burning Spear's 'Marcus Garvey'... produced a forthright statement of black pride that gave an electrifying resonance to the spirit of the times.

DENNIS BROWN

cancer in 1981 while only 36. In death he became one of the world's outstanding cultural icons.

New stars like Ernie Smith, Big Youth and Third World arrived in the early 1970s, while the smooth stylings of Dennis Brown and Gregory Isaacs gave birth to the 'lover's rock' genre. In 1975 drummer Lowell 'Sly' Dunbar and bassist Robbie Shakespeare, created the martial 'Channel One' beat that dominated reggae for the rest of the decade.

That same year Burning Spear's 'Marcus Garvey' combined hypnotic folkloric chanting with a swirling propulsive rhythm, and produced a forthright statement of black pride that gave an electrifying resonance to the spirit of the times. This sound became known as 'roots reggae', a genre heavily identified with Rastafarianism, and whose top performers included the Mighty Diamonds, Culture and Black Uhuru.

The Harder They Come hardly touched on the topic, and there were no dreadlocked reggae stars before 1973, yet by the end of the 1970s, rastafarianism and dreadlocks had become signature features of Jamaican music. Often it was just a commercial or lifestyle choice, as many spliff-puffing, Selassie-spouting, so-called dreads completely ignored the true religious tenets of rastafarianism. Such fake rastas still abound today.

The Wailers' success abroad made it fashionable for foreign artists like Paul Simon and Eric Clapton to record in Jamaica, while overseas companies like Virgin Records came searching for the next Bob Marley. Many Jamaican artistes now aimed not at the local charts but international record deals and focused on politicised 'conscious' lyrics instead of infectious 'riddims'. A lot of singers lost touch with the common man's everyday concerns, and reggae's dance appeal declined.

BOB MARLEY
REGGAE SUPERHERO

Bob Nesta Marley is by far the most famous figure Jamaican music has ever produced. Mention Jamaica, and foreigners who scarcely know in which hemisphere the country is located will cry in recognition 'Bob Marley!' Millions of people the world over know of reggae only because of him and have never heard of another Jamaican musician. It's a truly unique fame covering all corners of the earth, surpassing in universality the adulation accorded to other rock martyrs like Elvis Presley and John Lennon.

Marley is increasingly becoming to Jamaica what Robert Burns is to Scotland – most famous son, national bard, and symbol of cultural identity. The parallels between the two great Roberts are uncanny. Both were born to humble circumstances in a small country with a few million inhabitants. Both were free spirits who praised the intoxicating pleasures of ganja and whisky respectively. Both fathered numerous children from multiple mothers – roughly nine from seven for Marley and eleven from six for Burns. Both penned world anthems, with 'One Love' being arguably the closest modern equivalent to 'Auld Land Syne', and both died young, Marley at 36 and Burns at 37.

Burns' January 25 birthday is Scotland's national day, an occasion for 'bold john barleycorn' inspired admirers everywhere to praise Rabbie, and test the truth of 'Kings may be blest but Tam was glorious, o'er all the ills o life victorious'.

Marley's February 6 'earthday' already stirs up 'kaya' fuelled 'wake up and turn I loose' global tributes to 'Nesta', and might one day become as important to Jamaicans everywhere as 'Burns night' is to the Scots around the world. Time alone, time will tell.

Still it's not just music that has made Marley a great international icon. His songs are inseparable from the handsome, dreadlocked, mixed race, almost Christlike visage that made him visually an ideal global icon. Being obviously not pure anything meant every race could identify with him, in a way often not possible with someone like say Peter Tosh. In our still western media-dominated world, those accepted by European and American audiences become famous everywhere.

Musician Leroy Sibbles once had this to say:

> As great as Bob Marley was, I think Peter Tosh was just as good. But he couldn't make it as big as Bob, because Bob had a lighter complexion and the record companies were able to promote him more and he was accepted easier. Look at Toots. There's no one better than Toots – black, white, blue or pink. But he never reached the level of Bob Marley because of the same reason.

If Bob Marley looked like Peter Tosh and vice versa, whose music would be more popular today? It's an interesting question to ponder.

Then there is the martyr factor. In our image driven age, as the stand-up comics joke, dying young is a great career move. Most of the dominant twentieth century icons – James Dean, Marilyn Monroe, Elvis Presley, Che Guevera, Princess Diana for instance – died before 40, or in John F. Kennedy's case looked it. While their surviving contemporaries slowly dwindled into aged mortality, they in the public mind stayed forever young and glamorous. Watching Bunny Wailer at the New Kingston concert a few years back, some observers wonder how people would have reacted to a similarly grey and grizzled 60-year-old Bob Marley. Glory is a cold sun that warms no bones. However in the minds of the living, the early dead remain forever young and immune to the ravages of age – untarnished blank canvases on which we can paint our dreams of the ideal. Marlon Brando was a better actor than James

STATUE OF BOB MARLEY

Dean; Eisenhower was a greater leader than Kennedy and Johnny Cash was a superior artiste to Elvis Presley. However, in the popular mind, the accomplishments of fat old Marlon, bald Dwight, and wrinkled Johnny just can't compete with handsome, sleek, air-brushed Jimmy, JFK and Elvis.

None of this brings Marley's greatness into question, although some fervent admirers do get carried away. The man was a singer and songwriter after all – who like all musicians produced the occasional lousy tune – not some latter day biblical prophet. He certainly never professed such a role for himself.

Yet he was without a doubt one of the finest musicians of the twentieth century, and his global popularity is perhaps unparalleled. Americans, Asians, Europeans, Africans, the young, the old, the middle aged – everyone seems to like Bob Marley's music, and his lustre simply keeps growing. In 2000, *Time Magazine* chose *Exodus* as album of the century, and the BBC named 'One Love' song of the century. It's hard to top that for lasting global appeal.

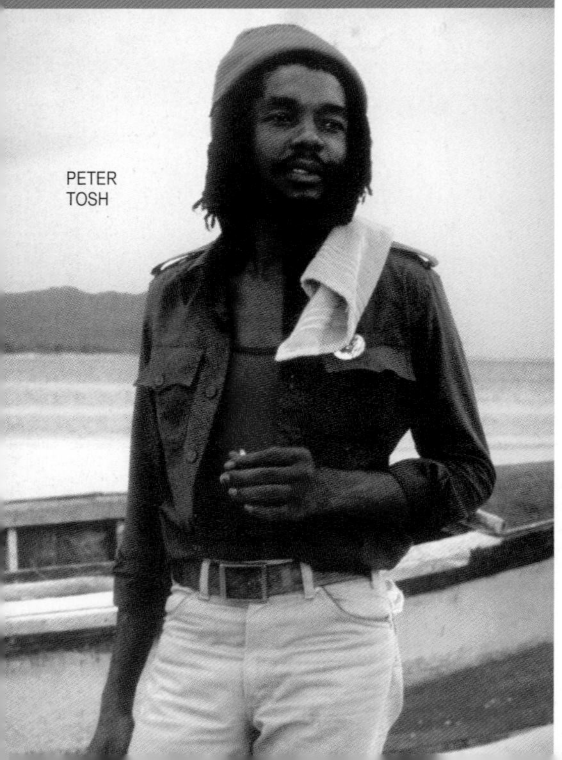

PETER TOSH

Deejay Inna Dancehall

Though some reviled them for being unmusical in the conventional sense, it was the deejays who increasingly moved the masses. Mike chanters like Dillinger, Trinity, Ranking Trevor, and the duo Michigan and Smiley had continued the traditions of U-Roy and Big Youth through the late 1970s. In the early 1980s the albino sensation Yellowman completely captured the imagination of the 'massives' with his fearless chanting, becoming the biggest star in the land.

In 1983 a show called 'Dancehall 83' was a huge success, and the name dancehall started popping up on shows and posters. The label went over to the Thursday night segment of the annual Reggae Sunsplash festival that featured deejays. Soon 'dancehall' came to refer to the predominantly deejay based sound of the era.

Singers like Beres Hammond, Barrington Levy, Freddie McGregor, Half Pint and Coco Tea continued to make good music. However, it was deejays like Josey Wales, Chaka Demus, Admiral Bailey, Red Dragon, Flourgon, Tiger, Lt Stitchie, Papa San, Ninja Man and Shabba Ranks who drew the biggest crowds.

In 1985 'Under Me Sleng Teng', featuring a Casio digital keyboard rhythm, became a smash hit, and the 'computer riddim' age was born. Many of the most popular dancehall 'riddims' over which deejays chanted were computer versions of old Studio One rhythms, and a slew of dancehall versions of ska and rocksteady classics became hits, including Shaggy's UK number one 'Oh Carolina'.

Whatever their artistic merits, computers had an undeniably positive commercial impact. While poor recording quality had previously been a big hindrance to local recordings abroad, the 'cleaner' digital sound led to unprecedented commercial success overseas for Jamaican music. Ini Kamoze's 1995 'Hot Steppa' topped the US charts, and Shaggy's *Hot Shot* was the world's biggest selling album in 2001. Sean Paul hit just as big in 2003 with 'Get Busy'.

Photos © Roy Sweetland/ Buzz Magazine

YELLOWMAN

In the early 1990s, dancehall became popular in Panama, which because of its Jamaican diaspora has always had a strong reggae tradition. Artistes like El General started translating Jamaican hits into 'Reggae en español', and their popularity spread to Puerto Rico and then to the rest of the Spanish-speaking New World. Hispanic and hip hop influences were incorporated, and a new genre emerged. Christened Reggaeton, it become the modern sound of Latin American youth. US commentators remarked on its uncanny ability to unite hitherto musically disparate Latino communities, something no previous sound had been able to accomplish. While their parents listened to the salsa or merengue or rumba or Tejano music of their own country, youngsters from Mexico, Guatemala, Honduras, Dominican Republic, Panama, Cuba and Puerto Rico are

BEENIE MAN
SIZZLA
NINJA MAN
FREDDIE MCGREGOR
BOUNTY KILLA
BERES HAMMOND

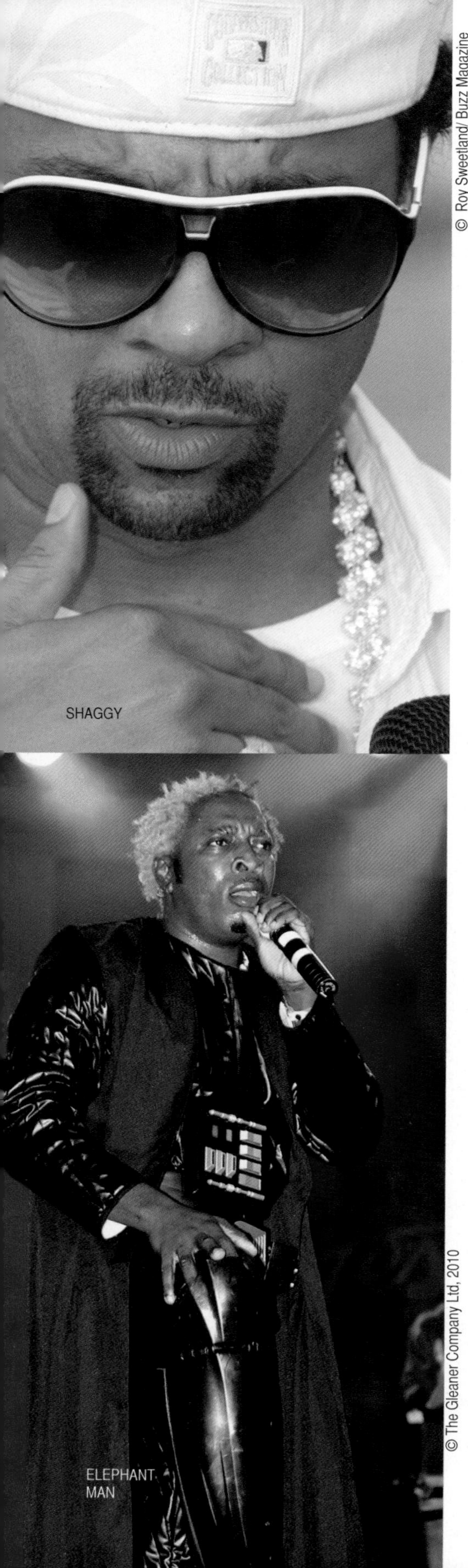
SHAGGY

© Roy Sweetland/ Buzz Magazine

ELEPHANT MAN

now jamming together to Reggaeton.

Of course to Jamaican ears, it still sounded mostly like Spanish dancehall, and thoughtful Jamaican musicologists puzzled once more over the astonishing power of the dancehall beat. Perhaps it was time to stop deriding it as 'primitive, slack and undisciplined', and to start trying to technically understand the source of its remarkable cross-cultural potency?

In about 1992 cable television arrived, pumping dozens of American pop culture belching channels into virtually every Jamaican household. BET, or Black Entertainment Television, helped make American hip hop popular, and big names of the day like Beenie Man and Bounty Killa started doing 'crossover' songs with US rap artists. Some claimed the Jamaican deejay style was starting to resemble hip hop, and that rap was killing dancehall. Yet rastafarian artistes like Sizzla and Capleton remained adamantly 'African' in outlook. Meanwhile singers and singjays like Luciano, Beres Hammond, Tony Rebel and Richie Stephens continued to make wonderful roots music.

While Jamaica is reggae country, for about two weeks every Easter it becomes a Soca land, embracing the modern Calypso-based sound of its cousin Trinidad. The young and not so young go wild at events like Beach Jouvert, and Bacchanal Fridays, culminating in the grand carnival parade on the Sunday after Easter. It may not quite match Port of Spain for all-encompassing bacchanal atmosphere, but hordes of glittering young women dancing down the road to pounding soca and dancehall is always lots of fun.

Paradoxically for a genre often condemned as misogynistic, dancehall has produced more significant female artistes than any other era of Jamaican music. The real groundbreaker was the highly controversial but brilliant Marion 'Lady Saw' Hall. There were significant reggae female stars before her, such as Marcia Griffiths, Phyllis Dillon, Judy Mowatt, Rita Marley and Patra. However, as the first to become a bona fide show headliner, Lady Saw sparked something of a cultural revolution.

Homo sum: humani nil a me alienum puto wrote the Roman poet Terence – 'I am a human being, so nothing human is strange to me'. Obsessive homophobia aside, this pretty much sums up today's dancehall scene. Jamaican music has never been more vibrant or varied. Current stars like Assassin, Mavado, Vybz Kartel, Elephant Man and Queen Ifrica keep putting out hits that cover the entire gamut of everyday life, from romantic love to social commentary to female empowerment to hardcore gangsterism to ghetto suffering to dance crazes to explicit sex.

Those who would write reggae's epitaph might have a long wait.

QUEEN IFRICA

LADY SAW – KICKING DOWN THE GLASS DOOR

LADY SAW

Marion 'Lady Saw' Hall is the most celebrated exponent of 'slackness' in Jamaican music history. As the first local woman performer to become a top billing main act and to write her own material, she is probably also reggae's most influential female artiste, kicking down the glass door for the likes of Macka Diamond, Tanya Stephens, Ce'cile and Queen Ifrica. Almost uniquely, Lady Saw is both a top notch 'riddim rider' deejay, and a highly accomplished singer. The acknowledged 'queen of dancehall' has in recent years moved away from 'slackness' and has even begun to appear at cultural shows under her real name Marion Hall.

Here she shares some insights on Jamaica and its music:

> What makes Jamaican music so popular around the world? I think it's because we produce music for all moods and emotions. Maybe it's because we Jamaicans are so in touch with our feelings and so direct about expressing them. But our music just seems to connect with people from all different backgrounds. I remember after a show in Switzerland how a lady came up to me crying and saying how my song 'I am not the world's most prettiest and I turned out fine' had touched her to the core, and how it summed up how she had always felt but never been able to express. Plus there's the beat of our music, it's the sweetest in the world. Even when people can't understand the lyrics they are just captivated by our riddims.

Music reflects society but it also influences it. I've had women come up to me and tell me how my songs like 'Hard Core' had taught them how to make their men happy in bed, and even had some tell me they lost their virginity to one of my songs. Now if it's adults saying that I have no problem and even feel good. But not if it is a young teenager. There's no doubt music lyrics can influence school children. Just look at the Gully and Gaza fights among our school boys. Yes young minds can be misled and should not be listening to some kinds of music that are okay for adults but not for them.

When I started out in the music business I did only clean songs – my first album was country and gospel. But I wasn't getting anywhere and saw these male artists having big dancehall hits with real slack songs. So I decided if you can't beat them join them. I don't know why I get so much criticism for doing as a woman what so many men were doing before me. But to be honest if they started to censor songs now because of the effect on school children, it wouldn't bother me. I know I can change to suit whatever is required by my audience. But when the audience demands hardcore and we give it to them, well you can't knock a man for eating food.

I don't know why Jamaicans like slackness so much and why we produce so many more hardcore songs than anywhere else. Maybe it's just our direct nature. We are not the type to go round and round and pretend. If is so it go, we going to say is so it go.

I've travelled all over and Jamaica to me is the most beautiful country in the world, and Jamaicans are the warmest people in the world. I just wish our governments could get the crime and violence under control. That is the thing really bothering me about this country. That and the high taxes – because we entertainers don't make as much as the government thinks we do!

DEEJAYS SPICE AND VYBZ KARTEL PERFORM THEIR CONTROVERSIAL SONG 'RAMPING SHOP'

RAMPING SHOP SLACKNESS: TRYING TO DRAW A LINE

Music is arguably the truest reflection of a nation's fundamental priorities, and this island has probably produced more sexually explicit recordings than the rest of the world combined, past and present. As an indication of how common such songs are, the December 17, 2008 Star Annual Music Readers' Picks included a 'Best Daggering Song' award, daggering being current slang for the sexual act. It's a category conceivable in few, if any other, countries.

Explicit songs – termed slackness in local slang – have always been part of Jamaican music. Planter-historian Bryan Edwards wrote that slave songs were 'fraught with obscene ribaldry' and accompanied with dances that were 'in the highest degree licentious and wanton'. While musicians were usually males, singers were often female. Lady Saw had nothing on this eighteenth century songstress!

> *Hipsaw! My deea! You no shake like a-me!*
> *You no wind like a-me! Go yonda!*
> *Hipsaw! My deea! You no jig like a-me!*
> *You no work him like a-me! You no sweet him like a-me!*
> – Moreton, (1793)

As for the 1930s duo Slim and Sam, our earliest named popular singers:

> Each song was also supposed to have a verse dealing with sex, which was not necessarily linked with the story, but was put in just the same…this was nothing new, because 'as far back as you look in folk music in this part of the world, you will find that there are some [sexual] overtones.

Mento tunes like 'All day all night Mary Ann, down by the seaside shifting sand', and 'The big bamboo stands up straight and tall, and the big bamboo pleases one and all' (orginally a Mighty Sparrow calypso) are still tourist staples – and you don't hear vistors complaining!

Ska and reggae continued the tradition. 'Tonight I'm going to wreck a p__ p__' sang Prince Buster to the tune of The Drummer Boy Christmas song. 'Dark like a dungeon, deep like a well, sweet as honey and nice no hell' crooned Scratch Perry, backed up by The Wailers, in Pussy Galore. The original conscious deejay U-Roy chanted 'Is Catty high, is catty low, will catty stand up to any blow?'

Though never heard on the radio, all were big sellers in their day, as were the famously obscene Lloyd and the Lowbite albums. Another banned underground hit of the early 1970s was 'Leggo Beast'. One hugely popular 1980s NFAP (Not Fit for Airplay) song went 'Soldering a wha de young gal want'.

Yet around 1990 risqué suggestiveness gave way to hardcore songs like 'Punany', 'Love Punany Bad', and 'Position'. It was Lady Saw who arguably broke down all barriers, with tunes such as 'Hard Core', 'Stab Up the Meat' and 'If Him Lef A Nuh My P____ Fault'. Musically and lyrically brilliant, these anthems of female sexual empowerment certainly could not be called sexist.

Since then, it's been just about anything goes in the dancehall. However an unwritten law still prevailed; slack songs were fine for adults in adult settings, but children were not supposed to hear them. What was not suitable for children, was not to be played on the radio, or in public spaces frequented by children.

Yet somewhere along the line this rule went out the window, and suddenly it seemed slackness was everywhere – blaring from bars, cars, buses and heard even at football matches. The sexually explicit songs were bad enough, but even worse were the macho gun-promoting songs that often seemed to endorse violence and murder. 'My war is like no other, when me done you have no sister and no brother' went a line from Mavado's 'Amazing Grace' song of praise to his gun.

Naturally many people, especially those with children, were not happy with this state of affairs, though somehow nobody seemed to be able to do anything about it. People began wondering if Jamaica had really become a truly 'anything goes' society with no limits at all, where the people would perhaps violently reject any attempt to rein in their right to do whatever they wanted whenever they wanted. Certainly this was the impression the hesitant authorities gave. No one seem willing or able to bell the cat.

Then, a firestorm of support was engendered by a newspaper column condemning a song called 'Ramping Shop', a duet where the female Spice entreated the male Vybz Kartel to 'Damage it fi spite…Send it up inna mi tripe'. Sensing an opening, the Media Broadcasting Commission jumped in to ban songs with explicit lyrics from airplay, and to crack down on suggestive dancing on television.

It's still not clear what the overall fallout has been. Many artistes have simply gone back to cutting cleaned up radio-friendly versions of 'Not Fit for Airplay' originals. Yet hard core slackness is still played not only in the dancehalls but on public transportation and roadside sound systems.

Still there is a general feeling that a much needed line has been drawn and a message has been sent that civilisation requires boundaries even in music.

STREET DANCES: URBAN FOLK CULTURE

BY DAVIA DAVIDSON

The sounds and fashions keep changing, but community based dances remain an integral part of Jamaican life, as they have been since time immemorial. Despite occasional crime upsurges and economic crises, their numbers keep growing, with street parties being held every night of the week.

Current ones include Passion Sundays, Early Mondays, Boasty Tuesdays, Weddi Weddi Wednesday 11:00 p.m. – 2:00 a.m., and then Passa Passa from 2:00 a.m. – 6:00 a.m., Bembe Thurdays and Dutty Fridaze, with late Friday and Saturday being club scene nights. It's a constantly shifting scene with new weekly sessions regularly popping up.

Despite the sometimes roughish locations, they are often frequented by uptowners. Not designed for tourist consumption, and with no cover charge, these are generally not money driven events. It's mostly just about enjoying music and dancing, a kind of urban folk culture.

From time to time, as with say Rae Town Sundays and Passa Passa Wednesdays, they catch the attention of an outside world searching for authentic experiences. The '15 minutes of fame' hype eventually dies down, and the 'flavour of the month' seeking spectators drift away. Yet the local beat goes on, and the constantly evolving dancehall scene keeps producing new rhythms and dances.

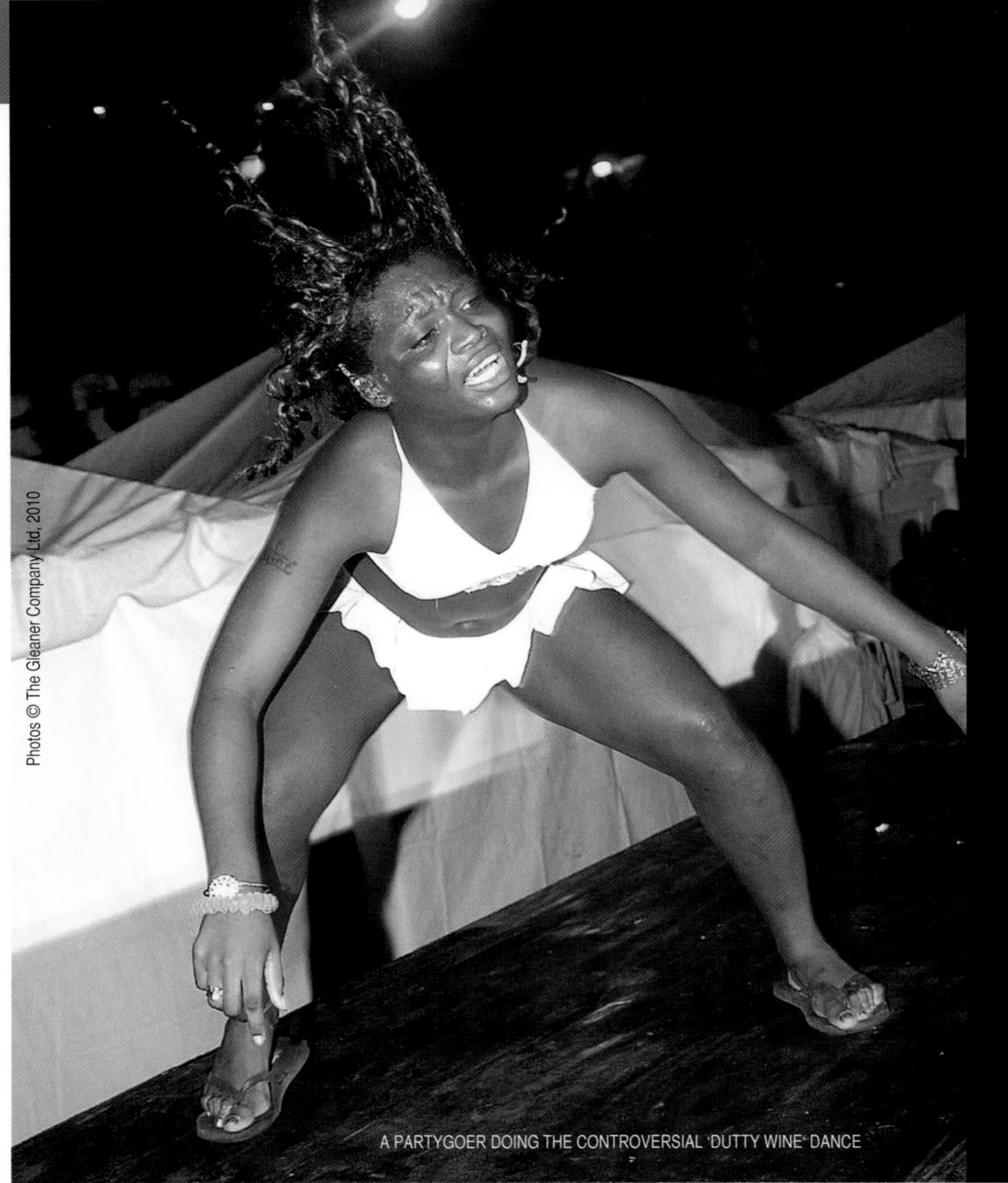

A PARTYGOER DOING THE CONTROVERSIAL 'DUTTY WINE' DANCE

Passa Passa, held in the West Kingston community of Tivoli Gardens every Wednesday night since 2003, was for a while arguably the greatest weekly street fest on earth.

In Jamaican vernacular 'passa passa' means mixed up complications and gossip (or suss). In the context of the party, it meant uptown meets downtown, well-off meets below the poverty line, and classy meets crass. It all combined into a high energy super session defined by pulsating rhythms, gyrating hips, coordinated moves in sync, and lots of skimpily dressed females. Passa Passa at its peak attracted thousands – including corporate heads, politicians, sports and media personalities – and made its audience feel part of a live music video.

Recognising its local and international appeal, businesses and the government jumped

on board. The 2008 'Emancipendence' grand gala parade included a Passa Passa float, featuring a giant doll in the pose of a woman dancing the 'Dutty Wine.'

Passa Passa DVDs were widely distributed overseas among the Jamaican diaspora and 'yardie wannabees,' making the local dancers and 'hot gal' profilers internationally known dancehall personalities in their own right.

The anything goes Passa Passa culture even spread abroad, not that it was welcomed everywhere. In 2006, Grenada's Education Minister called for a ban of Passa Passa parties, citing them as a contributor to the lewd behaviour of young women.

However, cultural evolution and political developments caused Passa Passa to gradually downsize, and it has more or less reverted to its community street dance roots.

One event that outgrew its roots and remains in the limelight, is the Dancehall Queen competition. Started in Montego Bay as local female dancers squaring off, it now attracts contestants from all over the world. Foreigners took the top three places in 2008, with the runner up being a Los Angeles attorney. The 'Jamaica Dance Hall Queen' competition has even been duplicated in Europe and North America.

How do they learn the latest dances? By watching street dance DVDs, logging on to the various dancehall dedicated websites, and coming to Jamaica to experience it 'live and direct.' The 2008 Beijing Olympics gave the island's street culture another massive boost, as a planet-wide audience of billions saw Usain Bolt and company celebrating their victories with dance moves like 'Nuh Linga,' 'Gully Creeper' and 'Tek Wey Yuhself.' In the lingo of the era, Jamaica to the world!

KEIVA (LEFT) AND JOHN HYPE (BOTTOM RIGHT) ARE TWO POPULAR DANCERS ON THE JAMAICAN DANCEHALL SCENE

Sports

GOOD AT MOST... GREAT AT SOME

As with most of the world, the most popular sport in Jamaica is what Americans refer to as soccer, but everyone else calls football. Drive anywhere in the country and you are sure to see a pickup game between young boys. Ask 'What was the most significant event to take place in the country in the 1990s', and many Jamaicans will answer 'Qualifying for the 1998 World Cup'. Sadly 'The Reggae Boyz', as the national team is known, have failed to make the finals since.

'JAMAICA IN BEIJING',
BARRINGTON WATSON PAINTING

...on a per capita basis Jamaica produces more top track performers than just about anywhere else

PREMIER LEAGUE FOOTBALL

The island's top competition, the Premier League, draws sizeable crowds on Sundays. Even more ardently followed are the schoolboy competitions, the Manning Cup in the corporate area and the Dacosta Cup in the rest of the island. Jamaica held the record as the smallest and least populous country ever to make it to the World Cup finals, until our Trinidadian cousins qualified in 2006. The island's best known 'ballers' over the years include Lindy Delapena, Alan 'Skill' Cole, Paul 'Tegat' Davis, Theodore 'Tappa' Whitmore, and Ricardo 'Bibby' Gardner. Yet curiously for a land that abounds in gifted athletes, no footballer produced here has made any significant impact on the world stage.

The same could not be said for track and field athletics, where on a per capita basis Jamaica produces more top performers than just about anywhere else. The list of Olympic champions past and present includes Arthur Wint, George Rhoden, Donald Quarrie, Deon Hemmings, Veronica Campbell, Usain Bolt, Shelly-Ann Fraser and Melaine Walker. Herb McKenley too was one of the best of his time. The legendary Merlene Ottey was also the most durable sprinter in history, reaching the finals in every Olympics from 1980 to 2000.

Two of the fastest men that ever lived are Jamaicans, with Asafa Powell recording the present third best 100 metres time of 9.74 seconds in 2008, and Usain Bolt setting the world record of 9.58 in 2009. Bolt also holds the 200 metres world record and has strong claims to being the greatest male sprinter of all time. These feats are especially satisfying since, unlike the mostly US-based stars of the past, Bolt and Powell are wholly home-grown and coached.

The font of all this success is the Boys' and Girls' High School Championships. In terms of attendance and atmosphere – 35,000 or so youngsters and oldsters ecstatically cheering on their alma maters – 'Champs' is one of the world's great annual track meets.

Jamaican athletics has come a long way, going from no gold medals in the 1966 Kingston

1998: THE REGGAE BOYZ

Commonwealth Games, to winning every track event under 400 metres in the 2006 Melbourne Commonwealth Games. At the 2008 Olympics, Jamaica won the men's 100 and 200 metres, all three medals in the women's 100 metres, gold and bronze in the women's 200 metres, the men's 4x100 relay in a world record time, and was well ahead in the women's 4x100 relay when the baton was dropped. After doing even better in the 2009 Berlin World Athletic Championships we are now officially the fastest country on earth.

The nation's unprecedented success in Bejing naturally excited the entire nation. Tens of thousands gathered to watch the proceedings on big screens at Half Way Tree. The sense of unity perhaps surpassed even the 1998 Reggae Boyz World Cup success. The victories of inner city denizens Shelly-Ann Fraser and Melaine Walker had a heightened significance, even inspiring peace marches in some troubled ghettos. Whether this Olympic euphoria can be transformed into a long-term change agent remains to be seen.

Jamaican athletics has come a long way, going from no gold medals in the 1966 Kingston Commonwealth Games, to winning every track event under 400 metres in the 2006 Melbourne Commonwealth Games

HERB MCKENLEY

Take away proven drug cheats like Marion Jones...not to mention Florence Griffith-Joyner of the untouchable world records...Jamaica would most likely have won many more Olympic medals over the past three decades.

THE FASTEST COUNTRY ON EARTH

It was the kind of scene that takes place everyday in Jamaica. A bunch of guys race across a field, one pulls away from the pack, holds out his hands in triumph, and slaps his chest in glee shouting 'A me dat!' Then he celebrates by dropping a few dance moves to the reggae music that's always pounding in the background somewhere. Except this time it happened in front of 91,000 roaring spectators and probably the largest television audience in history at the 2008 Bejing Olympics.

Of course Usain Bolt's record 100 metres run was not our only moment in the sun at Bejing. Shelly-Ann Fraser won the women's 100 metres, with Kerron Stewart and Sherone Simpson dead heating for second. Melaine Walker won the women's 400 metres hurdles. Bolt broke Michael Johnson's hithero untouchable world record in the men's 200 metres. Veronica Cambell-Brown and Kerron Stewart went 1–3 in the women's 200 metres. Bolt, Nesta Carter, Michael Frater, and Asafa Powell set a world record in the men's 4x100 relay. No country won more gold medals per capita.

The Olympic Games are a marvelous testimony to human adaptability. Though all originated in Africa, clearly some parts of the earth have produced bodies particularly suited for certain disciplines. Sprinting is dominated by those of West African descent, distance running by East Africans, and throwing events – like the discus, javelin, hammer and shot put – by Nordic and Eastern Europeans.

No doubt these are the results of culture, habitat, climate and countless other factors interacting over centuries. Yet on a simplistic level, is it far-fetched to suppose that yam-eating West Africans became fast by chasing down antelopes and outrunning lions on low level plains? Or that milk-drinking East African hill nomads developed stamina to keep up with herds over long distances at high altitudes? Or that war-loving, meat-eating Vikings from snowy climes came to excel at throwing spears and heavy objects at enemies?

Far from being proof of inherent genetic capabilities, all this argues for the infinite malleability of human beings. Over time we adjust to every situation. Could their terrified victims ever have dreamt that bloodthirsty Vikings would over a few centuries morph

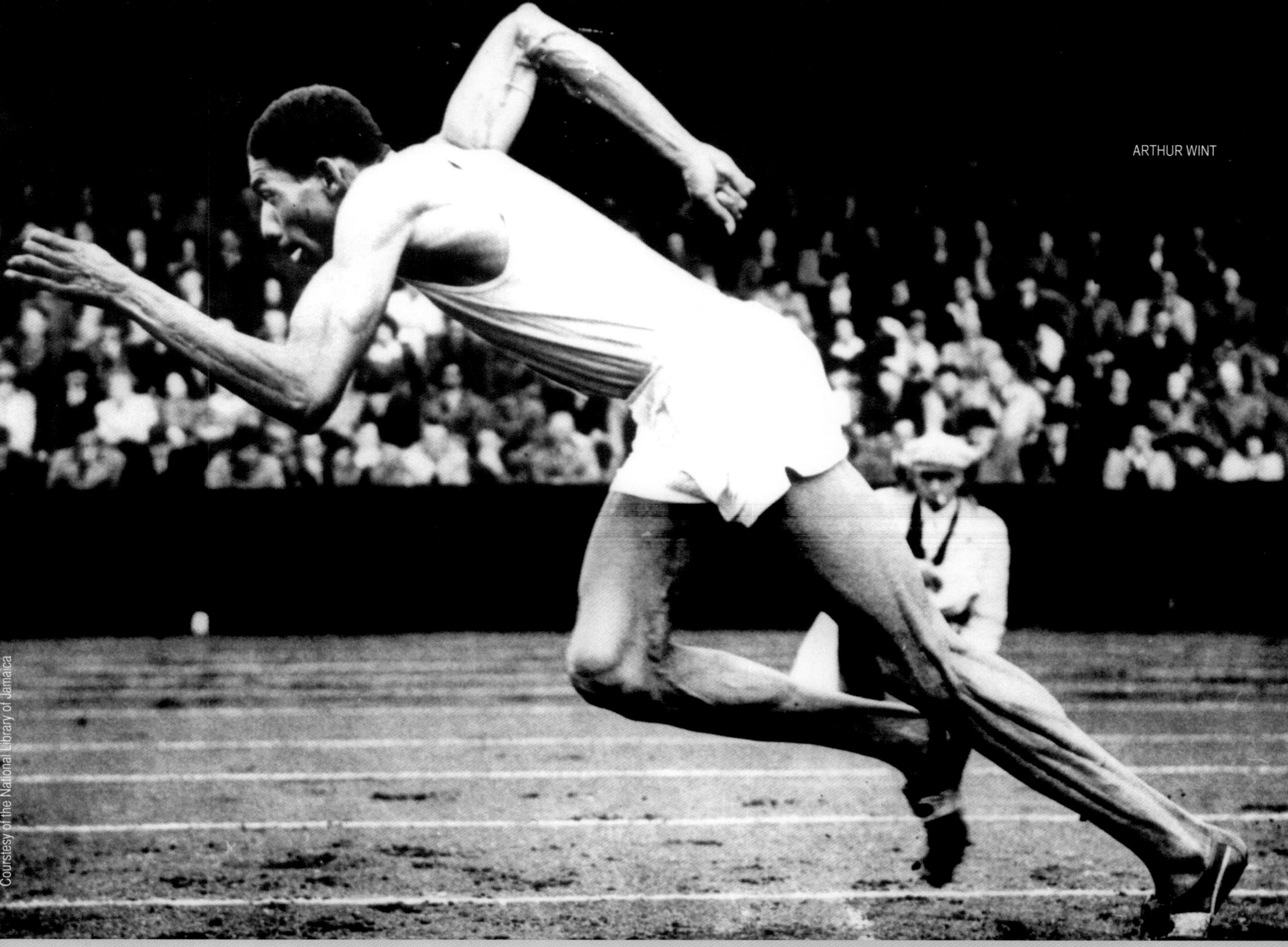
ARTHUR WINT

Courstesy of the National Library of Jamaica

into peace loving Swedes and Danes? Only the historically ignorant believe in permanent racial characteristics.

So what makes Jamaica the fastest country on earth? No one knows for sure. However, the 'It's all in the West African fast twitch muscle genes' argument does not compute. Maybe 350 million persons alive are West African, or of predominantly West African descent. Only 2.7 million, or less than one per cent, live here. Yet Jamaica won more gold sprint medals in Beijing 2008 than everywhere else put together.

Trelawny yam and dasheen are possible factors, but the crucial components may be tradition and expertise because Jamaica probably has the world's most vibrant track and field culture, and some of its finest coaches. Nowhere else are high school athletes national celebrities. Usain Bolt was a household name long before he competed abroad.

Elsewhere, the only dream of glory for youngsters who like to run fast are the Olympics – which to young minds can seem an out of reach fantasy. In Jamaica, every primary school sports day winner imagines themselves a star at the annual Boys' and Girls' High School Athletic Championships. The infrastructure built up around 'Champs' – Western and Eastern and Central and parish Champs and such – means Jamaica likely has a higher percentage of its population in ordered track and field programmes than anywhere else.

Most runners in other countries never see big crowds until they hit the international stage. Yet teenage Jamaicans run in front of passionate 30,000 strong crowds, which develops mental

Jamaica won more gold sprint medals in 2008 than everywhere else put together.
251

USAIN BOLT

ASAFA POWELL

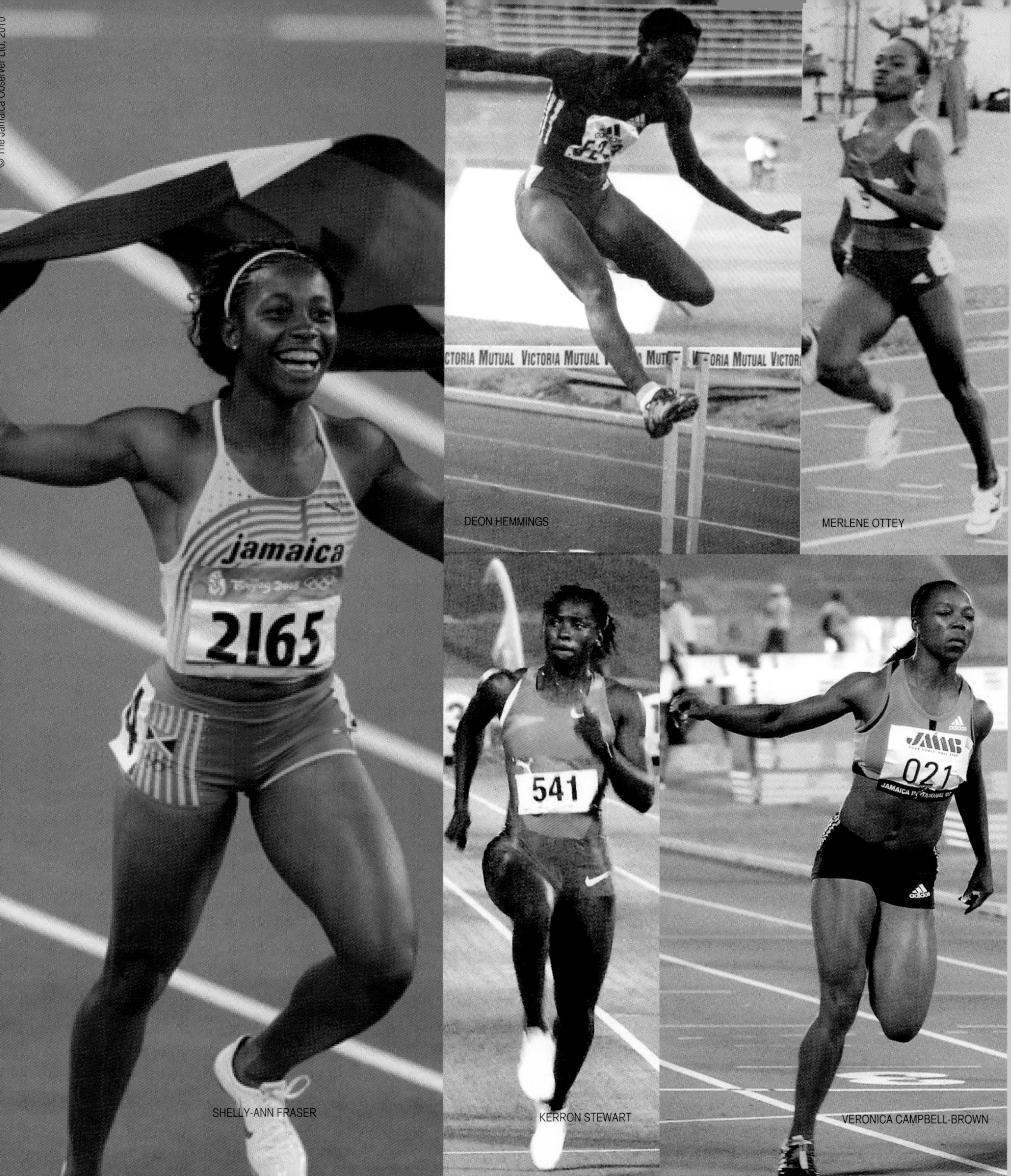

DEON HEMMINGS

MERLENE OTTEY

SHELLY-ANN FRASER

KERRON STEWART

VERONICA CAMPBELL-BROWN

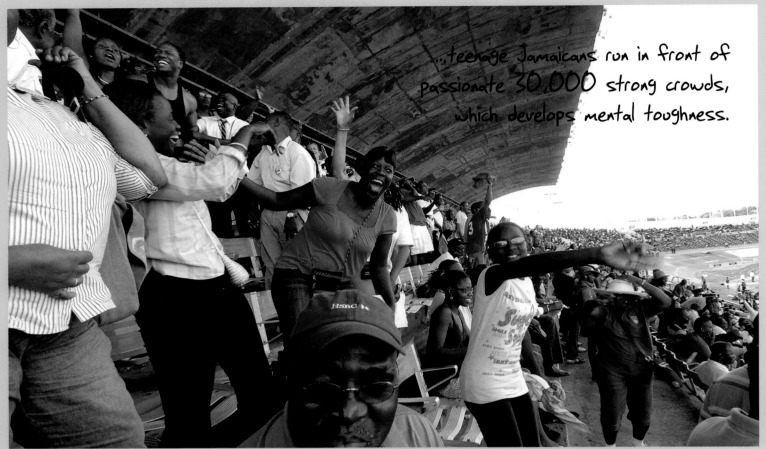

...teenage Jamaicans run in front of passionate 30,000 strong crowds, which develops mental toughness.

SPECTATORS ABOVE AND BELOW CHEER ON THEIR FAVOURITE HIGH SCHOOLS

toughness. Still, 'Champs' has been around for decades, so why was 2008 the first time Jamaica won either the men's or women's 100 metres, much less both? The answer may lie in drugs and coaches.

The Balco scandal levelled the playing field for poorer nations. Take away proven drug cheats like Marion Jones, Tim Montgomery and Justin Gatlin – not to mention Florence Griffith-Joyner of the untouchable world records plus other suspects never caught – and Jamaica would most likely have won many more Olympic medals over the past three decades.

Yet the biggest factor in moving Jamaica from track and field prominence to dominance might be coaching. For Jamaican-born sprinters

have been doing well for years, but for other countries. Locally-born Ben Johnson, Lynford Christie, and Donovan Bailey actually finished first in three consecutive Olympics from 1988 to 1996 (though Johnson was disqualified for a positive drug test), but they ran for Canada and Britain.

The difference now is that the innate talent is being properly harnessed at home. Stephen Francis, whose charges won two gold and three silver individual medals in Bejing, is perhaps the world's best all-round track and field coach. Glen Mills, who trained Usain Bolt to an unprecedented three Olympic world records, may be the best sprint coach. People like Maurice Wilson are rapidly moving up into their class. Coaches like these, allied with the University of Technology (UTech) and GC Foster athletic programmes, convinced Jamaican athletes they did not have to train abroad to succeed. The results are there for the world to see.

So it's not just raw ability and enthusiasm that has taken Jamaican track to the top, but applied technical knowledge and intelligent hard work. A nation that can make it at the Olympics, the biggest international event on earth, can surely make it anywhere it puts its mind to.

TREVOR BERBICK

Another great spectator favourite is horse racing. Meets are held on Saturdays and most Wednesdays, and off-track betting shops abound. A visit to Caymanas Park is a true study in fever pitch excitement as spectators roar on their choices down the stretch. It may not be Ascot or Belmont, but the fervour of Jamaican racing fans is unsurpassed, with champions like 'None Such', 'Legal Light' and 'Miracle Man' having passed into local folklore.

Basketball has gained considerable popularity among young males over the past decade. Though the craze has tapered off a bit since Michael Jordan retired, in terms of participation it's now one of the top three games among boys. The most popular sport among women is a relative of basketball called netball, which is played mostly in Commonwealth countries. Here Jamaica usually vies for world supremacy with Australia, New Zealand and England.

Jamaica also has a great tradition in boxing, with Mike McCallum, Trevor Berbick and Glen Johnson all winning world crowns. Though not technically born on the rock, legendary

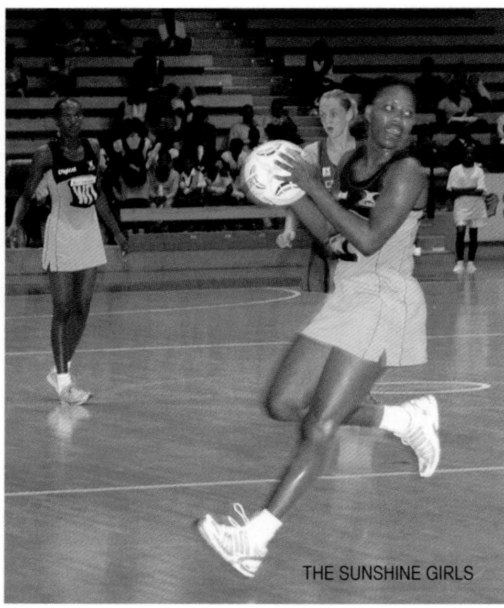
THE SUNSHINE GIRLS

heavyweight champ Lennox Lewis had Jamaican parents and now lives here, which makes him an honorary yardie in most eyes.

In the late 1980s, the Americans George B. Fitch and William Maloney witnessed a local Jamaican pushcart derby and realised that it was very similar to bobsledding. One thing, or drink, led to another, and the Jamaican Bobsled team was formed. They debuted disastrously at the 1988 Calgary Winter Olympics, crashing and overturning, but four black men from a snow-free country careening around the ice caused a media sensation, and inspired the 'loosely based on reality' 1993 movie *Cool Runnings*. Jamaica Bobsled returned to the 1992 Albertville Winter Olympics and stunned critics by finishing fourteenth, ahead of the US, Russia, France and Italy. The two-man team finished tenth, beating Sweden. In 2000 the Jamaicans won the gold medal at the World Push Bobsled Championships, but they failed to qualify for Turin 2006.

The sport that continually arouses the deepest emotions is cricket, with names like George Headley, Lawrence Rowe, Michael Holding, and

CHRIS GAYLE

Courtney Walsh continuing to echo down the years. Forty years ago cricket was like football today, tops in spectators and participants. Yet its extra dimensions made it truly 'more than a game'.

Though some are thousands of miles apart, Britain considered its English-speaking Caribbean territories a single entity. Hence the national cricket team was not Jamaica but the West Indies, encompassing Jamaica, Trinidad, Guyana, Barbados, Dominica, Grenada, St Lucia, St Vincent and The Grenadines, Anguilla, Antigua and Barbuda, Montserrat, St Kitts and Nevis, St Maarten and the Virgin Islands.

Its cricket team became the public embodiment of this identity. In Sir Frank Worrell's words, 'Only cricket unites the West Indies. To us it is more than just a game, it is a way of life.' As C.L.R. James wrote in: 'What do they know of cricket who only cricket know? West Indians crowding to Tests bring with them the whole past history and future hopes of the islands.' The region not only found its collective self in the sport, but played in a manner that defined the West Indian character – flamboyant, daring, and exuberant.

With its former territories now independent nations, only in cricket is 'West Indies' any more than a vaguely misleading geographic notion. Intellectuals interact to an extent through the University of the West Indies, and CARICOM brings politicians in regular contact. Yet the common man's only real interest in the wider Caribbean is cricket. Few Jamaicans can name the prime minister of Trinidad, Barbados, Antigua or Guyana. Yet they revere Brian Lara, Sir Garfield Sobers, Sir Viv Richards and Shiv Chanderpaul. The West Indies captaincy, currently held by Jamaican Chris Gayle, is still perhaps the region's most iconic position.

Cricket lovers may exaggerate the importance of this 'West Indian' identity; we're only talking about five million people after all.

COURTNEY WALSH

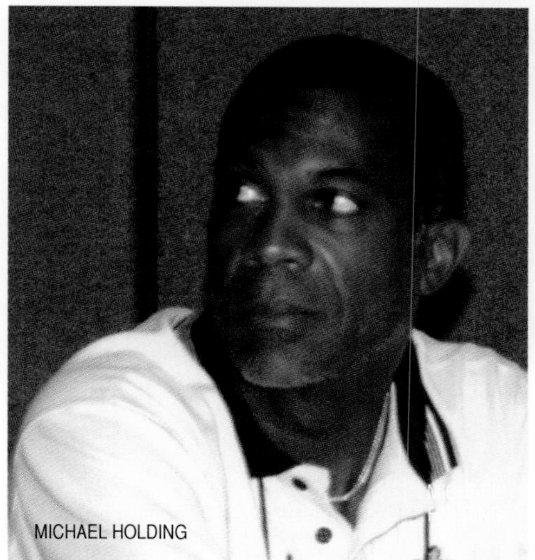

MICHAEL HOLDING

Still, anything that peacefully binds together otherwise far-flung nations, must be a force for good. It's a curious thing, 'Westindianness'. When the Trinidad and Jamaica football teams face off, fans taunt each other and abuse opposing players. Put those same spectators together to watch the West Indies, and they hug each other with joy at each West Indian triumph, no matter if it was Yardies or Trinis or Bajans responsible.

At the 2009 20/20 World Cup, the West Indian equivalent of 'God Save the Queen' and 'Advance Australia Fair' was David Rudder's 'Rally Round the West Indies'. So there was the intriguing spectacle of players singing along to the 'national' anthem of an imagined country that exists only in the minds of cricket fans – 'Rally, rally round the West Indies/ now and forever…/ pretty soon the runs are going to flow like water/ bringing so much joy to every son and daughter.'

Cricket has also mirrored the region's political development. In the socially stratified early twentieth century, the cricket field was the only arena in which different races interacted on level footing. A four was four, and a wicket a wicket, whether by white, black or Indian. When West Indies played England in 1928, it was the first time colonial underlings and imperial overlords

What do they know of cricket who only cricket know? West Indians crowding to Tests bring with them the whole past history and future hopes of the islands.

– C.L.R. James

faced each other as equals. The 1930 victory over England was a landmark that stretched, in C.L.R. James's famous phrase, 'Beyond a Boundary'.

The great George Headley was a notable regional symbol of pride, and black pride in particular. For like all aspects of British colonial life, cricket was racially segmented. Until the black-based Lucas cricket club was formed in 1898, cricket in Jamaica was an exclusively white affair, and it continued to be light skin-dominated. So when the black Headley proved himself one of the world's greatest batsmen in the early 1930s, it was more than just a sporting matter to a people yearning for someone to symbolise their aspirations. It upended the unspoken myth of British superiority and West Indian inferiority – if a black man could excel against whites in cricket, why not in other areas?

Cricket was thus an integral component of the emerging national consciousness. On Saturdays the urban masses went to Lucas Oval to see their hero Headley bat, and on Sundays they visited Edelweiss Park to be culturally entertained and hear Marcus Garvey speak. Some contend that Headley, the first black Jamaican to excel in international competition, inspired Edna Manley's 1935 landmark carving 'Negro Aroused'. Sir Frank Worrell played a similar role 25 years later as the first black West Indies captain. His successful leadership of the team in 1961 was arguably the final confirmation to Britain that its West Indian territories were ready for self-government.

STATUE OF GEORGE HEADLEY AT SABINA PARK

As globalisation alters the Jamaican and West Indian way of life, cricket continues to reflect social change in real time. One fundamental development was the early 1990s media liberalisation that made dozens of American cable channels available. Many wondered if modern schoolboys, flooded with instant gratification games like football and basketball, were losing the concentration and patience required for cricket. Perhaps not coincidentally, in 1994 the once dominant West Indies team lost a test series for the first time in almost 15 years, and then started to get beaten with depressing regularity.

At the same time, traditional five day test matches began to be marginalised by 50 over one day internationals and, recently, 20/20. Tests are still regarded as the sport's highest level. Yet few have five days to spend on anything in our rushed twenty-first century. So the shorter the form, the bigger the crowds and gate receipts. In a way tests, 50 overs, and 20/20 are like novels, movies and TV comedies. Profundity doesn't equal profit, nor vice versa.

Cricket has made a comeback of sorts. More games on local TV and better organisation in schools are unearthing promising young players like fast bowler Jerome Taylor. The shortened 20 over version, particularly the big money on offer in the Indian Premier League, also rekindled interest among boys. You now see more frequent roadside games, and the SDF national community 20/20 league draws big crowds.

So while many lament cricket's death, others see a renaissance around the corner. Some now view West Indies matches not as mere sporting contests, but as an interactive theatre where cultural shifts and clashes are being played out live. Every victory or outstanding achievement is a heartening glimmer of hope. Every humiliating defeat feels like another nail in the coffin of the sport and the West Indian idea.

A ball game may be a slender thing on which to base regional unity, but it's all West Indians have. What happens to a culture when its strongest unifying force dies? The English-speaking Caribbean wonders if it's in the process of finding out.

A DAY AT SABINA PARK

Connoisseurs say they love cricket because it presents a broader stage for drama, allows a greater canvas for artistic expression, and encompasses a wider range of emotions than any other outdoor game. To them cricket in its finer moments transcends sport, and enters the aesthetic realm, becoming not so much a game as an art form, where good strokeplay is analysed for correctness of form and virtuosity of performance.

Its language, incomparably the most varied in sport, reflects this. Beautiful, glorious, elegant, magnificent, graceful, delicate – such words might seem embarrassingly out of place in other games, but are a natural part of a cricket commentator's repertoire. Is there a more evocative phrase in sport than 'cricket, lovely cricket'?

Well maybe; but perhaps West Indians love cricket because it creates so many possibilities for them to indulge in their favourite pastime, namely carrying on excited, top of the voice discussions. For to attend an international match in the West Indies is to partake in a continuous group conversation, where everyone is not only permitted but encouraged to join in.

Nowhere is the inimitable West Indian approach to life so vividly expressed, for here is a gloriously uninhibited theatre of passion, laughter and national pride. This is the expansive good nature of the Caribbean at its best, with all visitors being instinctively welcomed as guests invited to share in the fun.

The chance to savour the moment sets cricket apart from other sports. Its measured tempo not only allows every beautiful stroke to be fully discussed and digested, but invites almost conscious participation as great innings and matches unfold ball by ball.

Naturally cricket fans are mainly caught up in the moment, cheering when West Indians make runs or take wickets, and despairing when the opposing team does. Yet the pause after every ball allows the action on field to be analysed and dissected in a unique way. It's not enough that

Lucky shot bwoy! Drive big man! The idiot give way him wicket!

a boundary was scored or a wicket was taken, its quality must be judged. So you hear shouts of 'Lucky shot bwoy'! or 'Classic cover drive big man!' or 'What a rhatid yorker!' or 'The idiot give way him wicket!'

A particularly beautiful stroke will elicit comparative superlatives. 'Look on that beautiful late cut man. Nobody ever play that shot like Brian Lara!' 'You crazy? Him is no portion of Lawrence Rowe!' 'Gary Sobers was better than both of them!' The jokes fly thick and fast. 'De man running from de ball so much him soon knock down the square leg umpire!' While the slower moments allow dreamy trips down memory lane as fans reminisce about great matches, such as Brisbane in 1960, Lord's in 1963, Adelaide in 1993, Sabina and Kensington in 1999, Antigua in 2003.

Jamaica being such a musical place, every action is greeted with an appropriate song from the ubiquitous sound system. Naturally a carnival-like atmosphere prevails when the West Indies are going well: men stand up and cheer, women dance and gyrate. When the Windies are down, as has been too often the case of late, the fans sink for a while into a gloomy depression. Yet in that irrepressible Caribbean way, gallows humour soon breaks out. When the West Indies were humiliatingly bowled out by England for a record low 47 in 2004, the crowd broke into choruses of 'Rock of ages' and 'No grave can hold my body down!'

Many of those watching cricket from the all-inclusive Mound, where you eat and drink all you want, will not even be aware of the score. Nubile, suntanning young women, endless supplies of Red Stripe beer and Appleton rum, and loud continuous music, all make it mighty hard to keep track of what is going on. Even after the 2004 disaster the crowd stayed on to party, causing a visiting Englishman to exclaim 'My God, imagine how they would have gone on if they had won!'

It's an atmosphere that's hard to beat, and when the Windies win, there's no happier place on the globe. In 2009 the West Indies gained revenge by dismissing England for 51, yet 70-year-old English visitor John Beckett had the time of his life. In his words 'You know, I have been to lots of places, almost everywhere really, and I have never enjoyed myself as much as I have over the past two days. I simply can't say enough about the warmth and generosity and humour of you Jamaicans. I can't wait to return.'

Including every possible mixture of black, white, yellow and brown, the mound crowd is about as perfect an example of racial harmony as can be found on the planet. It's this camaraderie of fans that is the most beautiful thing about the most beautiful game. Win, lose or draw, the spirit of cricket requires spectators to applaud excellent play, whether by their team or its opponents. Visitors are lightheartedly teased when their team is down and congratulated when on top.

Tears may be shed when the Windies lose, but except for the occasional self-inflicted bout of alcohol poisoning, visiting fans never fear for their safety. The best of outdoor games, yes. Yet still, thank God, but a sport.

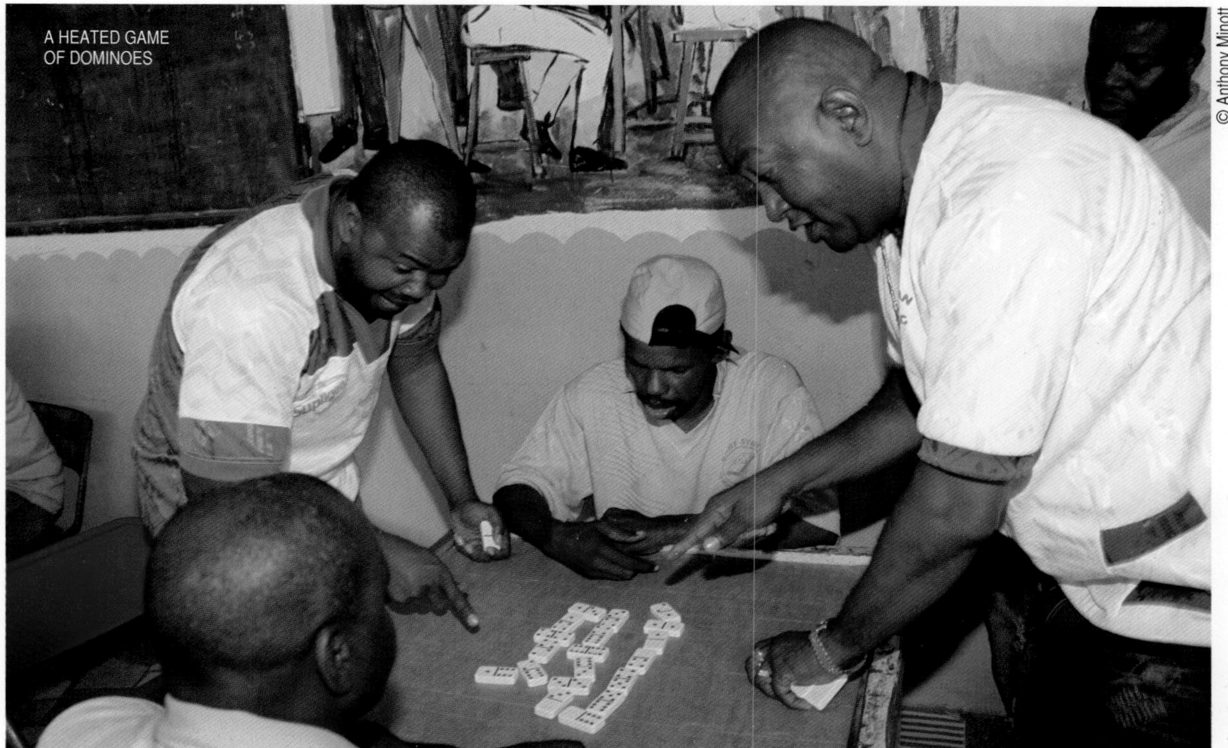

A HEATED GAME OF DOMINOES

© Anthony Minott

KNOCKING BONES

Walk anywhere in Jamaica and you sooner or later hear a series of sharp knocks of bone on wood interspersed by loud shouts, angry swearing and howls of laughter. Yes, it's that most ubiquitous of Jamaican male pastimes, a domino game. Though in many parts of the world a game for children, dominoes is in Jamaica perhaps the primary mode of male bonding. Jamaican men are notoriously homophobic, and regard any kind of public affection for other males as unnatural. Yet here domino games are always played between two pairs, and to many men their trusted domino partner, or 'pardy', is closer than blood.

Jamaican partner dominoes is played with 28 tiles ranging from the double six to the double blank. At the beginning of every match the tiles are vigorously shuffled and each person draws seven cards. Whoever disposes of all his cards first, wins the game for his team, with the first team to six games winning the rubber. The ultimate victory, or the most humiliating defeat, is a 'six love'.

The partner aspect gives it some similarity to bridge, and a domino world championship is staged in Jamaica every year with hundreds of entrants from all over the world. The best domino players are reckoned to be firemen, who reputedly do nothing between alarms but 'knock bones'.

What distinguishes Jamaican dominoes is, above all, the completely full rein given to emotions. Here is the most theatrical of table games. Not for Jamaicans the almost robotic focus of mah jong, the silent reserve of bridge and chess, or the serious intensity of poker. Domino onlookers usually give a non-stop commentary, respectfully saluting masterful strategic plays and mercilessly mocking egregious blunders.

Almost every play brings forth either the disappointed kissing of teeth, braggadocio warnings of doom, scornfully derisive laughter, the resigned silence of defeat, or ecstatic shouts of victory. The crowning glory is to 'bow' your hand in a series of thunderous slams. The pardys will then rise in triumph, pound the table in jubilation, and down a 'whites' or Red Stripe to celebrate. The bones are shuffled, and the drama begins again.

Revivalists' outsized exuberance and distinctive music has given them great cultural prominence.

Religion

SERIOUS BUSINESS

...the Jamaican outlook on life is remarkably celebratory...A common Jamaican reply to 'How are things?' is 'We giving thanks'.

Winter adds depth and darkness to life as well as to literature and in the unending summer of the tropics not even poverty or poetry seems capable of being profound because the nature around it is so exultant, so resolutely ecstatic, like its music. A culture based on joy is bound to be shallow.

– Derek Walcott

The West Indies is an unfinished society. It is incapable of producing anything important.

– V.S. Naipaul

Even from the limited view that judges life by western books, these West Indian Laureates have proven themselves wrong. Two Nobel Literature winners in a decade is pretty strong proof that this tiny region can create something others regard as possessing depth. The voices that won them acclaim are certainly West Indian products.

How much more absurd then are such views from any perspective extending beyond European literature. For no human beings have experienced life in such unsentimental reality, as the slaves forcibly transported from African homelands and worn out like beasts on sugar plantations.

Toiling under whips 'all day long in the burning sun' left little opportunity to reflect on books. Yet even when their freed descendants later learned to read, how could they take seriously any talk of 'ennobling art'? Did the culture that worked to death fellow human beings by the millions not also venerate Leonardo, Shakespeare and Mozart?

Deprived of any sense of societal continuity or individual significance, surely only a belief in a higher world to come kept plantation slaves from committing suicide en masse. Torn from language and culture, denied all familial ties and driven to death like nameless beasts – could there be more conclusive proof of the fundamental meaninglessness of life on earth? No people have been so brutally confronted with ultimate profundities. Theirs was and is no shallow joy, but a hard won philosophy of existence forged from the depths of blood, sweat and tears.

Despite such ancestral memories in the marrow, the Jamaican outlook on life is remarkably celebratory. The Buddhist or Hindu view of all life as suffering to which non-existence should be preferred, has no place here. Rather there is an almost universal sense of awe and gratitude that anything exists rather than nothing and that so much of what does exist is so wonderful. A common Jamaican reply to 'How are things?' is 'We giving thanks'.

The general religious mindset seems increasingly less Old Testament 'Thou shalt not' and more Sermon on the Mount 'Do unto others'. Certainly no pastor here is going to win any great following with 'Those who fornicate shall burn in hell!' sermons. Both preachers and congregations much prefer 'Do good and good will follow you' lessons.

Dostoevsky once wrote that 'For the secret of man's being is not only to live…but to live for something definite.' Having perhaps the most churches per square mile on earth, may or may not be a blessing, but a general unquestioning belief in a benevolent deity has left Jamaicans pretty free of existential anxiety.

Most Jamaicans are still inclined to view the Bible as the only book that really matters. Who can blame them, when it was for so long their only source of solace amidst unimaginable suffering? Even today virtually every household has a children's Bible from which stories are read at bedtime and many babies sleep with the Holy Scripture above their pillow. Most Jamaicans have an intimate familiarity with the Gospels and they often indulge in informal scripture quoting contests. A popular television show called 'Religious Hardtalk' is described by host Ian Boyne as 'arguing about the Bible'.

Completely secular events are rare here. The National Anthem 'Eternal Father Bless Our Land' is essentially a prayer and nearly every official function has a religious start. The swearing in of prime ministers begins and ends in prayer.

Even on the hardest core dancehall shows, artistes will admonish the crowd to 'Give thanks to the most high!' Most top dancehall and reggae artistes have released gospel-themed songs. In fact, many recently past big names like Papa San and Lt Stitchie have 'converted' and now deal only with 'Christian' lyrics.

In 2004 the song 'Hear My Cry O Lord' by the middle-aged Marvia Providence swept the dancehalls and inspired the 'Bun Bad Mind' response on the same rhythm by deejay Elephant Man. On dancehall night at Sumfest in front of the year's biggest music crowd, their combination on stage had even 'badman' fans 'praising the Lord' ecstatically. It was a living colour example of the extent to which religion is naturally integrated into everyday Jamaican life.

Out of Many, More

The Zemi religion died with the Tainos. So the oldest surviving faith here is Roman Catholicism brought by the Spanish, though the British made Anglicanism the state religion until 1872. Unlike nearby Catholic countries, where slaves were automatically baptised on arrival, Protestant West Indian planters were not concerned with what their slaves believed. So West African spiritual practices persisted and still survive in Myalism and Obeah.

As far back as 1660 King Charles II had decreed that British plantations should provide slaves with a Christian education. This had been loudly rejected by colonial slave owners. The Bible contained many stories of enslaved people rising up to gain freedom. Those who read them might start to think as well as obey – and so it eventually proved.

The American Revolution brought several hundred British Empire loyalists to the West Indies. Among them was the freedman George Liele, the first ordained black preacher in the US *and* founder of its first black Baptist churches. When the American War of Independence ended in 1783, he sailed to Jamaica rather than risk re-enslavement for his pro-British sympathies. He began preaching at Race Course in Kingston, gradually reached into the neighbouring canefields, eventually witnessing islandwide. In 1790 he built Jamaica's first Baptist Church at the corner of Victoria Avenue and Elletson Road, where he baptised 500 souls. It left him in such debt that he was jailed for over three years. He continued to suffer persecution of all sorts, including imprisonment for sedition, but evangelised and organised tirelessly until his death in 1828.

In 1813 one of Liele's converts named Moses Baker, appealed to the Baptist Missionary Society in England for support. John Rowe, the first English missionary, arrived the next year. Later came the indefatigable trio of Thomas Burnell, James Phillips and William Knibb. The general religious revival in Britain brought a number of other non-conformist (non-Anglican) missionaries to Jamaica, including Wesleyan Methodists, Presbyterians and Moravians.

Missionaries were generally the first whites to treat slaves like fellow human beings. They also preached a revolutionary doctrine that stressed the equality of all before the Heavenly Father and transferred 'ownership' from master to God. They constantly cited Galatians 3:28, 'There is neither Jew nor Greek, there is neither bond nor free, there is neither male nor female: for ye are all one in Christ Jesus.' The concept of emancipation was not explicitly expounded, yet the ideal of universal Christian brotherhood contradicted every tenet of slavery.

The dissenting missions gave freed blacks and coloureds an arena for self-expression and exercising responsibility, things hitherto absent from their political life. The passionate preaching and hymn singing were also new outlets of self-expression. Most slaves' first exposure to literature were Bible stories, which provided them with heroes they could identify with, such as 'David versus Goliath' and 'Daniel in the Lions' Den'. Here was spiritual, mental and emotional emancipation.

Fearing that Christianity would teach slaves to consider themselves human beings with rights, the governing Assembly tried to stifle the movement. Unqualified preachers were prohibited and slave gatherings between sunrise and sunset were banned. Planters blamed missionaries for the 1831 slave revolt and in January 1832 created the Colonial Church Union. In theory formed to protect the Anglican Church, its real objective was to defend slavery by forcing non-conformist congregations to disband. Mobs of prominent white men and their hirelings burnt down churches, arrested missionaries on trumped up charges, attacked their families and persecuted their followers. Seventeen chapels had been destroyed by early 1832.

This union was only broken in May 1833, when the new Governor, the Earl of Mulgrave, personally cashiered militia officers active in the movement. Ironically the CCU might have accelerated the emancipation progress, for the besieged missionaries dispatched William Knibb to Britain to lobby on their behalf. His vivid first-hand accounts of the outrages perpetuated against slaves and missionaries, fuelled the anti-slavery flame.

Fearing that Christianity would teach slaves to consider themselves human beings with rights, the governing Assembly tried to stifle the movement. Unqualified preachers were prohibited and slave gatherings between sunrise and sunset were banned.

WILLIAM KNIBB

UNACKNOWLEDGED NATIONAL HERO?

When the white English missionary William Knibb was posthumously awarded the Order of Merit in 1988, Devon Dick (author of the 1985 paper 'William Knibb: A National Hero?') wrote:

> He was for the black man and had great faith in the untapped resources of the negroes. No other person of his era demonstrated such faith in the prowess of the black people.
> For Knibb's work as Liberator of the slaves;
> For his work in laying the foundation of Nationhood;
> For his support of black people and things indigenous;
> For his display of great courage against tremendous odds;
> For being an inspiration then and now.

Knibb came to Jamaica in 1824 to replace his deceased brother as a missionary-schoolmaster. He became slavery's most uncompromising enemy.

> The cursed blast of slavery has, like a pestilence, withered almost every moral bloom. I know not how any person can feel a union with such a monster, such a child of hell. I feel a burning hatred against it and look upon it as one of the most odious monsters that ever disgraced the earth.

He made many enemies among slave owners and was placed under armed guard during the 1831 Sam Sharpe Rebellion. The 'Colonial Church Union' burnt down his Falmouth chapel, plotted to murder him and stoned his home. Under siege, the Baptists sent Knibb to Britain to report first-hand the situation in Jamaica. According to Devon Dick:

> To mobilise the entire British populace against

Courtesy of the National Library of Jamaica

slavery was a daunting task because the anti-slavery feeling was not widely diffused or intense in Britain. It was the pastime of idealists. To achieve his aim, Knibb travelled in five months six thousand miles, in the process attending 154 public services and addressing 200,000 people throughout Scotland, Ireland and England. No other person did a tenth of the volume of work that Knibb did.

The Baptist Missionary Society relied upon the goodwill of planters. So they felt unable to openly support the emancipation movement, with missionaries being instructed not to interfere in civil affairs. This was their stance until Knibb's speech at their public Annual Meeting on June 21, 1832.

> I call upon children, by the cries of the infant slaves who I saw flogged…I call upon parents, by the blood streaming back of Catherine Williams, who…preferred a dungeon to the surrender of her honour. I call upon Christians by the lacerated back of William Black…whose back, a month after flogging, was not healed. I call upon you all, by the sympathies of Jesus…

At this point, Mr Dyer, Secretary of the Society, pulled his tail coat by way of admonition. Yet Knibb continued:

> Whatever may be the consequence, I will speak. At the risk of my connexion with the Society and of all I hold dear, I will avow this…Lord, open the eyes of Christians in England, to see the evil of slavery and to banish it from the earth.

There was thunderous applause and Dyer himself proposed a public meeting as the next round in the struggle.

On August 15, 1832, in front of 3,000 Londoners, Knibb held up iron slave shackles and hurled them deafeningly to the floor:

> All I ask is, that my African brother may stand in the same family of man; that my African sister shall, while she clasps her tender infant to her breast, be allowed to call it her own; that they both shall be allowed to bow their knees in prayer to that God who has made of one blood all nations as one flesh.

Knibb's unassailably authentic reports did more than any other source to convince Britons that slavery must be speedily abolished. On August 1, 1834, it was theoretically terminated by Parliament. However, slaves had to endure a further six year 'apprenticeship' before they were granted full freedom. The planters ruthlessly abused this provision, but the protests of Knibb and others prompted Parliament to bring forward full emancipation from 1840 to August 1, 1838.

In September 1839, Knibb founded the weekly newspaper the *Baptist Herald and Friend of Africa*, giving freed slaves a voice of their own. He adopted James Phillipo's 'free village' system and helped raise money to purchase thousands of acres that enabled former slaves to own their own property. He also founded schools and organised teacher training. The humble Knibb never gloried in his success and always gave credit to others like Burchell, whom he thought hid their light under a bushel.

On August 1, 1839 – 124 years before Martin Luther King's 'I have a dream' speech – he declared (in words inscribed on a memorial plaque in the Falmouth Baptist Chapel):

> The same God who made the white made the black man. The same blood that runs in the white man's veins, flows in yours. It is not the complexion of the skin, but the complexion of character that makes the great difference between one man and another.

When Knibb died of fever in November 1845, 8,000 mourners attended his funeral. The inscription on his tomb includes:

> This monument was erected by the emancipated slaves to whose enfranchisement and elevation his indefatigable exertions so largely contributed.

Missionaries were active in settling and educating freed slaves and for a long time provided virtually the only schools open to blacks.

Emancipated slaves were released into a world without any supporting institutions and church ministers were often their sole source of legal advice. Missionaries were active in settling and educating freed slaves and for a long time provided virtually the only schools open to blacks. Yet not even religion escaped the island's ingrained class and colour stratification. The white plantocracy were mostly Anglicans, coloureds mainly Wesleyan Methodists and blacks overwhelmingly Baptist.

There was prejudice too among Baptists, imagined or real. English missionaries such as James Phillippo would use persons of African origin as assistants, but never as pastors. Such discrimination prompted the formation of the Native Baptist movement in the late 1830s. George William Gordon and Paul Bogle were both members, leading some to dub the 1865 Morant Bay Rebellion the 'Native Baptist War'.

Over time Christianity became 'Jamaicanised'. At times this meant simply ignoring doctrines incompatible with local habits, such as the concept of propagation only within marriage. In other instances African tradition and Christian orthodoxy were mixed. The most significant example was Revival, whose most prominent branches are Revival Zion and Pukumina (or Pocomania).

Revival's various African elements can be traced to Myal, Native Baptist movements and Kumina. Yet its name and impetus as a distinct folk religion came from the Great Christian Revival that swept across Ireland, England and the US before reaching Jamaica in 1860–61. Though originally a strictly Christian movement, in Jamaica it rapidly incorporated African derived customs. '60 Order' Revival Zionism represents the more Christian end of the spectrum, while '61 Order' Pukumina has more deeply African practices.

Revivalists are noted for their colourful dress (white or variously coloured robes and turbans), powerful drumming and singing and a characteristic wheeling dance that often induces spirit possession and talking in tongues. Orthodox Christians view their 'over-emotionalism' and 'heathenism' with suspicion. Yet though never large in numbers, Revivalists' outsized exuberance and distinctive music has given them great cultural prominence.

PENTECOSTS AT WORSHIP ON CHRISTMAS EVE

The strong indigenous element of Revival has inspired novels, poems, plays, dance-theatre and reggae music. Musicologist Kenneth Bilby says Revivalists invented an entirely new musical form by blending Protestant devotional songs – largely taken from nineteenth century British and American hymnals like the famous one by Ira Sankey – with polyrhythmic clapping and forceful drumming. Many popular reggae songs have affectionately satirised Revival, including 'Revival Time' by Chalice and 'Pocomania Day' by Lovindeer.

Revivalists have certain magical beliefs, called Obeah, which are influenced by books from the DeLaurence Company of Chicago. The

KUMINA DANCE

most popular of these are *The Sixth and Seventh Books of Moses* and *The Great Book of Magical Arts, Hindu Magic and Indian Occultism*, which in Jamaican folk memory are 'Obeah bibles'. Sold worldwide, these books are probably reworked eighteenth century magical texts.

What is generally called Obeah is not necessarily related to Revivalism and often refers to 'dark' supernatural powers of African derivative that some persons are said to possess. Anecdotal conversation suggests that belief in Obeah, often colloquially referred to as 'Science', remains fairly widespread. Many Jamaicans going through a bad patch still consult Obeah 'readers' to learn which bad-minded person has 'scienced' them and how they can lift the spell.

Obeah practitioners often double as 'balmists' or 'herbalists', folk healers who rely on native herbs mixed into concoctions called 'bush medicine'. These often have names like 'oil a come back' or 'oil a stay yah'. The secretive manner in which such subjects are discussed means no one really knows how extensively they are practised, or even exactly what 'Obeah' is nowadays.

Much of the African element in Revival comes from Kumina (hence Pu-Kumina) which still survives on its own. Kumina – which means to move or act rhythmically in the Ki-Kongo language – was brought here by the indentured Africans who came to Jamaica between the 1840s and 1860s mainly from the Congo. Kumina was also the basis of many of the beliefs, practices and musical traditions of Rastafarianism. Many of the Congo Africans originally settled in St Thomas parish, which remains the stronghold of Kumina and also of Obeah. 'Mind me go a St Thomas fe you' is a threat, usually taken seriously, to get an Obeah man to cast a spell.

Some Revival practices have become national customs. One of these is 'nine night', a wake – usually accompanied by much food and drink and often traditional music – held on the ninth night after death. It is feared that without

GOING HOME JAMAICAN STYLE

It was the singing, girl, the singing, it was that
that full my throat and blind my eye
with sunlight. Parson preach good and didn't
give we no long-metre that day…

But the singing was sermon and lesson and eulogy
and more and it was only when we raise
'How Great Thou Art' that I really feel
the sadness and the glory, wave after wave…

…It was then I know we was people
together, never mind the bad-minded and the carry down…
and I sing and the feelings swelling in my chest
till I had to stop and swallow hard...

Girl, I can't too well describe it.
Was like the singing was bigger than all of we
and making us better than we think we could be,
and all I asking you, girl, is when
my time come to go, don't worry
make no fuss bout pretty coffin
and no long eulogy, just a quiet place
Where gunman and drug addict don't haunt,
And if they sing me home like how they sing Gertie
I say thank you Jesus, my soul will sleep in peace

– 'It was the Singing', Edward Baugh

Tears and grief mixed with music and laughter – perhaps nothing so vividly illustrates the contradictions of Jamaica as its funerals, which in recent times have become both more ostentatious and more traditional. Cynics might say that the high murder rate gives them a lot of practice. Still Jamaicans on the whole appear almost comfortable dealing with death, having developed a set of rituals that seem to produce a satisfying catharsis for loved ones.

A central focus is the 'nine night' set up held on the eve of the actual funeral. This get together of family, neighbours and friends is always accompanied by lots of food, especially curry goat and mannish water and plenty of music. In the rural areas there are often traditional bands playing mento, pocomania and sankeys. In urban areas, especially the inner cities, sound systems pound out everything from hard core dancehall to gospel into the wee morning hours. Sometimes the only way to tell a 'nine night' set up from a regular dance is the casual dress at the former.

Like all else in Jamaica, funerals vary with class. 'Uptown' affairs tend to be quieter and less emotional, with private and restrained mourning. Among the working classes there is openly expressed anguish and often loud weeping and wailing, especially from women. Upper class services are also briefer in general, with a not too long message from the pastor and a few tributes and songs. 'Downtown' there is more room for scheduled tributes, with spontaneous ones encouraged and extended hymn singing. The preacher is also given full reign to minister to his flock in lengthy impassioned sermons. The contrast continues graveside, with the number and intensity of choruses around the tomb increasing as the 'class ladder' is descended.

Paradoxically, those of lesser means often seem to spend more on funerals. In recent years especially, the dancehall influenced 'bling don' culture has seen a proliferation of expensive coffins and glitzy outfits at internments. Loud music is sometimes played on the way to the cemetery, with attendees decked out in the latest party fashions, rather than traditional sober mourning attire. Some see similarities between this revelry and the jazz funerals in New Orleans, where a band accompanies the mourners to the cemetery.

Yet Jamaican popular funeral culture also shows some resemblance to that of the Akan of Ghana, where many Jamaican ancestors originated. So perhaps the recent 'dancehallisation' of funerals is a manifestation of the Akan world-view, where it is crucial to maintain harmony with the spirits of 'living dead' relatives and where the condition of the deceased in the other world is determined in part by the treatment they receive from relatives and friends.

such a ceremony the spirit of the deceased may not depart to heaven, but stay on earth to haunt the living as a malevolent ghost, or 'duppy'.

While small bands of actual Revival adherents still exist, over time Revival has tended to blend in with Pentecostalism, the largest and fastest growing religious movement in Jamaica.

The term Pentecostalism embraces many different religious denominations that emphasise charismatic Christianity and regard the Bible as literal truth. Born of a desire to return to the original simplicity of Christianity, its origins trace to a January 1, 1901 prayer meeting in Kansas, US led by Charles Parham. William J. Seymour, a one-eyed African-American preacher, took its teachings to Los Angeles and sparked the Azusa Street Revival.

There were earlier recorded examples, but the outpourings of the Holy Spirit at Azusa Street caught the attention of the press and attracted people from around the world, who spread the word. Evangelical missions that came to Jamaica as early as 1918 found much common ground with Revival and Native Baptist sects and the movement grew rapidly.

The basic Pentecostal doctrine centres on being 'born again', which entails conversion and adult baptism. The name is derived from the Day of Pentecost, when the Holy Spirit possessed the disciples and inspired them to speak in unknown tongues. Especially important are the first five books of the New Testament particularly the Book of Acts. The emphasis is not on doctrine, but on experiencing the Holy Spirit.

Virtually every existing form of religion is represented in present day Jamaica, but it is overwhelmingly Christian. Churches here are especially packed on Easter Sunday, Christmas Day and the night of December 31, as more Jamaicans welcome in the new year praising the Lord than partying to Auld Lang Syne.

Photos © Ray Chen/ Periwinkle

A CONGREGATION AT WORSHIP

Popular belief has it that Jamaica is listed in the *Guinness Book of World Records* for having the most churches per capita in the world. There is no such category, but this island would certainly be a leading contender. It also must be a world leader in the number of denominations, as Jamaican churches have a great tendency to throw off splinter groups, which create their own new distinctive house of worship.

Though doctrinal hair splitting is a favourite pastime, there is little religious tension here. The only exception might be the antagonism shown by some denominations towards the Roman Catholic Church, a possible offshoot of lingering British anti-Papism, although ironically Catholic organisations are estimated to be responsible for over 90 per cent of all charitable work in the island. Prominent among these are Food for the Poor, Missionaries of the Poor, Mustard Seed Communities and St Patrick's Foundation.

No discussion of religion in Jamaica could leave out its most famous indigenous belief system, Rastafarianism. Considering it began as a 'cult' of outcasts, the overall influence and worldwide reach of Rastafarianism is astonishing. This remarkable movement deserves a separate treatment of its own.

Courtesy of the National Library of Jamaica

ALEXANDER BEDWARD

DIP THEM BEDWARD!

One of the most remarkable episodes in Jamaican religious history was Bedwardism, a messianic cult movement which attracted thousands of followers from all over Jamaica, Cuba and Central America in the late nineteenth and early twentieth century. It was founded by the Native Baptist preacher Alexander Bedward, who began his mission in 1891 at the August Town Jamaica Native Baptist Free Church. His fame as a preacher and faith healer spread far and wide. Thousands came to be cleansed of their sins and cured of their ills, by being 'dipped in the healing stream' of the Hope River.

Bedward identified himself with Paul Bogle and began challenging not only the religious but the secular status quo. He was reported to have said:

> …the white wall has been closing around the black wall; but now the black wall has become bigger than the white wall. Let them remember the Morant War….

The colonial government arrested him for sedition in 1891. He was declared insane and put in an asylum, but was released on the intervention of his lawyers (committing 'troublemakers' to an asylum was a not infrequent tactic of the colonial authorities. Leonard Howell, one of Rastafarianism's founders, suffered the same fate).

Bedward resumed his activities and between 1895 and 1921 the phenomenon grew. In 1920 he announced he would ascend to Heaven on December 31. Thousands of people in Jamaica and many from Panama, Cuba and other parts of Central America, came to August Town to await the 'miracle'. Yet it failed to take place and Bedward announced the time was not right. Folk legend has it that he jumped out of a tree and broke his leg. However, if the incident did take place, it was one of his followers who suffered this fate.

On April 1921 Bedward decided to lead a march of his followers from August Town to Kingston for a 'manifestation'. The police arrested him and 685 of his followers. Bedward was committed to Bellevue once again and remained there until his death in November 1930.

A lunatic to some, he was a political visionary to others and provided a link to Garveyism and Rastafarianism. He was immortalised in at least two well known folk songs. One goes:

Dip them Bedward, dip them
Dip them in the healing stream
Dip them sweet but not too deep
Dip them fe cure bad feeling

The other tells of a scheming young man who made off with one of Bedward's virginal young lady followers.

Mongoose go inna Bedward kitchen
Pluck out one a him righteous chicken
Put it inna him waistcoat pocket
Sly Mongoose!

Mongoose say she a Bedward member
Bedward say him no quite remember
Mongoose say she join last December
Sly Mongoose.

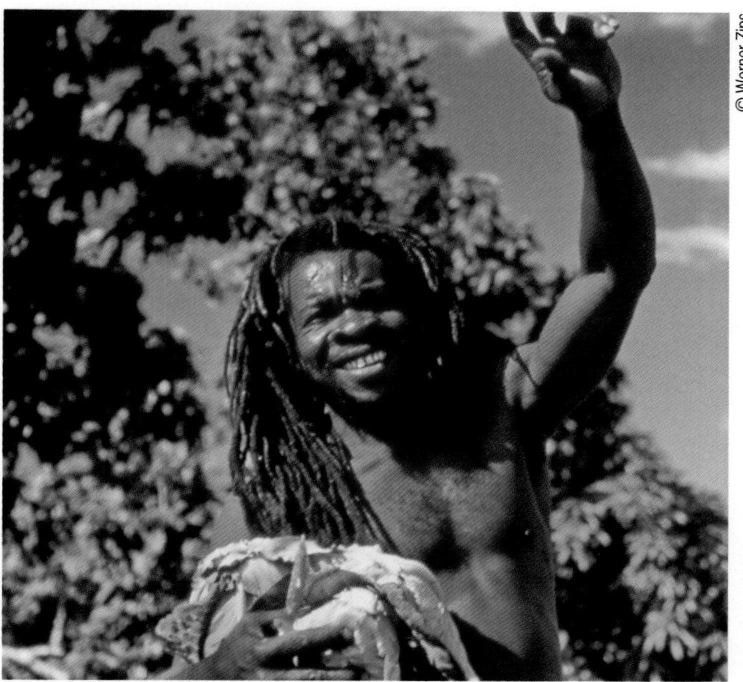
© Werner Zips

THE ROOTS OF RASTAFARI

The originating impulse of the Rastafari millenarian vision is often said to be Marcus Garvey's directive 'Look to Africa where a divine black king shall be crowned, for the day of deliverance is near' – a prophecy supposedly fulfilled by Haile Selassie's coronation as Ethiopian emperor on November 11, 1930. Yet there is no evidence Garvey ever uttered such words.

In *Rastafari Roots and Ideology*, sociologist Barry Chevannes gives a possible source of the 'divine black king' legend. After returning to Jamaica in 1927, Garvey staged concerts and plays before huge crowds at his Edelweiss Park cultural-political centre. One of the plays was 'The Coronation of the King of Africa', a fact and fiction dramatisation of UNIA work which ended with the crowning of an African king. It would not have been surprising if many made a connection between this play and

Though Rastas rejected the rejoicing, spiritual dancing and possession trance features of Revivalism, most aspects of Rastafarian music can be traced directly to Kumina.

Courtesy of the National Library of Jamaica

LEONARD HOWELL

Selassie's coronation, especially since most poor Jamaicans were then illiterate and there was no radio or television to interpret events.

Yet Rastafarians who insist that Garvey was their prophet are correct in spirit, if not in letter. A spirit can have no colour, he wrote in his 'Universal Negro Catechism'. Yet if white men worshipped a white deity, why should not blacks worship a black God?

It required only minor extrapolations of this eminently reasonable argument to see the earthly representative of this black God in the newly crowned emperor of Ethiopia. An independent sovereignty for at least 2,000 years and the only long-standing African empire to survive the colonial partition, Ethiopia was a long-standing symbol of African dignity and independence. Haile Selassie's coronation provided a new justification for political and spiritual faith in Ethiopia, which fused with Garvey's doctrine of racial redemption, black unity and a free Africa. Haile Selassie means 'Power of the Trinity'. Ras Tafari, or 'Prince of Peace', was his pre-coronation title.

Rastafarian ideology seems to be based on two books, *The Holy Piby* and *The Royal Parchment Scroll of Black Supremacy*. In 1935 these were extensively plagiarised in *The Promised Key* by Leonard Howell, who in time became the central figure in Rastafarianism's development.

Born June 16, 1898, Howell travelled to Panama and the US before returning to Jamaica in November 1932. This coincided with a marked upsurge of religious revivalism and he held his first public meeting on 'Ras Tafari, King of Abyssinia' in Kingston on January 1933. Citing Selassie's coronation attended by 72 nations paying homage and bearing gifts, Howell spoke of him as 'Christ returned to earth'. He said blacks in the west were really Jews, the Biblical lost tribe of Israel.

Many of Howell's initial converts, including his lieutenant Robert Hinds, were former disciples of Alexander Bedward. It would be simplistic to see Howellism as a continuation of Bedwardism, but there is undoubtedly a connecting thread.

Howell's early proselytising met with little success and in April 1933 he transferred his efforts to Trinityville in St Thomas, where he began to use the customs and drumming of the African originated Kumina-Revivalist cult in his ceremonies. Though Rastas rejected the rejoicing, spiritual dancing and possession trance features of Revivalism, most aspects of Rastafarian music can be traced directly to Kumina. Researchers say Kumina and Rasta Nyabinghi drumming are musically indistinguishable.

The term 'Nyabinghi' was first used to describe a liberation movement active in Uganda from 1850 to 1950. It was centred around a woman healer, Huhumusa, who was possessed by the spirit of Nyabinghi, a legendary Amazon queen. In 1937 Haile Selassie used the term to refer to an Ethiopian organisation that included warriors. Rastas then applied it to themselves.

There was one crucial distinction between Rastafarianism and the Kumina-Revivalist tradition. Revivalists were mainly concerned with personal salvation and ritual observance. In contrast, Rastafarians protested loudly about economic hardships and racial discrimination.

Rastafarianism was not a movement isolated from place and time, but part of a continuous matrix of black nationalism, folk religion and peasant resistance to the Jamaican plantation economy. It was infused with the spirit of the 1760 Tacky slave rebellion, the 1831 Sam Sharpe slave rebellion and the 1865 Paul Bogle Morant Bay rebellion. Tacky, Sam Sharpe and Paul Bogle were all religious leaders.

Rastafarianism gained prominence at a time

HAILE SELASSIE IN JAMAICA'S PARLIAMENT DURING HIS VISIT TO JAMAICA

© Werner Zips

NYABINGHI DRUMMERS

of fundamental social upheaval in Jamaica. This culminated in the 1938 Frome riots, a main spark of the movement for independence from Britain. Rastafari is perhaps best understood as a differing expression of the same continuing demand for freedom, a spiritual emancipation from perceived mental slavery.

In January 1934, Leonard Howell was charged with sedition and blasphemy, for allegedly selling postcards of Emperor Haile Selassie as passports to Ethiopia. He was imprisoned for two years. Police continued to harass the movement after his release and in 1940 Howell moved his followers to the old Pinnacle estate in the St Catherine mountains. It became the country's largest Rastafarian commune.

At first Rastafarian doctrines were obscure, but a firm core of beliefs emerged – Selassie was the living God, his crowning foretold African redemption and Marcus Garvey was his prophet.

Ironically Marcus Garvey, who emphasised black upliftment through education and presented himself neither as preacher nor prophet, was no friend of Rastafarianism. In 1933 he refused to allow Rasta leader Howell to distribute Selassie's picture at Edelweiss Park. In August 1934 the *Jamaica Times* reported that 'Mr Garvey also referred to the Ras Tafari cult... speaking of them with contempt'. Garvey was also critical of the Emperor during the 1935 Italian invasion of Ethiopia, blaming him for his country's lack of preparation. Another irony, given Rastafarianism's anti-papist streak, is that Garvey was Roman Catholic, marrying and being buried under its rites.

How did Selassie himself view his deification? In 1961, *Public Opinion* editor Clyde Hoyte wrote the Emperor's personal secretary to ask whether or not the Emperor considered himself to be

...the great triumph of Rastafarianism is to have channeled understandable feelings of resentment and oppression not into a creed of hate and violence, but into one preaching peace, love and the brotherhood of man.

God. Selassie's Press and Information Director General sent a reply to Hoyte:

> My August Sovereign desires to make a citation from the words of the Bible, in which it is said that man should not worship Man and there is one and only one God – the creator of the universe. Consequently, it is the fervent desire of his Imperial Majesty that the Ras Tafarians should discard this belief. On the other hand, my August Sovereign wants the Ras Tafarians to understand that He is always willing to maintain a friendly, fatherly and brotherly attitude towards them and also to be on their side whenever they need his help.

During Selassie's 1966 visit to Jamaica, where he was welcomed by huge crowds of followers, *Gleaner* editor Hector Wynter reportedly asked him when he was going to tell Rastafarians he was not God. 'Who am I to disturb their belief?' replied the emperor.

The Pinnacle commune grew ganja and baked bread and sold both in Kingston. So there was a considerable exchange of ideas between Howell's followers and other Rastas. Howellites are thought to have originated several important features of modern Rastafarianism, including the sacramental use of ganja. Some say this Sanskrit word for marijuana, as well as terms like collie (kali) weed and the use of chillum pipes, passed into local vernacular due to Howell's close association with a Jamaican Indian called Lalu. The concept of ganja as a holy herb is a Hindu one. It is widely used to enhance the religious experience in parts of India, despite government prohibition.

There are varying stories about the origin of 'dreadlocks'. Some say the style was inspired by news photos of Ethiopian warriors fighting the 1935 Italian invasion. Others state it was copied from the East African Masai, who became media prominent during the early 1950s Mau Mau rebellion. Barry Chevannes says the dreadlock trend had its beginnings in the late 1940s, when a group of young Rastafari converts formed the Youth Black Faith in Trench Town. Rastas cite biblical admonitions against the use of the razor as reason for not cutting their hair, as Tony Rebel sang in his 1994 hit 'Nazarite Vow'.

Rastafarians shunned alcohol and observed many food taboos of the ancient Hebrews, eating only fruits, roots, grains, vegetables and sometimes fish. Their food was always unsalted, or 'ital'. This has been linked to a belief among the indentured BaKongo, who came to Jamaica after emancipation, that eating salt prevented them from flying back to Africa. Rastafarians also considered the smoking of ganja a spiritual rite.

However 'the sacrament of the herb' often brought conflict with the law. Howell was apparently the island's first large-scale ganja farmer and Pinnacle became famous throughout Jamaica for its quality and quantity. Much of this was marketed in Kingston, prompting the police to raid and close down the settlement in 1954, an event commemorated in Louise Bennett's poem 'Pinnacle'.

Many Pinnacle Rastas moved to Kingston slums such as Back O'Wall and Moonlight City. In time Howell and a few followers drifted back to Tredegar Park, a few miles from Pinnacle. In his later years, as Rastafarianism became prominent worldwide, Howell gained a minor sort of fame and in December 1980 was featured in the US television programme '60 Minutes'. Howell died a few months later in February 1981.

Whatever his personal failings, Howell's legacy was on the whole a positive one. Rastafarianism may have its irrational aspects, but which religion is without a mystical side accessible only to true believers? Some say Haile Selassie as a man was not altogether worthy of the veneration accorded him, but in the end he was only a symbol. In essence Rastafarianism replaced the customary blue-eyed white Christian image of the Saviour, with a black one. Ethiopia and Africa became not so much physical destinations as conceptions of paradise.

Rastafarianism is an essentially tolerant faith and must be given some credit for the relatively good race relations Jamaica enjoys today. The avoidance of racial animosity in Rasta beliefs was not inevitable, and the great triumph of Rastafarianism is to have channeled understandable feelings of resentment and oppression not into a creed of hate and violence, but into one preaching peace, love and the brotherhood of man.

JAMAICA FESTIVAL

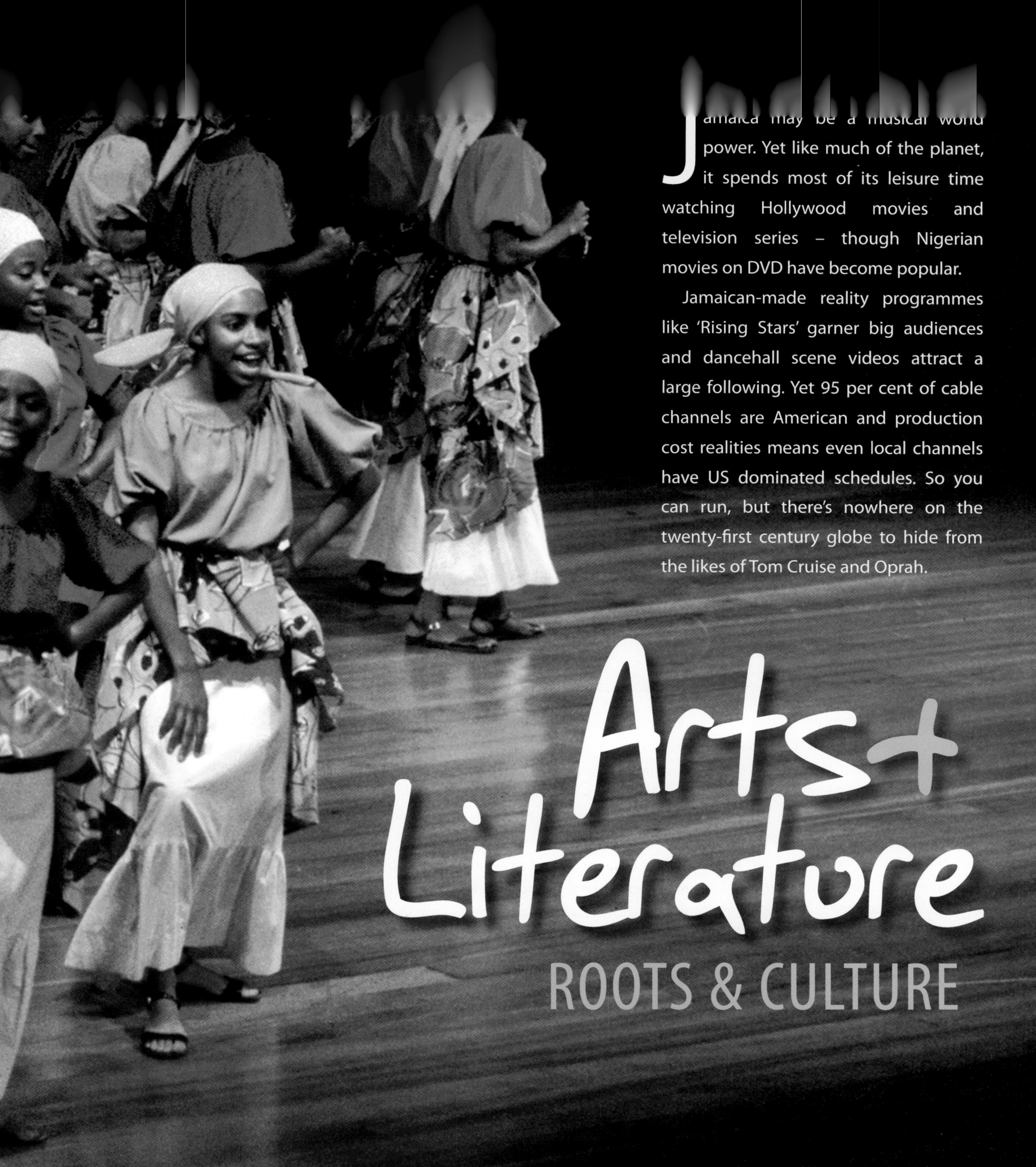

Jamaica may be a musical world power. Yet like much of the planet, it spends most of its leisure time watching Hollywood movies and television series – though Nigerian movies on DVD have become popular.

Jamaican-made reality programmes like 'Rising Stars' garner big audiences and dancehall scene videos attract a large following. Yet 95 per cent of cable channels are American and production cost realities means even local channels have US dominated schedules. So you can run, but there's nowhere on the twenty-first century globe to hide from the likes of Tom Cruise and Oprah.

Arts + Literature

ROOTS & CULTURE

...festival competition performances incorporate all phases of Jamaican culture in a quite natural manner.

In many countries the American video juggernaut has reduced indigenous entertainment to fossilised tourist displays. However, the annual Festival competitions are vivid evidence that Jamaican folk culture is vibrantly alive. Culminating between Emancipation Day on August 1 and Independence Day on August 6, these attract over 8,000 participants aged six to 80 in the categories of music, speech, drama, dance, folk arts, culinary arts and visual arts. A noticeable feature is the enthusiasm of school children entrants, who appear fully in tune with their cultural history. BET and MTV notwithstanding, they clearly still treasure their traditions.

Pleasingly varied and of consistently high quality, festival competition performances incorporate all phases of Jamaican culture in a quite natural manner. Century old traditions like Quadrille and Kumina, the latest emanations of the dancehall and everything in between, jostle on equal footing for judge and audience approval.

Adaptability to change while holding on to roots, has always been a hallmark of Jamaican culture in general and reggae in particular. So you see popular music videos with Jonkanoo themes and dancehall hits using motifs from folk songs like 'Sammy Dead O', a ska version of which topped the charts back in 1964.

All this is on display at the annual Grand Gala held at the National Stadium on Independence Day, August 6. It includes virtually every form of local music, poetry and dance imaginable, with performers ranging from primary school children to dancehall stars like Beenie Man. Yet despite the age differences of the artistes and the varying styles and forms on show, nothing seems out of place and the massive audience vociferously applauds every performance.

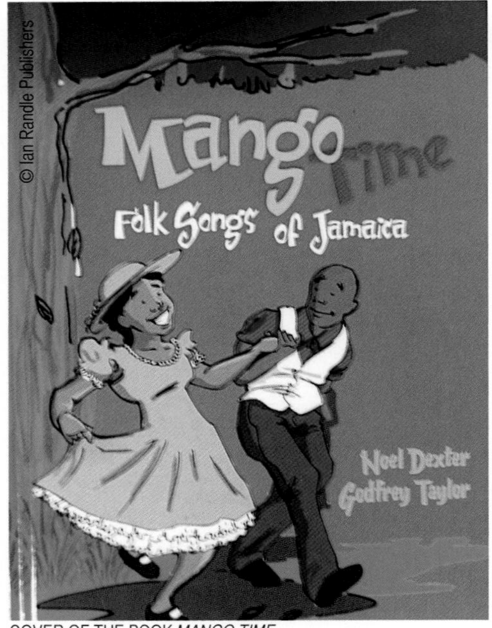

COVER OF THE BOOK *MANGO TIME*

The vibrancy of its folk heritage would be remarkable even if Jamaica was a large country with an ancient past. Yet for a nation so small and young to show such cultural confidence is nothing short of astonishing. From this perspective, reggae's worldwide popularity and influence is no accident, but merely reflects the compelling tenacity of the culture that produced it.

Perhaps the bedrock is a rich body of folk songs such as 'Sly Mongoose', 'Chi Chi Bud', 'Mango Time', 'Sammy Dead', 'Rookumbine' and 'Long Time Gal'. While such music was born out of an oral rural tradition, efforts have been made over the years to document and perform it on concert stages. In 1907 Walter Jekyll published his pioneering *Jamaican Song and Story*. Phillip Sherlock later daringly included the famous 1930s Kingston street minstrels Slim Beckford and Sam Blackwood on a concert programme at the Institute of Jamaica.

Slim and Sam created or gave lasting arrangements to many tunes now considered 'traditional'. Wycliffe Bennett remembered being

> ...caught up with the magic and the infectious laughter of the occasion. There was certainly a two-way flow of excitement between the performers and the audience and I was fascinated by their public use of the Jamaican idiom. This made them readily accessible to everyone. They understood the Jamaican mentality as well as other great performers of the Jamaican stage. I would certainly relate them to our comic tradition exemplified by...Ranny Williams and Louise Bennett.

Ranny Williams himself wrote in 1939 'Folklore is their business. All the incidents that have happened and are happening in Jamaica, they record them in songs that for plain broad humour, telling expression and true character study, cannot be beaten anywhere.'

The Cudjoe Minstrels, a group of upper class Jamaicans, presented Jamaican folk songs, stories and dancing between 1935 and 1940. They performed in blackface, not for burlesque purposes, but for the sake of the authenticity of a culture they genuinely cared for.

> The Cudjoe Minstrels...have seriously set themselves to collect these songs and to

sing them, because they love them…they look forward to a time when a Jamaican Festival will be held, with a programme wholly devoted to Jamaican Songs and Stories.

The first established folk group was the Frats Quintet, who starting in 1954 performed Jamaican folk and digging songs not only across Jamaica but in Latin America, North America and Europe. They were forerunners of present cultural groups like the Little Theatre Movement, the Cari Folk Singers, the Jamaica Folk Singers, the University Players, Ashe and the National Dance Theatre Company.

Since 1897 excellence in the fields of literature, art and science has been commemorated at the annual Musgrave Medals Award Ceremony, named after Governor Sir Anthony Musgrave, who founded the Institute of Jamaica in 1879. Gold is awarded for 'distinguished eminence', silver for 'outstanding merit' and bronze for 'merit'. Before 1941 silver medals rewarded 'distinguished merit', with bronze medals reserved primarily for competitions before 1962. The first gold was awarded in 1941 to Edna

Courtesy of the National Library of Jamaica

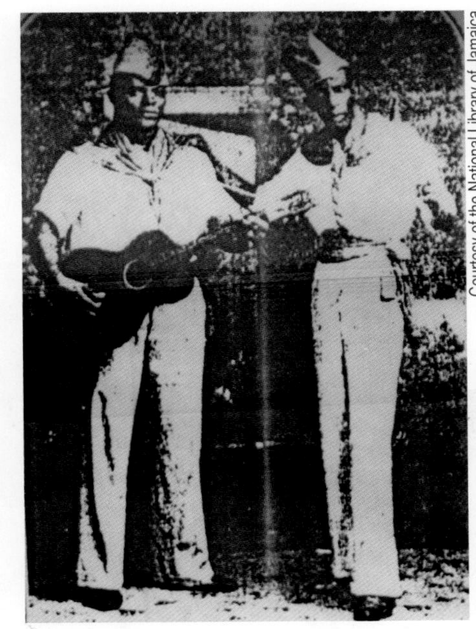

SLIM AND SAM

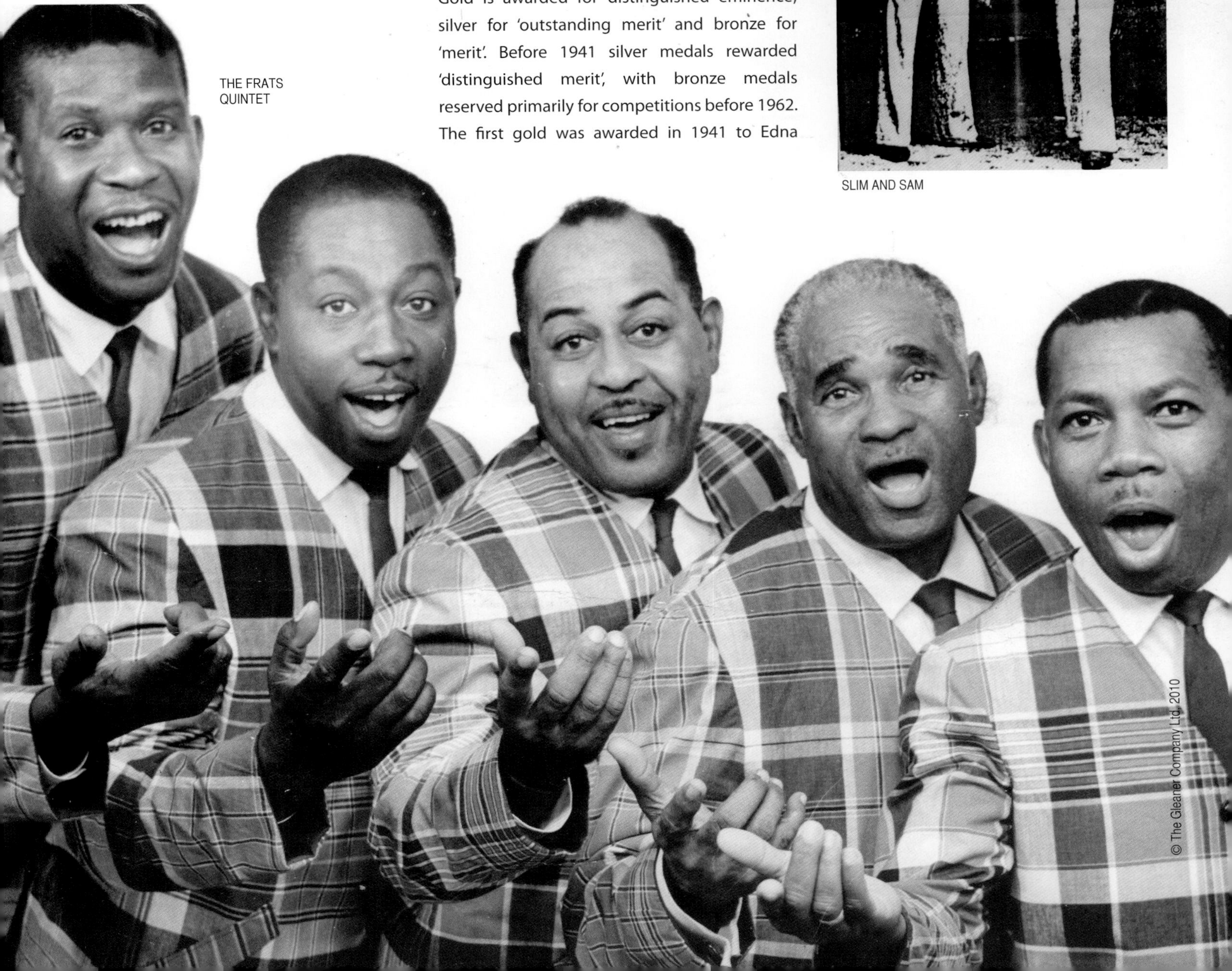

THE FRATS QUINTET

WARD THEATRE AND SCENE FROM PANTOMIME (ABOVE)

Manley in recognition of her work in promoting art and literature. As of 2008, 454 Musgrave medalists have been presented.

One long-standing bulwark of Jamaican self-expression in storytelling is Pantomime, an annual theatrical event that has opened on Boxing Day at the Ward Theatre every year since 1941. It usually runs until late April and in recent decades has attracted total crowds in the 75,000–80,000 range, not an insignificant figure in a population of 2.5 million.

Originally modelled after English Christmas pantomimes, it has become truly Jamaican over the years, combining traditional culture with the latest music and dances, while satirising leaders and current events. A number of pantomime songs have passed into the 'folk' repertoire with their original genesis largely forgotten. Among these is the wonderful 'Evening Time', composed by Barbara Ferland with lyrics by Louise Bennett, for the 1957 play 'Busha Bluebeard'.

Like its British parent, 'Panto' here often makes recurring use of stock folk figures, the most popular being Anancy. Originating in the Ashanti tribe of Ghana, this devious trickster spider is the hero of many tales and survives against the odds in a harsh world by his quick wit, cunning and ingenuity. He frequently appears with his wife Crooky and son Tacooma.

Then there is the 'roots' theatre phenomenon. These raunchy, humorous plays draw large live audiences and are local cable channel staples, with DVD taped copies also circulating widely here and abroad. While not Sophocles or Shakespeare – they nearly all focus on infidelity or 'bunning'– they give enjoyable and sometimes thought-provoking 'slice of life' looks at Jamaica.

With titles often taken from dancehall happenings – 'Passa Passa' and 'Chakka Chakka' for instance – they take a similar 'anything goes' approach to life. As with dancehall, many critics accuse 'roots' plays as being overly focused on sex and materialism. Still, their exuberant vitality is infectious, with the participatory audiences often being as entertaining as the plays. The writing quality has also improved significantly of late, with plots becoming more sophisticated and characterisations less one-dimensional.

For all their shortcomings, roots plays are the backbone of the surprisingly vibrant local theatre scene. They are as vivid a testimony as reggae of Jamaicans' irrepressible desire to express and enjoy their own realities. 'If you want to build a ship, don't instruct the men to go to the forest to gather wood. Instead, teach them to love the sea' Antoine de Saint Exupéry once remarked. Roots theatre has helped create a wider audience for more serious fare. Among those who have helped raise the dramatic bar are Fae Ellington, Oliver Samuels, Glen 'Titus' Campbell, Owen 'Blakka' Ellis, Tony 'Paleface' Hendriks, Father Richard Holung, Barbara Gloudon, Patrick Brown, Basil Dawkins and Balfour Anderson.

Similarly, dub poetry can be seen as an 'upliftment' of dancehall deejaying. Yasus Afari, one of its best known exponents, defines dub poetry as poetry set to music, with an emphasis primarily, but not exclusively, on the stripped down drum and base riddim. The concept originates in the word dub, which means to take out or put in.

It has revolutionised poetry by moving away from the formal European tradition and shifting

...their exuberant vitality is infectious, with the participatory audiences often being as entertaining as the plays...They are as vivid a testimony as reggae of Jamaicans' irrepressible desire to express and enjoy their own realities.

LOUISE 'MISS LOU' BENNETT AND RANNY WILLIAMS

Dub poetry employs the vernacular to express the intrinsic experiences of the people.

OLIVER SAMUELS

MUTABARUKA

to indigenous Afrocentric interpretations while still dealing with elevated thoughts and the higher aspects of life. It employs vernacular to express the intrinsic experience of the people and it also incorporates formal English to cover the full spectrum of emotions and thought.

Yasus Afari says he tries to make dancehall's undeniable power intellectually understandable. The goal is to both educate and entertain – edutainment – so the audience feels and ponders.

He sees both dancehall and dub poetry as forms of street poetry. Yet while the latter focuses on 'riding the riddim' and getting crowds excited and dancing to the beat, dub poetry places more emphasis on arresting the ear with the sounds of words and their meanings and messages. If you define the entire poetic spectrum as stretching from singing to singjaying to deejaying to chanting to

YASUS AFARI

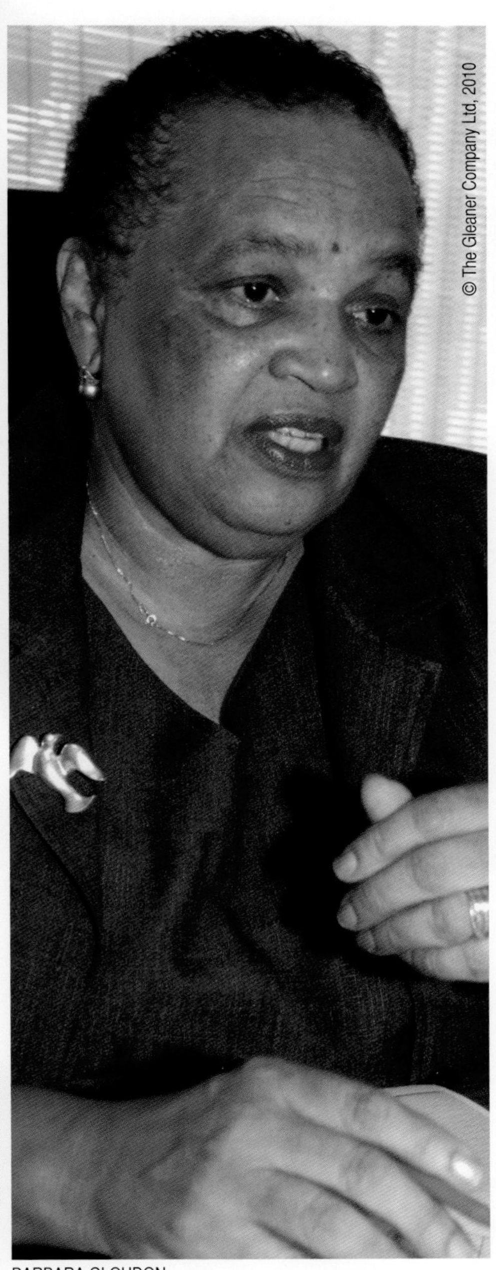
BARBARA GLOUDON

dub poetry to the spoken word, then dub poetry is delicately poised between the spoken word and deejaying, with a leaning and bias towards the former.

Bluntly put, dancehall focuses on the groin while dub poetry tries to appeal to the head. Still there are no hard and fast boundaries. Dancehall deejays like Beenie Man often borrow from dub poetry, while Ini Kamoze, Lt Stitchie and Papa San started out as dub poets. The singjay chanting of artistes like Tony Rebel, Anthony B and Sizzla often approaches dub poetry.

Many consider 1970s deejay Big Youth a pioneer of the form. Two other key early dub poets were the late Mikey Smith – who internationalised the art and Oku Onuora – who gave it its name. Other influential practitioners are Jean Binta Breeze – mother of cricketer Gareth Breeze, Mutabaruka, Linton Kwezi Johnson and Benjamin Zephaniah.

Dub poetry has moved far from its original parochial beginnings, having been translated into Spanish and French and its biggest market is said to be South Africa. Still it remains an authentic Jamaican art form that has become popular worldwide and whose influence in the field of poetry has probably been as significant as that of reggae in music.

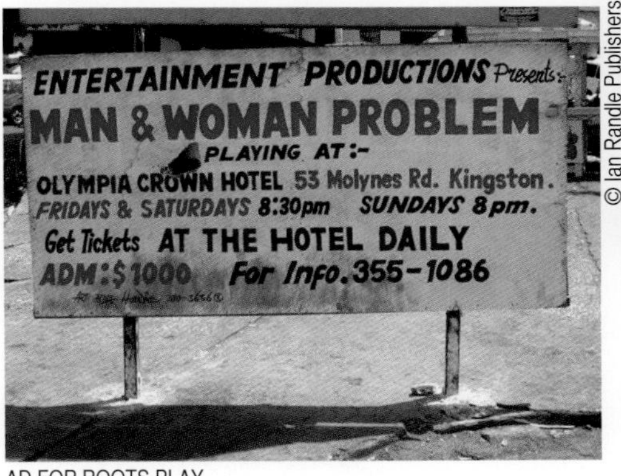

ENTERTAINMENT PRODUCTIONS Presents:
MAN & WOMAN PROBLEM
PLAYING AT:-
OLYMPIA CROWN HOTEL 53 Molynes Rd. Kingston.
FRIDAYS & SATURDAYS 8:30pm SUNDAYS 8pm.
Get Tickets AT THE HOTEL DAILY
ADM:$1000 For Info.355-1086

AD FOR ROOTS PLAY

MISS LOU

MOTHER OF JAMAICAN CULTURE

Louise 'Miss Lou' Bennett is undisputedly the most universally loved personality this nation has ever produced or likely will ever produce, engendering unabashed feelings of pride and affection in Jamaicans of all ages, colours, classes and creeds. For over 50 years, she tirelessly championed Jamaican folk customs on stage, radio and television. Yet apart from being our most celebrated entertainer, Miss Lou is also is the most popular poet in this island's history, outselling all others put together. Her impact on the national psyche was perhaps even more important than her artistic legacy, for she almost single-handedly gave Jamaicans pride in their cultural heritage. In musicologist Marjorie Whylie's words:

> All of us are the inheritors of the groundwork Louise did…Folk music only gained respectability after Louise came back from London and sang 'Rookumbine' on RJR….

Her extensive travels throughout Jamaica gave her a perhaps unsurpassed knowledge of native folklore. She collected and studied folk songs, ring-games, Anancy stories and riddles, becoming a primary resource for scholars and artists interested in such material. Marjorie Whylie called her 'the most generous soul I know… always so ready to assist with material or contacts or pointing you in a direction for tracing further material…a casual social visit with Louise…would make a good anthropological study.'

As her Norman Manley Award for Excellence citation noted:

> It is this truth grounded in her faithful observation and a genuine empathy with Jamaican folk life which makes Louise Bennett stand way above all her colleagues…. Her deep knowledge of Jamaica has helped to give her literary and theatrical work an authenticity that few other Jamaican artists have achieved.…Many of our other significant artists, working in their various media, are accessible only to an elite, cultivated or otherwise. Louise Bennett has achieved an excellence while reaching the entire society.
>
> But she does not flatter us. She is forever exposing our pretenses, our idiocies, our cosmic disproportions. She measures us against the values of common sense, of sanity, of reason; and yet in her compassion does not seem beyond us all. She speaks not so much to as for the whole Jamaican society.

Also as Rex Nettleford said:

> …those who indulge her rumbustious abandon and spontaneous inducement of laughter will sometimes forget that behind the exuberance and carefree stance, there are years of training – formal and informal – as well as this artist's own struggles to shape an idiom.

One reason I persisted in writing in dialect in spite of the opposition was because nobody else was doing so and there was such a rich material in dialect that I felt I wanted to put on paper some of the wonderful things that people say in dialect.

– Louise Bennett

It was Miss Lou's insistence on the inherent worth of Jamaican expression that established in the populace a respect for their language and tradition – the belief that 'patwa' wasn't merely corrupted English but a creation of immense vitality and humour. In her own words:

> Some thought Jamaican-English was vulgar, out-of-order language. It came out of the African heritage and at that time anything African was bad: hair, colour, skin, language, music. But I thought it was fascinating. Everything had a rhythm. It was a creation of the people. One reason I persisted in writing in dialect in spite of the opposition was because nobody else was doing so and there was such a rich material in dialect that I felt I wanted to put on paper some of the wonderful things that people say in dialect. You could never say 'look here' as vividly as 'kuyah'.

In her 1944 poem 'Bans O' Killing' she laughed at the snobbery which denigrated all common Jamaican speech:

> ...Meck me get it straight Mass Charlie
> For me no quite undastan,
> Yuh gwine kill all English dialect
> Or jus Jamaica one?
>
> Ef yuh dah-equal up wid English
> Language, den wha meck
> Yuh gwine go feel inferior, wen
> It come to dialect?
>
> Ef yuh kean sing 'Linstead Market'
> An 'Wata come a me y'eye',
> Yuh wi haffi tap sing 'Auld lang syne'
> An 'Comin thru de rye'

Her dialect performances were the direct precursors of deejay music and dub poetry. Tony Rebel, who uses Jamaican dialect as effectively as anyone in reggae, acknowledges Miss Lou as his greatest influence. While Luciano puts it this way:

> She has worked forward into my consciousness that I can be proud of my culture and proud of myself.

No single individual has been more responsible for the Jamaican nation's emancipation from colonial mental slavery. In Rex Nettleford words again:

> …she has carved designs out of the shapeless and unruly substance that is the Jamaican dialect – the language which most of the Jamaican people speak most of the time – and raised the sing-song patter of the hills and towns to an art acceptable to and appreciated by people from all classes....

Many people associate Miss Lou primarily with comedy. Yet while we rightly treasure those who bring the gift of laughter, we should not forget the serious side of Louise Bennett. Only a person with a very strong sense of racial pride and self-belief could have withstood the torrents of criticism she had to endure when she first championed the language and culture of her people.

Jamaicans today might be happily at ease with themselves and their customs, but it took a true 'lion heart' to speak out as she did at the height of 'only white is right' colonialism. Even though in much of her work she did 'tek kin teeth kibber heart bun' (Take skin teeth [a smile] cover heartaches), in poems like 'Dutty Tough' she addressed the issues of her day as seriously as any reggae artist and deejay ever did.

> Sun a shine an pot a bwile, but
> Things no bright, bickle no nuff
> Rain a fall, river dah flood, but,
> Water scarce and dutty tough.

In Tony Rebel's words 'Miss Lou was a sort of female Marcus Garvey'. She was a giant on whose shoulders all reggae artistes and dub poets now stand.

Storytellers

The high and low art debate centres more or less on the difference between reflective and entertainment art, but there is also a class component. Since it is usually those with leisure who have time to reflect, high art has traditionally been the province of aristocrats and the well-to-do. Given Jamaica's history where the rich were also generally light-skinned, while the poor were always black, it's not surprising that race enters into the argument here. The reality is that for a long time in this country, the patrons of painting, sculpture, classical music, formal dance and literature were primarily white and light brown.

This has caused these fundamentally elitist activities to seem even more irrelevant to most of the black working class. The fact is few Jamaicans know or even care about Jamaican writers or painters, or have seen a performance by the internationally acclaimed National Dance Theatre Company. Not a few 'roots' nationalists dismiss out hand as 'irrelevant' and 'non-Jamaican' any art and entertainment not deemed a product of the 'masses'.

A 'classicist' would respond that time is the only true judge of art and that however small the audience, it is 'formal' and not 'popular' art which posterity generally preserves. Few people read *The Iliad* 2,500 years ago and few read it today. Yet we know nothing now of the popular music that no doubt enthralled the ancient Greek 'hoi polloi', while Homer lives on.

Even though civilisations are remembered by what they wrote, authors usually have a tough time of it even in societies with strong literary traditions. It has been doubly so in a place like Jamaica, where for a long time most of the population was illiterate and the ruling class was noted for its philistine indifference and even hostility towards the written word.

Courtesy of the National Library of Jamaica

H.G. DE LISSER

The first books written either in or about Jamaica tended to be planter's biographies or visitor's travelogues. A few nineteenth century Englishmen set books in Jamaica, but these are now historical curiosities. It was not until the early twentieth century that books by Jamaicans about Jamaica began to be written. Two pioneers of this concept were Herbert de Lisser and Thomas McDermot.

A not quite full white Jew, de Lisser was, for good or ill, one of Jamaica's most influential public figures between the wars. Long time secretary of the Jamaica Imperial Association – an organisation of large land owners and merchants – he was also *Gleaner* editor for 40 years and used the newspaper to staunchly defend the colonial status quo. 'Everybody not a fool, or impertinent, will realise that they [the middle class] cannot rub shoulders with the great unwashed; we have no dislike of the latter, but...close physical association with them is not desirable' he wrote in 1928.

He relentlessly attacked Marcus Garvey and his fiction ridiculed figures like Garvey, Sam Sharpe and Paul Bogle. Yet his novel *Jane's Career* (1914) successfully manipulated creole speech, has perhaps the first black central character in a novel by a Jamaican writer and may be the first West Indian novel in which the peasant is given full status as a human person.

As one critic put it:

> de Lisser was certainly not the first, nor will he be the last Jamaican to celebrate his society in his creative work or to take an interest in its history, while at the same time entertaining views on race and class which would seem to exclude the majority of the island's population from full participation socially and culturally in their country's destiny.

The prolific de Lisser averaged a novel a year in his prime and his books were well reviewed in England. In 1920 he received the C.M.G., which made him the official giant of Jamaican letters in his day, since few Jamaicans in any sphere were so honoured.

His annual literary journal, the aptly named *Planters' Punch* (1920–44), featured his own efforts and those of his clique. It traditionally opened with a full page portrait of the invariably white wife or daughter of a local or visiting celebrity. Garvey called it '...not only a false representation, but an insult to the seven hundred thousand Negroes of the colony; and sowing the seed of racial antagonism....' In 1928 de Lisser authored the island's most famous bestseller, the slave plantation gothic potboiler *The White Witch of Rose Hall*.

© Ray Chen/ Periwinkle

ROSE HALL GREAT HOUSE TODAY

THE WHITE WITCH OF ROSE HALL

OSE HALL GREAT HOUSE IN THE 1800s

The Legend – John Rose Palmer, grandnephew of John Palmer who built Rose Hall between 1778 and 1790, married Anne May Patterson. Although half-English and half-Irish, the beautiful Annie was raised in Haiti and learned voodoo. A sexually insatiable murderess, Annie poisoned John Rose Palmer, stabbed a second husband and strangled a third, with a fourth possibly escaping. She then bedded and disposed of numerous slave lovers, before being strangled in her bedroom by her brutally mistreated slaves during the 1831–32 rebellion. She was buried in the garden where her grave can still be seen. Her husbands are buried under four palm trees on the beach across from the present great house. She wore a ring inscribed 'If I survive, I shall have five'.

The Facts – Rose Hall was named after Rosa Kelly, who had four husbands, the last being John Palmer. Rosa and John had been married for 25 years when she died in 1790 at 72. Her monument still stands in the Montego Bay Parish Church. John Rose Palmer married Anne Patterson in 1820 and died in 1827. Anne sold her claims to Rose Hall in 1830, never remarried, died peacefully in 1846 and was buried in the St James Parish Churchyard.

Rose Hall had fallen into disrepair. In August 1830 the missionary H.M. Waddell held services in the Great House, which he described as 'unoccupied save by rats, bats and owls.' In his 1863 account of the 1831–32 slave rebellion, he mentioned that the neighbouring Palmer estate Palmyra had furnished scenes and characters for a 1780 novel *Zeluco*. He claimed to have seen the iron collars and spikes used on slaves by a former lady owner and the bed on which her strangled body was found. Yet *Zeluco* contained no such scenes. Perhaps Waddell's story was a garbled slave version of long ago but still resonant cruelties. At any rate, Anne Palmer had not been born in 1780 and was still alive in 1832.

In 1868 James Castello, possibly inspired by Waddell, published a pamphlet called the 'Legend of Rose Hall'. It told of a church monument to the 'exemplary and dutiful' Mrs Ann Palmer, who in reality murdered three husbands – with the fourth escaping – and tortured slaves, who finally murdered her. In December 1870 the magazine *Leisure Hour* transported essentially the same story to two estates called Orange Hill and Citronia. As the story was in print, some believed it true and started to look for and find ghosts.

The tale became linked with the real monument in the Montego Bay Parish Church, though Castello's description is quite different from the actual one in appearance and inscription. In 1881 the earliest *Handbook of Jamaica* mentioned the 'exquisite' monument to the memory of Mrs Palmer of Rose Hall estate 'of whom tradition has said so much'.

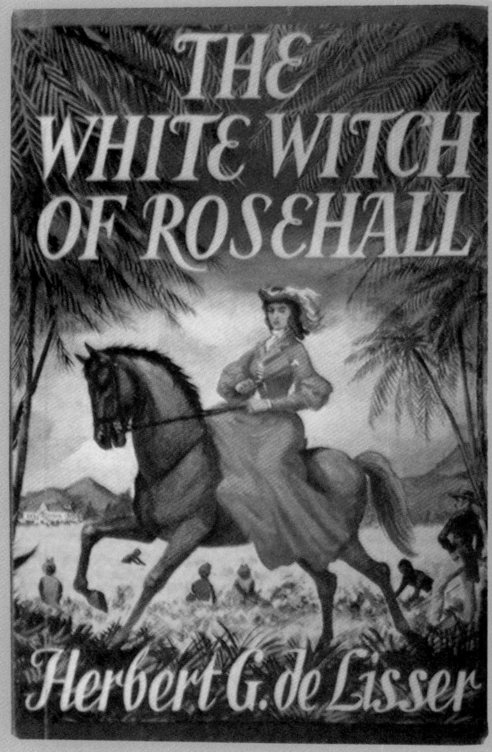

Desouza's *Tourist Guide* of 1891 told of five murdered husbands and a statue that showed strangulation marks. This was repeated in a handbook for the Jamaica exhibit at the 1893 Chicago Exhibition, with the statue's nostrils now seeming 'to exude blood'.

E.N. McLaughlin searched the records and published his findings in the June 17, 1895 *Gleaner*. He concluded that the whole tale was a myth 'aided by some forgotten tale of the old blood shedding days of Jamaica…but I am quite convinced that the legend has no more connection with the Palmers of Rose Hall…than it has with the man on the moon.'

There matters rested until 1911 when Joseph Shore's book *In Old St James* was published. Shore reprinted the 1868 pamphlet word for word and then gave his own embroidered version, which mentioned in passing Annie's 'powers of obeah'. In his 1915 *West Indian Tales of Old* Algernon Aspinall attributed the 'strangulation marks' on Annie Palmer's monument to a blue veined marble flaw near the neck, but accepted Castello's pamphlet as factual.

Herbert de Lisser elaborated on the obeah theme, throwing in such stuff as three-legged spectral horses and bear traps strewn in forests to catch would be escaping slaves. His widely popular novel gave the myth new impetus, the legend became established in Jamaican folklore as historical truth and its fame spread abroad. In the 1950s 'the famous sensitive' Mrs Eileen Garrett came to Jamaica to 'lay' Annie's ghost. She went into a trance and claimed to accomplish her mission, a transcription of proceedings being published in the *West Indian Review*. Annie also supposedly appeared to another psychic called Bambos at a séance held Friday, October 13, 1978. American country legend Johnny Cash even cut a 'Ballad of Annie Palmer' in the early 1970s.

Rose Hall Great House was refurbished into a major tourist attraction in the 1960s. The tale was embellished with fanciful stories of underground tunnels, bloodstains, ghostly mirrors, locked rooms and hauntings, which naturally pull in visitors by the bus load.

MONUMENT TO ROSA KELLY

© Ian Randle Publishers

Courtesy of the National Library of Jamaica

TOM REDCAM

McDermot's nom de plume was his last name reversed, Tom Redcam (the island's thespian hub, the Little Theatre, is located on Tom Redcam Drive). In Mervyn Morris's words (in 1972):

> Tom Redcam was no great artist; but he was a remarkable Jamaican... White (or near-white), [he] published 70 years ago [1899] attitudes which would seem exceptional from such a person even now…
> 'To anyone making a serious attempt to understand the present condition and future prospects of Jamaica, the condition of the blacks is of supreme importance. The 15,000 whites and the Hinterland of brown men, are interesting mainly, in fact solely, because of their relation to their 600,000 black fellows. In every sense, we white men and out brown cousins, are all the earnest minded among us, servants of the blacks. It is as our actions and opinions relate to them that they will stand applauded or condemned by the future historian.'

His *Becky's Buckra Baby* was an early attempt to inject Caribbean dialogue into a novel. He was better known as a poet, though his work now seems ornate and dated. However Redcam's influence on others was immense and he created the first West Indian novel series, the *All Jamaica Library*, selling books for a shilling each. It was a financial flop with only four titles being produced, but to quote Morris again:

> In encouraging Jamaicans not only to write for a Jamaican readership but also to write material 'dealing directly with Jamaica and Jamaicans' McDermot was pushing cultural nationalism further than many of us would think sensible even today [1972]…. For him the chief ambition…. In matters literary is to produce among his fellow Jamaicans, that which Jamaicans will care to read and may find some small reason for taking pride in as the work of a Son of the Island.

McDermot also encouraged perhaps the greatest of Jamaican writers, Claude McKay. McKay was born in 1890 to literate peasant farmers wealthy enough to vote. His talents was recognised early by Redcam and Walter Jekyll and with their help he published two books of dialect poetry, *Songs of Jamaica* and *Constab Ballads*, the second based on his experiences as a police officer. They were popular in Jamaica, well-reviewed abroad and earned him a Silver Musgrave Medal, then the country's highest literary honour. Yet, McKay felt patronised as a mere creole folk writer and nursed a desire to write on larger themes in English.

He emigrated to the US in 1912 and became an integral part of the Harlem Renaissance, the literary movement that brought black writers such as Langston Hughes to international attention. After visiting Russia in 1923, McKay became, in his words, 'a troubadour wanderer'

Courtesy of the National Library of Jamaica

CLAUDE MCKAY

and did not return to the US until 1934. Though published in the US, his four books of prose fiction were written in France, Germany, Spain and North Africa.

McKay's 1933 *Banana Bottom* is regarded by many as the country's finest novel. This classic evocation of Jamaican peasant life tells the story of the black girl Bita, from a relatively prosperous village background like McKay's, trying to reintegrate after being educated in England. The folk of Banana spurn the negative, but theirs is no blanket rejection of the European or white. They accept what they can use and welcome whatever can be integrated harmoniously into the basic rhythms of their community life. In the final resolution of her tensions, Bita is doing as an individual what her community has been doing for centuries, which is perhaps McKay's answer to the problem of Jamaican identity.

McKay is more famous as a poet and much of his work dealt with American themes. His best known piece 'If We Must Die' (1919) is often considered the inaugural address of the Harlem Renaissance.

If we must die, let it not be like hogs
Hunted and penned in an inglorious spot,
While round us bark the mad
and hungry dogs,
Making their mock at our accursed lot....

According to McKay:

> The World War had ended. But its end was a signal for the outbreak of little wars between labor and capital and, like a plague breaking out in sore places, between colored folk and white. Our Negro newspapers were morbid, full of details of clashes between colored and white, murderous shootings and hangings. Traveling from city to city and unable to gauge the attitude and temper of each one, we Negro railroad men were nervous...We stuck together, some of us armed, going from the railroad station to our quarters. We stayed in our quarters all through the dreary ominous nights, for we never knew what was going to happen. It was during those days that the sonnet, If We Must Die, exploded out of me. And for it the Negro people unanimously hailed me as a poet. Indeed, that one grand outburst is their sole standard of appraising my poetry.

The poem became an international anthem of resistance. It was even quoted by Winston Churchill in a Second World War address to the US Congress encouraging America to join the fight against Nazism.

Other prominent writers to emerge from this period were the poets George Campbell, M.G. Smith, H.D. Carberry and Basil McFarlane. The post-war era produced many significant novelists – some of whom also wrote poetry – including Roger Mais, V.S. Reid, John Hearne, Neville Dawes, Andrew Salkey, Sylvia Wynter,

TREVOR RHONE

PERRY HENZELL

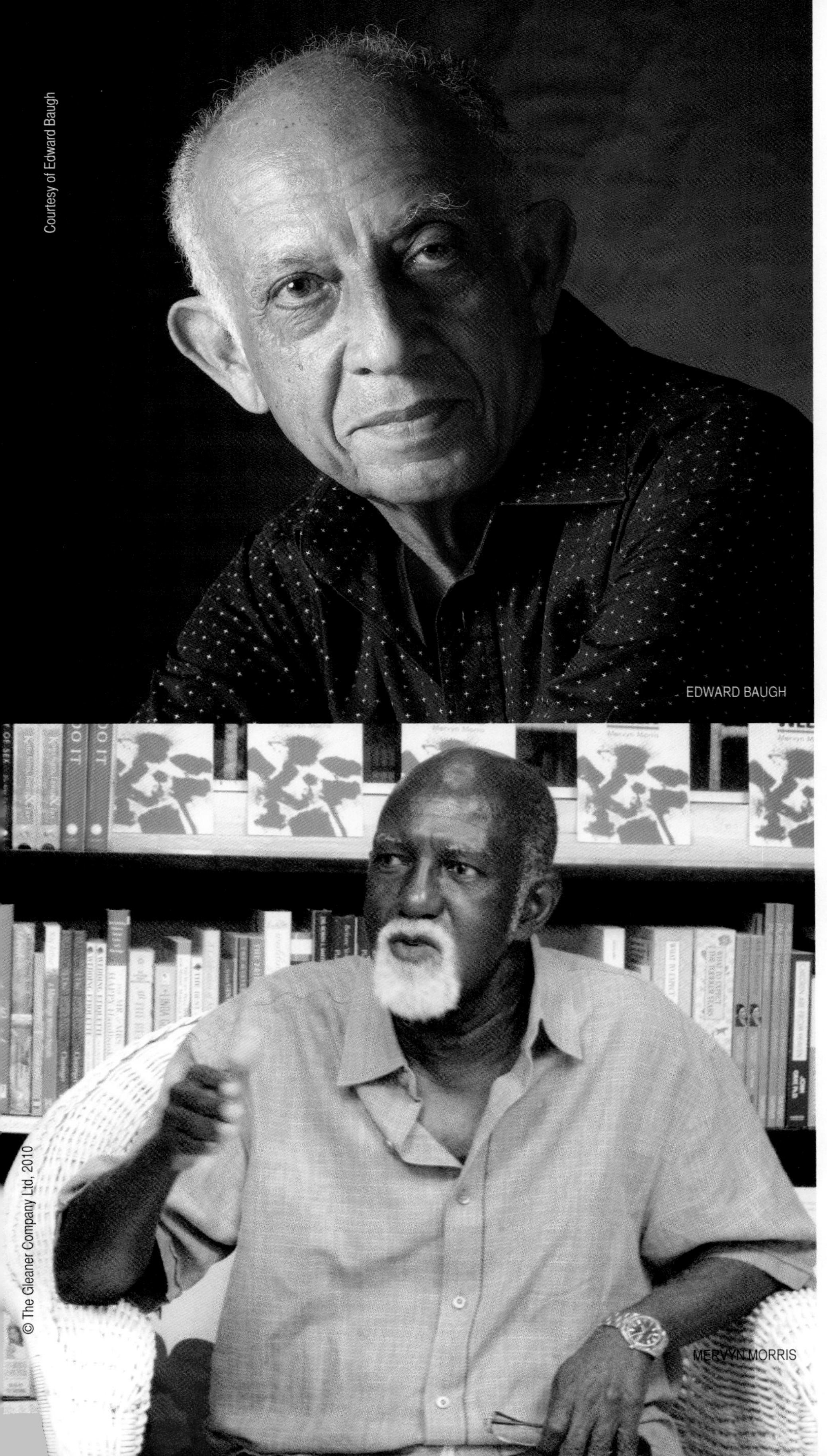
Courtesy of Edward Baugh

EDWARD BAUGH

© The Gleaner Company Ltd, 2010

MERVYN MORRIS

Orlando Patterson and Peter Abrahams. The latter was a South African who made Jamaica his home, while Patterson went on to become a prominent Harvard sociologist.

The most popular Jamaican-based writer of this period was the creator of the world's most famous spy. It was at Golden Eye in St Ann that Ian Fleming created James Bond, a name taken from the author of *Birds of the West Indies*. It's hard to say how much of the island got into these books, but Bond's womanising ways are certainly Jamaican.

Outstanding poets emerged in the 1960s and 1970s, among them John Figueroa, A.L. Hendriks, Louis Simpson, Edward Baugh, Mervyn Morris, Ralph Thompson, Dennis Scott and Anthony McNeil. The most influential locally inspired stories of the 1970s were Trevor Rhone's play 'Smile Orange', later made into a movie and the Perry Henzell directed film *The Harder They Come*. The latter is easily the island's best-known cinematic work.

From the 1980s onwards women began to dominate Jamaican writing, particularly in poetry and short fiction. Among the best known are Velma Pollard, Hazel D. Campbell, Olive Senior, Pamela Mordecai, Christine Craig, Opal Palmer Adisa, Jean Binta Breeze and Lorna Goodison, sister of noted playwright Barbara Gloudon and musicologist Bunny Goodison. Prominent male authors of poems or short stories include Earl McKenzie, Kwame Dawes and Geoffrey Phillips.

In recent times novelists have returned to prominence. Anthony Winkler's *The Lunatic* is considered something of a local modern classic. Other well-known names include Erna Brodber, Michelle Cliff, Joan Riley, Patricia Powell, Margaret Cezair-Thompson, Marlon James, Colin Channer, Kei Miller and Sadie Jones. Most of these are now based in North America or Britain, but draw extensively on Jamaican experiences in their fiction.

OLIVE SENIOR

ARCELIS GIRAMY SHARES HER POEMS AT CALABASH

ERNA BRODBER

Calabash Literary Festival, dubbed a mini-Woodstock on the Caribbean... a world-class Caribbean literary festival' by the New York Times, has helped to give Jamaican literature its highest profile in many years.

There have also been significant works blending the fictional and autobiographical. One was *Stonehaven* by Evan Jones – father of Sadie Jones and author of the famous poem 'Song of the Banana Man'. Another was Rachel Manley's *Drumblair*, which won the prestigious Governor General award in Canada.

A significant development of recent times has been the Calabash Literary Festival, founded in 2001 by Colin Channer, Kwame Dawes and Justine Henzell and held every last weekend in May at Jake's in Treasure Beach St Elizabeth. The *New York Times* dubbed it '…a mini-Woodstock on the Caribbean…a world-class Caribbean literary festival'. While according to the *London Times Literary Supplement* 'Calabash is a serious literary festival with serious literary merits. It combines this with good humour and merriment.'

Calabash has helped to give Jamaican literature its highest profile in many years. How much it says about the actual popularity of Jamaican books in Jamaica is unclear. Still, the existence of an annual book festival here attended by thousands of locals and foreigners, including the likes of Nobel Prize winner Derek Walcott, was unimaginable even ten years back. It's also worth noting that the Jamaican houses Ian Randle Publishers and LMH Publishers are two of the largest black publishers in the world outside the US.

Perhaps Jamaica's greatest literary triumphs have been those of its diasporic descendants. Zaidie Smith's *White Teeth* and Andrea Levy's *Small Island* were both hugely popular award-winning novels in Britain, while Malcolm Gladwell's *The Tipping Point* was a *New York Times* number one bestseller. All three have Jamaican mothers and they are only the most prominent of the writers with 'yard' parentage who have achieved success in the book world abroad. Not bad for a country which everyone says doesn't read.

Through Jamaican Eyes

It is often said that modern Jamaican art was born in the 1930s at Drumblair, home of Norman and Edna Manley. He was a father of Jamaica independence, while she became the island's most famous sculptor. The Manley's circle included the artist Koren der Harootian with whom she shared the first exhibition of modern art in Jamaica and other artists like Albert Huie, Ralph Campbell and David Pottinger. The novelist, photographer and painter Roger Mais was a regular at Drumblair, as were other writers and poets like Philip Sherlock and the young George Campbell and M.G. Smith. Another circle of taste and influence developed around the designer and patron Burnett Webster who exhibited the works of Manley, Koren and the photographer Dennis Glick in his design establishment. The sculptor Alvin Marriott began his career as a carver of 'deco' motifs on Webster's furniture.

At Drumblair, their discussions, poetry readings and critiques of each others' work gave birth to the modern Jamaican eye. According to Edna Manley:

> The great thing was to be able to see ourselves as Jamaicans in Jamaica and to try to free ourselves from the domination of English aesthetics. It came out in the poetry. You had poets in those days writing about daffodils, snow and bitter winds they had never experienced. I told them 'Why don't you describe the drought, when the sun gets up in the morning and

EDNA MANLEY

Courtesy of the National Library of Jamaica

ALBERT HUIE

> is king of the world all day and everything is parched? You can smell the Seymour grass and the sun goes down in a blaze of glory only to come up again tomorrow. The drought is on'. That is a very Jamaican and artistic and poetic theme. And we had the most terrific arguments over this.

Manley said the Jamaican establishment of the time 'thought we were bonkers'. The 'revolution' came in 1939 when a group of 40 liberals stormed the annual general meeting of the Institute of Jamaica. This had been created 'for the encouragement of arts, science and culture in Jamaica', but the board of directors were perpetuating a colonial outlook and approach.

> Our leader was a lawyer, Robert Braithwaite. He pointed to the portraits of the English governors on the wall and said 'Gentlemen! We have come to tell you to tear down these pictures and let Jamaican paintings take their place.' There was pandemonium. But we knew they could not ignore us anymore.

As early as 1934 Manley had called for the establishment of a National Art Gallery and her 1935 wood carving Negro Aroused would later become the first acquisition of the National Collection 'to form the nucleus of a permanent gallery'. Manley and other volunteers began to give art classes. This mushroomed into larger, more formal training courses that led to the eventual formation of the Jamaica School of Arts in 1950. Most of the country's established artists have been trained there. Now called the Edna Manley College of the Visual and Performing Arts, it houses the Schools of Art, Music, Dance and Drama.

Painting and sculpture in Jamaica evolved

Painting and sculpture in Jamaica evolved into two main groups: artists who were formally schooled and the self-taught 'Intuitives'.

into two main groups: artists who were formally schooled and the self-taught 'Intuitives'. The most prominent in the latter genre were John Dunkley known for his dark mysterious canvases and the Millers, father and son, elemental carvers of Negro heads of great power and beauty. After Dunkley's death in 1947 his mantle of leading Intuitive was inherited by Mallica 'Kapo' Reynolds, a Revivalist shepherd who painted mystical landscapes and visions and carved sculptures in wood that seemed to capture the

MALLICA 'KAPO' REYNOLDS

BARRINGTON WATSON

rhythms of Africa. Other early 'Intuitives' include the Rastafarians Everald Brown and Albert Artwell and Sydney McLaren, the naïf who delighted in depicting the hustle and bustle of the unruly streets of Kingston and rural towns like Morant Bay where he lived.

Leading figures in the formal school include: Albert Huie our greatest landscape painter, David Pottinger, Karl Parboosingh and his wife Seya, Gloria Escoffrey, Carl Abrahams, Barrington Watson, Osmond Watson, Christopher Gonzalez and the ceramicist Cecil Baugh. Over the last decades of the last century other notable talents came to the fore. Perhaps the best-known among the Intuitives are the painters Ras Dizzy, Leonard Daley and Roy Reid and the sculptor Woody Joseph; while among the trained formal school, the so-called 'mainstream', the surrealist Colin Garland, the expressionist Milton George and the abstractionists Eugene Hyde, Milton Harley and George Rodney imparted a decidedly internationalist flavour to our art.

Economy

A HISTORY OF GETTING BY

APPLETON ESTATE RUM FACTORY

Courtesy of the National Library of Jamaica

'Rich as a West Indian planter' was a proverbial British byword for extravagant wealth during the eighteenth and early nineteenth centuries. Yet Jamaica itself has never been even well-off, if one means by that a place where most inhabitants are free from struggle for their daily bread and live in relative comfort.

SLAVES TAPPING RUM

A BANANA FARM IN PORTLAND

A CANE FARMER BUNDLES CUT SUGAR CANE STALKS

The Tainos probably lived as well as hunter-gatherers can, before the Caribs and Spanish started attacking them. However the Spanish never developed the economy much beyond subsistence agriculture and trading in hides. The Buccaneers made Port Royal for a while 'the richest and wickedest city on earth', but little of that money trickled down to honest workers on the rest of the island. While a few white men lived in lap of luxury during the sugar heyday, the black slave masses endured unprecedented daily hardships.

The apparently ingrained inefficiency of this island was evident even from the supposed sugar boom years. Poor management and technological backwardness meant sugar estates were so in debt when emancipation came, that nearly all the compensation planters received for freeing their slaves went into paying off loans.

Things only got worse economically after 1838. While other West Indian lands adjusted to the new reality, Jamaican planters seemed to spend all their time grumbling about 'lazy workers' instead of innovating. While total British West Indies sugar production went up between 1839 and 1866, Jamaica's declined. The prophets of doom were loud in their lamentations and, not for the last time, newspapers trumpeted predictions that Jamaica was becoming another Haiti.

The banana industry that began in 1876 made Jamaica the world's largest banana exporter – until it was surpassed by Honduras in 1929 – and brought a certain level of prosperity to small farmers. In 1850 large-scale emigration began, first to Panama and later to other places like Cuba and the US. This lessened unemployment at home, while the money workers sent back invigorated the economy. Today Jamaica ranks near the global top in remittances received per capita and it is the country's biggest source

KNUTSFORD BOULEVARD, NEW KINGSTON

of foreign earnings. The downside is that the promise of largesse from family abroad has significantly weakened the work ethic of those still here and skewed salaries and the cost of living. Anecdotal evidence suggests that what employers can afford to pay unskilled labour is often dismissed as 'monkey money' by those waiting on a 'barrel from foreign'.

The reputation of Jamaicans abroad as hard-working, risk-taking entrepreneurs is in stark contrast to the general lackadaisicalness often witnessed here. Is it that those who go to North America or Europe are so much more highly motivated by the opportunities in these places? Or is it that those who go abroad are a self-selected minority more innately driven than the general population? They are certainly generally more educated. Some studies show that over 80 per cent of Jamaicans who earn university degrees here eventually emigrate, one of the world's highest percentages.

Jamaica doesn't have much of an export manufacturing sector to speak of, which may be just as well considering current developments in China and India. It's tough to compete with hundreds of millions of people willing to work for a dollar a day. In a sense Jamaica has already gone through the disruption many nations may face in the future.

What has been keeping this island's head above water is mainly bauxite and tourism. The island's bauxite deposits are among the richest in the world, though long-term planners wonder how long it will be before they run out. The 2009 global financial crisis saw a dramatic fall in global demand for aluminium and hence bauxite, making the future even more uncertain. One glimmer of hope is the island's copious reserves of limestone, which some think could become as important as bauxite.

On the tourism front, the country has been doing well and should do even better in the near future. The joyous victories of Jamaican athletes at the 2008 Olympics Beijing, in front of worldwide television audiences of billions,

THE JAMAICA STOCK EXCHANGE

A nation that so heedlessly lives above its means awaits inevitable bankruptcy.

provided priceless PR other places can only dream of. Tourism is also one of the few industries in which Jamaica is globally competitive. The Sandals and SuperClubs groups operate world-rated hotels. While over the past few years there has been an influx of Spanish-owned hotels such as the Riu chain.

With Kingston also becoming one of the busiest container transhipment ports in the western hemisphere, the Jamaican economy continues to putter along. Maybe the rich are getting richer. Yet the number of tertiary educated persons increases each year and the incidence of poverty almost halved over the past 15 years. The level of inequality has also declined, with the national Gini coefficient being relatively low by world standards.

In short, Jamaicans are better educated, better housed, better dressed, better fed and have greater access to cars, telephones, running water and electricity than at any time in history. Other places may be growing a lot faster. Yet the lack of any sense of urgency suggests that maybe getting by is enough for most Jamaicans. Certainly the single-minded dedication to excellence, indispensable to great success, is a scarce commodity here. Almost everyone who lives on this island for any length of time begins to take the not necessarily unhealthy outlook, that once your belly is full, nothing matters very much and very little matters at all.

Some hard-nosed economists even argue that with its sublime climate, matchless scenery and fertile soil, Jamaica's natural blessings are overly abundant and have in the long run been more of a blessing than curse. Places like Israel and Singapore, which have few natural resources and whose existence have been threatened by larger neighbours, have achieved miracles of productivity. Still Jamaica has not faced an invasion threat since the days of Horatio Nelson, so there's been no external spur urging the collective nose to the grindstone.

Morris Cargill, who as lawyer, businessman, politician, farmer and writer had as wide an experience of Jamaica as any, once put it this way:

> There is, in Jamaica today…a widespread lack of enthusiasm for hard, sustained and regular work, the result of which is relative poverty. A mere floating desire to be rich never made anyone wealthy….
> It has to be a more fundamental drive than that. And in Jamaica, whatever we may say, our actions disclose that amongst the majority that drive, at the present time at least, is lacking. How could it not be lacking in a country where there is no winter and no starvation and where a man without a penny in his pocket can still have a reasonable ration of women?

The Debt Trap

Democracy is based on the premise that given the consistent right to choose, a reasonably well-educated populace will in the long run choose well. The Jamaican people have had the good sense to maintain the institutions that make political choice possible. Yet they have also continually endorsed patronage politics and distributive financial policies, which have consistently failed to produce economic growth. Changes of party, leadership and ideology have made little difference. All financial paths have led but to an inexorably expanding national debt. Jamaica entered the 2008 global financial crisis, the worst economic downturn since the 1930s great depression, with a debt to GDP ratio of 113 per cent, the fourth highest in the world. This is clearly not sustainable. A nation that so heedlessly lives above its means awaits inevitable bankruptcy.

So what does our future hold? Will ever mounting debt burdens keep pushing the nation imperceptibly into Haitian style poverty, where the only law is the belly? Will a Jamaican government eventually default on its obligations, making the country a global financial pariah? Will poor people get fed up with elected governments and acclaim a populist strongman promising gain without pain? Or will the populace eventually learn from the past and elect an able government willing to make the tough fiscal decisions necessary for long-term growth?

The Scottish historian Alexander Tyler claimed that 'A democracy cannot exist as a permanent form of government. It can only exist until a majority of voters discover that they can vote themselves largesse out of the public treasury.'

Will Jamaica prove him right, or wrong?

THE BANK OF JAMAICA

A CRUISE SHIP DOCKED IN OCHO RIOS.

PIMENTO

Photos © Carlington Wilmot

FOOD
A LITTLE BIT FROM EVERYWHERE

Full-bodied, bold and sassy, there has never been anything shy about Jamaica, or its food. Our passion shows in the sizzle of our sauces, the exhilarating aroma of Blue Mountain coffee, the voluptuous succulence of mangoes, and the knee-buckling potency of our rum. Not to mention scorching scotch bonnet pepper, intoxicating ginger root and titillating pimento (all spice).

ACKEE AND
SALT FISH
IN ROASTED
BREADFRUIT

JERK PORK

© Ian Randle Publishers

THE BIRTH OF JERK

The name jerk derives from charqui, the Spanish version of the Quechua word charki, meaning dried meat. Legend says jerk evolved from Maroon earth ovens and Taino wood stick barbeques – *barabicu* means 'sacred fire pit' in Taino. Some speculate that the runaway male slaves who became Maroons interbred to some extent with Taino women, leading to fusion cuisine and otherwise.

In her book *Eat Caribbean*, Virginia Burke plausibly theorises that the Maroons' mobile guerrilla warfare required portable, non-spoilable food, and spicy jerk seasoning was their method of curing the meat of wild boars. Since smoke was a giveaway to pursuing British soldiers, cooking fires had to be covered. (Intriguingly, she says friends from Ghana claim the roots of jerk can be found there – and of course the original Maroons were Coromantees, who came from what is the present day Kromantse in Ghana).

After Emancipation, Maroons would go to rural markets and carry with them portions of 'jerk pork', sold from specially constructed pouches called *intetehs*, woven from palm leaves, but for a long time jerk remained a Maroon secret. It was only about 50 years ago that a version of jerk recipe came out of the mountains, and started to be prepared openly. This first happened in the lowland Portland hills below Maroon Town. As late as 1977, according to Kenneth Bilby, only two places outside Maroon communities sold jerk pork – Boston Bay and a spot across from the Port Antonio market. Colonel C.L.G. Harris says the proliferation of jerk stands across the island started when Maroons began to live outside the settlements.

Virginia Burke points out that the development of bottled seasoning such as Walkerswood, a by product of very early government sponsored research in Portland, has revolutionised jerk's access and appeal. Once jerk seasoning was available in a jar, everyone could make some version in the kitchen, leading to a quantum leap in the development of cuisine using jerk.

Good old-fashioned Jamaican dishes are rich in coconut milk, heavy on stick-to-your-ribs ground provisions, and come unapologetically laden with calories and warm memories.

Our cuisine is as distinctive as our culture. Practically all corners of the globe, including Africa, South East Asia, India, Canada, Spain, Brazil, and Britain, have contributed their little bit to pleasing the local palate. The end results are the delicious birthrights of the Jamaican belly: ackee and salt fish, curry goat, curry chicken, stew pork, tripe and beans, oxtail and beans, stew peas, mackerel rundown, escoveitch fish, jerk chicken, jerk pork, liver and onions, calalloo and salt fish, cabbage and salt fish, okro and salt fish, cornmeal porridge, peanut porridge, plantain porridge, banana porridge, hominy corn porridge, fried plantain, patties, coco bread, plantain tart, gungo or kidney bean rice and peas, mannish water, cow cod soup, pepperpot soup, red peas soup, pumpkin soup, fish tea, stamp and go, johnny cake, toto, gizzada , grater cake, plantain tart, blue drawers and tie leaf, festival, bammy, seasoned rice, turn cornmeal, sorrel, ginger beer, soursop juice, coconut water, busta, asham, jackass corn – and a whole lot more.

In its typically intrepid style, the island has wed ackee (though feared by others in the Caribbean), to salt fish (codfish) as the national dish. While Haitians who practise voodoo are awed that the bitter-tasting susumber (gully beans) they use in their ceremonies, are devoured by Jamaicans.

Lately the world has been smitten by jerk, the process of slowly cooking highly seasoned meats and vegetables over pimento wood. Jerk has become such an international hot commodity, that not long ago British celebrity chef Ainsley Harriott told BBC viewers to make jerk one of the 50 things they eat before they die.

Restaurateurs in foreign lands like Guatemala and India, who would be hard-pressed to tell a pimento from a peppercorn, are now luring patrons with the promise of jerk dishes to make the taste buds sing. Yet jerk, say those who know, is only jerk when it uses authentic Jamaican grown fresh ginger, thyme, scallions, scotch bonnet and pimento wood.

Traditional Favourites

Good old-fashioned Jamaican dishes are rich in coconut milk, heavy on stick-to-your-ribs ground provisions, and come unapologetically laden with calories and warm memories. Beyond jerk and ackee there are salacious goodies like mackerel rundown, otherwise called dip and fall back, oozing with coconut milk and spiced with onion, thyme and other seasonings.

One of the island's most famous soups, pepperpot, dates back to the Tainos. It is often made with callaloo, okra, kale, pig's tail (or salt beef), coconut meat, yams, scallions, and hot peppers. Versions of this soup are also found in other Caribbean islands.

Then there is the sweet delight of cornmeal and sweet potato puddings. Done the old-fashioned way, usually on Saturday nights for Sunday dinner, the pudding was baked in a puddin' pan on a coal stove with burning coal on top and underneath. Hence the phrase 'hell a top, hell a bottom, halleluiah inna middle'.

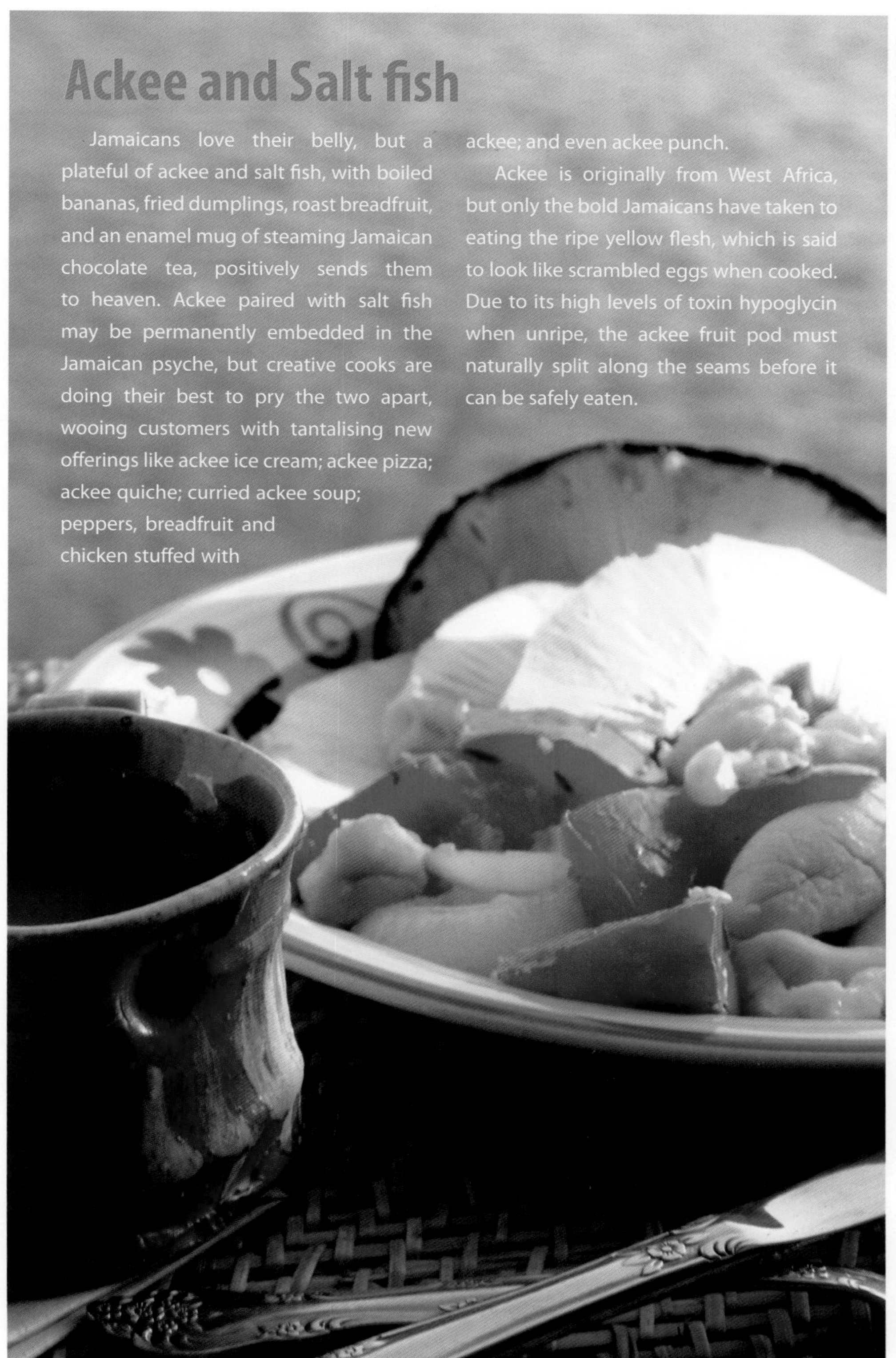

© Carlington Wilmot

Ackee and Salt fish

Jamaicans love their belly, but a plateful of ackee and salt fish, with boiled bananas, fried dumplings, roast breadfruit, and an enamel mug of steaming Jamaican chocolate tea, positively sends them to heaven. Ackee paired with salt fish may be permanently embedded in the Jamaican psyche, but creative cooks are doing their best to pry the two apart, wooing customers with tantalising new offerings like ackee ice cream; ackee pizza; ackee quiche; curried ackee soup; peppers, breadfruit and chicken stuffed with ackee; and even ackee punch.

Ackee is originally from West Africa, but only the bold Jamaicans have taken to eating the ripe yellow flesh, which is said to look like scrambled eggs when cooked. Due to its high levels of toxin hypoglycin when unripe, the ackee fruit pod must naturally split along the seams before it can be safely eaten.

© Diana McIntyre-Pike

FRUIT SHOP

© Carlington Wilmot

SCOTCH BONNET PEPPERS

Holidays bring their own scrumptious traditions. Baking black cake, a throwback to the British plum pudding, is a solemnly observed annual ritual. Serious bakers soak their fruits in rum for months or even a year. The cake is made just before Christmas, and is doled out at Christmas dinner and to visitors in thin slices, to stretch it through the season. Of course the great Jamaican Christmas drink is sorrel.

Easter is bun time, with everyone having a favourite brand among the huge variety available in supermarkets. For some Jamaicans abroad, Easter without bun and cheese is like Sunday without rice and peas, so many have relatives at home ship the baked goodies to them by post or courier. Easter bun derives from the English tradition of Hot Cross Buns at Good Friday. They are still eaten at Easter time in England, and some Yorkshire buns are even today indistinguishable from the local variety.

Jamaica's most well-known bread is the dense white variety called hardough, whose origin is unknown, but possibly Cuban. The dough break machine, important in its achieving the right texture, is utilised only in Jamaica, Cuba and Haiti. Norma Benghiat says that on a 1986 visit to Andalusia in Spain, she encountered bread identical to hardough, but made into rolls instead of loaves.

Now traditionalists may grumble, but fast food places like KFC and Burger King are massively popular with Jamaicans. Some even joke that Kentucky fried chicken is the new national dish! Yet dabble as they might with foreign fare, Jamaicans are never going to give up their yard food. After all, where would our Olympic gold medalists be without their regular performance enhancing doses of yam, banana, sweet potato and dasheen?

Kingston and the Corporate Area

Sure there are fancy restaurants in Kingston and in swanky resorts along the north coast and Negril. However, to 'taste the hand' of Jamaica, it's best to follow the trail of locals who can point the way to the best fried dumpling shop, pudding stop and porridge place.

Porridge-loving Kingstonians flock to Juicy Black in Maverley, just above Washington Boulevard and Molynes Road. On Sundays, cars line both side of the streets for his blend of cream of wheat and peanuts and hominy corn. Norma on Whitehall Avenue serves cheap, down home meals. While Rotty, described by cookbook author Rosemary Parkinson as the 'king of cookshops,' serves up traditional Jamaican fare from his cramped outpost in Stony Hill, north of the city.

Under the huge billboards, on the south east side of the Cross Roads square, Fatty (Curline Pitter) serves up heapings of boiled bananas, dumplings, brown stew chicken, callaloo and porridge while most of the city slumbers. Exotic dancers, entertainers and partygoers on their way home, or workers on the early shift, know they can get a hearty breakfast at Fatty's from as early as 3:30 a.m. When the barmaid is on time, regulars get into the spirit of things before the break of dawn.

Great pan chicken and pork can be found at the corner of Northside Plaza on Old Hope Road, on Red Hills Road, and on Mannings Hill Road.

PAN CHICKEN AT NORTHSIDE PLAZA

The Harbour View roundabout has seafood on the go, with fish, oysters, mussels, crab, conch, lobster and shrimp all available at reasonable prices. For delicious seafood in a relaxing on the waterfront atmosphere, Port Royal is the place to be. The once 'wickedest city' is known for places like Gloria's, Y-Knot and Fisherman's Cabin, where you can get any edible sea creature cooked in whatever style you want.

For a kick to the mojo, there's Harry Joseph and Sons Health Juice Centre on Grove Road. In this little corner, a stone's throw away from the buzzing Half Way Tree square, Harry (real name Morgan) packs a powerful punch with his 'Magnum' drink. Old-timers and dancehall DJs say a single shot of Magnum levels the playing field of love. Other roots drinks on Harry's long list include 'Front-end Lifter' and 'Summer'.

Along the North Coast

A well-known roadside eatery in Lucea, Hanover is Tapa Top Food Hut and Bar, whose hardy cookshop provisions includes cow foot and brown stew pork. A good ital breakfast can be purchased from the Rasta on the corner the Montego Bay Bus Park.

Just Cool on the roadside in Priory, St Ann (between St Ann's Bay and Runaway Bay), is the hot spot for sweet potato pudding. On any given day there are up to 25 puddings baking on the coal stoves, says owner Edgar Wallace. Not far away, in Salem, Runaway Bay, the Ackee Tree's Irish Moss provides a smooth, rich pick-me-upper. Midway between Kingston and Ocho Rios is the Faith's Pen collection of food shops that serve a very wide variety of popular Jamaican dishes.

Over in Portland, Dickie's Best Kept Secret is housed in a blue hut with yellow trimming, but don't look for a sign – there is none. This little restaurant, hanging over a cliff, coming from the St Mary side towards Port Antonio, serves up a robust Jamaican breakfast of fresh fruits, hardough bread, ackee, eggs and steaming tea sweetened with honey.

Closer to Port Antonio, just past the Blue Lagoon, the rich and famous quietly slip into Woody's Low Bridge Place for fish cake and fritters (stamp and go). Taxi drivers and those in the know make the trek up to the hills above the town for a late night snack at Jah T.

WOODY'S LOW BRIDGE

© Ian Randle Publishers

© Diane McIntyre-Pike

Along the South Coast

Sunday mornings find many Kingstonians driving to Hellshire beach in St Catherine to kick back and feast on fish, festival and bammy. Heading west, if it is mango time, you will see the mango vendors of Toll Gate, who have every variety available from East Indian to Julie to Bombay to Tommy Atkin. Just past the Clarendon–Manchester border, you encounter the fruit vendors of Porus, famous for ortaniques, tangerines, navel oranges, bananas, pineapples, papayas, star apples, naseberries, sweet sops and sour sops. Nearby Mandeville, the smoky huts of Melrose yam park beckon to passersby, where vendors boast that they sell the best roast yam and salt fish anywhere.

In Mandeville the excellent Bloomfield Great House

© Diane McIntyre-Pike

LITTLE OCHI

...a row of pots bubble under the zinc roofs...

Restaurant has a lovely view and very tasty food at reasonable prices. A nice excursion is lunch at Bloomfield, followed by a drive through the scenic Mile Gully and Devon region, and evening tea at the quaint Villa Bella Hotel in cool Christiana.

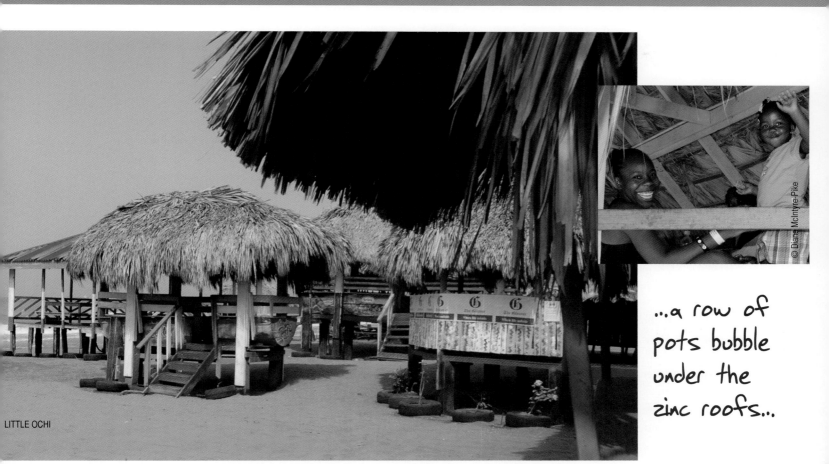

West of Manchester past Holland Bamboo in St Elizabeth, a row of pots bubble under the zinc roofs at Howie's, starting with porridges in the mornings, and continuing through the day with hearty fare like peanut soup and fish tea. A little further on is Middle Quarters, famous for its peppered shrimps, with Billy's Grassy Park serving some of the best. Located 14 miles out at sea off the coast of Parottee is Floyd's Pelican Bar. Owner, Floyd Peck, says he was instructed in a dream to build his establishment in the sea. The collection of shacks at Scott's Cove Park near 'Border' between St Elizabeth and Westmoreland serve seafood of all varieties.

© Jeffrey Marshall

MELROSE YAM PARK

Places to Eat

Food Festivals

In the last decade, Jamaicans have started paying homage to local food with various festivals and events across the island. One of the first, the Boston Jerk Festival in Portland, draws tens of thousands of people at the beginning of each July. A second jerk festival, held in Ewarton, St Catherine, at the end of July, also draws an enthusiastic crowd.

There are also two breadfruit festivals in St Thomas and St Mary; yam festival in Trelawny; bussu festival in Portland; ackee festival in Linstead, St Catherine; curry festival in Westmoreland; Nyammings and Jammins in Montego Bay; chicken festival in Yallahs, St Thomas; and various fish and seafood festivals, including one at the popular Little Ochi in Alligator Pond, Manchester.

Jamaica's passion for food is also highlighted in events like the Kingston Restaurant Week each November, and the decade old Jamaica Observer's Table Talk Awards, which applauds excellence in food – from innovative dishes to best service.

In the meantime, boiled cow's tongue, mackerel pizza with cassava base, plantain chutney, cashew wine and other innovative creations continue to flow from amateur cooks and students across the country. They show off their goods each April and May in the Jamaica Cultural Development Commission (JCDC) Festival of Food competitions.

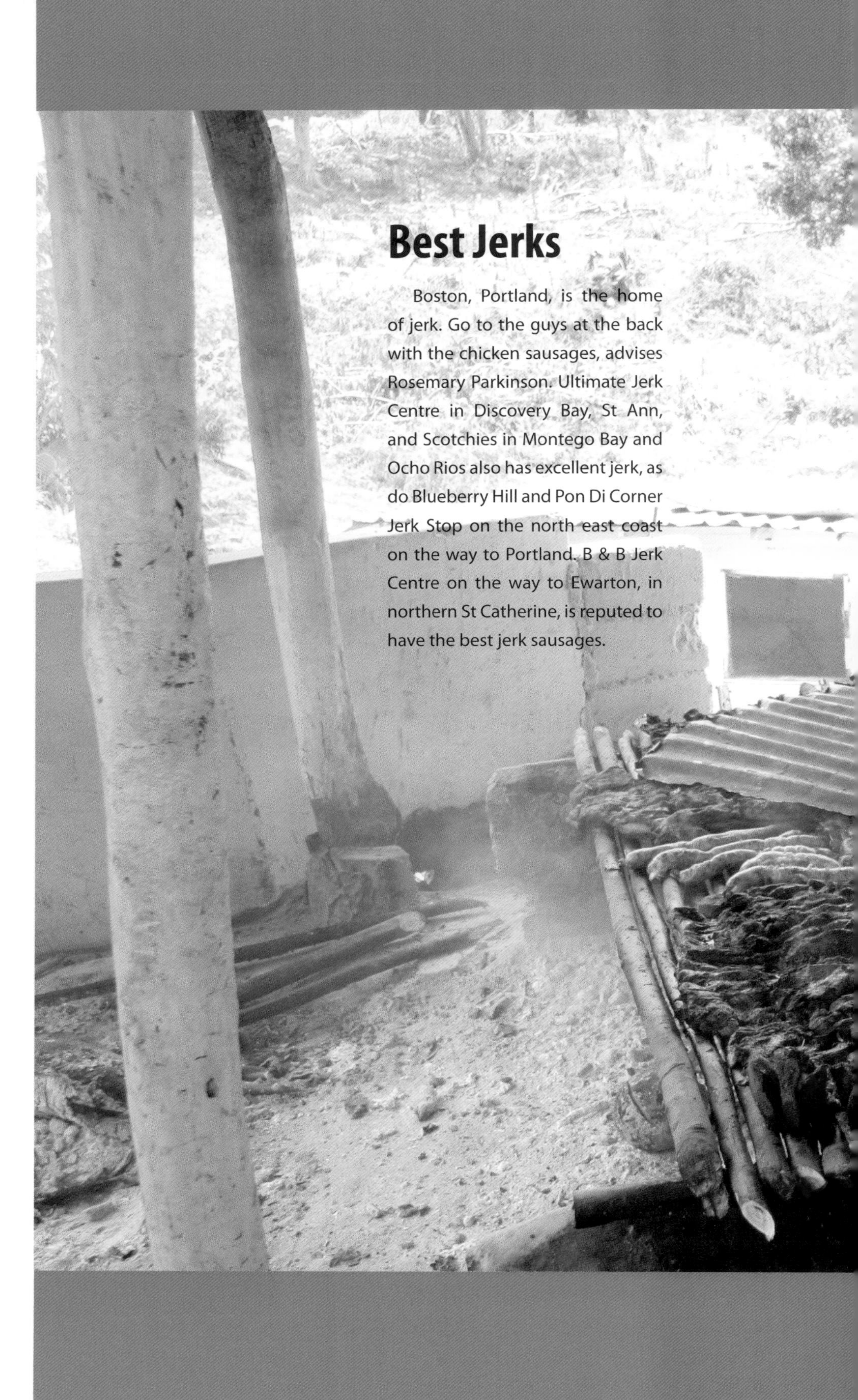

Best Jerks

Boston, Portland, is the home of jerk. Go to the guys at the back with the chicken sausages, advises Rosemary Parkinson. Ultimate Jerk Centre in Discovery Bay, St Ann, and Scotchies in Montego Bay and Ocho Rios also has excellent jerk, as do Blueberry Hill and Pon Di Corner Jerk Stop on the north east coast on the way to Portland. B & B Jerk Centre on the way to Ewarton, in northern St Catherine, is reputed to have the best jerk sausages.

Scenery

AROUND THE BEAUTIFUL ISLE

In her best selling book, *1,000 Places to See Before You Die: A Traveler's Life List*, Patricia Schultz includes five Jamaican choices. She calls Jamaica Inn in Ocho Rios 'a civilised anachronism'. Reggae Sumfest in Montego Bay is 'the party of parties'. Rock House and Rick's in Negril is 'high style, low attitude and sunset served on the rocks'. Strawberry Hill in Irish Town is 'on top of the world in the Blue Mountains', and the Pork Pit restaurant in Montego Bay is 'a beachside introduction to the world of jerk'.

Well far be it from me to contradict someone who's been everywhere and seen everything, but while it's a pleasant enough eatery, few people who live here would rank the Pork Pit in the 1,000 most memorable places to visit in Jamaica. Anyway, 'you pays your money, and you takes your choice.' With that caveat in mind, here's an alternative list of five Jamaican must sees.

A SECTION OF SEVEN MILE BEACH, NEGRIL

Port Antonio and its Environs

For the best jerk and scenery, it's Port Antonio and surrounding environs. The most beautiful part of the world's most beautiful island must be special indeed, and 'Porty' is. World-travelling movie star Errol Flynn washed up here when his yacht was blown ashore by a storm, and called it

> More beautiful than any woman I've ever seen. Never had I seen a land so beautiful. Everywhere there is a blanket of green so thick that the earth never shows through. Now I knew where the writers of the Bible had got their description of paradise. They had come here to Jamaica. When God created Eden, this is what he was aiming at.

He was so taken, that he bought Navy Island, and made it his home. After Flynn's death his widow, actress Patrice Wymore, remained in Jamaica, and once won the national champion farmer title!

Port Antonio became a sort of boom town in the late 1800s and early 1900s after sea captain Lorenzo Dow Baker started shipping bananas to the US. This 'green gold' inspired the famous 'Day O' or 'Banana Boat song':

BLUE LAGOON

FRENCHMAN'S COVE

Six hand, seven hand, eight hand bunch!
Daylight come and me want to go home
Come, Mr Tally Mon, tally me banana
Daylight come and me want to go home
Me say day O, me say day ay O!
Daylight come and me want to go home.

WORKERS LOADING BANANAS IN THE EARLY 1900s

It also gave birth to one of Jamaica's best known poems, Evan Jones's 'Song of the Banana Man', the last verse of which reads

So when you see dese ol clothes
brown wid stain,
An soaked right through wid de Portlan rain,
Don't cas your eye nor turn your nose,
Don't judge a man by his patchy clothes,
I'm a strong man, a proud man, an I'm free,
Free as dese mountains, free as dis sea,
I know myself, an I know my ways,
An will sing wid pride to de end o my days
(Sung)Praise God an m'big right han'
I will live an die a banana man.

Legend has it that when Flynn saw bananas brought down the river on bamboo rafts, he suggested to boatmen that they carry passengers on the scenic trip. However, local raftsmen scoff at this story. However it began though, rafting on the Rio Grande River which

More beautiful than any woman I've ever seen. Never had I seen a land so beautiful....When God created Eden this is what he was aiming at.

might be described as floating down the heart of paradise, is one of the most memorable experiences any visitor can have in Jamaica.

For sheer loveliness it's only rivalled by the Blue Lagoon, a limestone sink estimated to be about 200 feet deep. Its luminous azure waters are ringed by jungle like green foliage, creating a spectacular picture postcard setting, used in many movies. Those lucky enough to get caught in a rain storm while eating dinner there – and frequent rain is the usual price of natural beauty – will experience an almost surreal Hollywood romance yet real life atmosphere.

The area suffers from an embarrassment of riches, including San San beach, Fairy Hill beach, Reach Falls, Somerset Falls and the Nonsuch Caves. One unmissable highlight is Boston Bay, the original home of jerk and still reckoned by connoisseurs to be the best. Sorry Pork Pit!

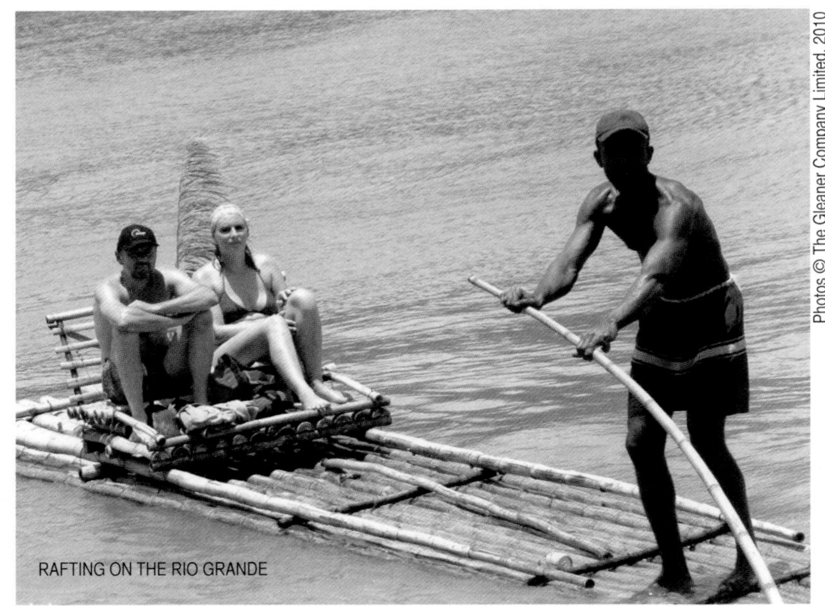

RAFTING ON THE RIO GRANDE

Negril

'More than a beach' is one of the Jamaica Tourist Board's slogans, but if it's a beach you want, there are few, if any, better than Negril's famous seven mile long stretch. Walking on its powder soft white sand and floating in the balmy crystal clear water is about as close to heaven as human beings can get. At such moments life does indeed seem a wonderful thing. The non-high rise atmosphere, and buzzing reggae-filled night life, give Negril a funky 'with it but laid back' atmosphere unmatched by any other Jamaican resort town. Yet it's the soft blue sea that transports you to ecstasy, and yes, sunset in the West End at Rick's Cafe is spectacular.

WHILE GEORGIAN ARCHITECTURE IS CELEBRATED AT THE STRAWBERRY HILL RESORT (BELOW), THERE ARE MANY HOMES ACROSS THE ISLAND WHERE IT HAS BEEN NEGLECTED (RIGHT)

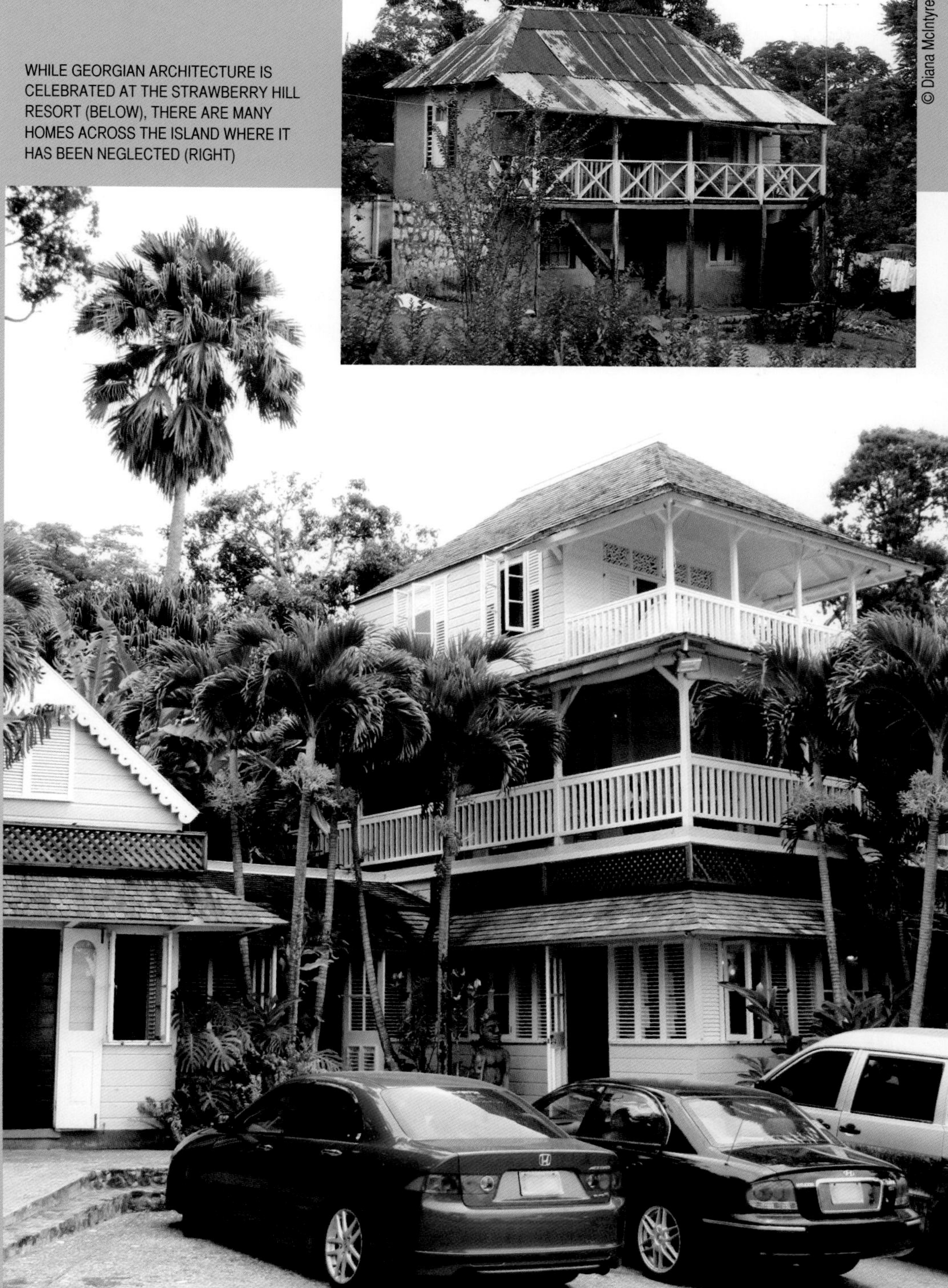

Kingston

NOT EVEN TRYING

Kingston may be a fascinating place culturally, but the national capital is never going to win any most beautiful city awards. In fact Jamaica is pretty much an architectural wasteland. Sure a few buildings stand out because of the non-descript surroundings, but a book of *Great Jamaican Architectural Masterpieces* will be about as thick as *Famous Singaporean Reggae Singers*. As to the surviving Great Houses, in novelist John Hearne's words:

> They are for the most part, relatively modest gentlemen's houses modified from English originals for comfortable living in the tropics. The title 'Great' is, for most of them, a harmless but aesthetically indefensible flight of colonial hyperbole.

People here don't even seem to try. Driving through the countryside, you notice lots of houses basically unpainted or even unrendered. In most countries, elite neighbourhoods are generally spotlessly manicured with neat fences, but the abodes of the rich here are distinguished mainly by bigger houses and larger lots. Even

BUXTON HALL, MICO TEACHERS' COLLEGE

in the poshest neighbourhoods, such as Cherry Gardens and Jack's Hill, you still often see potholes, crumbling curbs, unfinished walls and wandering cows.

What accounts for this striking national lack of architectural ambition? One possible explanation is the wonderful scenery. Just as truly beautiful women don't need to wear make up, maybe the Jamaican landscape is so gorgeous, that even the ugliest – or most striking – house seems hardly noticeable. Perhaps the logic is that we're surrounded by loveliness no matter what, and it's function not form that really matters. So as long as the wall is sturdy enough, why trouble yourself about a coat of paint? For this is nothing if not a land of least effort. If you don't have to, why bother?

HISTORICAL BUILDING ON EAST STREET, KINGSTON

The Cockpit

Rugged and largely inaccessible, the 500 square mile Cockpit Country in southwest Trelawny is the most mysterious part of Jamaica. The seventeenth-century British named it after the then popular cock-fighting arenas, which were hot, humid and dangerous places. Consisting of a regular array of round-topped conical hills and sinks, the karst terrain is often being likened to an inverted egg carton. As it is unfavourable to human settlement, some semblance of the country's original flora and fauna remains, creating an island-within-an-island of specially-adapted biodiversity found nowhere else on earth.

Covered in dense vegetation, this isolated region provided a perfect hideout for Maroons. One southern section is known as the District of Look Behind in reference to the Maroon habit of ambushing British redcoats. Another is called Me No Sen, You No Come. Every January 6 in Accompong, named after the brother of the legendary leader Cudjoe, the Maroons celebrate the anniversary of the 1739 peace treaty with feasting, dancing and drumming.

No roads traverse the Cockpits, which are accessible only from the surrounding settlements. They are best explored from Windsor, Troy, or Accompong, but only with trained guides, as it's easy to become hopelessly lost in the endless hills that all look alike. There are numerous caves, the best known being Windsor, which stretches three miles underground. The harsh landscape has a rugged grace, with razor-sharp limestone hills dropping precipitously to the valley floor. The trails stop where virgin forests remain, and penetrating this area is not recommended, as there is a constant danger of plunging through the thin limestone covering into bottomless sinkholes.

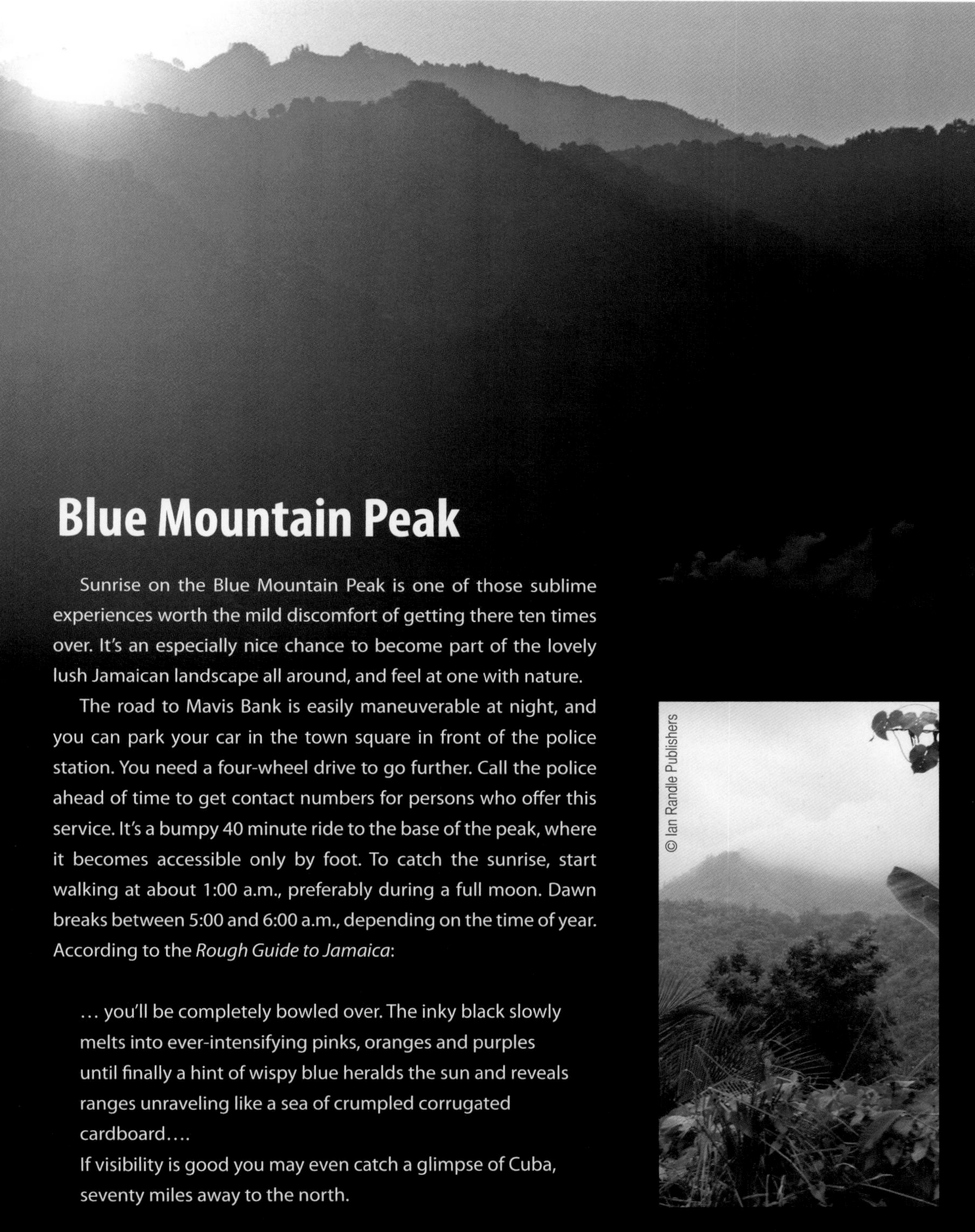

© Ray Chen/Periwinkle

© Ian Randle Publishers

Blue Mountain Peak

Sunrise on the Blue Mountain Peak is one of those sublime experiences worth the mild discomfort of getting there ten times over. It's an especially nice chance to become part of the lovely lush Jamaican landscape all around, and feel at one with nature.

The road to Mavis Bank is easily maneuverable at night, and you can park your car in the town square in front of the police station. You need a four-wheel drive to go further. Call the police ahead of time to get contact numbers for persons who offer this service. It's a bumpy 40 minute ride to the base of the peak, where it becomes accessible only by foot. To catch the sunrise, start walking at about 1:00 a.m., preferably during a full moon. Dawn breaks between 5:00 and 6:00 a.m., depending on the time of year. According to the *Rough Guide to Jamaica*:

> … you'll be completely bowled over. The inky black slowly melts into ever-intensifying pinks, oranges and purples until finally a hint of wispy blue heralds the sun and reveals ranges unraveling like a sea of crumpled corrugated cardboard….
>
> If visibility is good you may even catch a glimpse of Cuba, seventy miles away to the north.

Treasure Beach

'Back in time' is what the Treasure Beach area of St Elizabeth often feels like it reminding many of Negril 30 years ago. The beaches may not be as white, nor the waters as calm and blue, as on the North Coast, but the laid back old time charm more than makes up for this. The surrounding areas are also a treat. Lover's Leap – with the obligatory story of star-crossed sweethearts jumping hand in hand to death – has a very enchanting view, especially at sunrise or sunset. While a drive through nearby the hills of Malvern is filled with captivating mountain side vistas. A great way to cap a rambling day in 'Sainty' is dinner just across the Manchester border at Little Ochi in the fishing village of Alligator Pond. Eating just-caught fish, crab, shrimp or lobster on the beach as the sun goes down, with mellow music on the nearby sound system – well it doesn't get much better.

Historical Moments – Trevor Munroe

Reggae Songs – Omar Davies

Dancehall Songs – Mel Cooke

Gospel Songs – Tommy Cowan and Carlene Davis

Sports Personalities –Tony Becca

All-Time West Indies Team – Simon Crosskill

All-Time Relay Squads – Paul Auden

All-Time Football Starting Squad – Geoffrey Maxwell

Art of the National Gallery – David Boxer

Books – Carolyn Cooper

Food + Drink – Grace Cameron

Plants + Trees – Thelma McCathy

Travel Off the Beaten Path – Robert Lalah

Proverbs – Vivien Morris-Brown

Jamaican Poems – Wayne Chen

Heritage Sites – David Buckley

Folk Songs – Hazel Ramsay-McClune

Birds + Butterflies – Vaughan Turland

National and Ecological Beauty – Jill Byles

Unforgettable Jamaican Experiences

Jamaican Comic Songs – Ity and Fancy Cat

The Experts Speak

JAMAICA TOP TENS

EMANICPATION SQUARE, SPANISH TOWN

Top Ten Historical Moments that Shaped the Jamaica Nation

PROFESSOR TREVOR MUNROE, Professor of Government and Politics, UWI

1494 Columbus arrives: Written Jamaican history begins.

1655 English takeover: Jamaica becomes English speaking.

1690 First Maroon War: Cudjoe and his warriors show slaves are willing to fight for their freedom.

1831 Sam Sharpe Rebellion: One of the first recorded examples of non-violent passive resistance makes it clear that plantation slavery is no longer tenable in the British Empire.

1838 Emancipation: The majority of Jamaicans are for the first time free to think and act in their own self-interests.

1865 Morant Bay Rebellion: Paul Bogle shows that the Jamaican peasantry is willing to fight for its rights.

1927 Marcus Garvey returns to Jamaica: The political education of the Jamaican masses begins.

1938 Frome Riots and Kingston protests: The Jamaican masses show they are the dominant force in the country.

1944 Universal Suffrage: For the first time, all Jamaicans are politically equal.

1962 Independence: Jamaicans take complete charge of their own destiny.

Top Ten Reggae Songs (1957–1982)

DR OMAR DAVIES, Former Finance Minister of Jamaica and Acknowledged Music Expert

1. 'Get Up, Stand Up' by The Wailers
2. 'Easy Snappin'' by Theophilus Beckford
3. 'One Love' by Bob Marley
4. 'Satta Massagana' by The Abyssinians
5. 'Schooling the Duke' by Don Drummond
6. 'Got To Go Back Home' by Bob Andy
7. 'Can't Blame The Youth' by Peter Tosh
8. 'Nanny Goat' by Larry & Alvin
9. 'Oh Carolina' by The Folkes Brothers
10. 'Carry Go, Bring Come' by Justin Hinds & The Dominoes

BOB ANDY

Top Ten Dancehall Songs (1983–2009)

MEL COOKE, Entertainment Writer, *Jamaica Gleaner*

1. 'Love Punaany Bad' (Shabba Ranks) – The late 1980s quintessential homage to 'that little piece of renking meat…', the essential tune for any dancehall session's early morning 'bubbling time'.
2. 'Greetings' (Half Pint) – The 1986 dancehall hail on the Powerhouse label, recorded in England.
3. 'Action' (Terror Fabulous and Nadine Sutherland) – Written and produced by Dave Kelly, hit the Billboard charts in 1994, named in *Vibe Magazine's* top 20 duets of all time in 2007.
4. 'Minivan' (General Trees) – The first deejay tune to hit number one for the year (RJR top 100, 1985).
5. 'Driver' (Buju Banton) – A revival of the Unmetered Taxi rhythm by Sly and Robbie, the 2006 song was the centrepiece of Buju's Sting performance that year, which in turn was Sting's major drawing card; used in the JLP general election 2007 campaign.
6. 'Bogle; (Buju Banton) – The early 1990s dance tune of dance tunes and, as Peter Ashbourne pointed out at the 2008 Global Reggae Conference at UWI, Mona, done to a beat with a distinctive double kick that has become the backbone of modern dancehall (until the fusions of producers like DASECA and Stephen McGregor).
7. 'Look' (Bounty Killer) – On Dave Kelly's 'Bug' rhythm, among the first set of CD singles released in Jamaica, mid-1990s.

SHABBA RANKS

8. 'Welcome to Jamrock' (Damian 'Jr Gong' Marley) – Title track from the outstanding 2005 album, a genuine, lasting hit 'a yard' and abroad.
9. 'Eagle and the Hawk' (Bounty Killer) – The ultimate 'bad man' braggadocio tune of the mid-1990s that doesn't go into figuratively splashing marrows and rifle recoils.
10. 'Stab Up De Meat' (Lady Saw) – Ripped up and reconfigured what a DJ is when released in the early 1990s, announced the arrival of a true original.

BUJU BANTON

DAMION MARLEY(JUNIOR GONG)

Top Ten Jamaican Gospel Songs (alphabetically)

TOMMY COWAN AND CARLENE DAVIS, Music Producer and Well-known Gospel Singer

PAPA SAN

'All Christian Soldiers' – Joan Flemmings

'Can't Even Walk' – Grace Thrillers

'Hail Him Up' – Papa San

'Hear My Cry' – Marvia Providence

'Hold My Hand Today' – Glacia Robinson

'Hurry Up' – Sister Scully

'Man from Galilee' – Otis Wright

'Jesus is the Winner Man' – Lester Lewis

'This Island Needs Jesus' – Carlene Davis

'Turn Your Radio On' – Claudelle Clarke

CARLENE DAVIS

Top Ten Jamaicans in Sport of All-Time

TONY BECCA, *Jamaica Gleaner* Senior Sports Editor

LAWRENCE ROWE

1. George Headley – the man who scored 2,190 runs with ten test centuries in 22 test matches, averaged 60.83, and who was known simply as 'Mass George'.

2. Usain Bolt – three gold medals and three world records in one Olympic Games, without question, the best single performance by any Jamaican in any sport, and arguably the greatest sprinter of all time.

3. Herb McKenley – although a bit disappointing in his medal count, he was arguably the greatest athlete of his time, silver medal after a photo finish in the 100 metres at the Olympic Games, two silver medals in the 400 metres at the Olympic Games, and the fastest leg in a 1,600 metres relay when he paced Jamaica to victory in the Helsinki Olympics of 1952.

4. Arthur Wint – Jamaica's first gold medal winner at the Olympic Games when he won the 400 metres in London in 1948, silver medallist in the 800 metres in London and in Helsinki, gold medal winner in the 1,600 metres relay.

5. Michael Holding – a member of the champion West Indies team, arguably the greatest cricket team of all time, arguably, and despite two like Valentine and Courtney Walsh, the greatest bowler in Jamaica's cricket history, and the man who is believed, by many, to have bowled the greatest over in the history of the game.

6. Veronica Campbell – 200 metres gold medallist at back-to-back Olympic Games in Athens and in Beijing, gold medal winner in the women's 400 metre relay in Athens, and bronze medal winner in the 100 metres.

7. Lawrence Rowe – world record performance of 214 and 100 not out in his first Test match, 302 versus England, rated one of the finest innings by a West Indian in Test cricket, next to Headley, Jamaica's best batsman, and after Headley and before Bolt, probably, and definitely so the rebel tour of South Africa, the most loved Jamaican sportsman or sportswoman of all time.

8. Merlene Ottey – the queen of Jamaica's sports for many, many years, silver medallist in the women's 100 and 200 metres at the Atlanta Olympics in 1996, silver medallist in the 100 metres and gold medallist in the 200 at successive World Championships in Stuttgart and in Gothenburg in 1993 and in 1995, and the woman with the most medals, eight, at the Olympic Games.

9. Michael McCallum – the 'body snatcher', Jamaica's first world boxing champion.

10. Courtney Walsh – like Holding, a member of the great West Indies team of the 1980s and the early 1990s, a former world record holder for the highest number of wickets in Test cricket, 519 wickets, including a hat-trick, when he retired after a long, consistent, and glorious career. He is also numbered among the people's favourite.

CHAMPION MEN'S 4X100 METRES RELAY TEAM AT THE BEIJING OLYMPICS 2008

All-Time West Indies Team

SIMON CROSSKILL, TV Personality and Sports Commentator

George Headley
Gordon Greenidge
Viv Richards
Brian Lara
Gary Sobers
Clive Lloyd
Jeff Dujon
Malcolm Marshall
Andy Roberts
Mikey Holding
Lance Gibbs

All-Time Jamaica Relay Squads

DR PAUL AUDEN, Team Doctor for Several National Track and Field Teams and Acknowledged Track and Field Expert

Men's 4X100 Metres	Women's 4X100 Metres	Men's 4X400 Metres	Women's 4X400 Metres
Usain Bolt, Asafa Powell, Donald Quarrie, Lennox Miller	Shelly-Ann Fraser, Merlene Ottey, Kerron Stewart, Juliet Cuthbert	Herb McKenley, Arthur Wint, George Rhoden, Burt Cameron	Lorraine Graham, Sherika Williams, Novlene Williams, Grace Jackson
RESERVES: Raymond Stewart, Herb McKenley	RESERVES: Veronica Campbell, Sherone Simpson	RESERVES: Gregory Haughton, Davian Clarke	RESERVES: Sandi Richards, Deon Hemmings

All-Time Jamaica Football Starting XI and Squad

GEOFFREY MAXWELL, Former Jamaica National Football Coach

[Orville Edwards]

Paul Thomas   Larry Wynter   Jackie Bell   Frank Brown

Henry Largie

Syd Bartlett   Herkley Vaz

Allan Cole

Art Welsh   Noel Tappin

Reserves: Vester Constantine – GK, Delroy Scott – Def., Edward Dawkins – Def, Asher Welsh – For., Tegat Davis – For., Peter Marston – Mid Field, Lascelles Dunkley – Mid Field.

Top Ten at the National Gallery of Jamaica

DAVID BOXER, Director Emeritus and Chief Curator

I must begin at the beginning: the superb art of our first known inhabitants the Taino. The gallery has on display the four supreme masterpieces in wood of these gifted carvers. Rarest and oldest is the dujo done a millennium ago but my favourite for its sheer sculptural force is the **Pelican with a cohoba platform** (cohoba is the hallucinogenic drug used in zemi worship) done perhaps 700 years ago.

I started paying more attention to Isaac Mendez Belisario when it was proven that he was Jamaican born and not simply the itinerant British artist that we once thought him to be. His oils seem a fascinating blend of the trained artist (he was trained in watercolours) and the untutored naïf. Still for its sheer rarity and importance I would select the **Actor Boy Lithograph** in the collection.

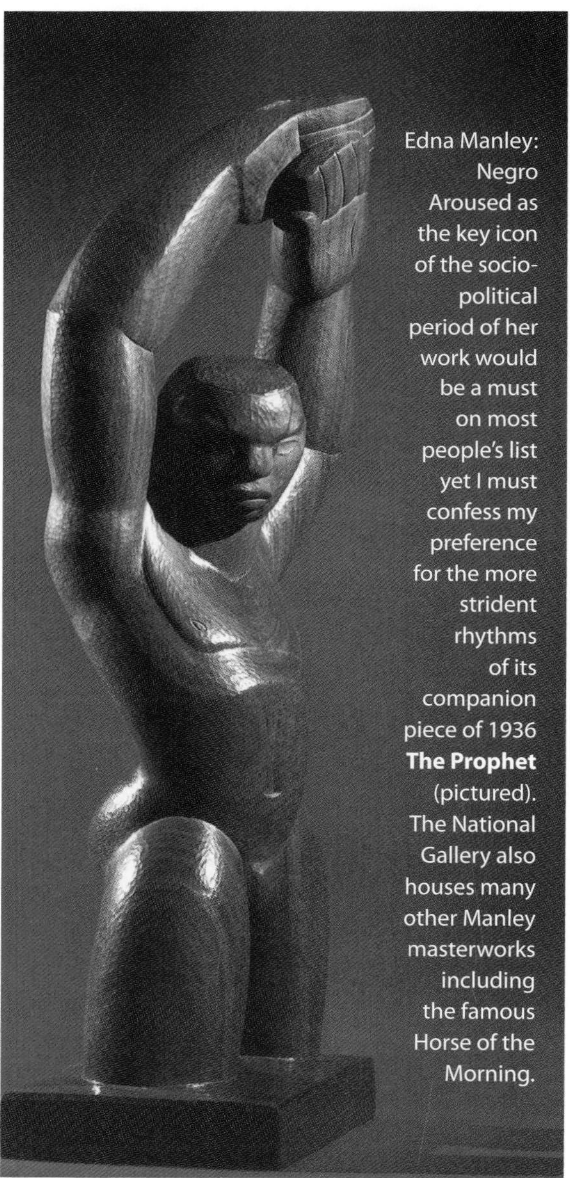

Edna Manley: Negro Aroused as the key icon of the socio-political period of her work would be a must on most people's list yet I must confess my preference for the more strident rhythms of its companion piece of 1936 **The Prophet** (pictured). The National Gallery also houses many other Manley masterworks including the famous Horse of the Morning.

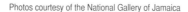

Photos courtesy of the National Gallery of Jamaica

Photos courtesy of the National Gallery of Jamaica

A maverick in painting, Carl Abrahams is the quintessential 'Jamaican eccentric.' But what a painter! He was also our most important religious painter. The gallery owns several examples of his religious works and all are superb. Perhaps the finest is his wonderful **Thirteen Israelites.**

Barrington Watson introduced a certain 'academic grandeur' into Jamaican realism in the late fifties. His **Mother and Child** is easily the most popular painting in the gallery and as such would appear in everyone's 'top ten.'

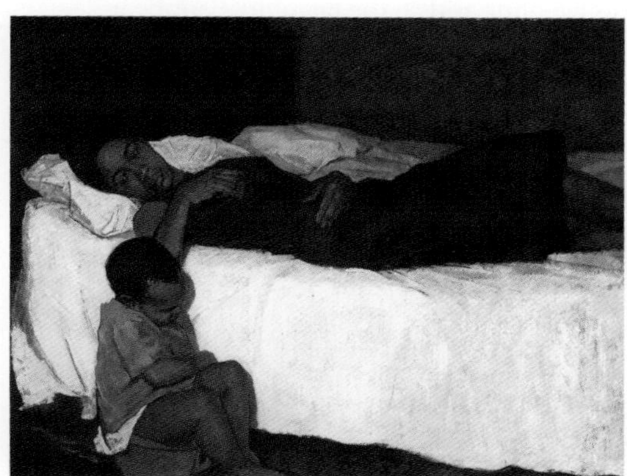

John Dunkley is for my money the supreme Jamaican painter. His mysterious and enigmatic works constantly amaze me and the very best sends shivers down my spine no matter how frequently I see them. We are fortunate to have six superb examples of his painting and a great sculpture. The **Banana Plantation**, which I persuaded his widow, Cassie Dunkley to donate to the gallery, is my absolute favourite.

ANGEL

Mallica Reynolds otherwise known as Kapo is certainly our best known Intuitive artist. He was equally adept at painting and sculpture, so I have named works of each medium for this top ten. In sculpture his **Angel**, with the poignant hollowing out of the body just outranks the magnificent Three Sisters and in painting I would rank his **Peaceful Quietness** which came from the collection of that astute collector the late Deryck Roberts, pays homage to that most 'spiritual' of trees, the Cotton tree as the finest Kapo in our collection.

PEACEFUL QUIETNESS

Colin Garland. This master fantasist whose works at times verges on the surreal, was a master craftsman. The Gallery has a fine selection of many of his best known paintings. It is difficult to choose between them but his Fairyscape, his Eventide and In the Beautiful Caribbean must rank near the top. My absolute favourite however is his **End of an Empire**.

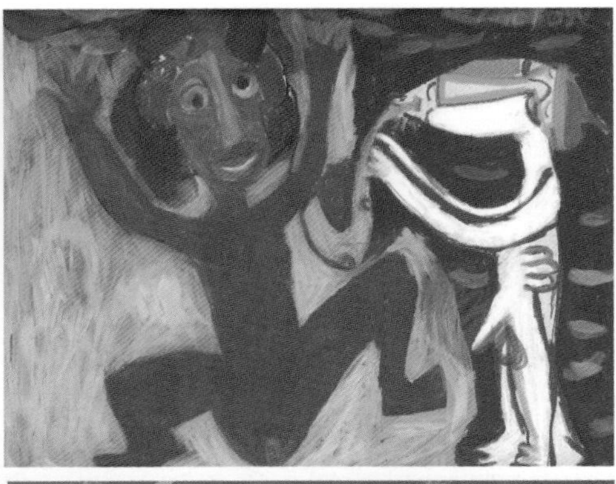

All photos courtesy of the National Gallery of Jamaica

Recently deceased, Milton George remains the most misunderstood Jamaican artist. He was a highly imaginative expressionist. The Gallery owns a wonderful suite of images **Fourteen Pages from My Diary** (four pages are shown) which is a set of variations on the theme of the nude female model being observed and painted by the painter, who is clearly Milton himself. This is erotic art with humour, and passion and an ecstatic use of colour.

CROP TIME

COCONUT PLACE

Albert Huie is perhaps the most popular of Jamaican painters excelling in traditional landscape and portrait painting. He is at his very best, I feel, when figures are integrated into the landscape as in his **Crop Time** and **Coconut Piece**. They are both magnificent and I hate to make a choice.

10

Top Ten Jamaican Books

CAROLYN COOPER, Professor of Literatures in English, UWI

Because I'm foolhardy, I took up Kevin's challenge to produce a list of 'Top Ten Jamaican Books.' Unlike conventional music 'top tens,' my list has nothing to do with volume of sales. And it's not a ranking order: I simply registered the books in the arbitrary way they presented themselves. Given my vocation, it's not surprising that it's all literature: five novels, two volumes of poetry, a memoir, a collection of autobiographical stories, and three plays under two covers.

I'm now teaching Lorna's magnificent memoir and that's probably why it appeared first. Then these are all books I've read. I do have lots of other candidates languishing on my shelves that I'm sure other people would have picked; but they are not in my consciousness. So here are the ten that dreamed me:

From Harvey River, Lorna Goodison

The Harder They Come, Michael Thelwell

Waiting in Vain, Colin Channer

Nanny Town, Vic Reid

Lionheart Gal, Sistren Theatre Collective

Jane and Louisa Will Soon Come Home, Erna Brodber

It Was the Singing, Edward Baugh

The Lunatic, Anthony Winkler

Old Story Time and Other Plays, Trevor Rhone

Louise Bennett, Selected Poems, edited by Mervyn Morris

FRIED DUMPLINGS

Ten of Jamaica's Favourite Food + Drink

Plus one more for the brawta (something extra)

GRACE CAMERON, Editor of *Jamaica Eats Magazine*

You haven't really lived until you've had your vocal chords yanked by the spicy flame from a well cut piece of Boston (Portland, Jamaica) jerk pork. These days jerk, which has become synonymous with Jamaican and Caribbean food, is on the lips of people around the world, and the zany and ever popular BBC television chef Ainsley Harriott has named jerk one of the 50 things to eat before you die.

Still, there's more to Jamaican cuisine than being rendered temporarily speechless by the pimento-encrusted heat of jerk. Therefore, for this top ten list of favourite Jamaican foods, we're putting jerk in the Hall of Fame and whetting your appetite with some other island favourites.

1. PATTY

If you want to drive a Jamaican into the gastronomic stratosphere, mention patty – Jamaican patty, that is. Patty holds memories of childhood and the simplicity of life in its flaky, golden crescent shape. Thought to be a descendant of the English pasties, the Jamaican patty has migrated with islanders around the world and is wowing a new set of admirers. Note: Those who are truly patty savvy also know that a soft, fluffy coco bread makes a decadent patty sandwich.

2. FRIED DUMPLING

We just can't say enough about these tasty morsels with the golden crust and chewy

10

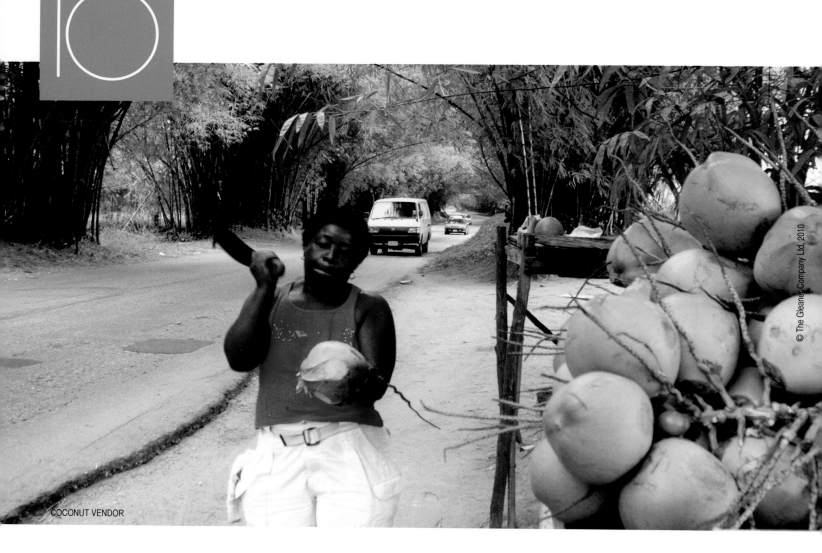

COCONUT VENDOR

interior. Not everyone can make a good fried dumpling though and in the wrong hands dumplings, also called Johnny cakes, can become round little missiles, tough enough to 'stone dawg'. It's believed that the name Johnny cake evolved from workers on the plantation who used to take journey cakes with them into the fields for a long lasting, hearty snack. Journey cake eventually became Johnny cake.

3. RUM

The spirit of Jamaica may be traced to two sources – churches and rum bars. Jamaica is said to have more churches and rum bars per capita than anywhere else on earth. The two, sometimes squaring off across the road from each other, vie lustily for the attention of Jamaicans. While church congregations pray for the souls of wayward islanders, the spirited conversations in rum bars tackle complicated political, social and sporting issues. Still the competition may not be as stiff as one may think. Worshippers have been known to cross the street, exchanging one spirit for the other.

4. GUINEP

Many young children have their first taste of guinep after their mother would remove the skin, crack the seed and place it in their mouth. This was done to allow the child to eat the velvety coating without accidentally swallowing the seed. A true delight is discovering a twin guinep seed.

5. RUM AND RAISIN ICE CREAM

While almost one-third of the world's ice cream eating population prefers vanilla, with chocolate, butter pecan and strawberry rounding out the top 50 per cent of ice cream flavours, Jamaicans are far more adventurous. Over the years, we've hankered for the heady, rum-infused ice cream, punctuated with plump, rum-soaked raisins. Rum and raisin leaves an impress on less than one per cent of ice cream eaters elsewhere, but with some of the world's best rums brewed on the Rock, who can blame us for going gaga over rum and raisin. Plus, Jamaicans who grew up in the 1950s, 1960s and 1970s will happily recall enduring the torture of churning the handle of the ice cream maker, anticipating the ecstasy of the rich, velvety texture.

6. CURRY GOAT AND WHITE RICE

And it has to be white rice. A perennial favourite at wakes and Nine Night ceremonies, this is a must-have at many festivities. For many important events, it is common to kill a goat or two to feed the hungry crowd. Still, don't display your ignorance by asking for curry (and it is curry and not curried) goat with rice and peas. It's just not done. If not white rice, then ask for boiled bananas (green, of course) with it.

7. GINGER BEER

When my brother got married in Toronto, Canada, a couple decades ago, my grandmother insisted on adding a spark of the Caribbean to the occasion and made up a batch of her famous ginger beer. Well, when it came to the serving, we discovered most of the bottles of ginger beer were gone. My guess is that they were 'pinched' by the mainly Caribbean guests who needed a little warmth of the Caribbean to ward off the chill of the northern clime.

8. COCONUT WATER

By this we do not mean coconut drink (which has been created by 'foreigners' with the addition of sugar). Coconut water, pure and simple, slakes the thirst of many Jamaican and Caribbean people. What's more, the water from the young, green coconut is a good 'heart' wash, say health experts. And, of course, the 'jelly' from the green coconut is a must-eat after you've finished draining the water from the hard green shell.

RICE AND PEAS WITH GUNGO (PIGEON) PEAS

9. STEW PEAS AND RICE

Ackee and salt fish may be the national dish, but stew peas and rice is a strong contender for the palate of Jamaicans. The only debate is – with or without the pig's tail. While the rasta man (and vegetarians) prefers to keep it *irie*, foregoing pig's tail and salt beef, the remainder of the population happily chows down on this rib-sticking stew dish.

10. ACKEE AND SALT FISH

Although people in the rest of the world have avoided eating the ackee (it can be poisonous if it not allowed to ripen and open on its own) Jamaicans have fallen hard for the fruit wrapped in the bright orange-red pod. Islanders have wedded ackee (which looks like scrambled eggs when cooked) with salt fish (cod) and made it their signature dish. Add fried dumplings, and most Jamaicans are in heaven.

11. RICE AND PEAS

Sunday dinner is just not complete without rice and peas at the table. Stories abound of Jamaican women preparing to-die-for meals of tempting roast beef, chicken that leave diners clucking for more, scrumptious pasta, salads and more. Yet, their men folk kept waiting for the rice and peas even after stuffing themselves full with the feast at hand. More times than not, rice and peas is made with red peas (kidney beans), but around the Christmas and New Year's holidays, gungo (pigeon) peas come into their own. Rice and peas, or beans and rice as it may be called elsewhere, is enormously popular in the Caribbean. In islands like Cuba, black bean is the bean of choice. Rice and peas is thought to come from the dozens of bean stews found in Africa, Asia, Europe and the Americas.

A HIBISCUS FLOWER

Top Ten Jamaican Plants + Trees

THELMA MCCARTHY of the 'Growing Things' Television Programme

Ackee: National dish. Very popular, versatile food. Attractive tree. Beautiful, distinctive fruits.

Breadfruit: Very popular staple food. Attractive tree and fruits.

Blue Mountain Coffee: Needs no justification

BLUE MOUNTAIN COFFEE

Sugar cane: Historical association. Source of our unique rum. Common sight across the country.

Scotch bonnet pepper: Developed here. Exceptional, distinctive flavour. Made popular in several uniquely Jamaican sauces and condiments.

Sorrell: Popular drink defines Jamaican Christmas. Beautiful flowers and fruits.

Croton: Seen in all types of gardens (formal and informal) throughout the island. Brilliant hues.

Hibiscus: Same as croton.

Lignum vitae: National tree/ flower. Extremely durable, dense wood used in furniture, carvings.

Logwood: Historical importance. Nectar gives our honey its distinctive flavour.

LOVERS' LEAP

Top Ten Off the Beaten Path Travel Spots

ROBERT LALAH
Assistant Features Editor, *Jamaica Gleaner*

Somehow I was lucky enough to wind up in a job that allows me to travel all around the country. I don't take this lightly, especially because my journeys allow me to meet some great people. Over the past few years, I've discovered many spots in Jamaica, (many of them obscure) that I knew very little about, prior to my visit. It's hard to choose the best of the lot, but I have managed to put together a list of ten of the places that have really stuck with me over time. Here they are, in no particular order.

LOVERS' LEAP, ST ELIZABETH

The first time I went there, I was blown away by the view. You're so high up that the waves far below seem to move in slow motion. It's the perfect example of the beauty that can be found in nature.

BATH, ST THOMAS

The area gets its name from the resident mineral fountain that is believed to possess natural healing powers. People travel great distances to take a dip in the water that, according to folks who live nearby, can cure everything except bad mind.

PENLYNE CASTLE, PORTLAND

I'll never forget my first trip to Penlyne Castle. It sure was not for the faint hearted. But, after driving up a single lane, seemingly vertical mountain for far too long, I finally got to this quaint, cool community where the residents are among the most welcoming I have come across.

MOCHO, ST JAMES

Now Mocho is obviously not the most glamourous name for a town, but the small community in the hills of St James is so serene and beautiful that the name is no issue. It's a very small farming community tucked away in the hills, close to Garlands. There are perhaps less than a hundred residents and they all rely on a small spring for all their water. But nobody complains. You see, they are all like family and their surroundings so beautiful, that they can hardly find a thing to complain about.

SHIRLEY CASTLE, PORTLAND

The people of Shirley Castle make the area special. The first time I visited, I was struck by how friendly and welcoming the residents were. I was invited home by a few people for dinner and drinks and had to make a promise that I would return soon. Up there you don't think about the country's crime trouble or the worries of the economy. It's so serene and the air so clear, it's hard to harbour a single negative thought.

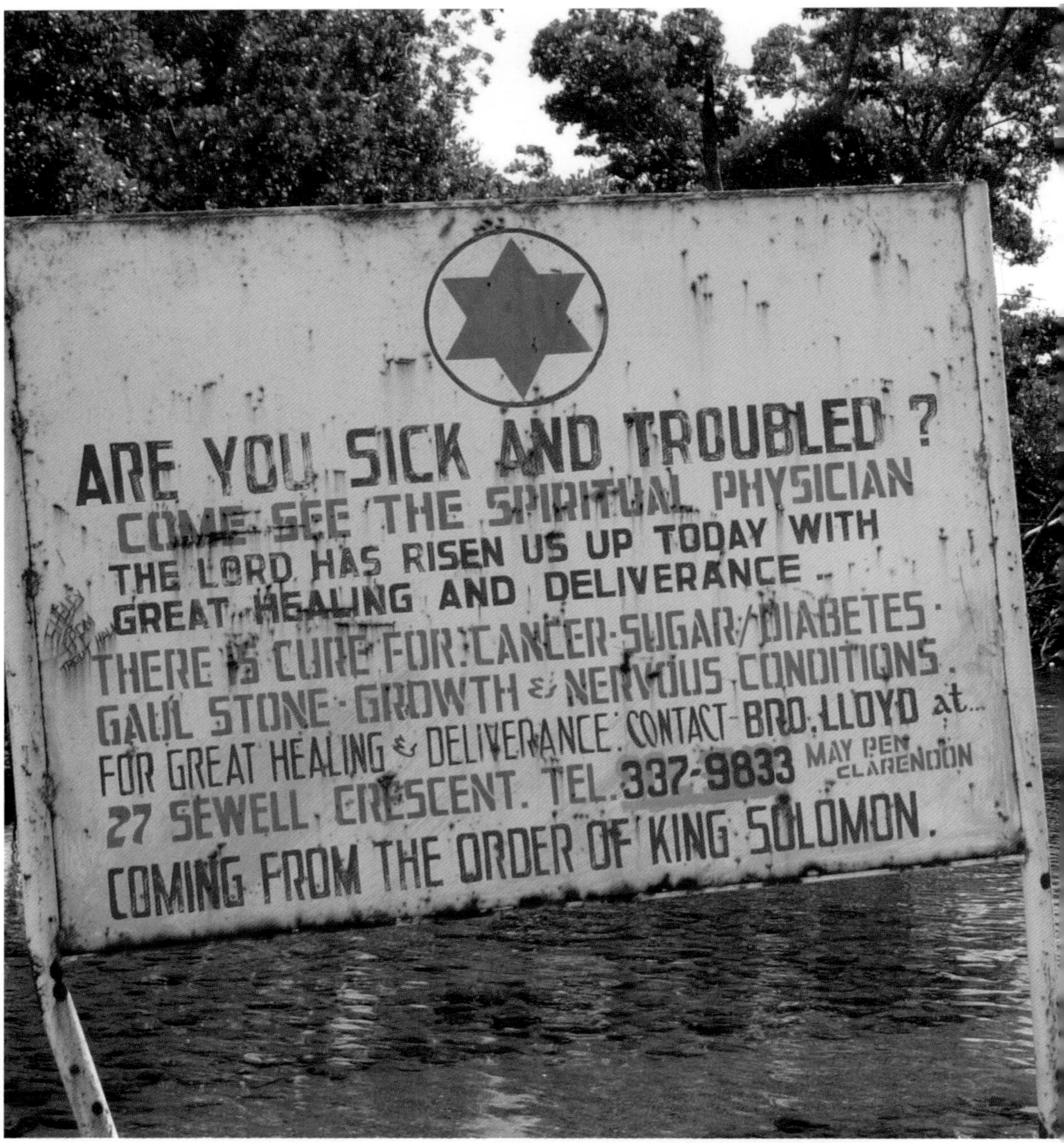

SALT RIVER, CLARENDON

This is another natural body of water that is widely thought to possess mystical healing powers. It's quite open and right next to a somewhat secluded roadway. Access is easy and there are always people around willing to tell you about all the people who supposedly have been healed after a few sessions of splashing around in the river.

SALT RIVER

NONSUCH, PORTLAND

I first stumbled upon Nonsuch quite by accident. I was completely lost and was just driving around looking for someone to ask directions when I came across a crowd at a small graveyard. Turns out the entire community had come together to bury a woman who had lived there for several years. There were men digging, women cooking and children helping their moms. Nobody paid for anything. It's just what they do, just like a big family. I was moved by that.

TOMBSTONE, ST ELIZABETH

A town with two often ignored tombstones by the side of the road. There's a story about the tombs, actually there are several, but most people agree that the tombs mark the graves of a British soldier and his beloved horse. A chat with residents will reveal a whole lot more.

SPANISH TOWN, ST CATHERINE

Yes, Spanish Town. Despite what you might have heard, the historical sights and monuments in the old capital are fascinating and well worth a visit.

GODWELL, CLARENDON

Who knew that a giant hole in the ground could have been so captivating? The stories that circulate about the giant well are too many to mention here. All I will say is that residents swear that nobody has ever been able to get to the bottom of the well. They say scientists have come from all over and have never found the bottom. It's hidden in bushes and you'll need a guide to find it, but a visit there is an experience you'll never forget.

Ten Pungent Proverbs

VIVIEN MORRIS-BROWN
Author of *The Jamaica Handbook of Proverbs*

1. New broom sweep clean, but old broom know the corners.

2. Patient man ride donkey.

© Diana McIntyre-Pike

3. Parson christen him pickney (children) first.

4. When you dig a hole for somebody, dig two.

5. Fisherman never say fi him fish stink.

6. Sorry fi mawga (scrawny) dog, mawga dog turn round bite you.

7. Every day you carry bucket go a well, one day the bucket bottom a go drop out.

8. Wha sweet nanny goat a go run him belly.

9. Me throw me corn, me no call no fowl.

10. If fish come from river bottom and tell you say shark down there, believe him.

Ten Great Jamaican Poems

WAYNE CHEN, Businessman and Chairman of the National Gallery of Jamaica

'Song of the Banana Man' by Evan Jones

'Uncle Time' by Dennis Scott

'If We Must Die' by Claude McKay

'Colonization in Reverse' by Louise Bennett

'Little Boy Crying' by Mervyn Morris

'Nigger Sweat' by Edward Baugh

'Hello Ungod' by Anthony McNeill

'I Saw My Land in the Morning' by M.G. Smith

'Bedspread' by Lorna Goodison

'Mi Cyaan Believe It' by Mikey Smith

THE SONG OF THE BANANA MAN

Touris, white man, wipin his face,
Met me in Golden Grove market place.
He looked at m'ol' clothes brown wid stain ,
An soaked right through wid de Portlan rain,

UNCLE TIME

Uncle Time is a ole, ole man…
All year long 'im wash 'im foot in de sea,
long, lazy years on de wet san'
an' shake de coconut tree dem…

IF WE MUST DIE

If we must die, let it not be like hogs
Hunted and penned in an inglorious spot,
While round us bark the mad and hungry dogs,
Making their mock at our accursed lot.

COLONIZATION IN REVERSE

Wat a joyful news, miss Mattie,
I feel like me heart gwine burs
Jamaica people colonizin
Englan in Reverse

LITTLE BOY CRYING

Your mouth contorting in brief spite and
Hurt, your laughter metamorphosed into howls,
Your frame so recently relaxed now tight
With three-year-old frustration, your bright
eyes…

I SAW MY LAND IN THE MORNING

I saw my land in the morning
And oh, but she was fair,
The hills flamed upwards scorning
Death and failure here.

MI CYAAN BELIEVE IT

Mi cyaan believe it
mi seh mi cyaan believe it
room dem a rent mi apply widdin but as me go
in cock-roach rat and
scorpion also come in

NIGGER SWEAT

No disrespect, mi boss,
just honest nigger sweat;
well almost, for is true
some of we trying to fool you

HELLO UNGOD

Ungod my lungs blacken
the cities have fallen
the easy prescriptions
have drilled final holes in my cells

FORT CHARLOTTE
A beautiful horseshoe bay, mapped by Captain Bligh, and guarded by an eighteenth-century fort.

Top Ten Heritage Sites

DAVID BUCKLEY, Author of *The Right to be Proud: A Brief Guide to Jamaican Heritage Sites*

SPANISH TOWN SQUARE
One of the finest Georgian squares in the New World. This was the seat of government for both the Spanish and the English.

ROSE HALL GREAT HOUSE
Perhaps the grandest such in the English-speaking Caribbean, with a fascinating legend associated with it.

FORT CHARLES
A careenage for the Spanish, a part of Admiral George Rodney's experience, and the headquarters of the British Navy in the Western hemisphere.

NEW SEVILLE
A major site in the New World, where three races co-existed for a number of years.

DEVON HOUSE
The restored and refurbished nineteenth century home of Jamaica's first black millionaire.

MORANT BAY COURTHOUSE
Here, National Heroes Paul Bogle and George William Gordon were tried and executed for their part in the 1865 Morant Bay Rebellion.

NATIONAL HEROES PARK
All seven National Heroes are commemorated here for their contribution to the history of Jamaica.

SAINT ANDREW PARISH CHURCH
Built in 1661, the second oldest Protestant church in Jamaica, and attended by governors since 1872.

KENILWORTH
An impressive example of the value of sugar to the British Empire.

Ten Great Folk Songs

HAZEL RAMSAY-MCCLUNE
Former Researcher at the African-Caribbean Institute of Jamaica, Jamaica Memory Bank

FOLK SINGERS

1. MOUT A MASSY

Mine yu time mout a massy mine yu time.
(Criticises those who act holier than thou, but who use their mouths to spread confusion and bad mind.)

2. MI CAWFEE

Mi bowl a bwiling cawfee in de mawnin.
(Everyone else likes tea and lemonade, but all the singer wants is a bowl of boiling coffee.)

3. MANUEL ROAD

Guh dung a Manuel Road gal an boy
fe go bruck rock stone.
(Tells the story of women breaking the stones used to build roads. This later became a ring game which teaches you to keep the rhythm in time, if not your finger will be crushed.)

4. DIS LONG TIME GAL

Dis long time gal me nevah see yu, come mek me hol' u han'.
(A greeting song; I have not seen you for the longest time, let's dance and sing and be friends forever, till you see a john crow eating blossoms – which you will never see.)

5. GUAVA ROOT

Guava root a medicine fe go cure
de young gal fever.
(Before we had Hospitals and Doctors, there were good old bush remedies to cure everything.)

6. YELLA YAM

When yu roast de yella yam,
and yu slice it in a two
How nice it will be, wid de ackee an de saltfish;
An de white flour dumpling, and de coconut ile;
What a glorious day,
when we roast de yella yam.
(Needs no explanation.)

7. MISSA POTTA

Ah plant a piece a red peas a red Sally lan, Mary Jane an pigeon come eat it out Sah.
(Someone is unable to pay their rent because pigeons have eaten their grain, and the owner is not willing to listen to a hard luck story.)

8. LINSTEAD MARKET

Carry me ackee go a Linstead market,
not a quatty wut sell.
(A woman is not selling any of her ackees, and there are mouths at home to feed.)

9. ROCKY ROAD

Dem big mout gal me nuh chat to dem, sing Charley Marley call yu.
(Poking fun at each other in the Mento style.)

10. RUN MOSES

Run Moses run, Missa Walker da come,
If yu buck yu right foot, buck yu lef foot,
try doan look back.
(A slave is running away, and being urged on by his friends and well wishers – 'don't stop, keep going'.)

Ten Great Jamaican Birds and Butterflies

VAUGHAN TURLAND, BirdLife Jamaica

Of Birds and Butterflies

Jamaica has 28 endemic birds. That's more than any other island in the Caribbean!

With the exception of the Black-billed Streamertail hummingbird which is confined to the eastern parishes, our other endemics can generally be found in forested areas throughout the island.

Jamaica is an excellent birding location with a wide range of habitats that you can visit, from wet montane forest to dry limestone forest and coastal wetlands.

Fourteen Important Bird Areas (IBA) have been defined in Jamaica by Birdlife International. Among these are the rugged and mysterious Cockpit Country (63,935ha.), Jamaica's last wilderness; the wetlands of The Black River Morass (17,770ha.) and Blue Mountains (40,065ha.).

In all, around 300 species have been recorded here including winter visitors, transients and vagrants. These migrants can start to arrive in August and will remain here until April/May.

For birders from North America, winter is a good opportunity to see migrant species that do not occur in their home territory; whilst for visitors from Europe, the winter season is an ideal time to visit and to catch the mainly North American influx of warblers, wetlands and shore birds. Many of the species that come to Jamaica at this time add to our own resident populations.

In spring, we have a small number of species that migrate or come onshore to breed here: Black-whiskered Vireo, Caribbean Martin, Antillean Night Hawk, Least Tern, White-tailed Tropic Bird.

RED-BILLED STREAMERTAIL

The Red-billed Streamertail has velvety black and iridescent green plumage. It is Jamaica's national bird. Locally known as the Doctor Bird, Scissors Tails or Streamertail it is pretty easy to find anywhere there is a nectar-bearing flower or bird feeder. Don't forget, it's only the male that has the tails. So watch out for the less brightly coloured and much politer female.

Photos courtesy of Vaughan Turland

JAMAICAN TODY

The Jamaican Tody is a master of camouflage. In its forest home, its coarse, 'churring' call is often heard but because of its leaf green plumage it can be difficult to see. This is perhaps the most popular bird on our tours. Strangely, the Tody is an earth dwelling bird and a pair can frequently be seen excavating a burrow in soft earth to build their nest.

YELLOW-SHOULDERED GRASSQUIT

The male Yellow-shouldered Grassquit just glows in the sun. This lovely endemic is widespread and usually found at the forest edge. Its distinctive descending call notes make it easy to pinpoint.

Jamaican Endemic Birds

Ring-tailed Pigeon
Crested Quail Dove
Yellow-billed Parrot
Black-billed Parrot
Jamaican Lizard Cuckoo
Chestnut-bellied Cuckoo
Jamaican Owl
Jamaican Mango
Red-billed Streamertail
Black-billed Streamertail
Jamaican Tody
Jamaican Woodpecker
Jamaican Elaenia
Jamaican Pewee
Sad Flycatcher
Rufous-tailed Flycatcher
Jamaican Becard
Jamaican Vireo
Blue mountain Vireo
Jamaican Crow
White-eyed Thrush
White-chinned Thrush
Arrowhead Warbler
Jamaican Spindalis
Jamaican Euphonia
Yellow-shouldered Grassquit
Orangequit
Jamaican Blackbird

YELLOW-BILLED PARROT

The endemic Yellow-billed Parrot can be distinguished from our endemic Black-billed Parrot, because, well, it has a yellow bill and the other has…you guessed. Both species of the Amazona genus are usually found in the mountainous, forested interior where they can be heard chattering through the day. But, check out Hope Gardens in Kingston where a small flock of Yellow-bills lives. You won't be disappointed.

JAMAICAN MANGO

The Jamaican Mango is just resplendent in its mix of iridescent magenta, purple, blue with hints of green and orange. It is the largest of our endemic hummingbirds and also the noisiest. Always first at the feeder, it fights off all comers. Found all over the island, though not so common as the Streamertails.

All photos courtesy of Vaughan Turland

JAMAICAN ORIOLE

The Jamaican Oriole, although not a full endemic, has iconic status. It is the 'Yellow Bird' of the Harry Belafonte song. Affectionately known as Banana Katie, its call, 'You thief, you thief,' can be heard in parks, gardens and woods as it searches for food.

Photos courtesy of Vaughan Turland

Butterflies

There are around 130 species of butterfly that can be seen in Jamaica. Of these, at least 28 are presently classified as endemic species. A couple of these are very seldom seen. Eight spectacular swallowtails are included in the species list. Three of these are endemic and three are endemic sub-species. The largest of the endemics is the spectacular Homerus Swallowtail with a wingspan of more than six inches which is restricted to just a very few locations in the rugged, forest interior of the island.

At the other end of the scale is the Pygmy Blue which is so small that it hard to see as it flies between flowers in its specialised coastal habitat.

The great thing about butterflies in Jamaica is that you can see them on every day of the year no matter where you are on the island.

HOMERUS

Homerus, the largest swallowtail in the Americas can only be found at a few remote locations in conditions nearing 100 per cent humidity. Endemic to Jamaica, it glides along forest paths majestically, then soars above the tree tops. Classified as endangered it is protected by international convention. It is a true wonder of the natural world.

GOLDEN SWALLOWTAIL

This endemic Golden Swallowtail (male shown) occurs mostly below 600m (2000 ft) in wet limestone forest. It occurs just about island wide and can be seen in most months. It lays its eggs on Citrus, especially tangerine and orange.

BLUE SWALLOWTAIL

The endemic, Blue Swallowtail, was once common in Kingston but now is restricted to just a very few breeding localities in central western forests and south east Jamaica. It is the smallest of our Swallowtails. Flying rapidly, it hardly seems to settle long enough to be properly viewed. Periodically, there are huge expansions in the population and it can be seen in early May swarming, around flowering trees in pursuit of nectar.

PRICKLY ASH SWALLOWTAIL

The Prickly Ash Swallowtail is widely distributed but not common. It can be found in wet forest and forest fringes above 200m (600ft) and up to 900m (3000ft). When the day is shady, it can be seen at rest with its wings fully open. It is an endemic sub-species.

PORTLAND BIGHT

Top Ten Spots of Natural and Ecological Beauty

JILL BYLES, Natural History Society of Jamaica

Grand Ridge of the Blue Mountains, including High Peak (highest in the Caribbean at 2,082m), Holywell (nature reserve and recreational area), Cinchona Gardens (botanical history, spectacular views). On the upper slopes some of Jamaica's little remaining endemic forest and less well known birds are found. There are peaks and valleys of outstanding scenic beauty, which give rise to most of Jamaica's major rivers, often with enticing rock pools and waterfalls.

John Crow Mountains and Rio Grande Valley: rafting, Maroon history, trails and waterfalls, isolated areas of rare biological species, including Giant Swallowtail butterfly (*Pterourus homerus*).

Ecclesdown: forested area where many bird species may be seen. Bordered by Drivers River with pristine, blue pools above the Reach Falls.

Eastern St Thomas coast including Morant Cays, a sea bird nesting site: good beaches, reefs, geological and historic points of interest, outstanding views especially Bowden Harbour from above.

Portland Bite: includes approximately 6,000 hectares of dry limestone forest, the Salt River, mangroves protecting the coast and forming islands and waterways, secluded beaches and white sand cays such as Pigeon Island.

Black River Morass, which includes the Broad River: tranquil boating, good bird and crocodile watching. Fishermen in small dugout canoes set specially woven shrimp traps.

Bluefields Bay, adjoining coast and back drop of hills: inspired the Naturalist Philip Henry Gosse in the 1840s. A variety of bird species can be seen along the coast, and on forest trails into the hills. Good views as one climbs.

The Cockpit Country: Western boundary settled by Maroons. Unique geological limestone formation resembling cock fighting pits. Pits are often isolated from their neighbours resulting in them being uniquely biodiverse. Giant Swallowtail butterfly (*Pterourus homerus*) and Black billed parrot may be seen.

ENDEMIC JAMAICAN PEEWEE

Bull Head Mountain (845m) and Mason River, in the middle of the island: a recently replanted forest reserve and high altitude inland wetland, respectively. A carnivorous plant can be found at Mason River.

North East Portland coast and the foothills of the Blue Mountains including Blue Lagoon: vivid, contrasting colours, lush vegetation, white sand coves and rocky islets.

Ten Unforgettable Jamaican Experiences

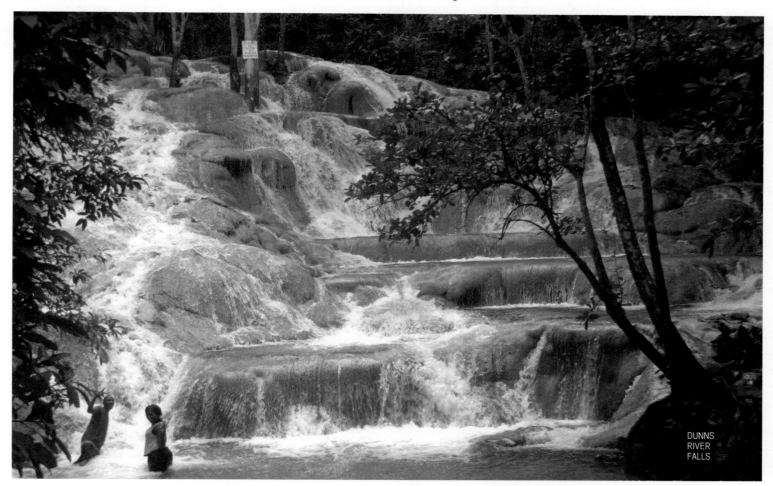

DUNNS RIVER FALLS

RAFTING ON THE RIO GRANDE

Float down the heart of paradise. Relax in absolute calm amidst stunning scenery. Lunch along the way on a dry river bed. Take a dip in the crystal clear water. It just doesn't get any better than this – except maybe on the moonlight lovers' cruise. Talk about the ultimate romantic experience.

DUNN'S RIVER FALLS

Get up close and personal with nature. Climb to the top of the mossy green rocks amidst cascading water, then clamber back down to the golden sands and dive into the inviting blue Caribbean sea.

DANCEHALL NIGHT AT REGGAE SUMFEST

NATIONAL GRAND GALA

Folk culture may be under threat and in need of artificial support in much of the world, but it's alive and thriving in this island. Every Independence Day, the young, old and in-between celebrate every aspect of their culture in a jampacked National Stadium. It's all there, from Kumina to Quadrille to Mento to Ska to Rocksteady to Reggae to Dancehall – the full and authentic soul of Jamaica.

DANCEHALL NIGHT AT REGGAE SUMFEST

The hardcore, contemporary essence of one of the world's great popular musics. For good and for bad, it's the thrillingly uncensored reality of today's Jamaica. In the searing peaks when both deejays and audience are giving full rein to their feelings, everything becomes as one in a seething sea of maximum emotional intensity. This is as musically real as it gets.

BOYS' AND GIRLS' HIGH SCHOOLS ATHLETIC CHAMPIONSHIPS

'Champs' is the unbridled exuberance of youth at its joyous best. It's an unsurpassed atmosphere of crackling electricity, as 35,000 delirious fans cheer on their alma maters with non-stop full volume drumming, chanting and singing. While on the track, the next generation of Usain Bolts and Veronica Campbells is blossoming before your very eyes.

WEST INDIES CRICKET AT THE SABINA PARK MOUND

Endless supplies of Red Stripe Beer and Appleton Rum, sun tanning beauties all around, and cricket lovely cricket. You will never encounter a more mixed and inviting crowd, and when the West Indies win, there's no happier place on the planet.

GRAND MARKET

Silver bells and silent night? Not in Jamaica. Christmas Eve here is a Grand Market Night of music and vibes, with thousands of youngsters and oldsters thronging town centres to shop, eat, dance, and just soak up the festive atmosphere. Stores and street vendors open through the night and jerk pan chicken smoke fills the air while roadside sound systems pour forth oldies reggae and dancehall. It's laughter, happy faces, openly expressed love, and joy to the world.

ROOTS PLAY

Nearly all the plots centre around 'bun and jacket' infidelity, but it's non-stop jokes both on and off the stage. The real kick is the unself-conscious audience participation that creates a delightful communal ambience.

HELLSHIRE BEACH, SUNDAY MORNING

'Let's go and have some fun, on the beach, where there's a party'. Not to mention lashings of delicious fresh fried fish and festival, and sounds of laughter everywhere from families just enjoying life.

A SCENE FROM ROOTS PLAY 'BASHMENT GRANNY'

Top Ten Jamaican Comic Songs

ITY AND FANCY CAT
Comedic Duo

'Duppy Gunman' (1974) – Ernie Smith

'Ram Goat Liver' (1974) – Pluto Shervington

'Like You and My Sweetheart to be Friends' (1975) – Bim and Clover

'Hol A Fresh' (1987) – Red Dragon

'Wear Yu Size' (1987) – Lt Stitchie

'Wild Gilbert' (1988) – Lovindeer

'Maddy Maddy Cry' (1991) – Papa San

'Tan So Back' (1991) – Professor Nuts

'It Wasn't Me' (2000) – Shaggy and Rik Rok

'Bun Him' (2005) – Macka Diamond and Black-er

THE BLUE LAGOON

Notes

INTRODUCTION

PAGE

xviii From the song 'Nowhere no Better than Yard' by Josey Wales.

I. PEOPLE:

OUT OF MANY, ONE OF A KIND

PAGE

2 Jamaican slang for boastful.

2 Michael Rosenberg, *Detroit Free Press*, August 17, 2008.

2 Kevin O'Brien Chang, *Jamaica Gleaner*, August 24, 2008.

2 Ity and Fancy Cat are Jamaica's most popular comedy duo as of 2009.

3 http://news.bbc.co.uk/2/hi/science/nature/7668250.stm.

5 Cassidy, *Jamaica Talk*, 31, 49.

5 Olive Senior, *Encyclopedia of Jamaican Heritage*, 246, 276.

5 World Bank, 2007.

5 According to former Technology Minister Phillip Paulwell.

7 'The Meaning of Kiss-teeth', Esther Figueroa and Peter L. Patrick. http://privatewww.essex .ac.uk/~patrickp/papers/KSTpapwww.pdf

8 'Women in Dancehall. A Response by Lloyd Lovindeer' *Jamaica Journal* 23 no. 1, (February–April 1990).

9 For the record, the author believes that the state has no business in the nation's bedroom, and that consulting adults of any persuasion should be free to do as they wish in the privacy of their homes.

11 Costa Rica and the Dominican Republic ranked first and second in the study that measured well being in 143 countries representing 99 per cent of the world's population. http://www.happyplanetindex.org/.

13 WHO, World Health Statistics 2008.

13 Jamaican slang for irresponsible, philandering male.

14 Senior, *Encyclopedia of Jamaican Heritage*, 374.

14 http://news.bbc.co.uk/2/hi/uk_news/education/8085011.stm.

14 UNESCO Institute for Statistics (UIS) 2007.

14 http://en.wikipedia.org/wiki/List_of_countries_by_suicide_rate. Jamaica recorded 51 suicides in 2009, meaning a national rate of about 1.9 per 100,000 – Jamaica Constabulary Force Statistics. This compares to Lithuania's world leading 38.6, Trinidad's 12.8 and the US's 11.1.

14 Suicides in Jamaica 2009 – 46 male, 5 female. Jamaica Constabulary Force Statistics

14 Winkler, *Trust the Darkness*, 167.

15 UNDP, 2000.

15 United Nations Population Division (2000) World Marriage Patterns 2000.

15 Statin, 2000.

16 That is, the smallest country that sells more cultural products to other countries than it imports.

16 For some reason a sexual mystique built up around women of East Indian descent, colloquially summed up by 'coolie white liver'. Though highly controversial and politically incorrect, this term of indeterminate origin is still commonly used. Senior, *Encyclopedia of Jamaican Heritage*, 43.

16 'The offspring of a black and white was a mulatto, of a mulatto and white a quadroon, of a quadroon and white a mustee, and of a mustee and white a mustephinoo. A child of a mulatto and negro was a sambo, and that of a negro and sambo a negro'. Senior, *Encyclopedia of Jamaican Heritage*, 125.

18 http://www.jamaica-gleaner.com/pages/history/story003.html

19 Clayborne Carson and Peter Holloran 'A Knock at Midnight: Inspiration from the Great Sermons of Reverend Martin Luther King, Jr.,' *Inspiration from the Great Sermons of Reverend Martin Luther King, Jr.*, chapter titled 'American Dream'.

19 Neita, *Hugh Shearer: A Voice for the People*, 178.

19 Neita, *Donald Sangster*, unpublished manuscript.

20 Knight and Palmer, *The Modern Caribbean*, 120.

20 Neita, *Hugh Shearer: A Voice for the People*, 299.

22 'An Uptown Story,' *Sunday Gleaner*, March 26, 2006.

24 'Hugh Shearer: Ja's greatest PM?' *Sunday Gleaner*, July 11, 2004.

24 Beverly Manley, *The Manley Memoirs*, 93, 99, 94, 123.

24 Rachel Manley, *In My Father's Shade*, 149.

25 'Interview with Kevin O'Brien Chang,' *Sunday Observer*, January 28, 2001.

27 Erika Smilowitz, 'Una Marson: Woman before Her Time,' *Jamaica Journal* 16 no. 2, (May 1983).

II. EARLY YEARS: THE HANDS OF CHANCE

PAGE

33 http://edition.cnn.com/2004/WORLD/americas/08/02/columbus/index.html.

34 Senior, *Encyclopedia of Jamaican Heritage*, 111.

34 Sherlock and Bennett, *The Story of the Jamaican People*, 43.

34 Senior, *Encyclopedia of Jamaican Heritage*, 474.

34 Ronald L. Vanderwal, 'Problems of Jamaican Pre-History' *Jamaica Journal* 2 no. 3, (September 1968).

34 Munroe and Bertram, *Adult Suffrage and Political Administrations in Jamaica 1944-2002,* 12.

34 Senior, *Encyclopedia of Jamaican Heritage*, 95.

34 Carey Robinson, *The Iron Thorn*, 18–20, 35.

34 Senior, *Encyclopedia of Jamaican Heritage*, 96.

35 Black, *History of Jamaica*, 43.

36 Cordingly, *Life Among the Pirates: The Romance and the Reality*, 75.

37 Black, *History of Jamaica*, 81.

39 Senior, *Encyclopedia of Jamaican Heritage*, 72.

39 Black, *History of Jamaica*, 70.

39 Sowell, *Conquest and Culture*, 190.

39 Sherlock and Bennett, *The Story of the Jamaican People*, 43.

39 Sowell, *Conquest and Culture*, 154.

40 For an excellent discussion of both ancient slavery and the African Slave Trade see Reynolds, *Stand the Storm*; and Sowell, *Conquest and Culture*.

40 Reynolds, *Stand the Storm*, 29.

40 Black. *History of Jamaica*, 73.

40 Senior, *Encyclopedia of Jamaican Heritage*, 446.

41 Ahmed Reid, 'Abolition Watch: Jamaican Port Cities,' *Jamaica Journal* 31 nos. 1–2, (June 2008).

41 Verene Shepherd and Ahmed Reid, 'An Overview of the Transatlantic Trade in Africans and Its Abolition,' *Jamaica Journal*. 31 nos. 1–2, (June 2008).

41 Thomas, *The Slave Trade*, 804.

41 Sowell, *Conquest and Culture*, 160.

41 Reynolds, *Stand the Storm*, 73, 111.

41 Ibid., 84.

41 Verene Shepherd and Ahmed Reid, 'An Overview of the Transatlantic Trade in Africans and Its Abolition,' *Jamaica Journal* 31 nos. 1–2, (June 2008).

41 Reynolds, *Stand the Storm*, 76.

42 Everett, *History of Slavery*, 152–53.

42 Ibid., 134–53.

42 Black, *History of Jamaica*, 58, 72.

42 Senior, *Encyclopedia of Jamaican Heritage*, 6.

43 Ibid., 132–33.

44 Sylvia Wynter, 'Lady Nugent's Journal,' *Jamaica Journal* 1 no. 1, (1967).

45 *The Rough Guide to Jamaica*, 2007, 401.

45 Sowell, *Conquest and Culture*, 159.

46 Perhaps the first was Gaspar Yanga, who led a Mexican slave rebellion in 1570 and established a Maroon community. He fought the Spanish to a standstill and a peace treaty was signed in 1618. He is now National Hero of Mexico.

46 Senior, *Encyclopedia of Jamaican Heritage*, 474.

46 Agorsah, *Maroon Heritage: Archeological, Ethnographic and Historical Perspectives*, 74–6.

46 Robinson, *The Iron Thorn*, 27, 35.

47 Ibid.,100.

47 Agorsah. *Maroon Heritage: Archeological, Ethnographic and Historical Perspectives*, 91–92.

47 Robinson, *The Iron Thorn*, 130.

48 Carl A. Lane, 'Concerning Jamaica's 1760 Slave Rebellions,' *Jamaica Journal* 7 no. 4, (December 1973).

48 C. Roy Reynolds 'Tacky, and the Great Slave Rebellion of 1760,' *Jamaica Journal* 6 no. 2.

48 Robinson, *The Iron Thorn*, 130, 155, 254.

49 Black, *History of Jamaica*, 80.

49 L. Alan Eyre, 'Jack Mansong, Bloodshed or Brotherhood,' *Jamaica Journal* 7 no. 4, (December 1973).

50 Senior, *Encyclopedia of Jamaican Heritage*, 343.

52 Mary Reckord, 'The Slave Rebellion of 1831,' *Jamaica Journal*.

52 Senior, *Encyclopedia of Jamaican Heritage*, 442–43.

52 Sherlock and Bennett, *Story of the Jamaican People*, 219–22.

52 Curtin, *Two Jamaicas*, 85.

54 Alan Eyre, 'Dusky Doctress: A Jamaican Perspective on Mary Grant-Seacole,' *Jamaica Journal* 30 no. 1–2, (December 2006).

55 http://news.bbc.co.uk/1/hi/uk/3475445.stm

56 *The Best of Skywritings*, 345.

56 Trevor Munroe and Arnold Bertram, *Adult Suffrage and Political Administrations in Jamaica 1944–2002*, (Kingston: Ian Randle Publishers, 2006), 80.

56 Ibid., 30–31.

56 'Robert Osborn – Brown Power Leader,' *Jamaica Journal* 11 nos. 1–2, (1977).

57 Senior, *Encyclopedia of Jamaican Heritage*, 261.

58 Sherlock and Bennett, *The Story of the Jamaican People*, 230.

58 Senior, *Encyclopedia of Jamaican Heritage*, 200.

58 H. P. Jacobs, 'The Last Africans: A Review Article,' *Jamaica Journal* 8 no. 4.

58 Black, *History of Jamaica*, 117–19.

60 Ansell Hart, 'Colour Prejudice in Jamaica,' *Jamaica Journal* 4 no. 4, (December 1970).

62 Heuman, *The Killing Time*, 131–34.

62 Glory Robertson 'A Conflict of Heroes,' *Jamaica Journal* 2 no. 2, (June 1968).

63 Munroe and Bertram, *Adult Suffrage and Political Administrations in Jamaica 1944–2002*, 41–43.

III. MODERN TIMES:

CHARTING A NATIONAL DESTINY

PAGE

65 Insanally, et al, *Regional Footprints: The Travels and Travails of Early Caribbean Migrants*, 61–63, 69.

66 Greenwood, et al, *Emancipation to Emigration*, 157.

66 Sherlock and Bennett, *The Story of the Jamaican People*, 280.

66 Munroe and Bertram, *Adult Suffrage and Political Administrations in Jamaica 1944–2002*, 44–48.

66 Bryan, *The Jamaican People 1880–1902*, 15 .

67 Moore and Wilmot, eds., *Before and After 1865: Education, Politics and Regionalism in the Caribbean*, 115.

67 Sherlock and Bennett, *The Story of the Jamaican People*, 283.

67 Munroe and Bertram, *Adult Suffrage and Political Administrations in Jamaica 1944–2002*, 49.

67 Sherlock and Bennett, *The Story of the Jamaican People*. Page 285

67 Glenford Howe, *Race, War and Nationalism: A Social History of West Indians in the First World War*, 2.

68 Munroe and Bertram, *Adult Suffrage and Political Administrations in Jamaica 1944–2002*. Page 51

68 Lewis, *Marcus Garvey: Anti-Colonial Champion*, 28.

68 Munroe and Bertram. *Adult Suffrage and Political Administrations in Jamaica 1944–2002*, 54.

68 Ibid., 56.

68 Carnegie, *Some Aspects of Jamaica's Politics, 1918–1938*, 88.

68 Moore and Wilmot, eds., *Before and After 1865: Education, Politics and Regionalism in the Caribbean*, 121.

68 Rupert Lewis, 'Robert Love,' *Jamaica Journal* 11 no. 1–2, (1977).

68 Lewis, *Marcus Garvey: Anti–Colonial Champion*, 25.

68 Ibid., 197.

68 http://www.jamaica-gleaner.com/pages/history/story003.html

68 Mrs Amy Jacques-Garvey, 'Political Activities of Marcus Garvey in Jamaica,' *Jamaica Journal* 6 no. 2, (June 1972).

68 Sewell, *Garvey's Children*, 18.

69 Fax, *Garvey: The Story of a Pioneer Back Nationalist,* 23–4.

69 Sewell, *Garvey's Children*, 28.

71 Sherlock and Bennett, *The Story of the Jamaican People*, 301.

71 Tony Martin 'International Aspects of the Garvey Movement,' *Jamaica Journal*, (August–October 1987).

72 http://www.jnht.com/heritage_site.php?id=218

72 Beverly Hamilton, 'Marcus Garvey – Cultural Activist,' *Jamaica Journal*, (August–October, 1987).

73 Lewis, *Marcus Garvey: Anti-Colonial Champion*, 72.

73 Ibid., 197–98.

73 Glenford Howe, *Race, War and Nationalism: A Social History of West Indians in the First World War*, 3, 16, 18, 41.

73 Lewis, *Marcus Garvey: Anti-Colonial Champion*, 215.

74 Ibid., 270.

74 Ibid., 213.

74 Sewell, *Garvey's Children*, 87.

74 Ibid., 83.

74 Carnegie, *Some Aspects of Jamaica's Politics, 1918–1938*, 81.

74 Rupert Lewis, 'Robert Love,' *Jamaica Journal* 11 nos. 1–2, (1977).

74 Lewis, *Marcus Garvey: Anti-Colonial Champion*, 226.

74 Munroe and Bertram, *Adult Suffrage and Political Administrations in Jamaica 1944–2002*, 59.

75 Carnegie, *Some Aspects of Jamaica's Politics, 1918–1938*, 179.

75 Hill, *Bustamante and His Letters*, 62.

75 Sealy, *Sealy's Caribbean Leaders*, 100.

75 Gladys Bustamante, *The Memoirs of Lady Bustamante*, 121.

75 Some see similarities between Bustamante's role and that of Captain Arthur Andrew Cipriani (1875–1945) in Trinidad.

75 Eaton, *Alexander Bustamante and Modern Jamaica*, 53–54.

75 Gladys Bustamante, *The Memoirs of Lady Bustamante*, 87.

75 Lewis, *Marcus Garvey: Anti-Colonial Champion*, 265.

76 Gladys Bustamante, *The Memoirs of Lady Bustamante*, 77, 85–86.

77 Ibid., 93.

77 Ibid., 76.

79 Sealey, *Sealey's Caribbean Leaders*, 109.

79 'The Autobiography of Norman Washington Manley,' *Jamaica Journal* 7 nos. 1–2, (March–June 1973).

80 Vivian Blake 'In Pursuit of Excellence,' *Jamaica Journal* 25 no. 1, (October 1993).

80 For useful insights into the personalities of Bustamante and Manley see *Sealey's Caribbean Leaders*, 147.

80 Barbara Gloudon, 'Hon. Lady Gladys Bustamante O.J. Interviewed,' *Jamaica Journal* 17 no. 4.

80 'Elsie Hunter, during her first marriage to Robert Clarke, gave birth to Bobby Clarke, Bustamante's father. In her second marriage to Alexander Shearer, she gave birth to Margaret Shearer, Norman's mother, and Ellie Shearer, Edna's mother.' George E. Eaton, *Alexander Bustamante and Modern Jamaica*, 1.

80 Ibid., 250.

81 Gladys Bustamante, *The Memoirs of Lady Bustamante*, 102.

81 Eaton, *Alexander Bustamante and Modern Jamaica*, 97.

81 Ibid., 82.

81 Gladys Bustamante, *The Memoirs of Lady Bustamante*, 101.

81 Neita, *Hugh Shearer: A Voice For The People*, 80–81.

81 Black, *History of Jamaica*, 156.

82 Sealy, *Sealy's Caribbean Leaders*, 163.

82 Eaton, *Alexander Bustamante and Modern Jamaica*, 89.

83 Sealy, *Sealy's Caribbean Leaders*, 115.

83 Ibid., 163.

83 Senior, *Encyclopedia of Jamaican Heritage*, 51.

83 Gladys Bustamante, *The Memoirs of Lady Bustamante*, 170.

84 Neita, *Hugh Shearer: A Voice for the People*, 192.

85 Ibid., 229.

86 Neita, *Donald Sangster*, unpublished manuscript.

86 World Bank Statistics, Jamaica Constabulary Force Statistics.

86 Neita, *Hugh Shearer: A Voice for The People*, 378.

91 http://en.wikipedia.org/wiki/Reporters_Without_Borders

91 Interviews with author.

IV. MUSIC:

HEARTBEAT OF A NATION

PAGE

97 Bolland, *The Birth of Caribbean Civilization*, 636.

97 George Simpson, 'The Rastafari Movement in Jamaica,' *Jamaica Journal* 25 no. 2, (December 1994).

98 Olive Lewin, 'Traditional Jamaican Music – Mento,' *Jamaica Journal* 26 no. 3.

98 Randolph Williams, 'The Story of Two Men and a Guitar,' *Jamaica Journal* 16 no. 3, (August 1988).

98 Sonjah Stanley Niaah 'Kingston's Dancehall Spaces' *Jamaica Journal* 29 no. 3.

101 *Tougher Than Tough* – liner notes

106 'Mad Hot Reggaeton,' *New York Times*, July 15, 2005. http://www.nytimes.com/2005/07/17/fashion/sundaystyles/17reggaeton.html?scp=2&sq=reggaeton&st=cse

110 Senior, *Encyclopedia of Jamaican Heritage*, 335.

110 Godfrey Taylor, 'Slim and Sam: Jamaican Street Singers,' *Jamaica Journal* 16 no. 3, (August 1988).

V. SPORTS:

GOOD AT MOST, GREAT AT SOME

PAGE

125 This oft repeated phrase originated in Thomas Hughes' 1857 novel *Tom Brown's School Days*: 'What a noble game it [cricket] is too!' 'Isn't it? But it's more than a game, it's an institution.'

126 Arnold Bertram, **'**Headley, Garvey and the National Movement**,'** *Sunday Gleaner*, May 31, 2009.

VI. RELIGION:

SERIOUS BUSINESS

PAGE

131 'For religion, after all, is the serious business of the human race.' Arnold Toynbee.

133 Fischer, *A History of Reading*, 250–51.

133 Munroe and Bertram, *Adult Suffrage and Political Administrations in Jamaica 1944*–2002, 33.

133 Billy Hall, 'George Liele: Should be a National Hero,' *Jamaica Gleaner*, April 8, 2003.

133 C.S. Reid, **'**Early Baptist Beginnings,**'** *Jamaica Journal* 16 no. 2, (May 1983).

133 Senior, *Encyclopedia of Jamaican Heritage*, 123–24.

134 Devon Dick, 'William Knibb: A National Hero?'

136 'Exploring the 1865 Native Baptist War,' *Jamaica Gleaner*, May 19, 2008.

136 Senior, *Encyclopedia of Jamaican Heritage*, 417.

136 Ibid., 417–18.

137 http://www.amazon.com/Magical-Indian-Occultism-Ceremonial-Talismanic/dp/0766101185

137 Senior, *Encyclopedia of Jamaican Heritage,* 217.

137 Ibid., 353.

138 'Funeral Rites and Popular Culture,' *Sunday Gleaner*, April 29, 2007.

138 Samuel Twumasi Ankrah, *The Death and Funeral Rites in Contemporary Akan Society: An Appropriate Christian Response*, 2002.

139 Followed by 281,353 Seventh Day Adventists, 188,770 Baptists, 93,612 Anglicans, 67,204 Roman Catholics.

There were 24,020 Rastafarians.

139 http://en.wikipedia.org/wiki/Pentecostalism

140 Lewis, *Marcus Garvey: Anti-Colonial Champion*, 35.

141 Senior, *Encyclopedia of Jamaican Heritage*, 54–56.

141 Robert Hill, 'Leonard P. Howell and Early Rastafari,' *Jamaica Journal* 16 no. 1, (1983): 25.

141 Chevannes, *Rastafari Roots and Ideology*, 94.

142 Ibid., 94.

142 *Encyclopedia Britannica* vol. 4, 1993, 581.

142 Robert Hill, 'Leonard P. Howell and Early Rastafari,' *Jamaica Journal* 16 no. 1, (1983).

142 Bisnauth, *History of Religions in the Caribbean*, 188.

142 Robert Hill, 'Leonard P. Howell and Early Rastafari,' *Jamaica Journal* 16 no. 1, (1983).

142 Ibid.

142 *The Guinness Who's Who of Reggae*, 223.

142 Robert Hill, 'Leonard P. Howell and Early Rastafari,' *Jamaica Journal* 16 no. 1, (1983).

142 Chevannes, *Rastafari Roots and Ideology*, 39.

142 Bryan, *The Jamaican People: 1880–1902*, 41–45.

142 Chevannes, *Rastafari Roots and Ideology*, 39.

142 Bilby and Leib, 'Kumina, the Howellite Church and the Emergence of Rastafarian Traditional Music in Jamaica,' *Jamaica Journal* 19 no. 3, (1985).

142 George Simpson, 'The Rastafari Movement in Jamaica,' *Jamaica Journal* 25 no. 2, (December 1994).

142 Prahlad, *Reggae Wisdom: Proverbs in Jamaican Music*, 276.

142 Robert Hill, 'Leonard P. Howell and Early Rastafari,' *Jamaica Journal* 16 no. 1, (1983).

142 Bisnauth, *History of Religions in the Caribbean*, 185.

143 Ibid., 32.

144 Lewis, *Marcus Garvey: Anti-Colonial Champion*, 89.

144 Ibid., 172.

145 Neita, *Donald Sangster*, unpublished manuscript.

145 Crewe, *Touch The Happy Isles*, 286.

145 Bilby and Leib, 'Kumina, the Howellite Church and the Emergence of Rastafarian Traditional Music in Jamaica,' *Jamaica Journal* 19 no. 3, (1985).

145 Maureen Warner-Lewis, 'Jamaica's Central African Heritage,' *Jamaica Journal* 28 nos. 2–3.

145 Senior, *Encyclopedia of Jamaican Heritage*, 207–8.

145 Chevannes, *Rastafari Roots and Ideology*, 152.

145 Ibid., 34.

145 Ibid., 122.

VII. ARTS AND LITERATURE: ROOTS AND CULTURE

PAGE

148 Godfrey Taylor, 'Slim and Sam: Jamaican Street Singers,' *Jamaica Journal* 16 no. 3, (August 1988).

148 Randolph Williams, 'The Story of Two Men and a Guitar,' *Jamaica Journal* 16 no. 3 (August 1988).

149 Augustus Braithwaite, 'The Cudjoe Minstrels: A Perspective' *Jamaica Journal* 43.

149 Cheryl Ryman 'The Frats Quintet,' *Jamaica Journal* 22 no. 1, (February–April 1989).

149 Senior, *Encyclopedia of Jamaican Heritage*, 372.

150 Ibid., 16.

151 'Roots Plays Tone Down,' *Jamaica Sunday Gleaner*, January 22, 2006.

155 Pamela O'Gorman, 'Marjorie Whylie's contribution to the development of drumming in Jamaica,' *Jamaica Journal* 24 no. 1, (June 1991).

155 *Jamaica Journal* 6 no. 2, (June 1972).

155 Bennett, 'Introduction,' *Jamaica Labrish*.

156 Ibid.

157 Carnegie, *Some Aspects of Jamaica's Politics, 1918–1938*,173.

157 Lewis, *Marcus Garvey: Anti-Colonial Champion*, 231.

157 Rupert Lewis, 'The Politics of Interim,' *Jamaica Journal* 21 no. 2, (May–July 1988).

157 Mordecai and Mordecai, *Culture and Customs of Jamaica.*

157 Rhonda Cobham, 'The Literary Side of H.G. de Lisser1878–1944),' *Jamaica Journal* 17 no. 4 (November 1984–January 1985): 9.

157 *Companion of the Order of St Michael and St George*.

157 Carnegie, *Some Aspects of Jamaica's Politics, 1918–1938*, 171.

157 Lewis, *Marcus Garvey: Anti-Colonial Champion*, 253.

159 Glory Robertson, 'The Rose Hall Legend,' *Jamaica Journal* 2 no. 4.

159 Geoffrey S. Yates, Assistant Archivist, Jamaica Archives, 'Rose Hall – Death of a Legend,' c. 1965. http://jamaicanfamilysearch.com/Samples2/mpalmer.htm.

159 Senior, *Encyclopedia of Jamaican Heritage*, 426.

160 Mervyn Morris, 'The All Jamaica Library,' *Jamaica Journal* 6 no. 1, (March 1972).

162 Mervyn Morris, 'Contending Values – The Prose Fiction of Claude McKay,' *Jamaica Journal* 9 nos. 2–3, (1975).

165 *Insight Guide*, 262–63.

166 'The National Gallery of Jamaica,' *Jamaica Journal* 16 no. 4, (November 1983).

VIII. ECONOMY:

A HISTORY OF GETTING BY

PAGE

170 Parry, Sherlock and Maingot, *A Short History of the West Indies*, 172.

170 http://www.migrationinformation.org/feature/display.cfm?ID=137#3

171 Planning Institute of Jamaica (PIOJ). The January 2009 National Geographic showed that 41.4 per cent of Jamaican doctors leave to practise in the US, UK, Canada or Australia, the highest percentage of any country studied.

172 *World Bank Report 2007.*

173 Professor of Economy, UWI, Dr Damien King.

IX. FOOD:

A LITTLE BIT FROM EVERYWHERE

PAGE

176 'Sweet Heat: For Jamaicans, It's About Jerk,' *New York Times*, July 2, 2008.

176 Burke, *Eat Caribbean*, 120.

176 *The Best of Skywritings*, 147.

178 Benghiat, *Traditional Jamaican Cookery*, 124.

178 *The Best of Skywritings*, 143.

X. SCENERY:

AROUND THE BEAUTIFUL ISLE

PAGE

186 Errol Flynn, *My Wicked, Wicked Ways*, 1976.

186 http://www.jamaica-gleaner.com/pages/history/story0033.html

188 John Hearne, 'The Jigsaw Men,' *Jamaica Journal* 6 no. 1, (March 1972).

Bibliography

76 King Street. *Journal of Liberty Hall: the Legacy of Marcus Garvey*. Volume 1. 2009 Kingston: Arawak Publications, 2009.

Abrahams, Roger, and John Szwed. *After Africa*. London: Yale University Press, 1983.

Afari, Yasus. *Overstanding Rastafari: Jamaica's Gift to the World*. Kingston: Senya Cum, 2007.

———. *Eye Pen: Philosophical Reasoning and Poetry*. Kingston: House of Honour Publishing, 1998.

Agorsah, E Kofi, ed. *Maroon Heritage: Archeological, Ethnographic and Historical Perspectives*. Kingston: Canoe Press, 1994.

Arnold, Guy. *Africa: A Modern History*. London: Atlantic Books, 2005.

Austin-Broos, Diane. *Jamaica Genesis: Religion and the Politics of Moral Order*. Kingston: Ian Randle Publishers, 1997.

Baker, Christopher. *Jamaica* 3rd ed. Australia: Lonely Planet Publications Pty Limited, 2003.

———. *Passport Illustrated Travel Guide to Jamaica*. Illinois: NTC Publishing Group, 1995.

Barrett, Leonard. *The Rastafarians*. Boston: Beacon Press, 1997.

Barrow, Christine, ed. *Caribbean Portraits*. Kingston: Ian Randle Publishers, 1998.

Barrow, Steve and Peter Dalton. *Reggae*. London: Rough Guides Limited, 1997.

———. *Reggae* 2nd ed. London: Rough Guides Limited, 2001.

Bayer, Marcel. *Jamaica: A Guide to the People, Politics and Culture*. Kingston: Ian Randle Publishers, 1993.

Beckles, Hilary, and Verene Shepherd, eds. *Caribbean Freedom: Economy and Society from Emancipation to the Present*. Kingston: Ian Randle Publishers, 1993.

———. ed. *Caribbean Slave Society and Economy*. Kingston: Ian Randle Publishers, 1991.

Bell, Brian, and Lesley Gordon, eds. *Jamaica*. Hong Kong: Apa Productions GMBH and Company, 1983.

Bennett, Louise. *Jamaica Labrish: Jamaica Dialect Poems*. Kingston: Sangster's Book Stores, 1966.

Bertram, Arnold. *P.J. Patterson: A Mission to Perform*. AB Associates and Supreme Printers and Publishers Limited, 1995.

Bisnauth, Dale. *History of Religions in the Caribbean*. London: Africa World Press, 1996.

Black, Clinton. *History of Jamaica. Kingston*: Longman Publishers, 1988.

Bolland, O. Nigel. *The Birth of Caribbean Civilization*. Kingston: Ian Randle Publishers, 2004.

Booker, Cedella, and Anthony Winkler. *Bob Marley: An Intimate Portrait by His Mother* London: The Penguin Group, 1997.

Bowman, John, and Ferrell, Robert, eds. *The Twentieth Century: An Almanac*. New York: World Almanac Publications, 1985.

Bryan, Patrick W. *Edward Seaga and the Challenges of Modern Jamaica*. Kingston: University of the West Indies Press, 2009.

Buissert, David. *Jamaica in 1687*. Kingston: The Mill Press, 2008.

Burke, Virginia. *Eat Caribbean*. London: Simon & Schuster, 2005.

Burnett, Paula, ed. *Caribbean Verse*. London: Penguin Group, 1986.

Bustamante, Gladys. *The Memoirs of Lady Bustamante*. Kingston: Kingston Publishers, 1997.

Cameron, Linda, ed. *The Story of the Gleaner: Memoirs and Reminiscences*. Kingston: Gleaner Company Limited, 2000.

Cargill, Morris, ed. *Ian Fleming Introduces Jamaica*. London: Andre Deutsch Limited, 1965.

———. *Jamaica Farewell*. New York: Barricade Books Inc., 1995.

———. *Public Disturbances: A Collection of Writings 1986–1996*. Kingston: The Mill Press, 1998.

Carnegie, James. *Some Aspects of Jamaica's Politics, 1918–1938*. Kingston: Institute of Jamaica, 1973.

Cassidy, Frederic. *Jamaica Talk: Three Hundred Years of the English Language in Jamaica*. London: Macmillan Education, 1961.

Charles, Pearnel. *Jamaica and the People's Struggle for Survival*. Kingston: PC Publishers, 2007.

Chen, Ray, ed. *The Shopkeepers: Commemorating 150 Years of the Chinese in Jamaica 1854-2004*. Kingston: Periwinkle Publishers, 2005.

Chevannes, Barry. *Rastafari: Roots and Ideology*. Syracuse: Syracuse University Press, 1994.

Clarke, John, ed. *Marcus Garvey and the Vision of Africa*. New York: Random House, 1973.

Cooper, Carolyn. *Noises in the Blood: Orality, Gender, and the Vulgar Body of Jamaican Popular Culture*. Durham: Duke University Press, 1995.

Cordingly, David. *Life Among the Pirate: The Romance and the Reality*. London: Warner Books, 1995.

Crew, Quentin. *Touch the Happy Isles*. London: Michael Joseph, 1987.

D'Costa, David, ed. *Public Disturbances*. Kingston: The Mill Press Limited, 1998.

De Lisser, Herbert. *The White Witch of Rose Hall*. Kingston, Kingston Publishers, 1928.

Dostoevsky, Fyodor. *Great Short Works*. New York, Harper and Row, 1968.

Duncan, Peter, and Ferguson, Renee, ed. *Berlitz Pocket Guides: Jamaica*. London: Berlitz Publishing Company Limited, 1996.

Eaton, George. *Alexander Bustamante and Modern Jamaica*. Kingston: LMH Publishing, 1995.

Everett, Susanne. *History of Slavery*. New Jersey: Chartwell Books, 1991.

Fanon, Frantz. *Black Skin, White Masks*. New York: Grove Press Inc., 1967.

Fax, Elton. *Garvey: The Story of a Pioneer Back Nationalist*. New York: Dodd Mead and Co, 1972.

Ferguson, James. *The Story of the Caribbean People*. Kingston: Ian Randle Publishers, 1999.

Fermor, Patrick Leigh. *The Traveller's Tree: A Journey through the Caribbean Islands*. London: Penguin Group, 1950.

Fischer, Steven Roger. *A History of Reading*. London: Reaction Books, 2003.

Franklyn, Delano. *The Right Move: Corporate Leadership and Governance in Jamaica*. Kingston: Arawak Publications, 2001.

Gambrill, Linda, ed. *A Tapestry of Jamaica: The Best of Skywritings*. Kingston: MacMillan Publishing Company, 2003.

Gambrill, Anthony. *In Search of the Buccaneers*. Oxford: MacMillan Publishing Company, 2007.

Gauldie, Robin. *Globetrotter Travel Guide: Jamaica*. London: New Holland Publishers, 1998.

Godfrey, David. *Reckoning with the Force*. Kingston: The Mill Press, 1998.

Goffe, Leslie Gordon. *When Banana was King*. Kingston: LMH Publishers, 2007.

Gray, Obika. *Demeaned But Empowered: The Social Power of the Urban Poor in Jamaica*. Kingston: University of the West Indies Press, 2004.

Greenwood, Robert et al. *Emancipation to Emigration*. Oxford: MacMillan Caribbean, 2003.

Hacker, Andrew. *Two Nations: Black and White, Separate, Hostile, Unequal*. London: Macmillan Publishing Company, 1992.

Hall, Douglas. *In Miserable Slavery*. Kingston: University of the West Indies Press, 1999.

Harden, Blaine. *Africa: Dispatches from a Fragile Continent*. Boston: Houghton Mifflin Company, 1991.

Harriot, Anthony. *Police and Crime Control in Jamaica*. Kingston: University of the West Indies Press, 2000.

———. ed. *Understanding Crime in Jamaica*. Kingston: University of the West Indies Press, 2003.

Harris, Donald J. *Jamaica's Export Economy: Towards a Strategy of Export-led Growth*. Kingston: Ian Randle Publishers, 1997.

Hart, Richard. *Slaves Who Abolished Slavery: Blacks in Bondage*. Kingston: University of the West Indies Press, 2002.

Headley, Bernard. *A Spade is Still a Spade: Essays on Crime and the Politics of Jamaica*. Kingston: LMH Publishing Limited, 2002.

Hearne, Leeta, ed. *The Memoirs of Lady Bustamante*. Kingston: Kingston Publishers Limited, 1997.

Heuman, Gad. *The Killing Time: The Morant Bay Rebellion in Jamaica*. London: Macmillan Publishers Ltd, 1994.

Higman, B.W. *Jamaican Food: History, Biology, Culture*. Kingston: University of the West Indies Press, 2008.

Hill, Frank. *Bustamante and His Letters*. Kingston: Kingston Publishers, 1976.

Howard, David. *Kingston: A Cultural and Literary History*. Kingston: Ian Randle Publishers, 2005.

Howe, Glenford. *Race, War and Nationalism: A Social History of West Indians in the First World War*. Kingston: Ian Randle Publishers, 2002.

Insanally, Annette et al. *Regional Footprints: The Travels and Travails of Early Caribbean Migrants*. Kingston: University of the West Indies Press, 2006.

Jamaica Journal. 1968–2009

James, Marlon. *John Crow's Devil*. New York: Akashic Books, 2005.

Johnson, Anthony. *Kingston: Portrait of a City*. Kingston: Tee Jay Ltd., 1993.

Johnson, Howard, and Karl Watson, eds. *The White Minority in the Caribbean*. Kingston: Ian Randle Publishers, 1998.

Jones, Ken. *Bustamante: Notes, Quotes, Anecdotes*. Kingston: Kenneth Jones, 2009.

Katz, David. *People Funny Boy*. Edinburgh: Payback Press, 2000.

Knight, Franklin, and Colin Palmer, eds. *The Modern Caribbean*. Chapel Hill, NC: University of North Carolina Press, 1989.

Kurlansky, Mark. *A Continent of Island: Searching for the Caribbean Destiny*. Reading, MA: Addison-Wesley Publishing Company, 1992.

Larkin, Colin, ed. *The Guinness Who's Who of Reggae*. London: Guinness Publishing Ltd, 1994.

Ledgister, F.S.J. *Class Alliances and the Liberal Authorian State: The Roots of Post-Colonial Democracy in Jamaica, Trinidad and Tobago and Surinam*. Trenton, NJ: Africa World Press, Inc., 1998.

Lee, Easton. *From Behind the Counter: Poems from a Rural Jamaican Experience*. Kingston: Ian Randle Publishers, 1998.

Lee, Helene. *The First Rasta: Leonard Howell and the Rise of Rastafarianism*. Chicago: Lawrence Hill Books, 2003.

Levi, Darrell. *Michael Manley: The Making of a Leader*. Kingston: Heinemann Publishers Ltd, 1989.

Lewin, Olive. *Rock It Come Over: The Folk Music of Jamaica*. Kingston: University of the West Indies Press, 2000.

Lewis, Matthew. *Journal of a Residence among the Negroes of the West Indies*. 1861.

Lewis, Rupert. *Marcus Garvey: Anti-Colonial Champion*. Trenton NJ: Africa World Press, 1998.

———. and Patrick Bryan. *Garvey: His Work and Impact*. Trenton NJ: Africa World Press, 1991.

Mackie, Christine. *Life and Food in the Caribbean*. Kingston: Ian Randle Publishers, 1995.

Maingot, Anthony, J.H. Parry and Phillip Sherlock. A *Short History of the West Indies*. London: Macmillan Publishers Ltd, 1987.

Manley, Beverley. *The Manley Memoirs*. Kingston: Ian Randle Publishers, 2008.

Manley, Rachel. *Drumblair*. Kingston: Ian Randle Publishers, 1996.

———. ed. *Edna Manley: The Diaries*. Kingston: Heinemann Publishers (Caribbean) Ltd., 1989.

———. *In My Father's Shade*. London: Black Amber Books, 2004.

Marley, Rita and Hettie Jones, *No Woman No Cry*. London: Pan Macmillan Ltd, 2004.

Marriot, Louis. *Who's Who and What's What in Jamaican Art and Entertainment.* Kingston: Talawa, 1995.

Miller, Errol. *Marginalization of the Black Male*. Jamaica: Canoe Press, University of the West Indies, 1994.

Moore, Brian and Swithin Wilmot, eds. *Before and After 1865: Education, Politics and Regionalism in the Caribbean*. Kingston: Ian Randle Publishers, 1998.

Morris, Margaret. *Tour Jamaica*. Kingston: The Gleaner Company Ltd., 1985.

Morris, Mervyn. *Is English We Speaking and Other Essays*. Kingston: Ian Randle Publishers, 1999.

———. and Carolyn Allen. *Writing Life: Reflections by West Indian Writers*. Kingston: Ian Randle Publishers, 2007.

Morris-Brown, Vivien. *The Jamaica Handbook of Proverbs*. Mandeville, Jamaica: Island Heart Publishers, 1993.

Mordecai, Martin, and Pamela Mordecai. *Culture and Customs of Jamaica*. Santa Barbara, CA: Greenwood Press, 2000.

Moyne Commission. *Report of the West India Royal Commission 1945*. Barbados: Reprinted by Government Printing Department, 2000.

Munroe, Trevor, and Arnold Betram. *Adult Suffrage & Political Administrations in Jamaica 1944–2002*. Kingston: Ian Randle Publishers, 2006.

Munroe, Trevor. *Jamaican Politics: A Marxist Perspective in Transition*. Kingston: Heinemann Publishers Ltd., 1990.

———. *For a New Beginning*. Kingston: CARICOM Publishers Ltd, 1994.

———. *Jamaican Politics: A Marxist Perspective in Transition*. Kingston: Heinemann Publishers Ltd, 1990.

Neita, Hartley. *Hugh Shearer: A Voice for the People*. Kingston: Ian Randle Publishers, 2005.

Nettleford, Rex, ed. *Jamaica in Independence: Essays on the Early Years*. Heinemann Publishers (Caribbean) Ltd., 1989.

Orizio, Riccardo. *Lost White Tribes: Journey among the Forgotten*. London: Secker and Warburg, 2000.

Osborne, Francis. *History of the Catholic Church in Jamaica*. Kingston: Loyola University Press, 1987.

Panton, David. *Jamaica's Michael Manley: The Great Transformation (1972–92)*. Kingston: Kingston Publishers Limited, 1993.

Parry, J.H. et al. *A Short History of the West Indies*. Oxford: MacMillan Publishers, 1987.

Patterson, Orlando. *The Children of Sisyphus*. London: Longman Group, 1986.

Payne, Anthony. *Politics in Jamaica*. London: C. Hurst and Company Publishers Ltd, 1988.

Popenoe, David. *Life Without Father*. Cambridge: Harvard University Press, 2000.

Potash, Chris, ed. *Reggae, Rasta, Revolution*. New York: Simon and Schuster Macmillan, 1997.

Prahlad, Anand. *Reggae Wisdom: Proverbs in Jamaican Music*. Jackson, MS: University Press of Mississippi, 2001.

Reader, John. *Africa: A Biography of a Continent*. New York: Alfred A. Knopf, 1998.

Reid, Basil. *Myths and Realities of Caribbean History*. Tuscaloosa: University Alabama Press, 2009.

Reynolds, Edward. *Stand the Storm: A History of the Atlantic Slave Trade*. London: Allison & Busby, 1989.

Robinson, Kim, Harclyde Walcott, and Trevor Fearon. *The How to Be Jamaican Handbook*. Humor Us Publications, 1987.

Runge, Jonathan. *Rum and Reggae: The Insider's Guide to the Caribbean*. New York: Villard Books, Random House Inc., 1993.

Salewicz, Chris. *Rude Boy: Once Upon a Time in Jamaica*. London: Victor Gollancz, Orion Publishing Group, 2000.

Seaga, Edward. *My Life and Leadership, Volume I: Clash of Ideologies 1930–1980*. Oxford: Macmillan Education, 2009.

Sealy, Theodore. *Caribbean Leaders*. Kingston: Kingston Publishers Ltd., 1991.

Senior, Olive. *A-Z of Jamaican Heritage*. Kingston: The Gleaner Company Ltd., 1983.

———. *Encyclopedia of Jamaican Heritage*. Jamaica: Twin Groups Publishers Ltd., 2003.

Sewell, Tony. *The Legacy of Marcus Garvey: Garvey's Children*. London: Macmillan Publishers Ltd, 1990.

Sherlock, Phillip, and Hazel Bennett. *The Story of the Jamaican People*. Kingston: Ian Randle Publishers, 1998.

Sives, Amanda. *Elections, Violence, and the Democratic Process in Jamaica: 1944–2007*. Kingston: Ian Randle Publishers, 2010.

Small, Geoff. *Ruthless: The Gobal Rise of the Yardies*. London: Warner Books, 1995.

Smith, M.G. *The Plural Society in the British West Indies*. Kingston: Sangster's Book Stores Ltd, 1974.

Statistical Institute of Jamaica. *Statistical Yearbook of Jamaica*. Kingston: Statistical Institute of Jamaica, 2006.

———. *Jamaica Survey of Living Conditions*. Kingston: Statistical Institute of Jamaica, 2006.

Sowell, Thomas. *Conquests and Culture*s. New York: Basic Books, 1999.

———. *Race and Culture: A World View*. New York: HarperCollins Publishers, 1994.

Stephens, Evelyne, and John Stephens. *Democratic Socialism in Jamaica*. London: Macmillan Education Ltd, 1986.

Stolzoff, Norman. *Wake the Town and Tell the People: Dancehall Culture in Jamaica*. London: Duke University Press, 2000.

Stone, Rosemarie, ed. *The Stone Columns: The Last Year's Work*. Kingston: Sangster's Book Stores Ltd., 1994.

Sunshine, Catherine A. *The Caribbean: Survival, Struggle and Sovereignty*. Washington: Epica, 1980.

Theobalds, Sabina and Ingrid Walter. *A Sea Of Wisdom* 2nd ed. Canada: Walter and Company, 2004.

Thomas, Hugh. *The Slave Trade*. New York: Simon & Schuster, 1997.

Thomas, Polly, and Adam Vaitlingam. *The Rough Guide to Jamaica* 3rd ed. London: Rough Guides Limited, 2003.

Thompson, Alvin. *The Haunting Past: Politics, Economic and Race in Caribbean Life*. Kingston: Ian Randle Publishers, 1997.

Tortello, Rebecca. *Pieces of the Past*. Kingston: Ian Randle Publishers, 2007.

Walvin, James. *The Life and Times of Henry Clarke of Jamaica, 1828–1907*. London: Frank Cass and Company Ltd., 1994.

Williams, Eric. *From Columbus to Castro: The History of the Caribbean 1492–1969*. New York: Random House, Inc., 1984.

Wilson, Anne. *Essential Jamaica*. London: AA Publishing, 1992.

Winkler, Anthony. *The Lunatic*. Kingston: Kingston Publishers Limited, 1987.

———. *Trust the Darkness*. Oxford: Macmillan Publishers Ltd., 2008.

Wong Ken, David. *The Runnings*. Kingston: Alternative Energy Ltd, 2003.

Wright, Philip, ed. *Lady Nugent's Journal of Her Residence in Jamaica from 1801 to 1805*. Kingston: University of the West Indies Press, 2002.

Zach, Paul. *Insight Guides Jamaica*. London: APA Publications, 2004.

Zips, Werner. *Black Rebels: African Caribbean Freedom Fighters in Jamaica*. Kingston: Ian Randle Publishers, 1999.

SUNSET IN NEGRIL

Index